elk's  n

Written by
Joshua Hale Fialkov

Art by
Noel Tuazon

Colors by
Scott Keating

Lettered by
Jason Hanley

Chapter title art by
Datsun Tran

Edited by
Jason Rodriguez

Villard Books · New York

A Villard Books Trade Paperback Original

Copyright © 2007 by Hoarse and Buggy Productions
Introduction © 2007 by Charlie Huston

Published in the United States by Villard Books, an imprint of The Random House Publishing Group, a division of Random House, Inc., New York.

VILLARD and "V" CIRCLED Design are registered trademarks of Random House, Inc.

This work was originally published in serial form as comic books published by Hoarse and Buggy Productions and Speakeasy from 2005 through 2006.

ISBN 978-0-345-49511-2

Printed in the United States of America

www.villard.com

9 8 7 6 5 4 3 2 1

First Edition

Contents

Introduction
Charlie Huston

What do you believe in?
How far are you willing to go in service of that belief?
No, really, how fucking far?
I only ask because Joshua Hale Fialkov is going to force you to ask that question of yourself.
God. Country. Family. Food, clothing, and shelter. What would you do to defend these things?
Stop.
Stop reading now.
Think.

Would you die?
Think.

Would you kill?
Think.

Does this seem irrelevant to your day to day life?

The extremes of existence, who the fuck can be bothered with that kind of theoretical shit when there's groceries to put on the table? Once I take care of the basics for me and mine, I'm done in, I got nothing left for questions like that. I'm just looking to have a drink and put my feet up and read a comic book.

I get it. I really do. But if that's the way you feel about it, best put this particular comic book down.
See, Joshua Hale Fialkov has looked at the world. He's looked and he's seen that some people are asking themselves what they believe in and how far they'll go. Fuck, some people don't have to ask themselves. They just *know*. And they have no understanding of people who do not share their certainty.
The certainty of the founders of Elk's Ridge.

What do you believe in?
How far are you willing to go?

Those questions, the answers to those questions, they forge heroes. And they birth monsters. Which is which depends on what side of the fire you're standing on.

Read the fucking book.
Burn, baby, burn.
And learn something about yourself.

Charlie Huston
Madison, Wisconsin
September 29, 2006

Charlie Huston is the author of No Dominion, A Dangerous Man, Already Dead, *and* Caught Stealing. *He has also written* Moon Knight *for Marvel Comics.*

elk's run

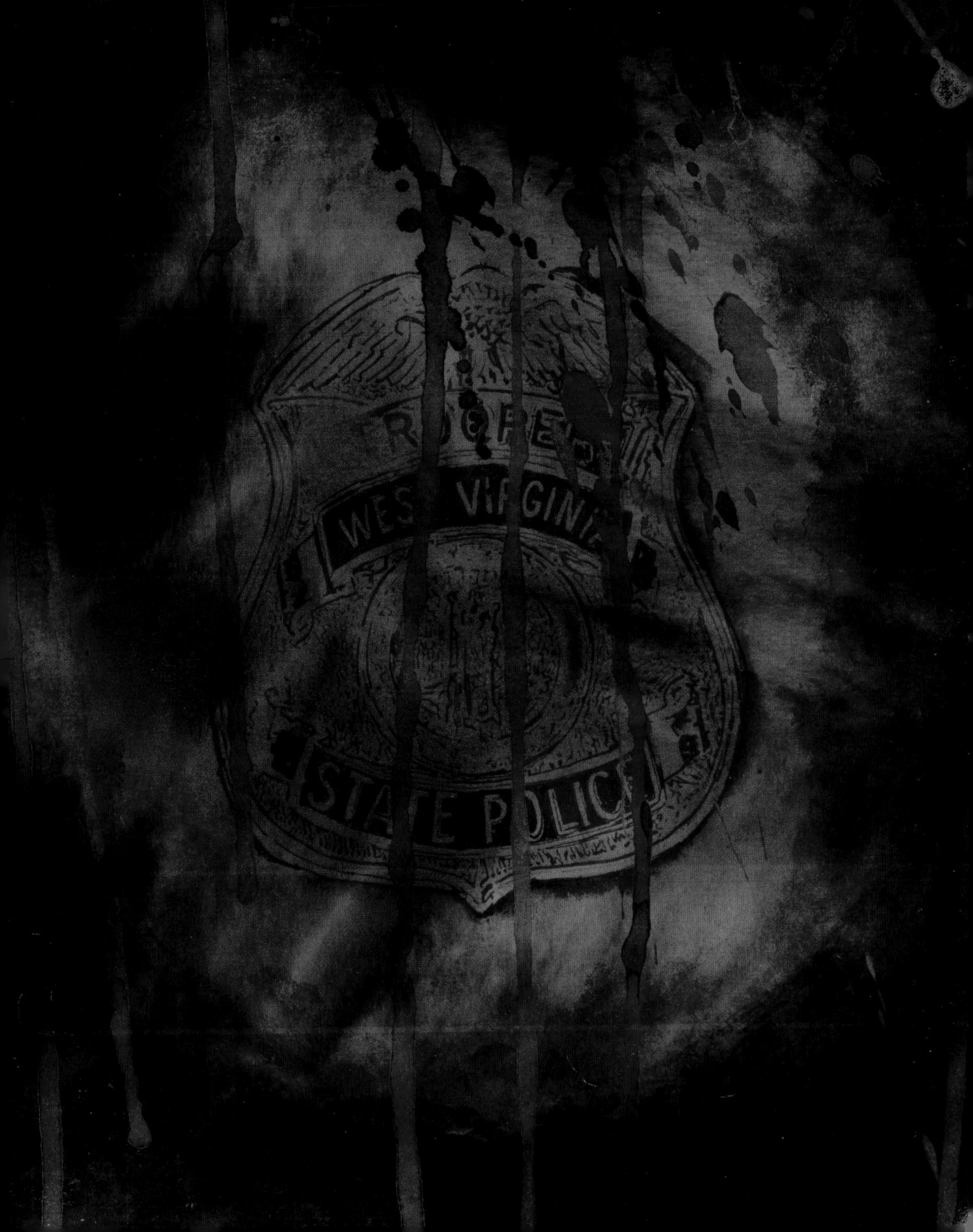
WEST VIRGINIA
STATE POLICE

Chapter One: A Few Pebbles

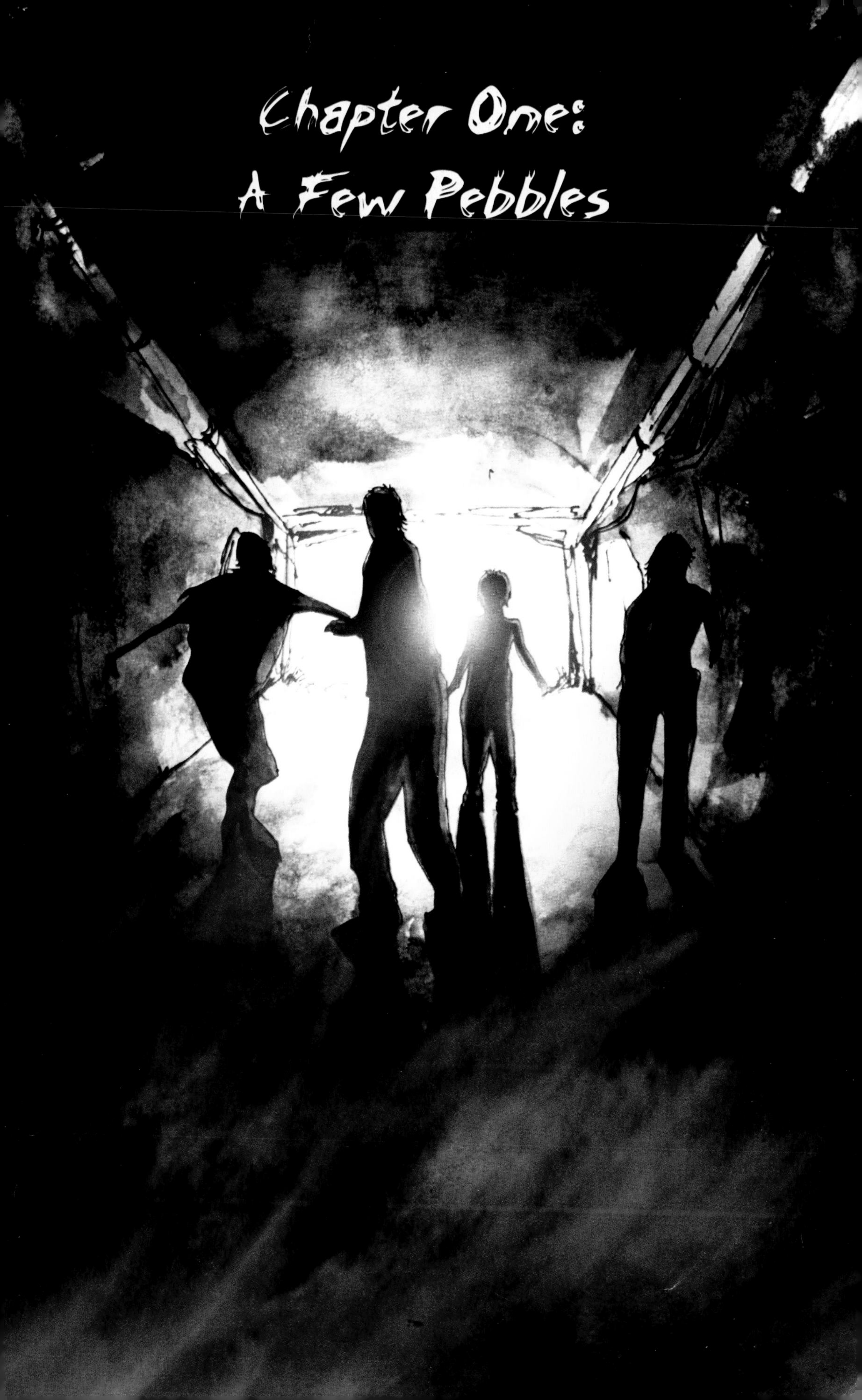

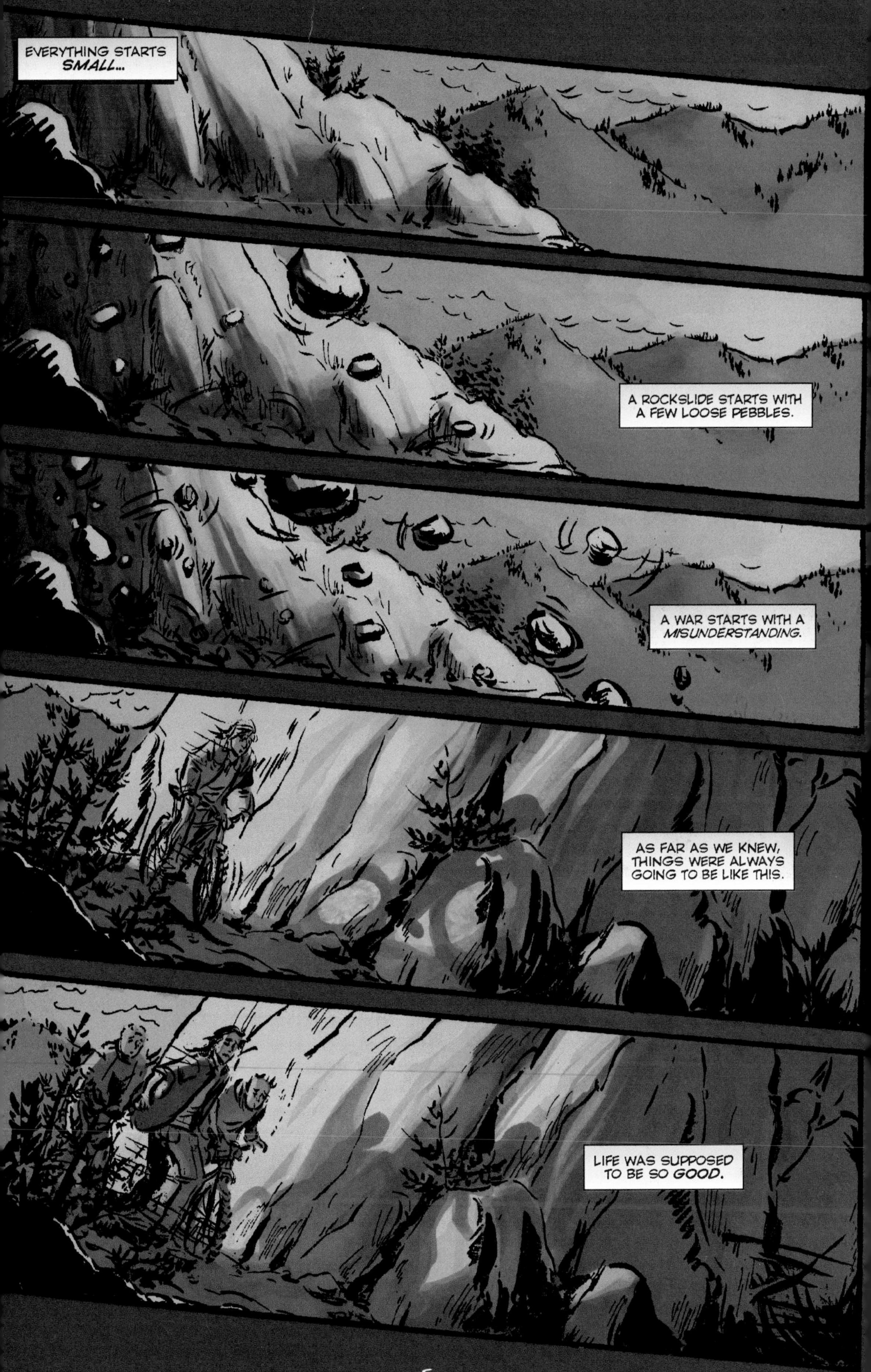
EVERYTHING STARTS SMALL...
A ROCKSLIDE STARTS WITH A FEW LOOSE PEBBLES.
A WAR STARTS WITH A MISUNDERSTANDING.
AS FAR AS WE KNEW, THINGS WERE ALWAYS GOING TO BE LIKE THIS.
LIFE WAS SUPPOSED TO BE SO GOOD.

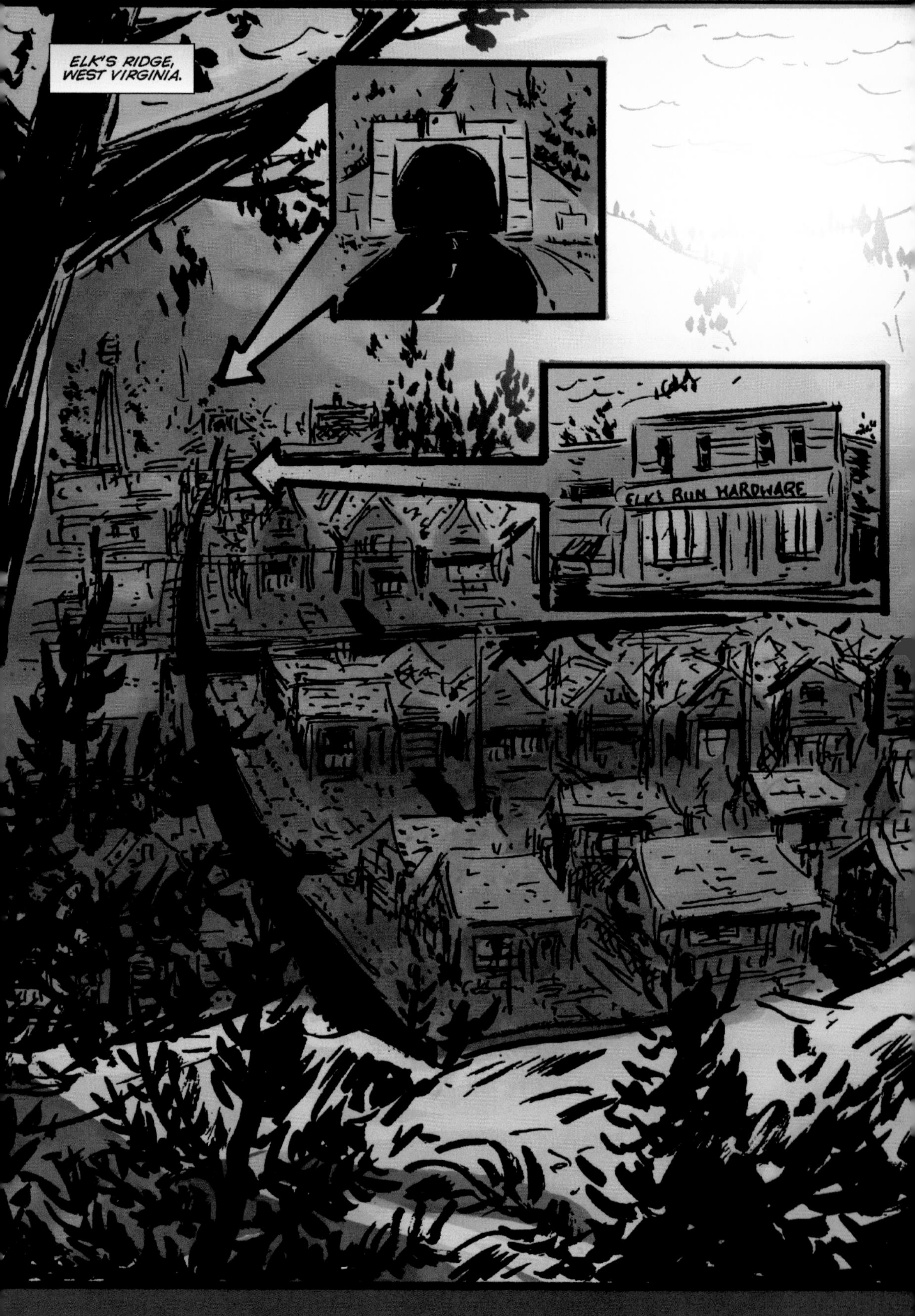
ELK'S RIDGE,
WEST VIRGINIA.
ELK'S RUN HARDWARE

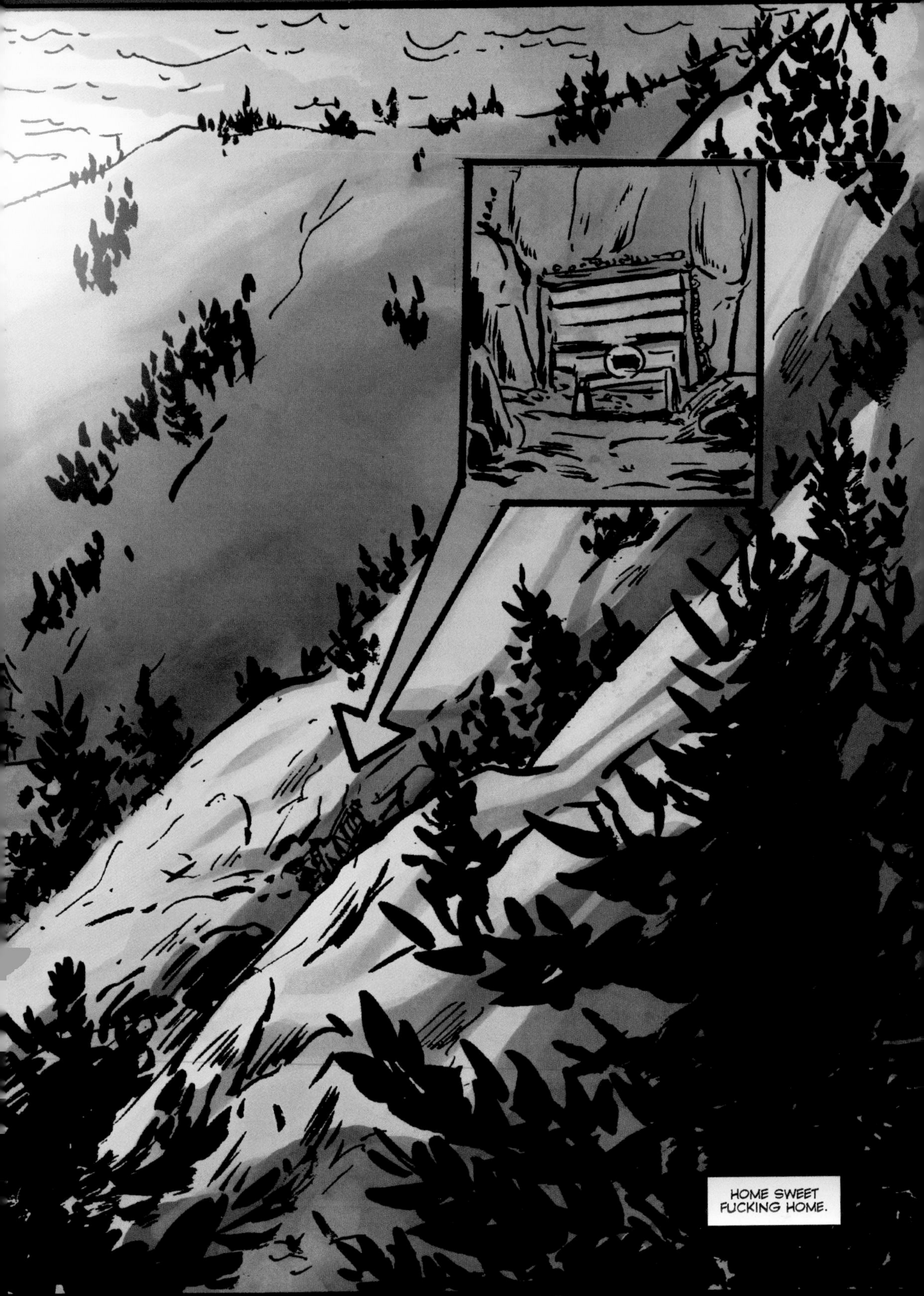
HOME SWEET
FUCKING HOME.

THIS TOWN USED TO BE A MINE. THEY CARVED IT INTO THE MOUNTAIN AS A PLACE FOR THE MINERS TO *LIVE.*
MADE MR. GRONSKI'S GRANDFATHER A *TON* OF MONEY.
THEN THERE WERE SOME *CAVE-INS.* A BUNCH OF WORKERS GOT KILLED.
LET ME GIVE YOU A QUICK LESSON IN *MINING.*
Gin Pole
Carrier and Bucket
Holst Cable
To Hoist
High
Line
Trip Cable
Dump
Muck
Shaft
Frozen Alluvial Gravel
Drift
IF THERE'S COAL OR WHATEVER THAT YOU CAN GET TO EASILY, NO PROBLEM. YOU HIRE *WHOEVER.*
BUT, AFTER YOU GET MOST OF THE *EASY* STUFF, YOU START WORKING OUT HOW MUCH IT COSTS TO REPLACE ALL THE WORKERS WHO'RE GONNA *DIE* VERSUS WHAT YOU'LL MAKE IN *COAL.*
MY DAD SAYS THERE WAS AN ACTUAL *EQUATION* THEY USED TO WORK OUT THE VALUE OF A WORKER VERSUS HOW MUCH COAL HE COULD YIELD.
THAT'S WHAT MY DAD SAYS ANYWAY.
ANYWAYS, WHEN EVERYONE MOVED INTO TOWN, THEY BLOCKED OFF THE ENTRANCE. 'CAUSE THEY SAY IT'S *HAUNTED.*
DO NOT ENTER
"AND SOMETIMES, WHEN IT'S REALLY *LATE* AT NIGHT..."
DO NOT ENTER
"YOU CAN HEAR ELIJAH'S *GHOST* CALLING OUT YOUR NAME."

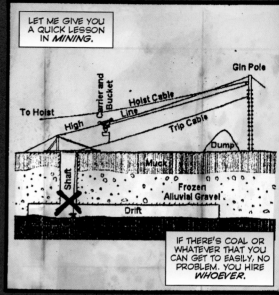

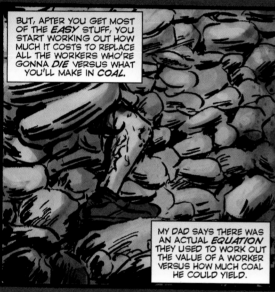

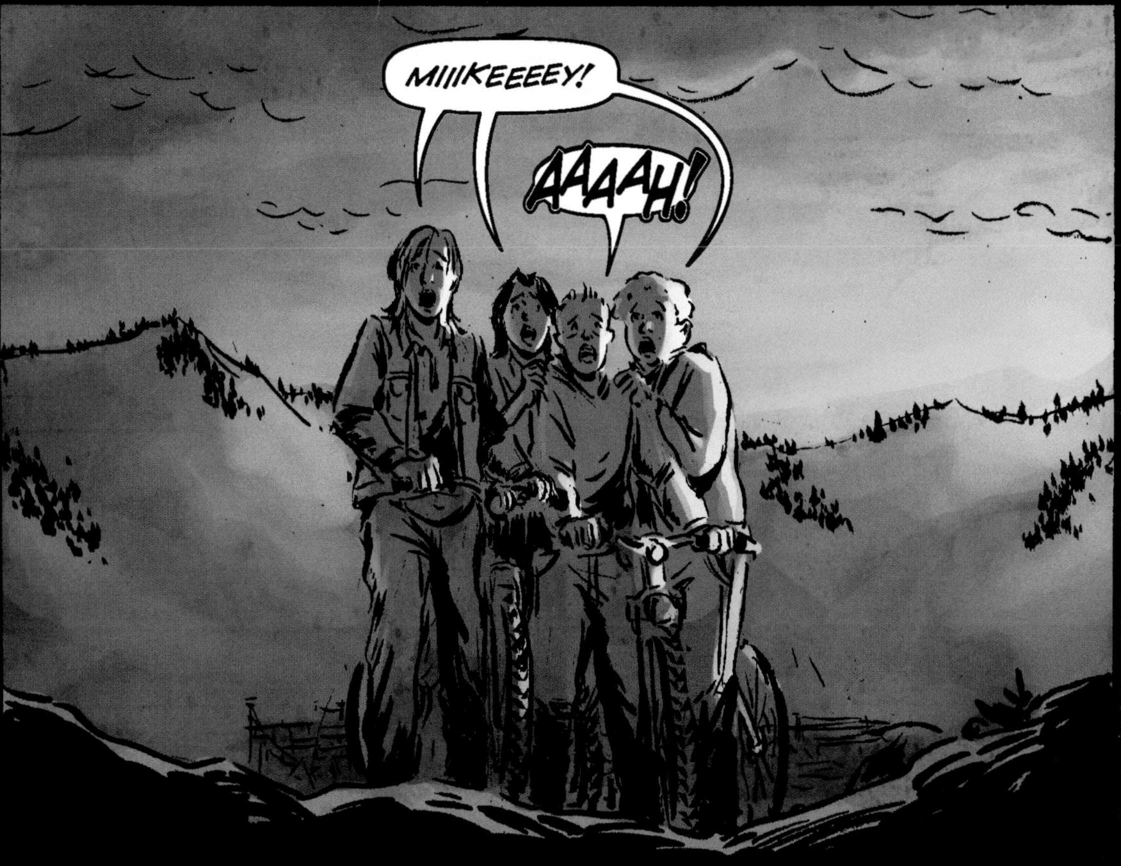
MIIIKEEEEY!
AAAAH!

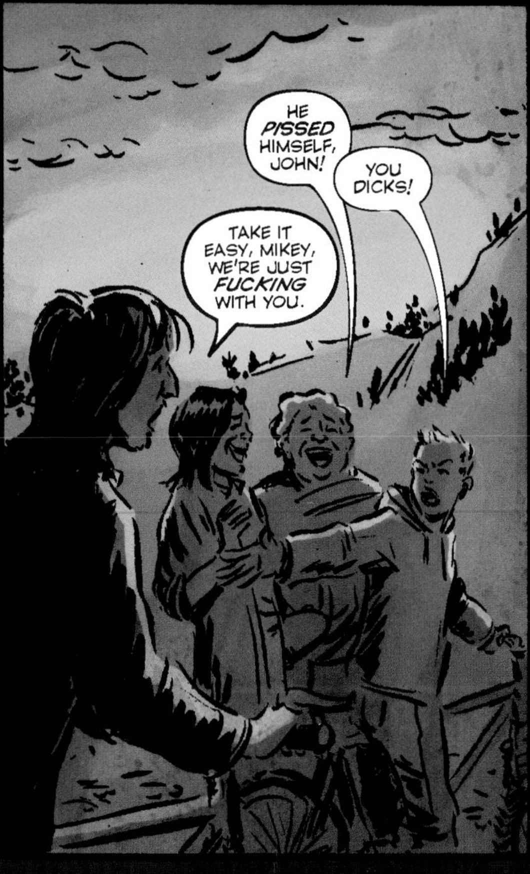
HE PISSED HIMSELF, JOHN!
YOU DICKS!
TAKE IT EASY, MIKEY, WE'RE JUST FUCKING WITH YOU.

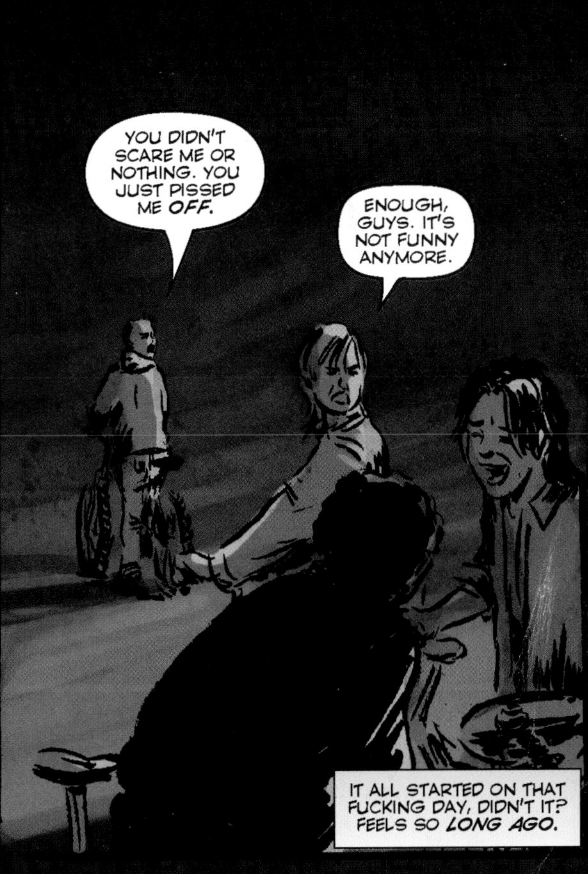
YOU DIDN'T SCARE ME OR NOTHING. YOU JUST PISSED ME OFF.
ENOUGH, GUYS. IT'S NOT FUNNY ANYMORE.
IT ALL STARTED ON THAT FUCKING DAY, DIDN'T IT? FEELS SO LONG AGO.

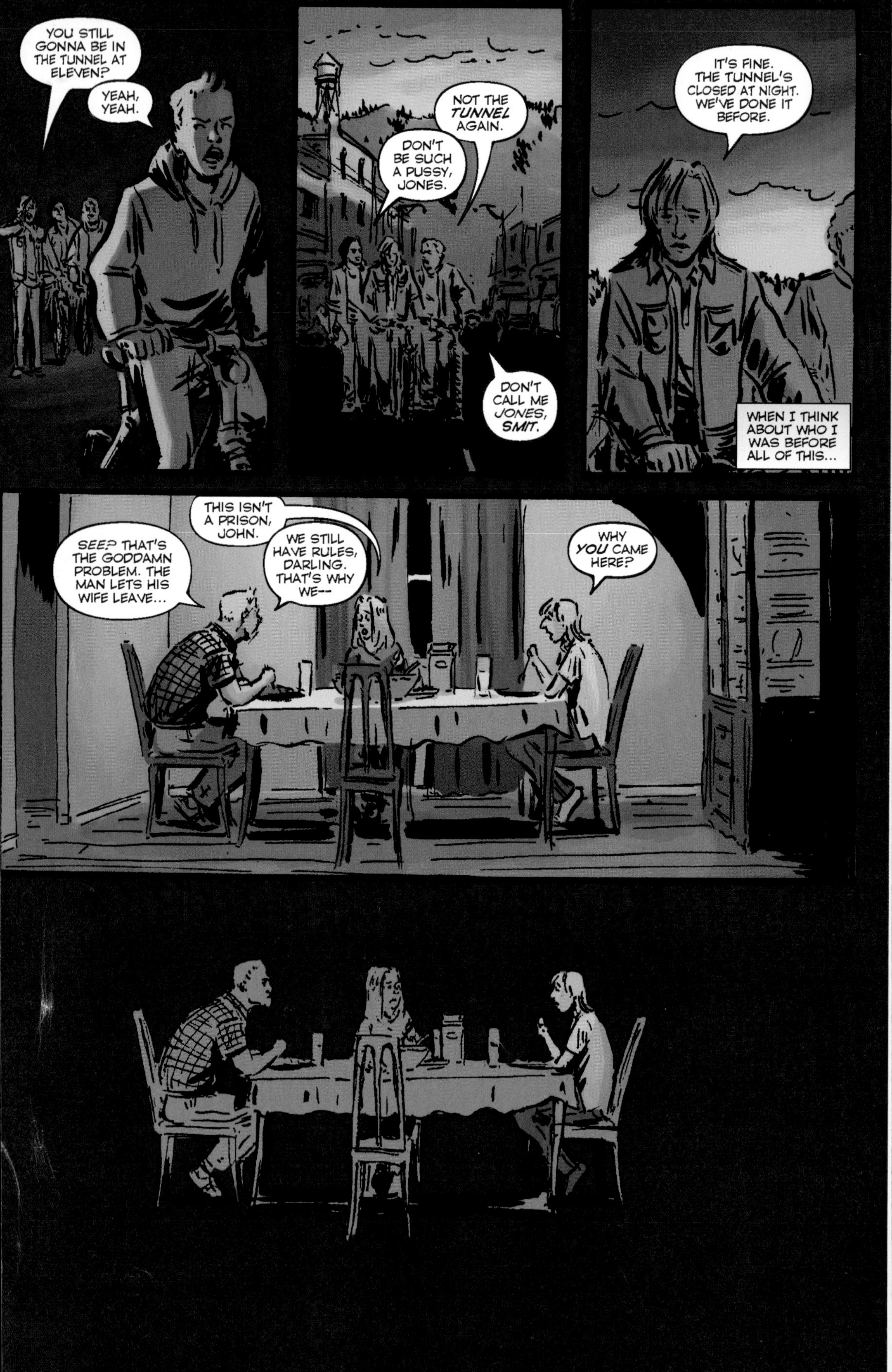

YOU STILL GONNA BE IN THE TUNNEL AT ELEVEN?
YEAH, YEAH.
NOT THE TUNNEL AGAIN.
DON'T BE SUCH A PUSSY, JONES.
DON'T CALL ME JONES, SMIT.
IT'S FINE. THE TUNNEL'S CLOSED AT NIGHT. WE'VE DONE IT BEFORE.
WHEN I THINK ABOUT WHO I WAS BEFORE ALL OF THIS...
SEE? THAT'S THE GODDAMN PROBLEM. THE MAN LETS HIS WIFE LEAVE...
THIS ISN'T A PRISON, JOHN.
WE STILL HAVE RULES, DARLING. THAT'S WHY WE--
WHY YOU CAME HERE?

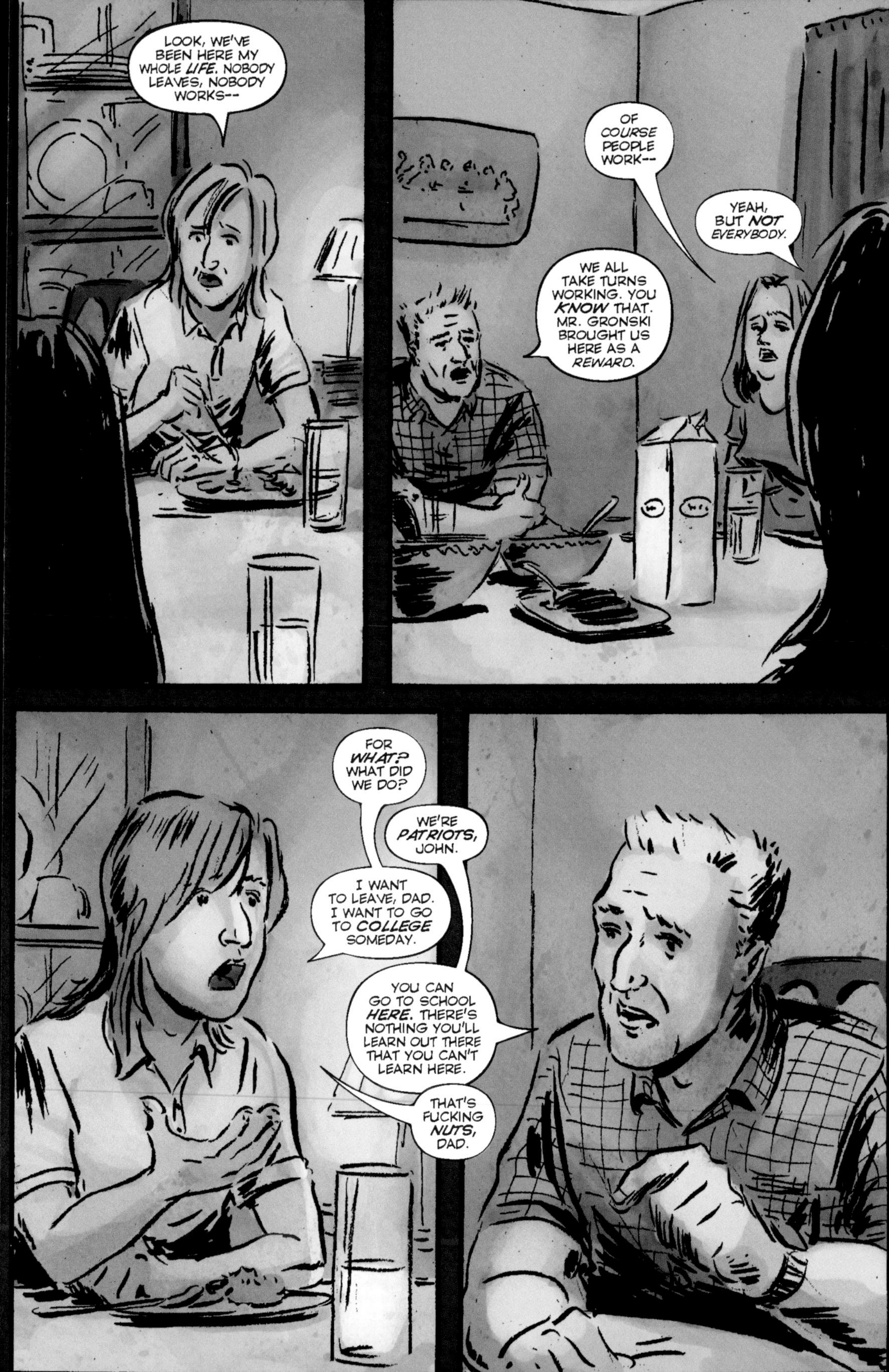
LOOK, WE'VE BEEN HERE MY WHOLE LIFE. NOBODY LEAVES, NOBODY WORKS--
OF COURSE PEOPLE WORK--
YEAH, BUT NOT EVERYBODY.
WE ALL TAKE TURNS WORKING. YOU KNOW THAT. MR. GRONSKI BROUGHT US HERE AS A REWARD.
FOR WHAT? WHAT DID WE DO?
WE'RE PATRIOTS, JOHN.
I WANT TO LEAVE, DAD. I WANT TO GO TO COLLEGE SOMEDAY.
YOU CAN GO TO SCHOOL HERE. THERE'S NOTHING YOU'LL LEARN OUT THERE THAT YOU CAN'T LEARN HERE.
THAT'S FUCKING NUTS, DAD.

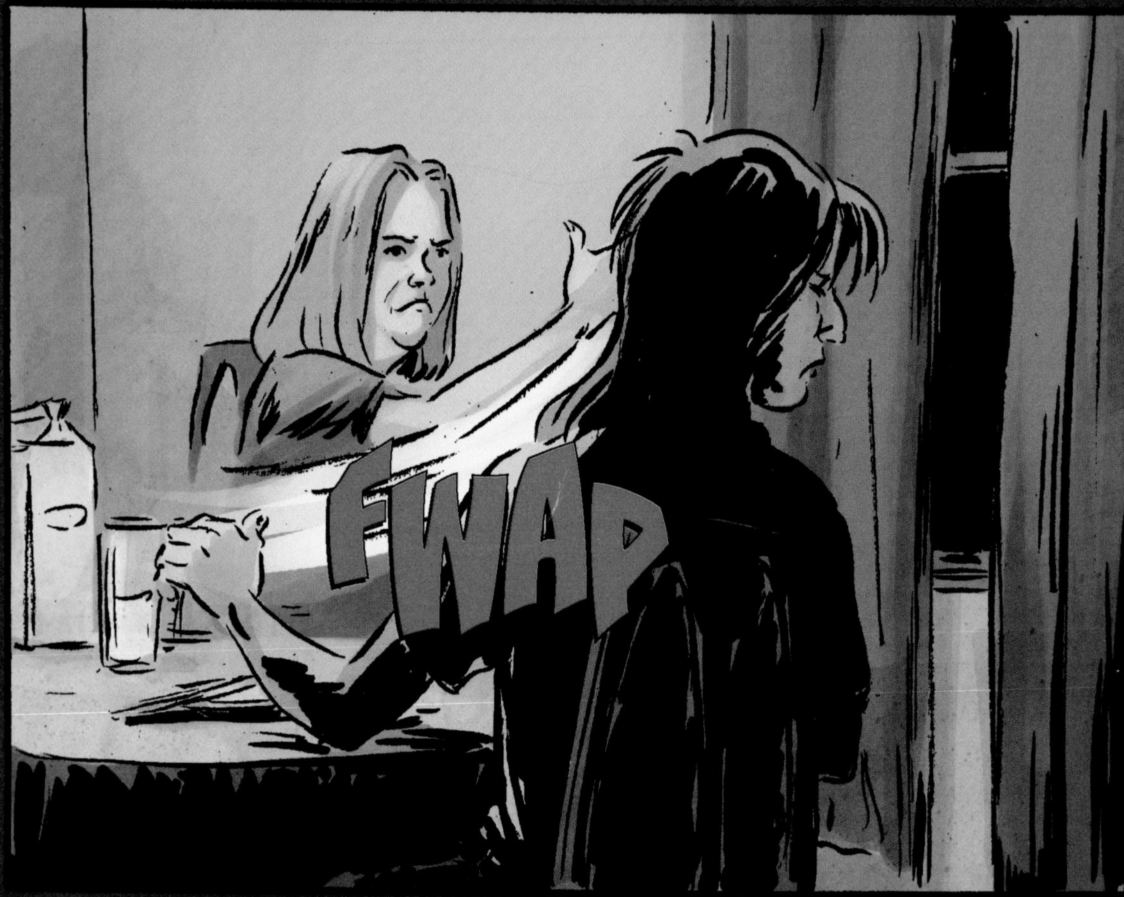
FWAP

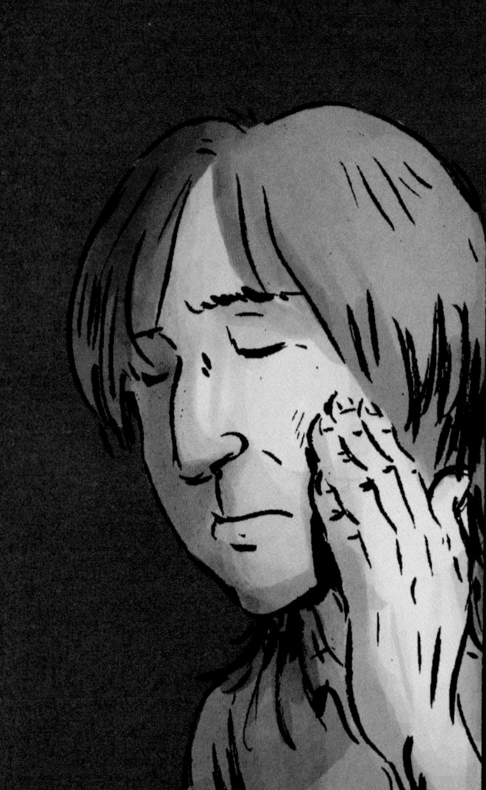

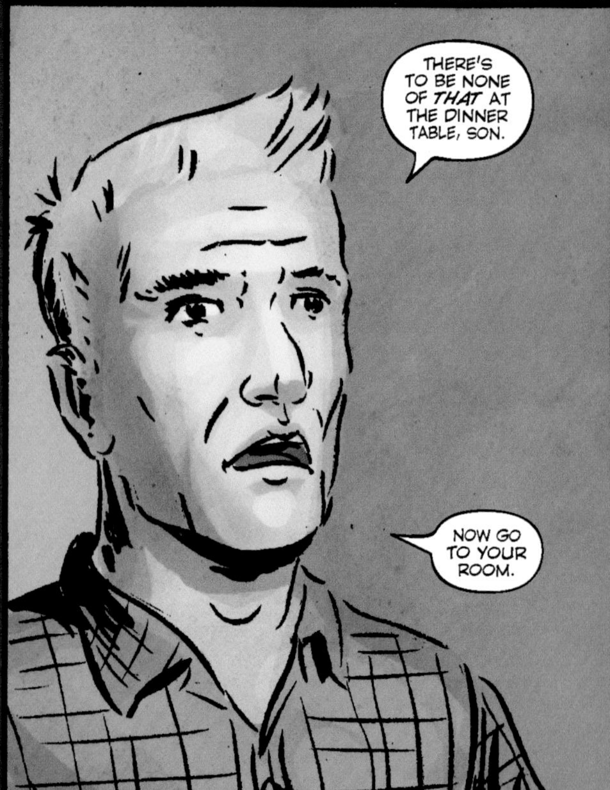
THERE'S TO BE NONE OF *THAT* AT THE DINNER TABLE, SON.
NOW GO TO YOUR ROOM.

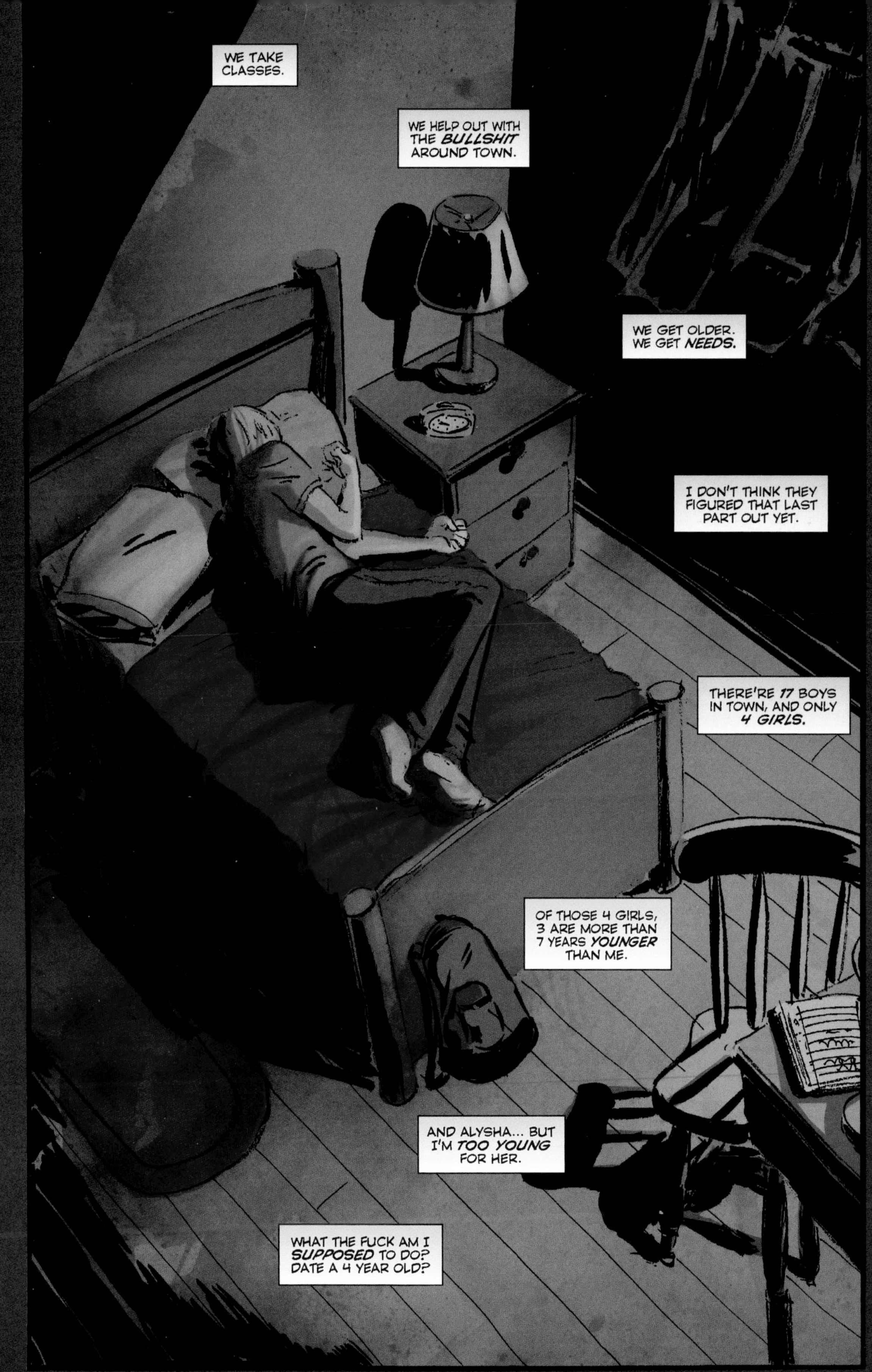
WE TAKE CLASSES.
WE HELP OUT WITH THE BULLSHIT AROUND TOWN.
WE GET OLDER. WE GET NEEDS.
I DON'T THINK THEY FIGURED THAT LAST PART OUT YET.
THERE'RE 17 BOYS IN TOWN, AND ONLY 4 GIRLS.
OF THOSE 4 GIRLS, 3 ARE MORE THAN 7 YEARS YOUNGER THAN ME.
AND ALYSHA... BUT I'M TOO YOUNG FOR HER.
WHAT THE FUCK AM I SUPPOSED TO DO? DATE A 4 YEAR OLD?

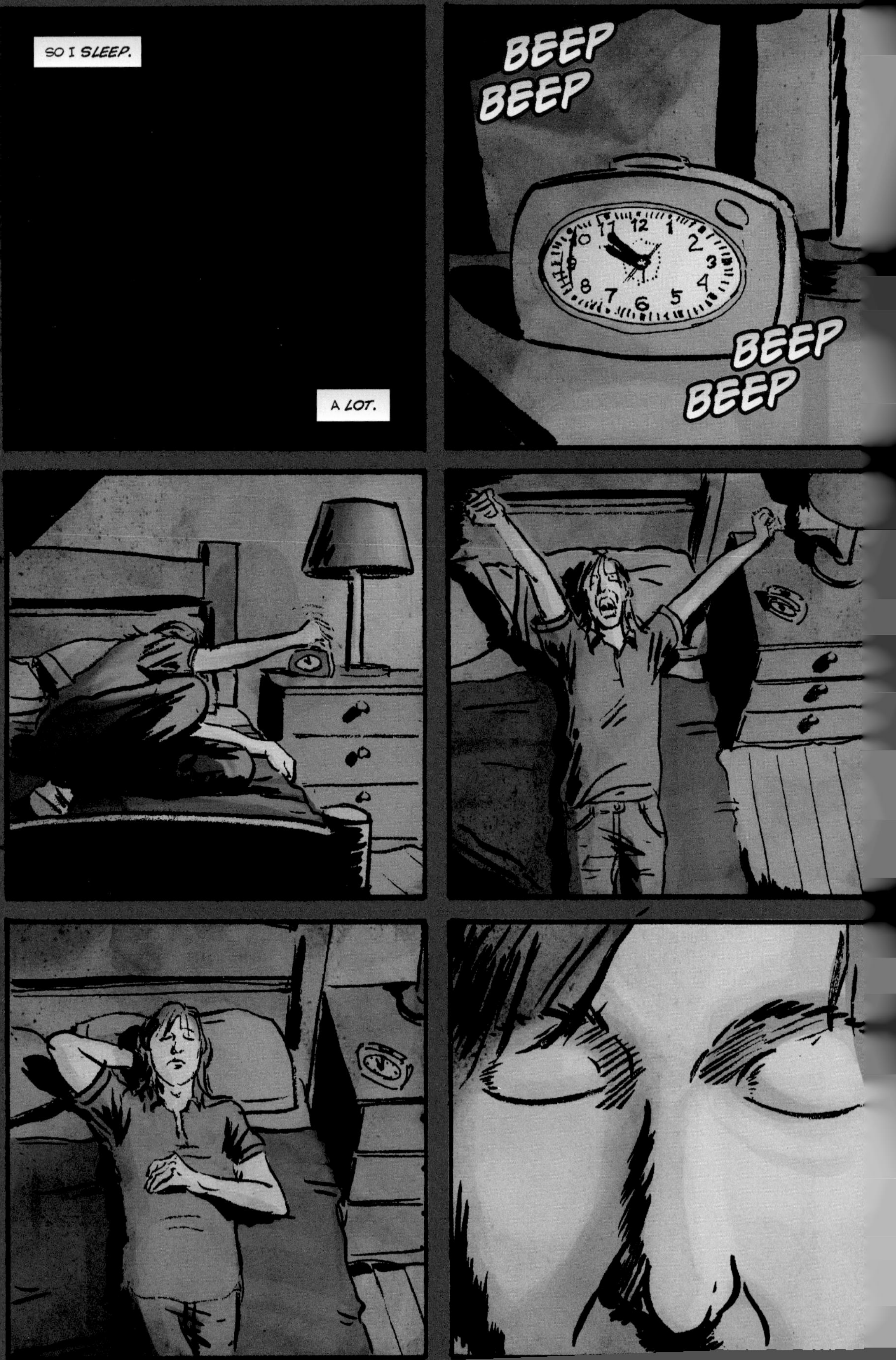
SO I SLEEP.
A LOT.
BEEP
BEEP
BEEP
BEEP

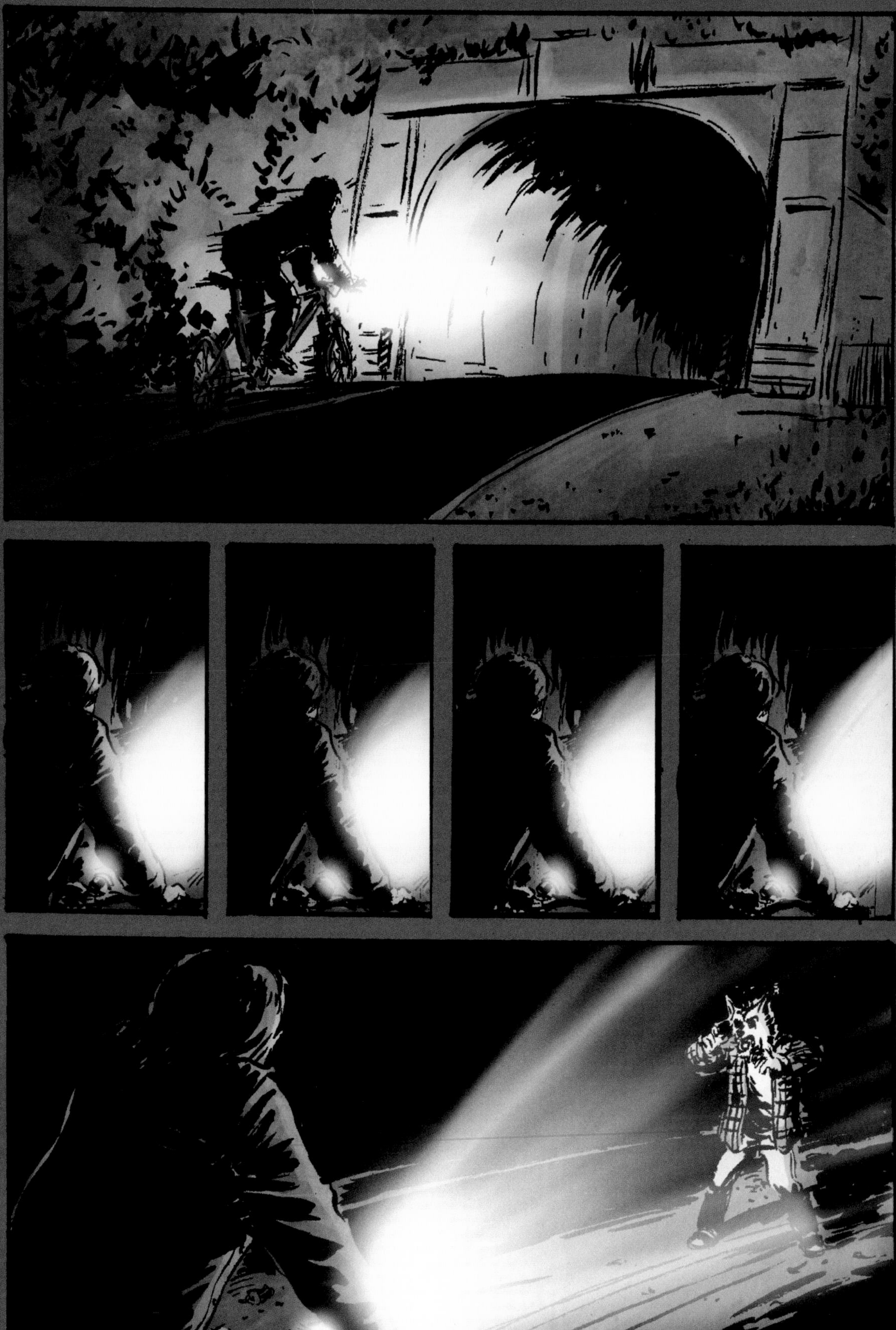

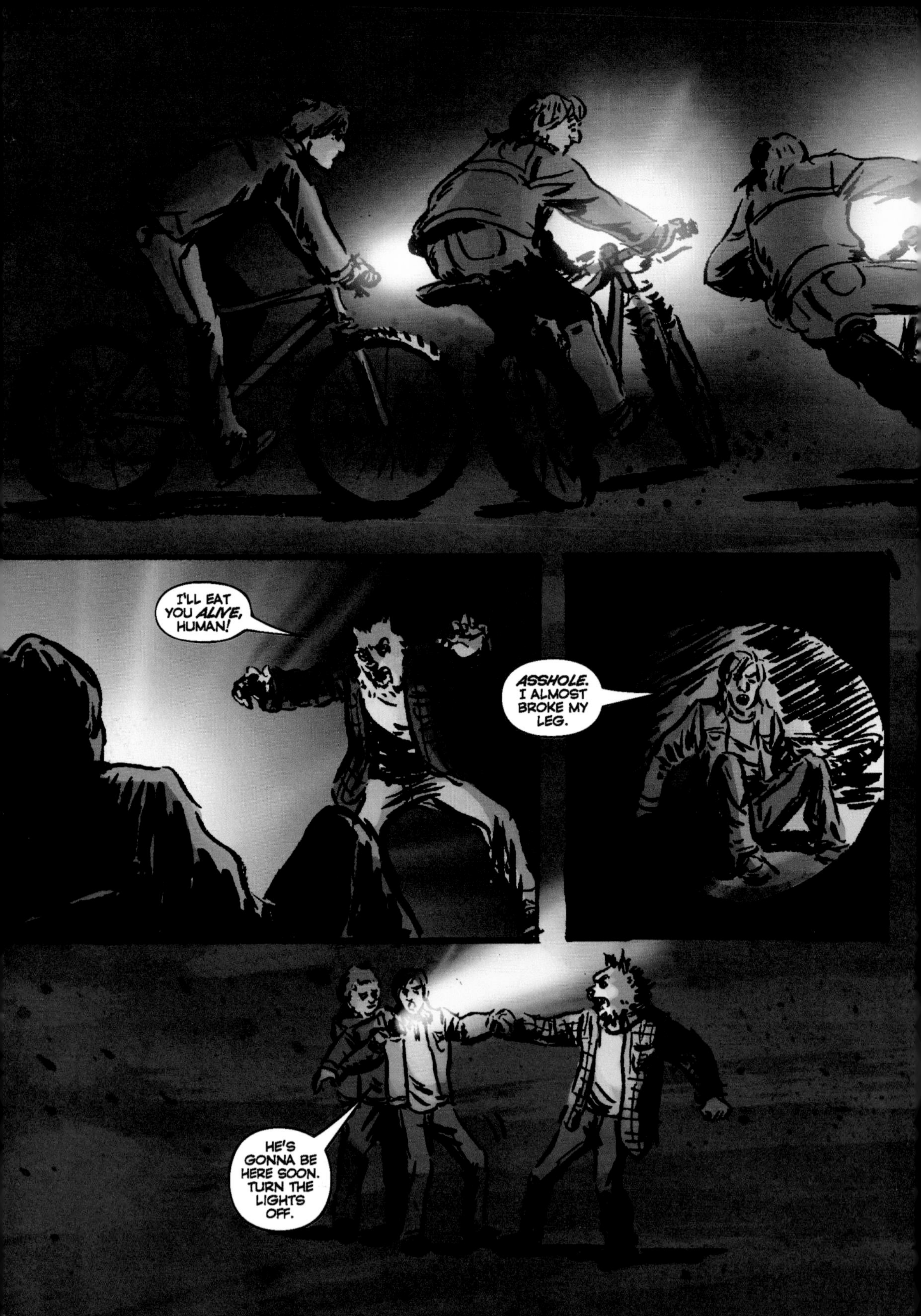
I'LL EAT YOU *ALIVE*, HUMAN!
ASSHOLE. I ALMOST BROKE MY LEG.
HE'S GONNA BE HERE SOON. TURN THE LIGHTS OFF.

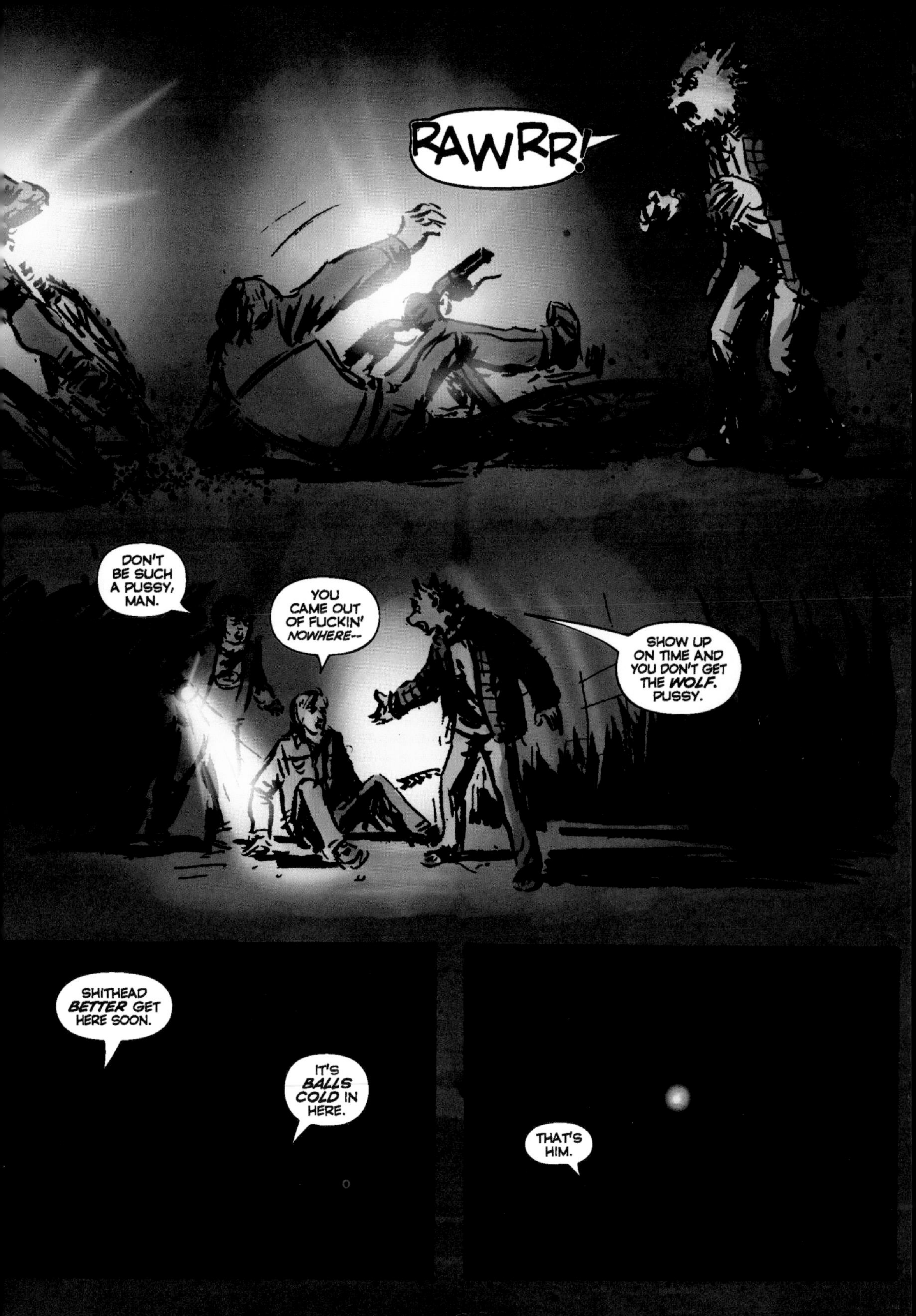
RAWRR!
DON'T BE SUCH A PUSSY, MAN.
YOU CAME OUT OF FUCKIN' *NOWHERE*--
SHOW UP ON TIME AND YOU DON'T GET THE ***WOLF.*** PUSSY.
SHITHEAD ***BETTER*** GET HERE SOON.
IT'S ***BALLS COLD*** IN HERE.
THAT'S HIM.

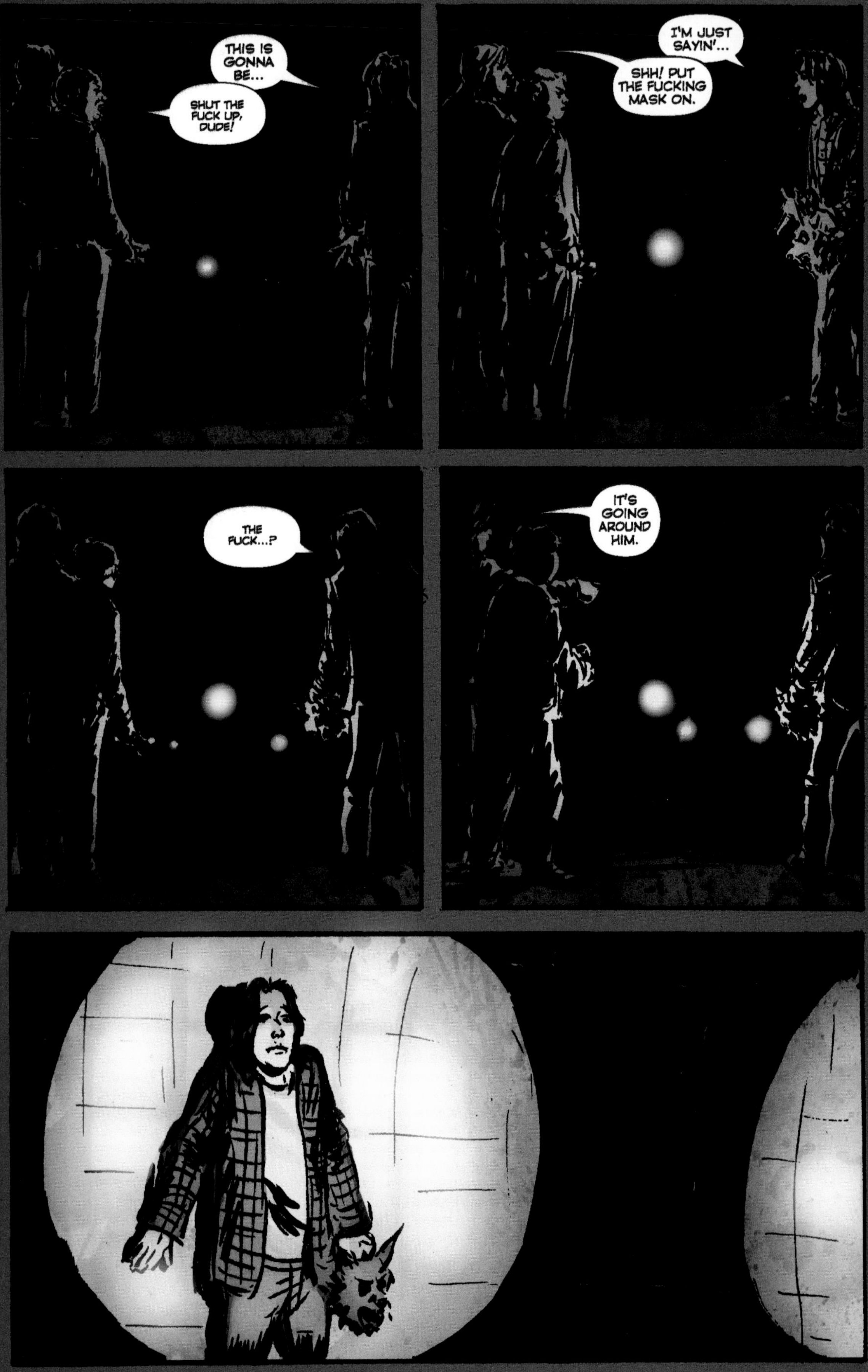
THIS IS GONNA BE...
SHUT THE FUCK UP, DUDE!
I'M JUST SAYIN'...
SHH! PUT THE FUCKING MASK ON.
THE FUCK...?
IT'S GOING AROUND HIM.

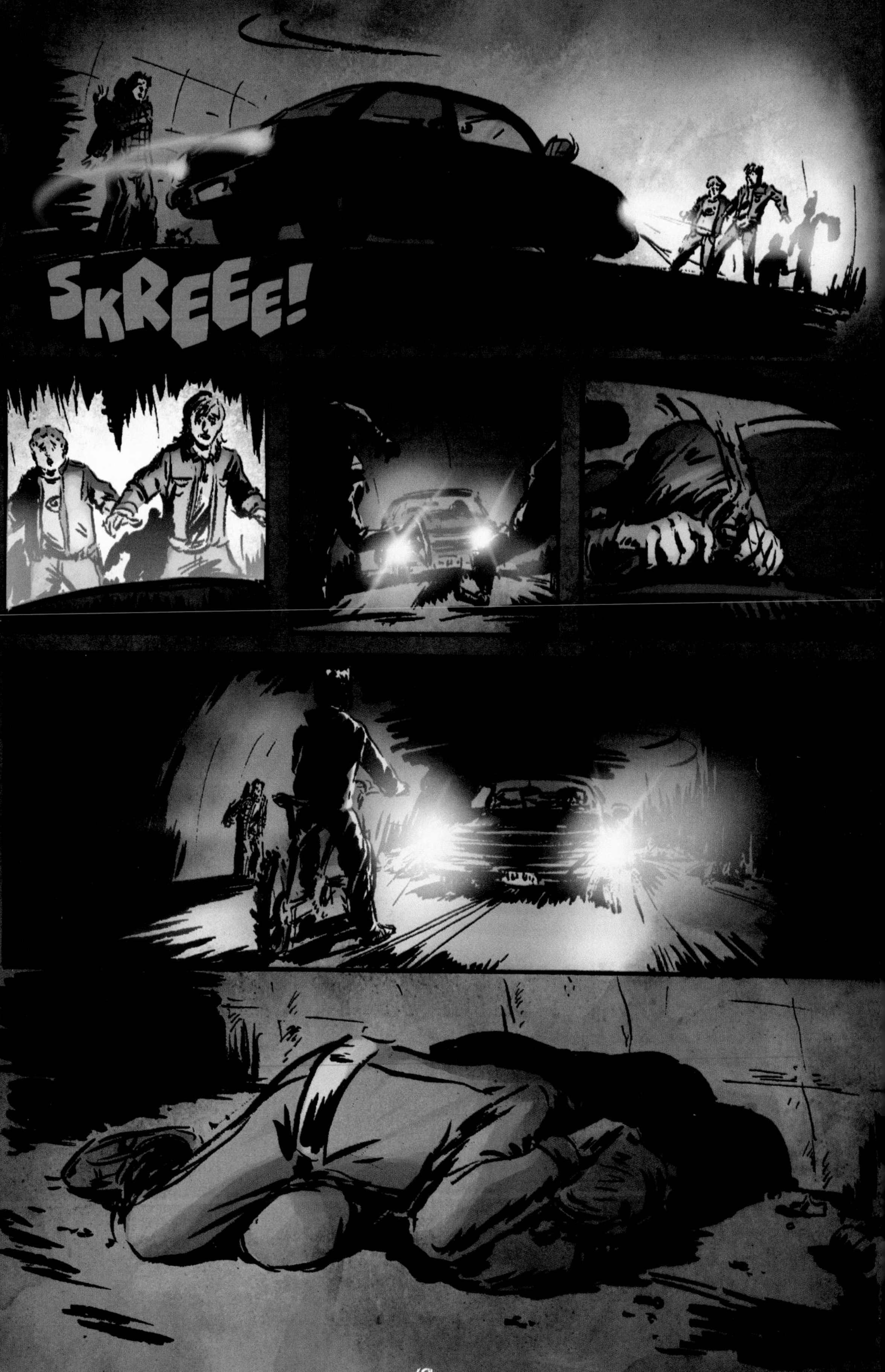
SKREEE!

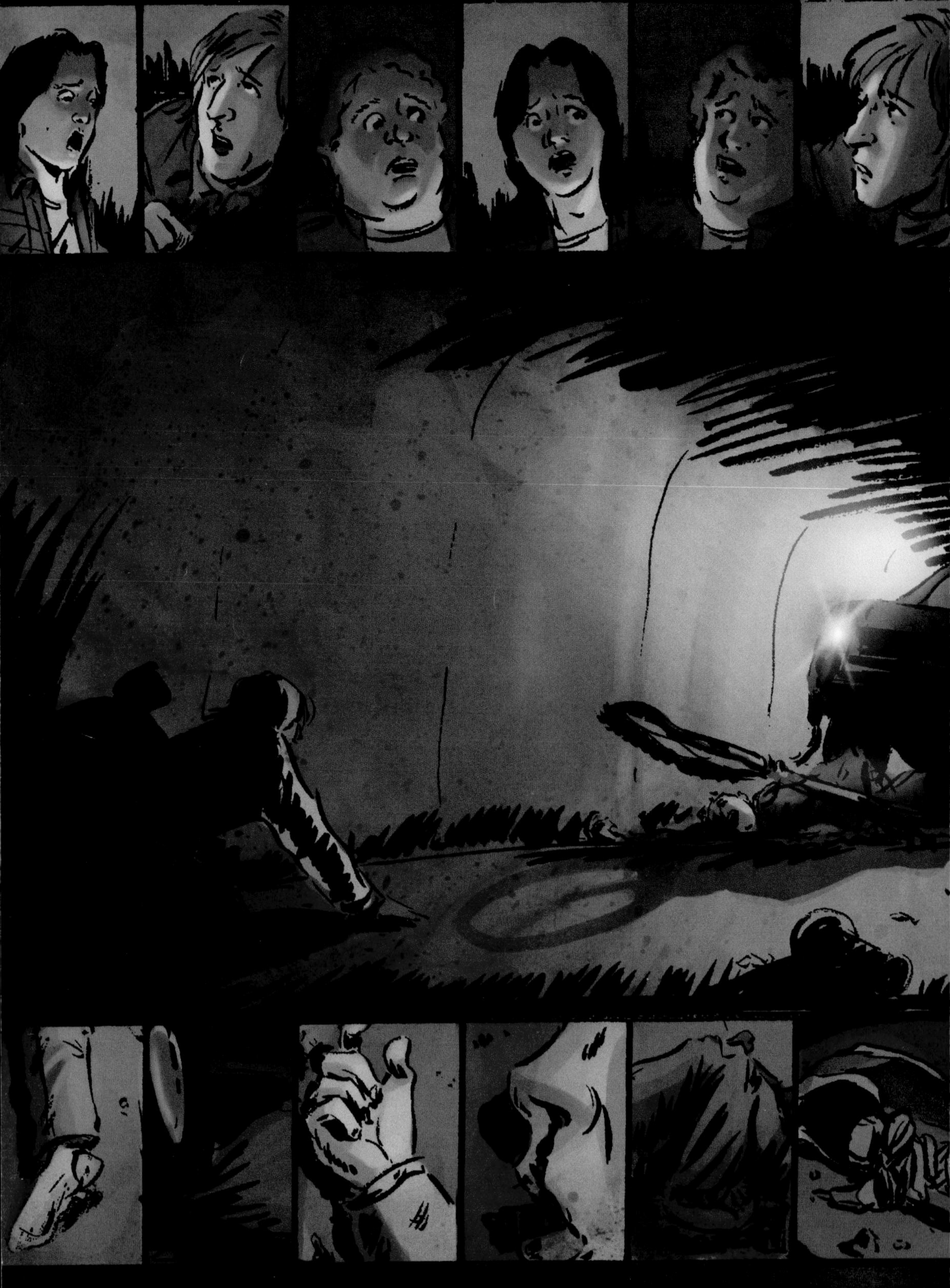

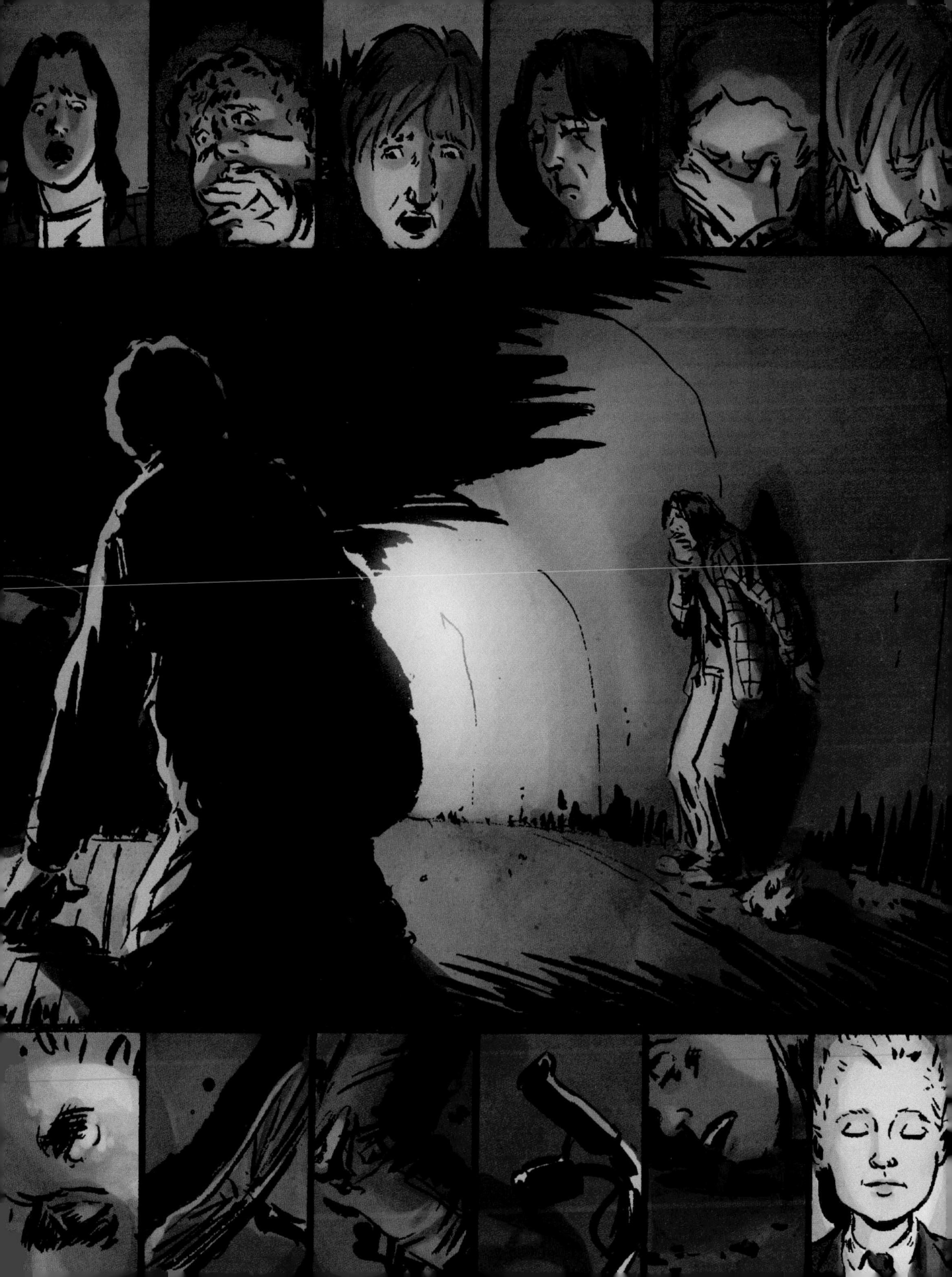

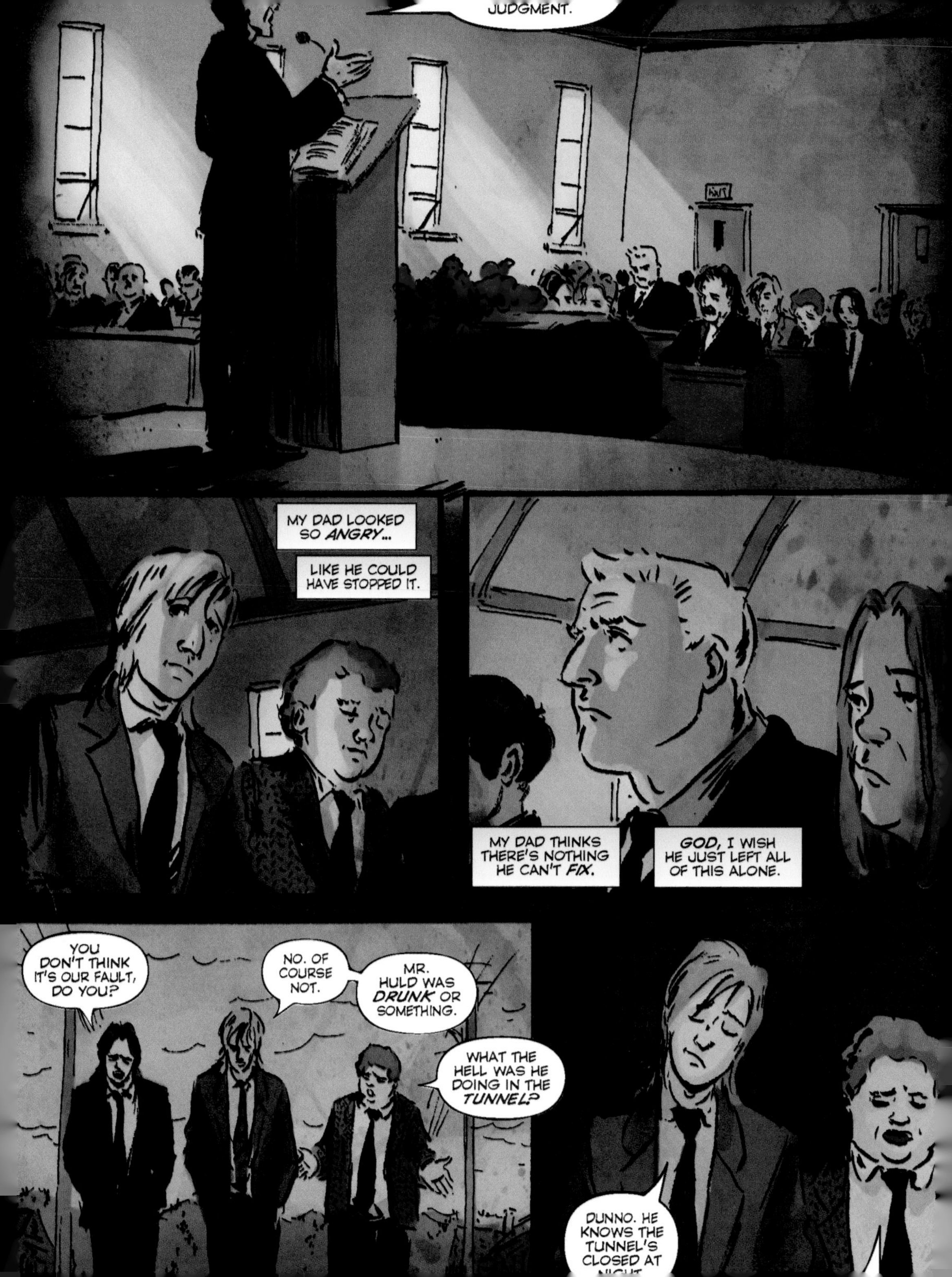
JUDGMENT.
MY DAD LOOKED SO *ANGRY*...
LIKE HE COULD HAVE STOPPED IT.
MY DAD THINKS THERE'S NOTHING HE CAN'T *FIX*.
GOD, I WISH HE JUST LEFT ALL OF THIS ALONE.
YOU DON'T THINK IT'S OUR FAULT, DO YOU?
NO. OF COURSE NOT.
MR. HULD WAS *DRUNK* OR SOMETHING.
WHAT THE HELL WAS HE DOING IN THE *TUNNEL?*
DUNNO. HE KNOWS THE TUNNEL'S CLOSED AT

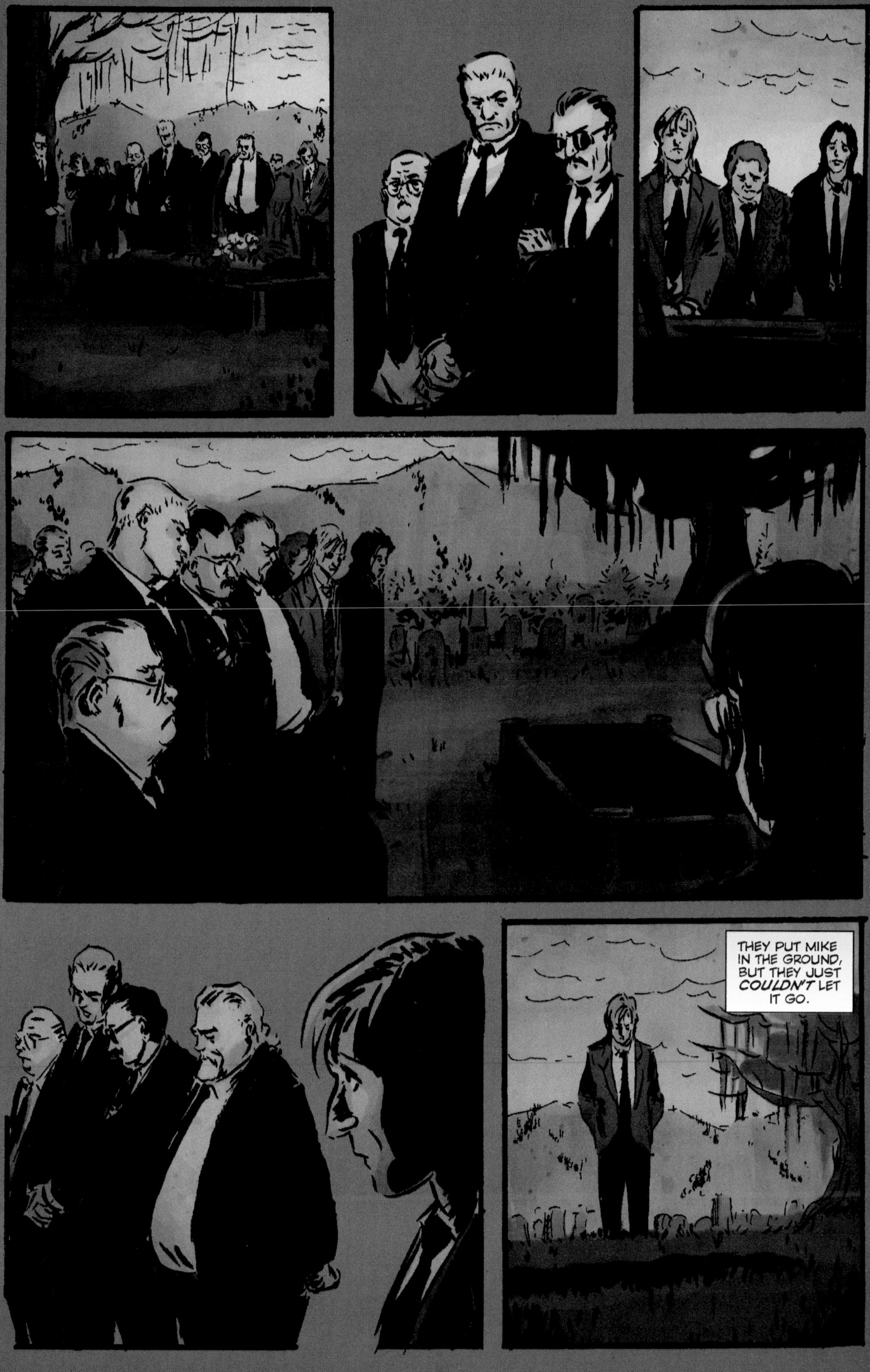
THEY PUT MIKE IN THE GROUND, BUT THEY JUST *COULDN'T* LET IT GO.

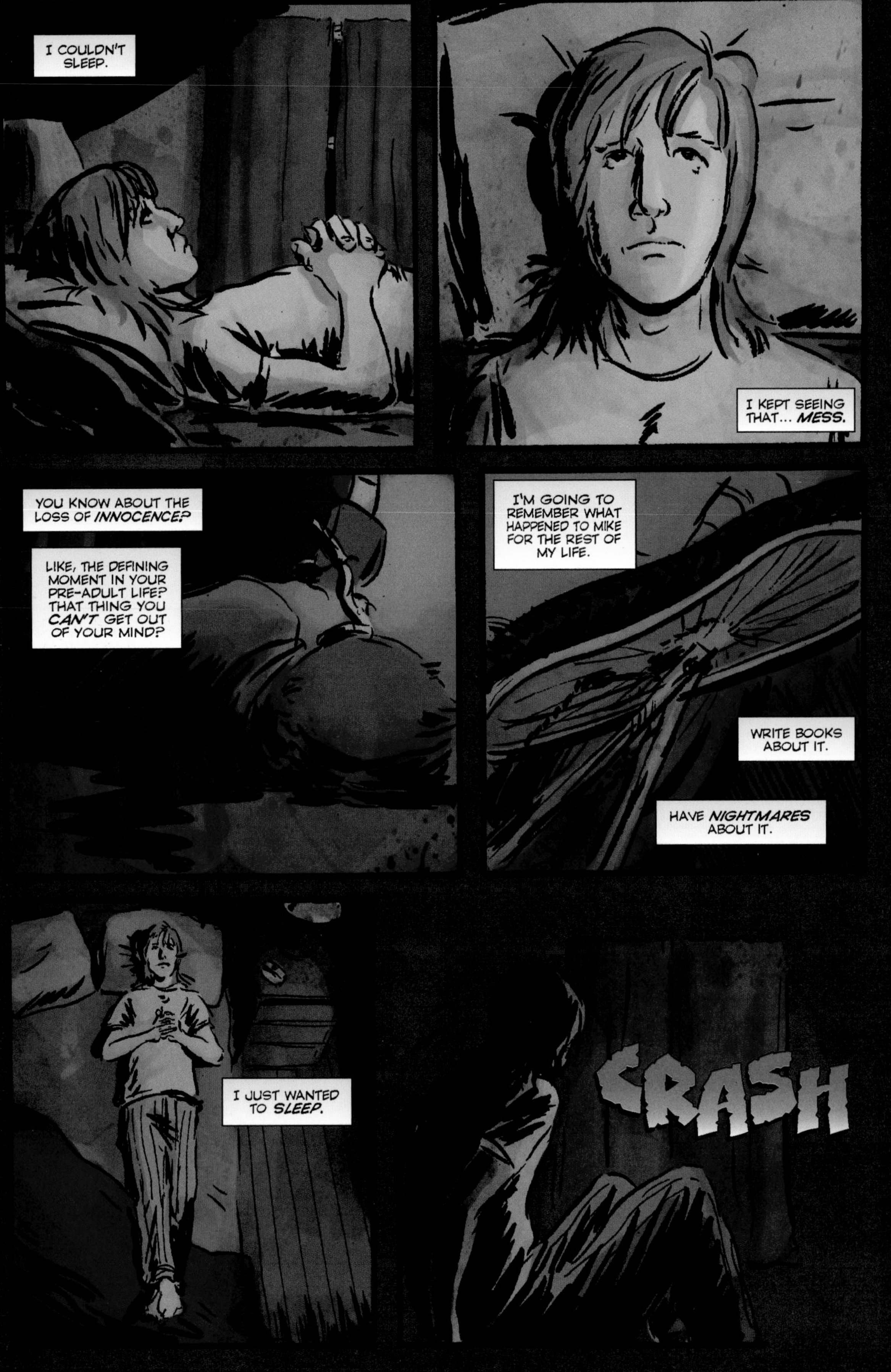
I COULDN'T SLEEP.
I KEPT SEEING THAT... *MESS.*
YOU KNOW ABOUT THE LOSS OF *INNOCENCE?*
LIKE, THE DEFINING MOMENT IN YOUR PRE-ADULT LIFE? THAT THING YOU *CAN'T* GET OUT OF YOUR MIND?
I'M GOING TO REMEMBER WHAT HAPPENED TO MIKE FOR THE REST OF MY LIFE.
WRITE BOOKS ABOUT IT.
HAVE *NIGHTMARES* ABOUT IT.
I JUST WANTED TO *SLEEP.*
CRASH

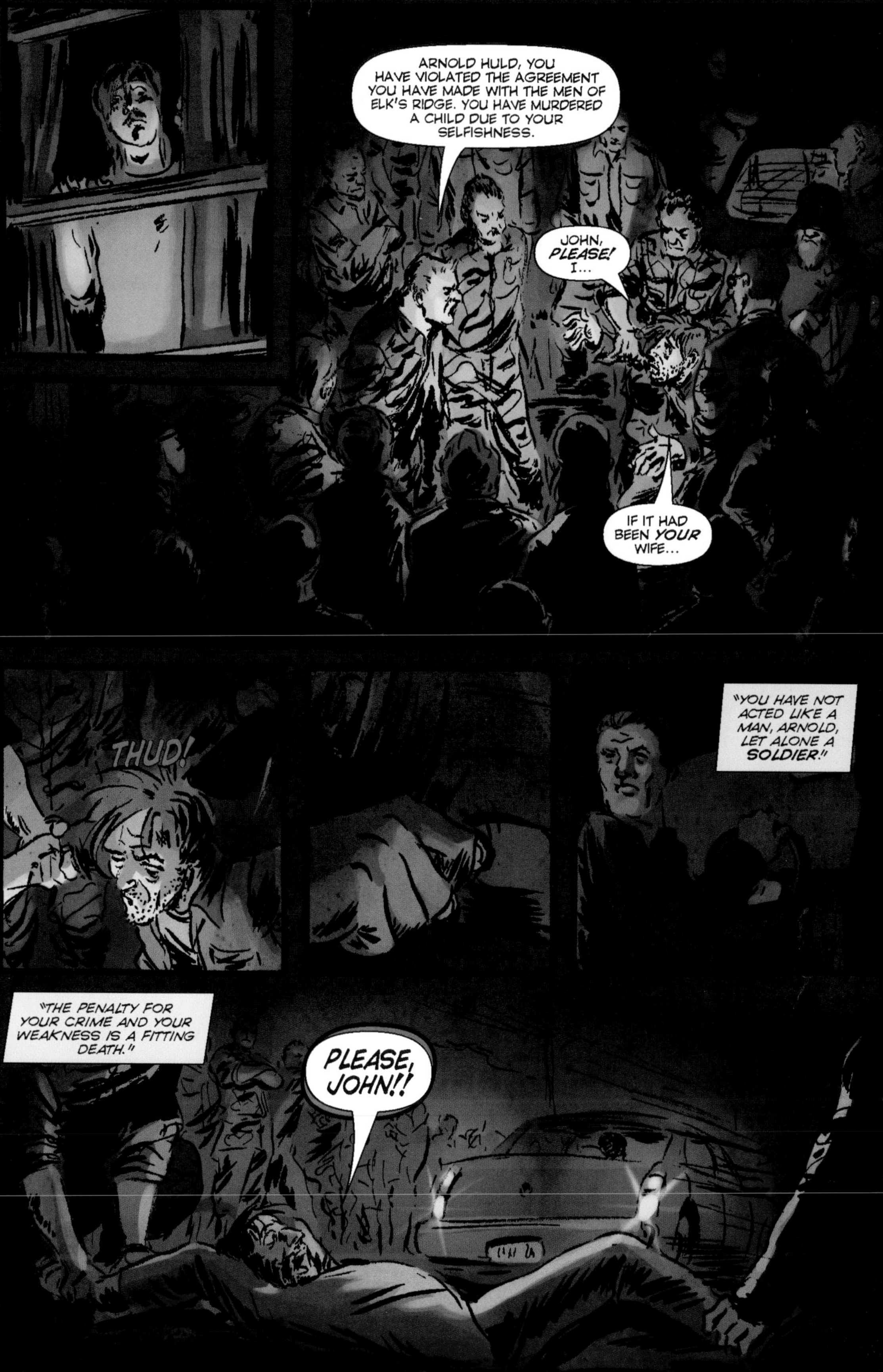
ARNOLD HULD, YOU HAVE VIOLATED THE AGREEMENT YOU HAVE MADE WITH THE MEN OF ELK'S RIDGE. YOU HAVE MURDERED A CHILD DUE TO YOUR SELFISHNESS.
JOHN, *PLEASE!* I...
IF IT HAD BEEN *YOUR* WIFE...
THUD!
"YOU HAVE NOT ACTED LIKE A MAN, ARNOLD, LET ALONE A **SOLDIER**."
"THE PENALTY FOR YOUR CRIME AND YOUR WEAKNESS IS A FITTING DEATH."
PLEASE, JOHN!!

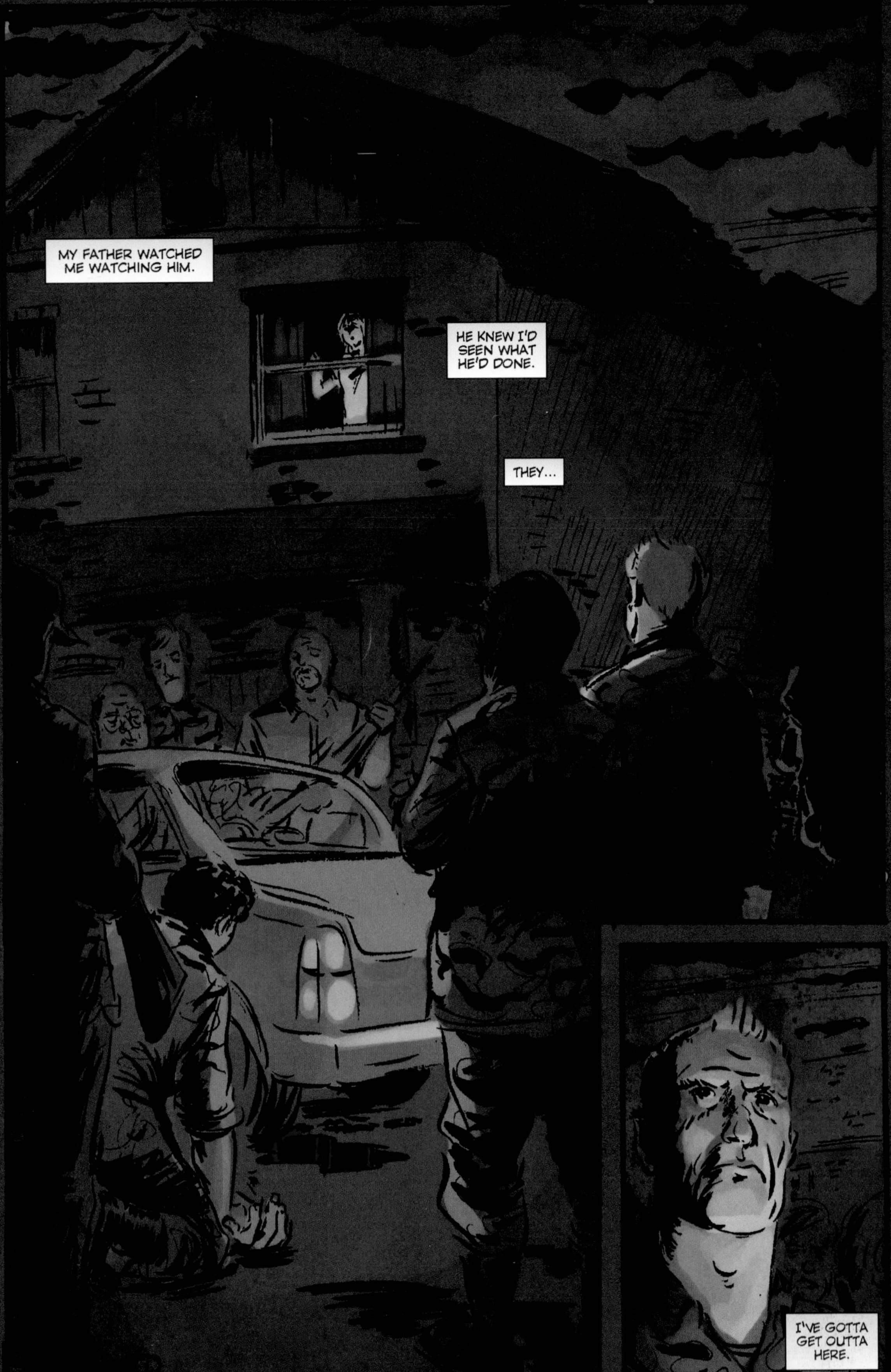
MY FATHER WATCHED ME WATCHING HIM.
HE KNEW I'D SEEN WHAT HE'D DONE.
THEY...
I'VE GOTTA GET OUTTA HERE.

END OF CHAPTER ONE...

Chapter Two: The Coming War

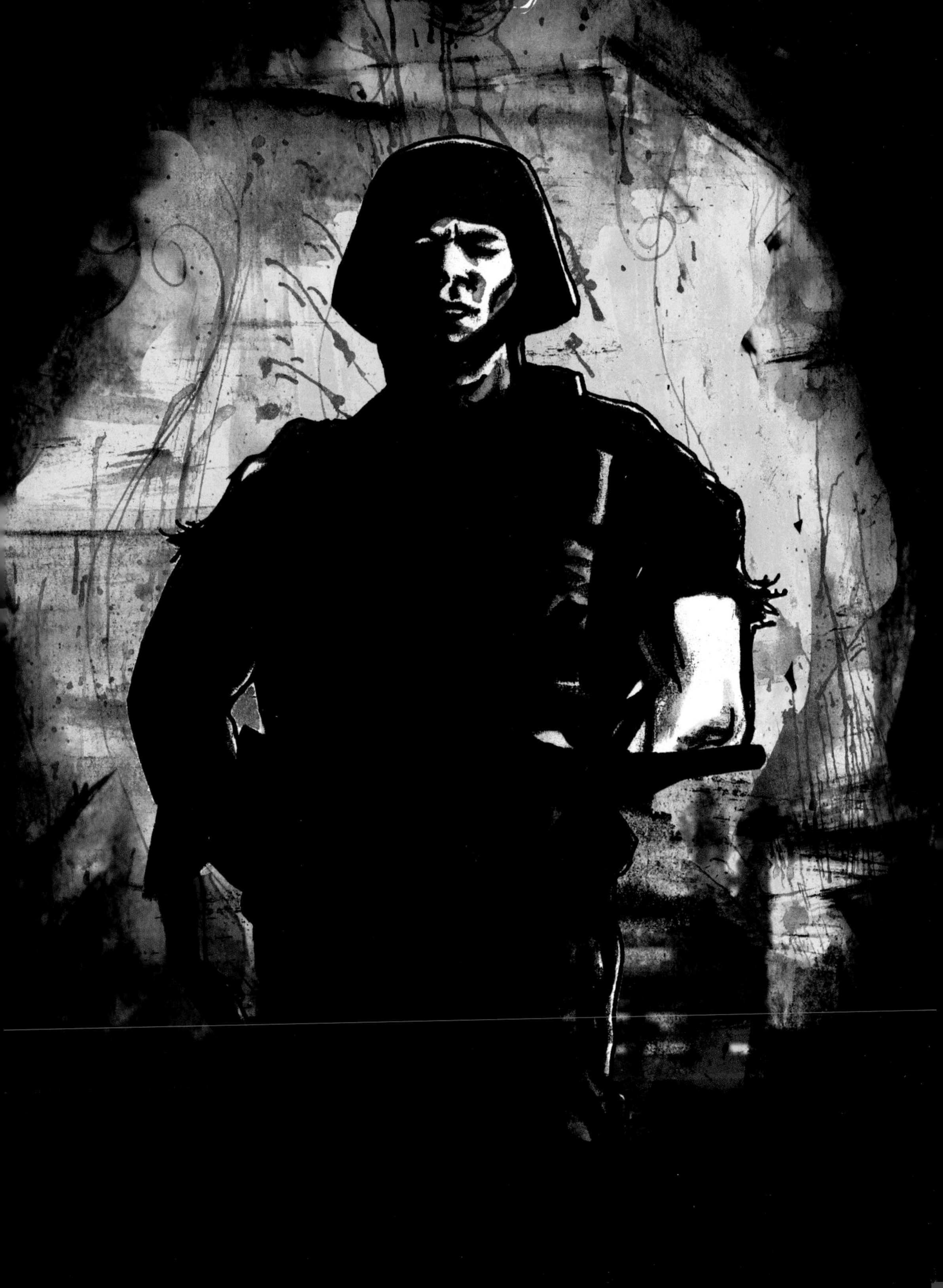

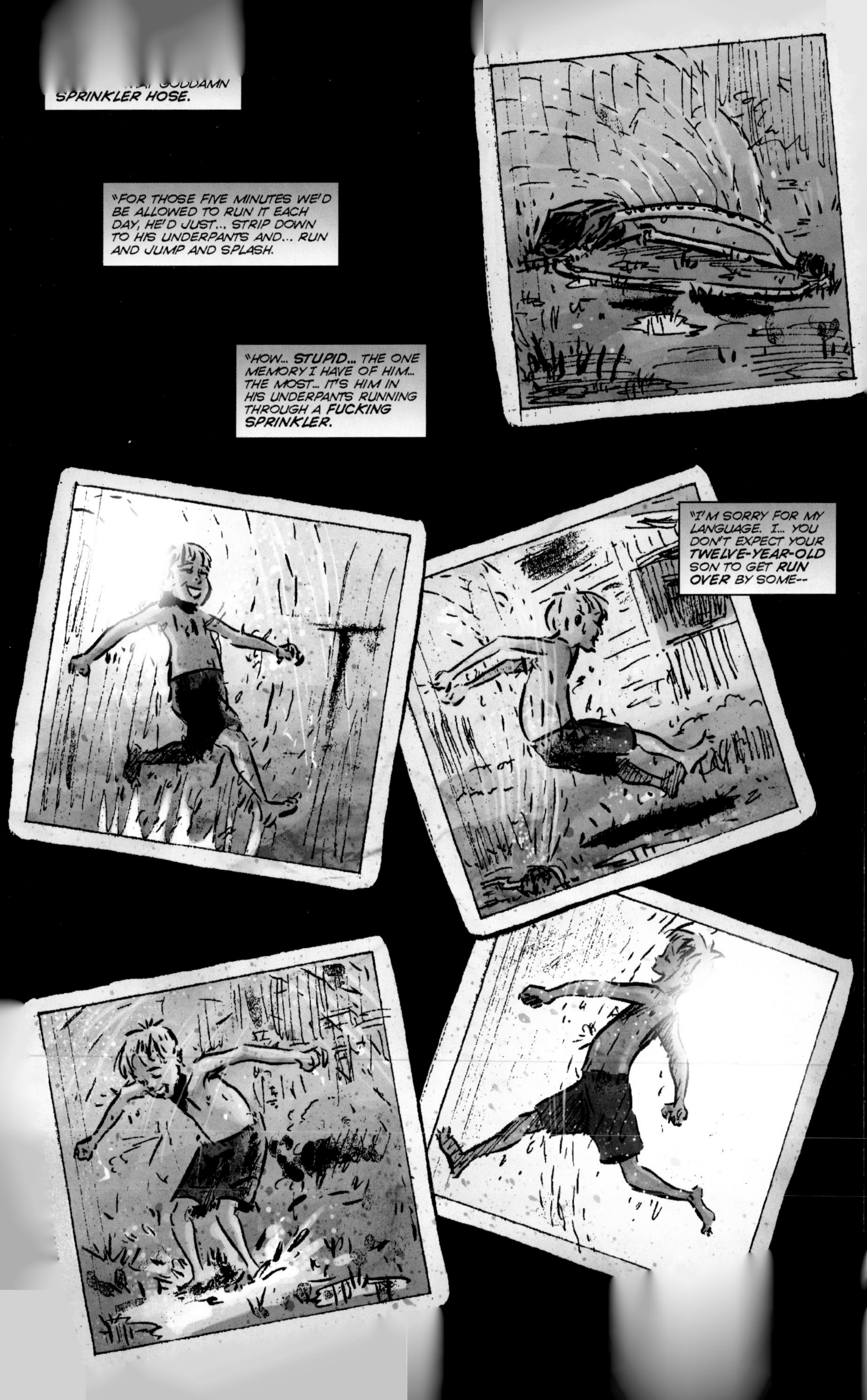
GODDAMN SPRINKLER HOSE.
"FOR THOSE FIVE MINUTES WE'D BE ALLOWED TO RUN IT EACH DAY, HE'D JUST... STRIP DOWN TO HIS UNDERPANTS AND... RUN AND JUMP AND SPLASH.
"HOW... STUPID... THE ONE MEMORY I HAVE OF HIM... THE MOST... IT'S HIM IN HIS UNDERPANTS RUNNING THROUGH A FUCKING SPRINKLER.
"I'M SORRY FOR MY LANGUAGE. I... YOU DON'T EXPECT YOUR TWELVE-YEAR-OLD SON TO GET RUN OVER BY SOME--

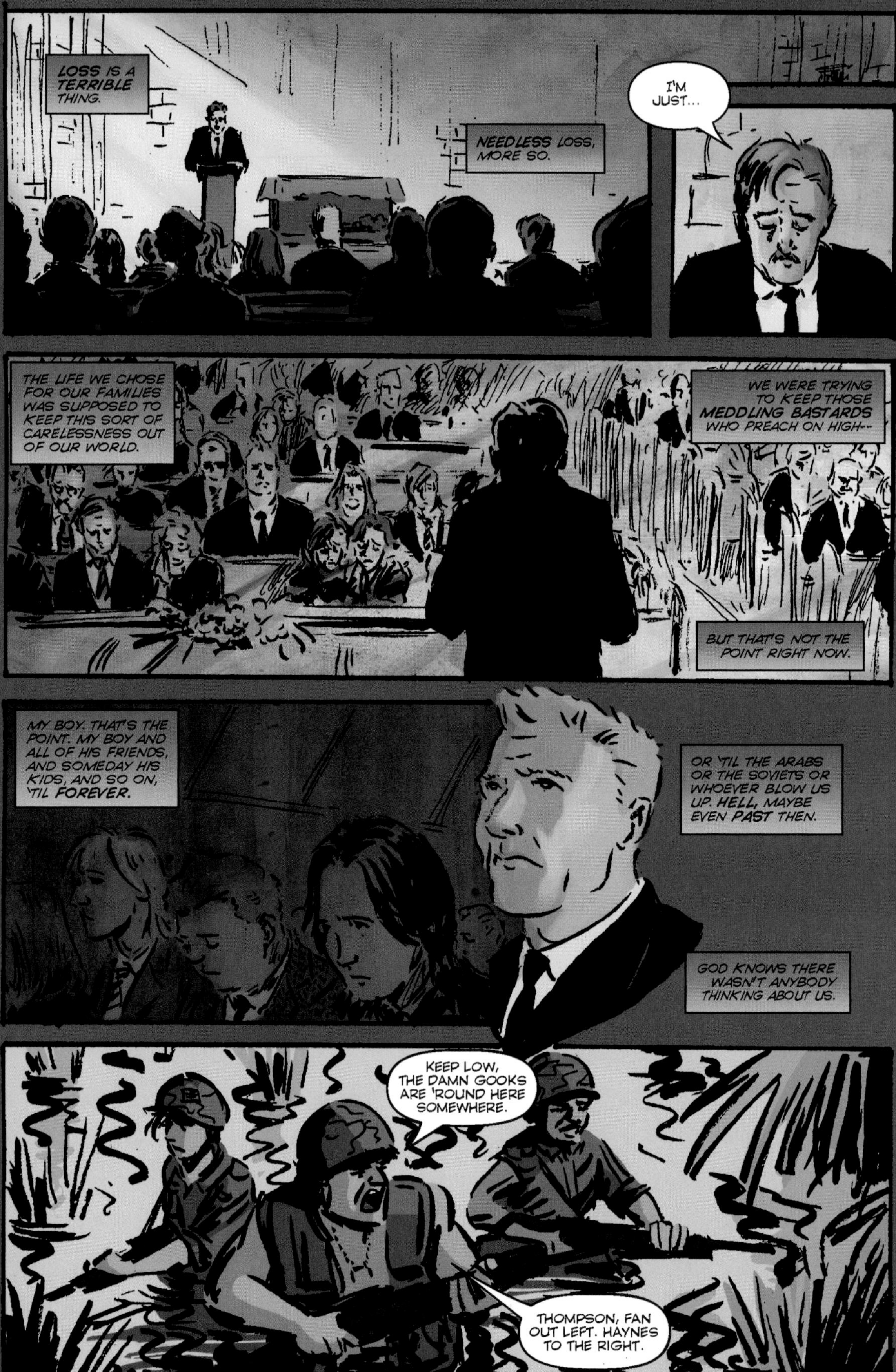
LOSS IS A TERRIBLE THING.
NEEDLESS LOSS, MORE SO.
I'M JUST...
THE LIFE WE CHOSE FOR OUR FAMILIES WAS SUPPOSED TO KEEP THIS SORT OF CARELESSNESS OUT OF OUR WORLD.
WE WERE TRYING TO KEEP THOSE MEDDLING BASTARDS WHO PREACH ON HIGH--
BUT THAT'S NOT THE POINT RIGHT NOW.
MY BOY. THAT'S THE POINT. MY BOY AND ALL OF HIS FRIENDS, AND SOMEDAY HIS KIDS, AND SO ON, 'TIL FOREVER.
OR 'TIL THE ARABS OR THE SOVIETS OR WHOEVER BLOW US UP. HELL, MAYBE EVEN PAST THEN.
GOD KNOWS THERE WASN'T ANYBODY THINKING ABOUT US.
KEEP LOW, THE DAMN GOOKS ARE 'ROUND HERE SOMEWHERE.
THOMPSON, FAN OUT LEFT. HAYNES TO THE RIGHT.

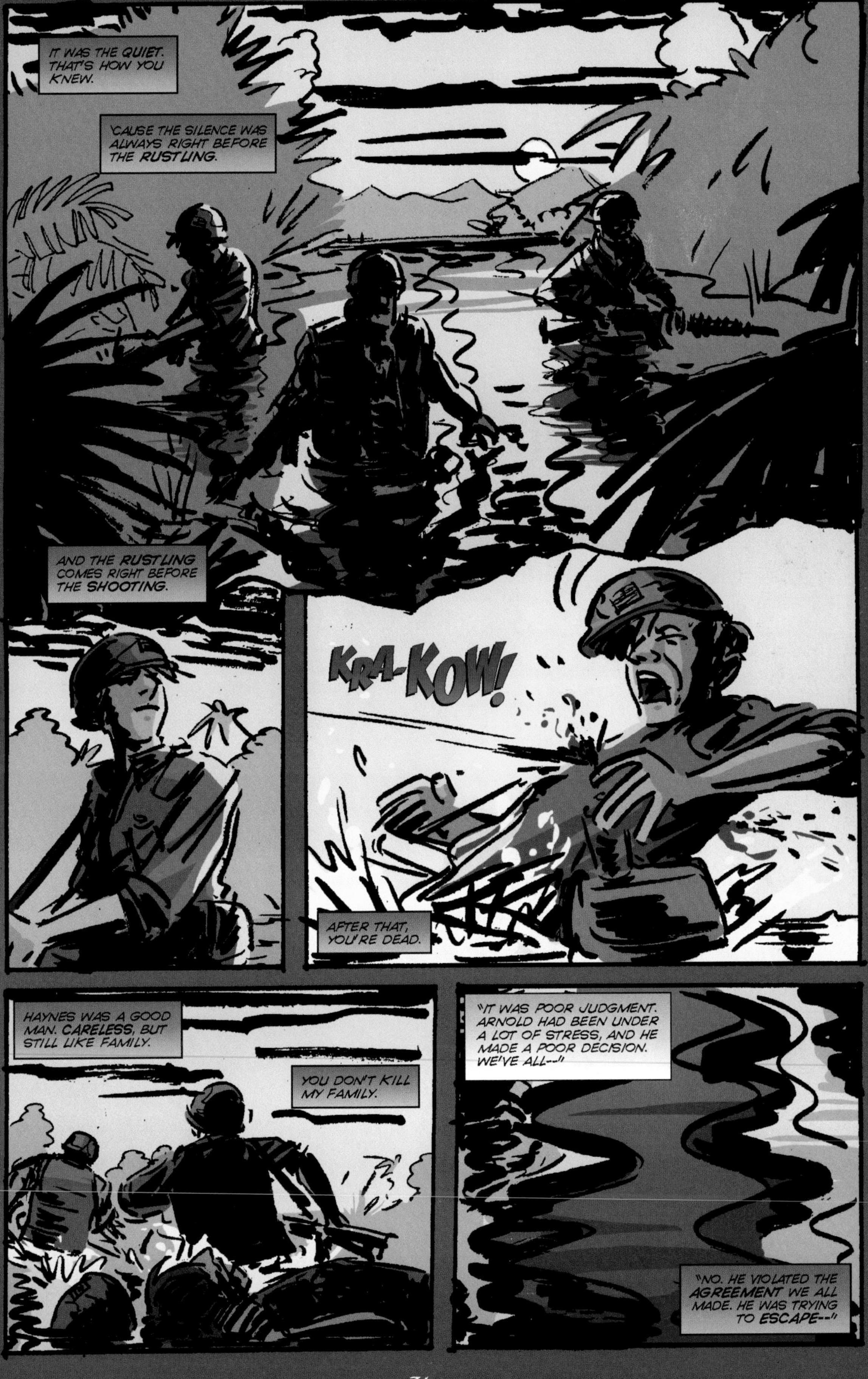
IT WAS THE QUIET. THAT'S HOW YOU KNEW.
'CAUSE THE SILENCE WAS ALWAYS RIGHT BEFORE THE RUSTLING.
AND THE RUSTLING COMES RIGHT BEFORE THE SHOOTING.
KRA-KOW!
AFTER THAT, YOU'RE DEAD.
HAYNES WAS A GOOD MAN. CARELESS, BUT STILL LIKE FAMILY.
YOU DON'T KILL MY FAMILY.
"IT WAS POOR JUDGMENT. ARNOLD HAD BEEN UNDER A LOT OF STRESS, AND HE MADE A POOR DECISION. WE'VE ALL--"
"NO. HE VIOLATED THE AGREEMENT WE ALL MADE. HE WAS TRYING TO ESCAPE--"

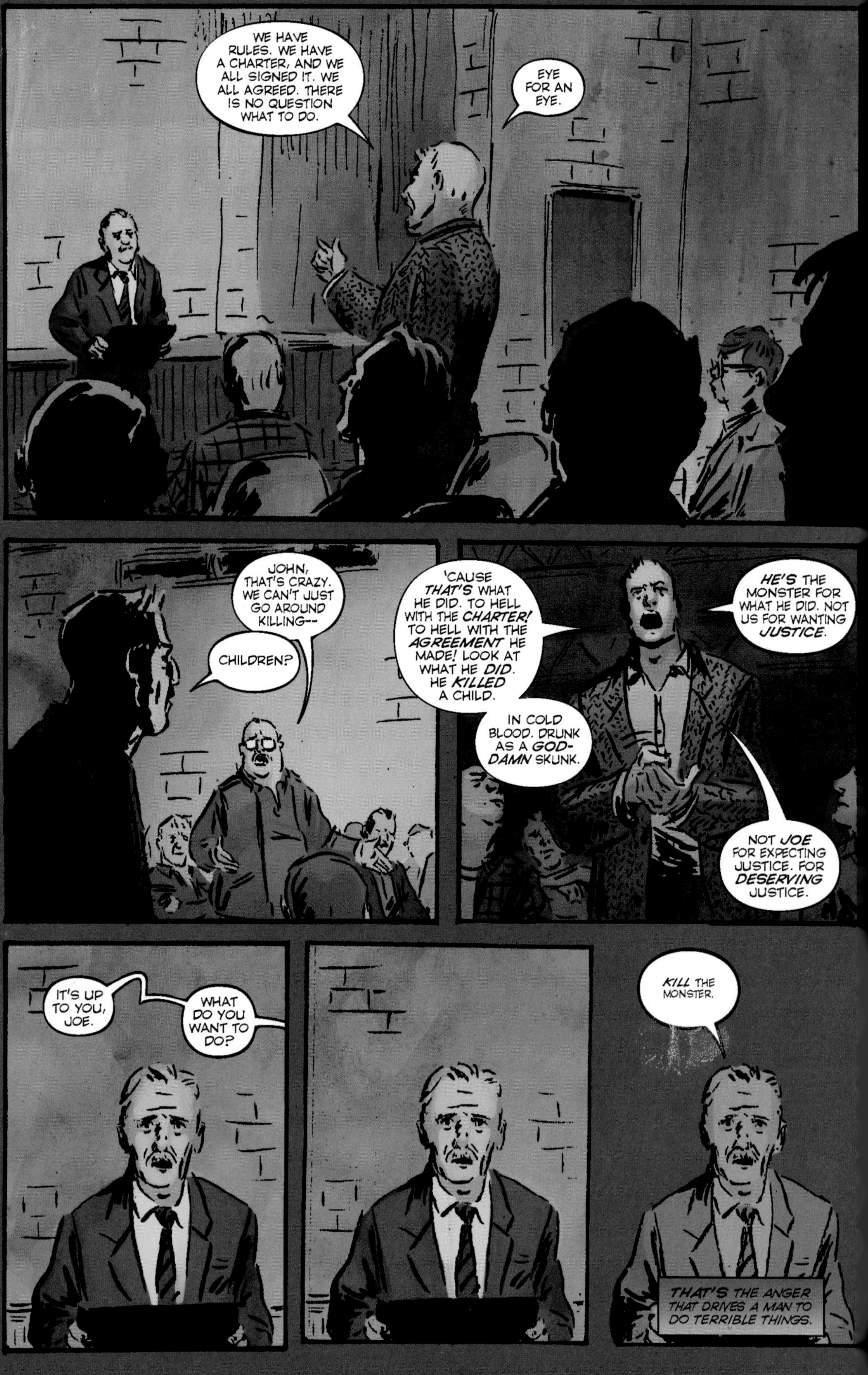
WE HAVE RULES. WE HAVE A CHARTER, AND WE ALL SIGNED IT. WE ALL AGREED. THERE IS NO QUESTION WHAT TO DO.
EYE FOR AN EYE.
JOHN, THAT'S CRAZY. WE CAN'T JUST GO AROUND KILLING--
CHILDREN?
'CAUSE THAT'S WHAT HE DID. TO HELL WITH THE CHARTER! TO HELL WITH THE AGREEMENT HE MADE! LOOK AT WHAT HE DID. HE KILLED A CHILD.
IN COLD BLOOD. DRUNK AS A GOD-DAMN SKUNK.
HE'S THE MONSTER FOR WHAT HE DID. NOT US FOR WANTING JUSTICE.
NOT JOE FOR EXPECTING JUSTICE. FOR DESERVING JUSTICE.
IT'S UP TO YOU, JOE.
WHAT DO YOU WANT TO DO?
KILL THE MONSTER.
THAT'S THE ANGER THAT DRIVES A MAN TO DO TERRIBLE THINGS.

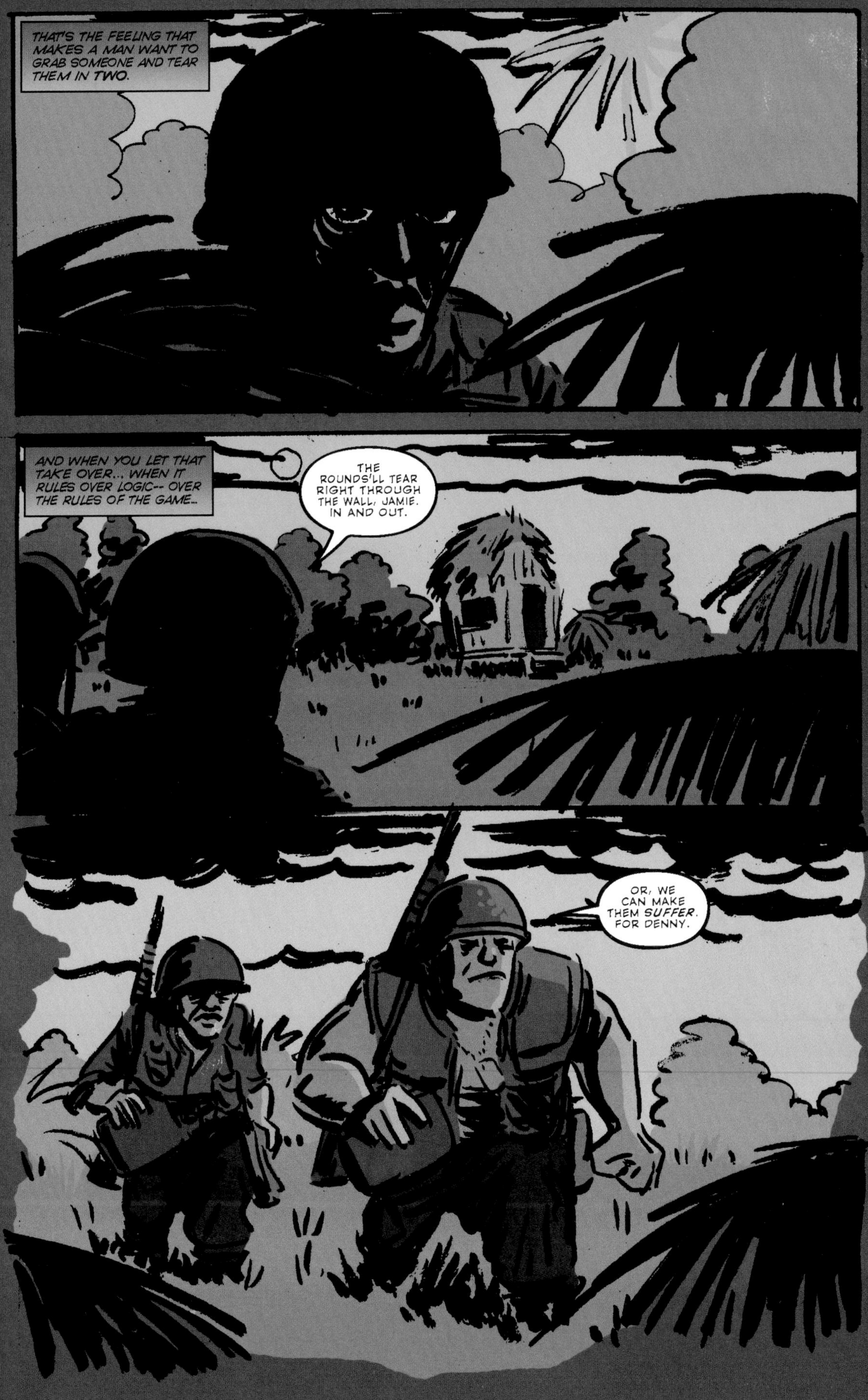
THAT'S THE FEELING THAT MAKES A MAN WANT TO GRAB SOMEONE AND TEAR THEM IN TWO.
AND WHEN YOU LET THAT TAKE OVER... WHEN IT RULES OVER LOGIC-- OVER THE RULES OF THE GAME...
THE ROUNDS'LL TEAR RIGHT THROUGH THE WALL, JAMIE. IN AND OUT.
OR, WE CAN MAKE THEM SUFFER. FOR DENNY.

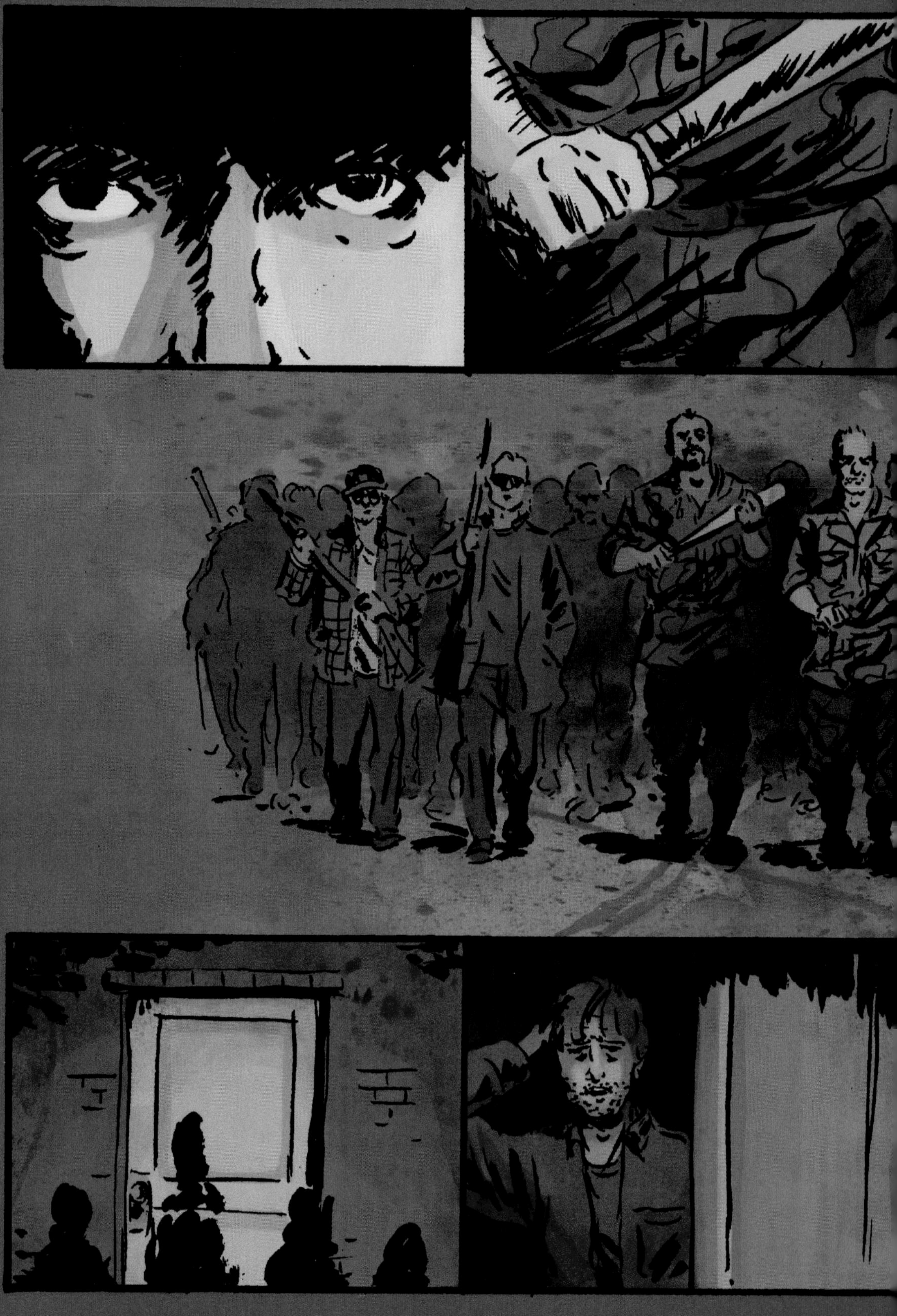

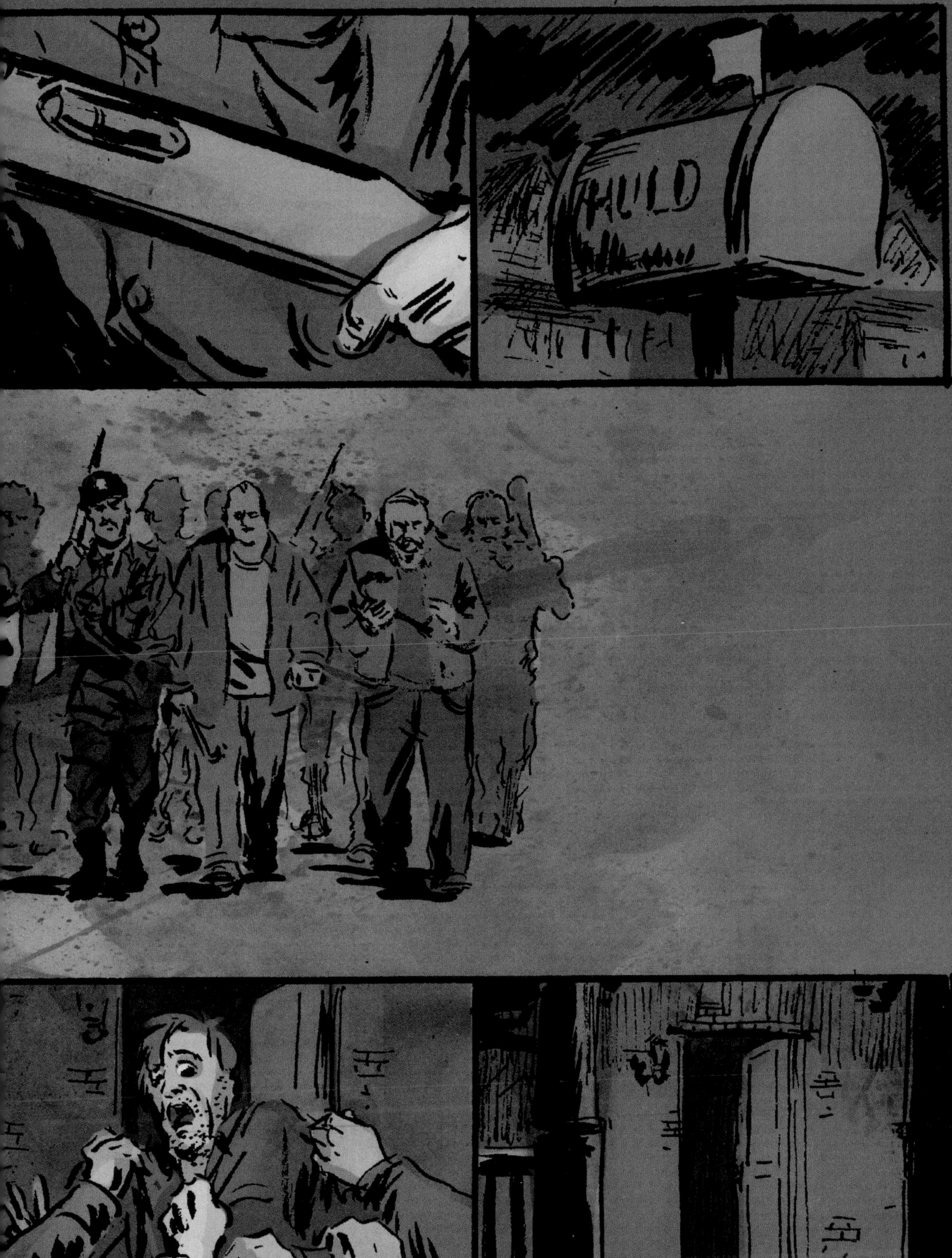
HULD

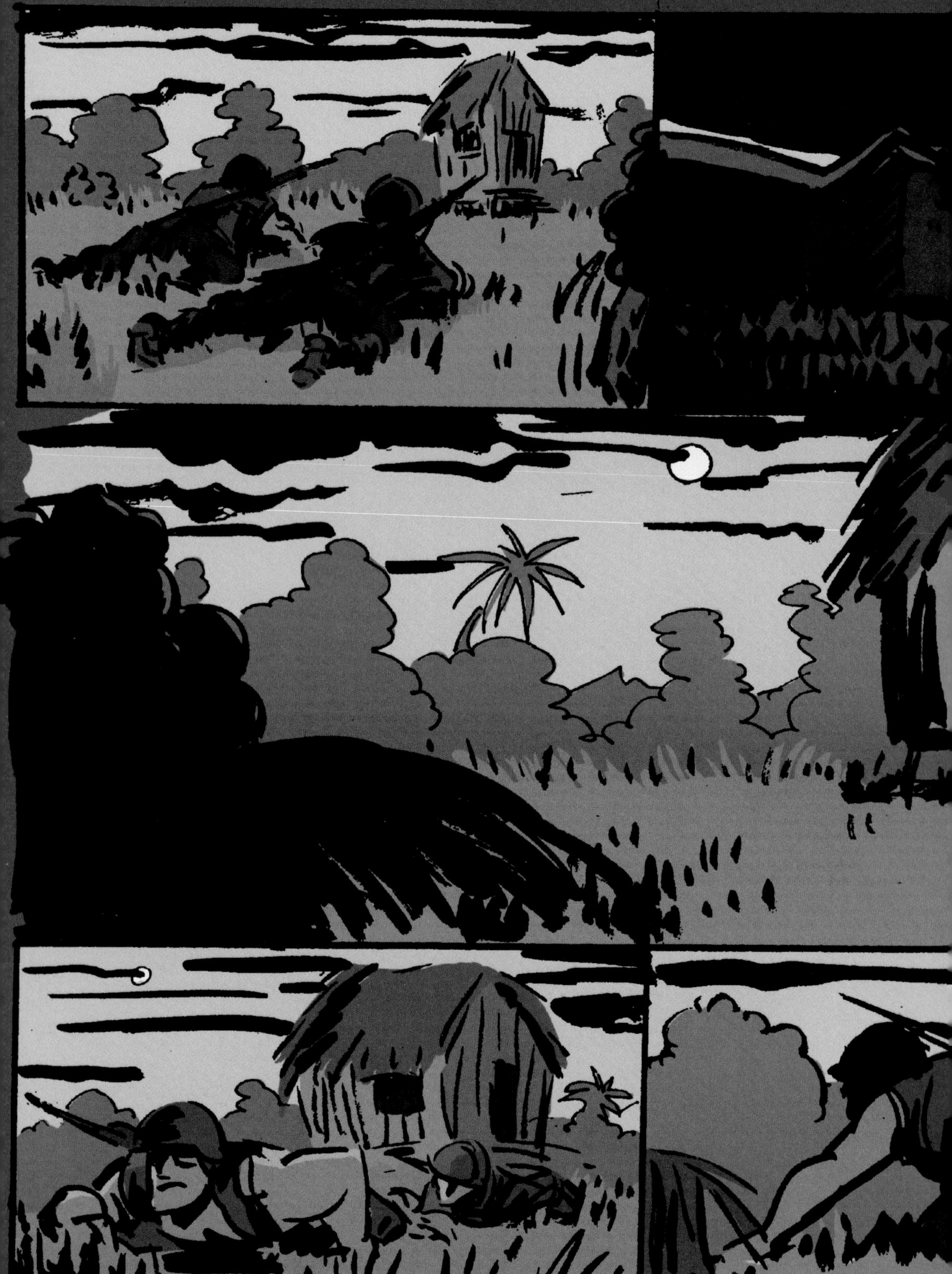

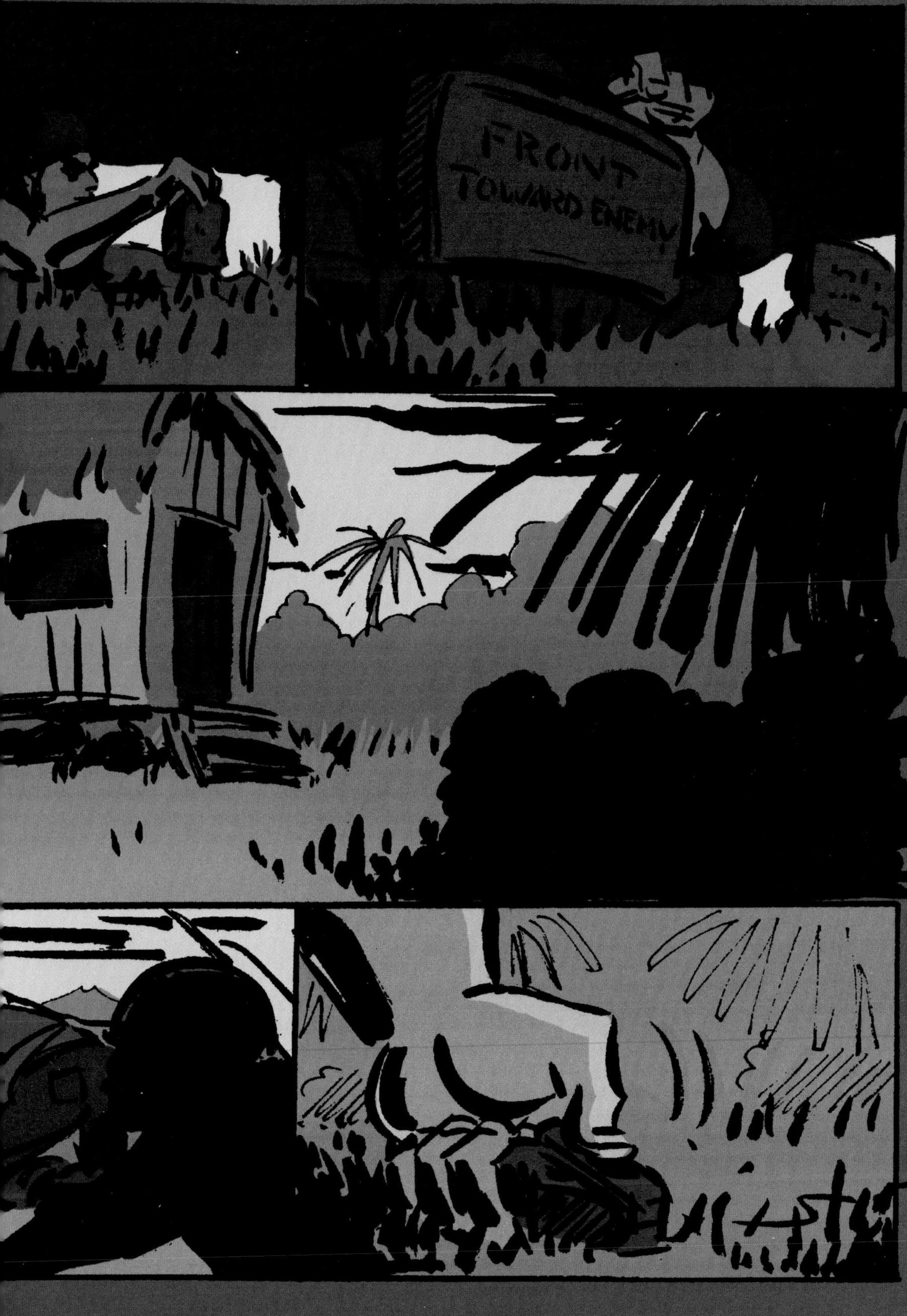
FRONT
TOWARD ENEMY

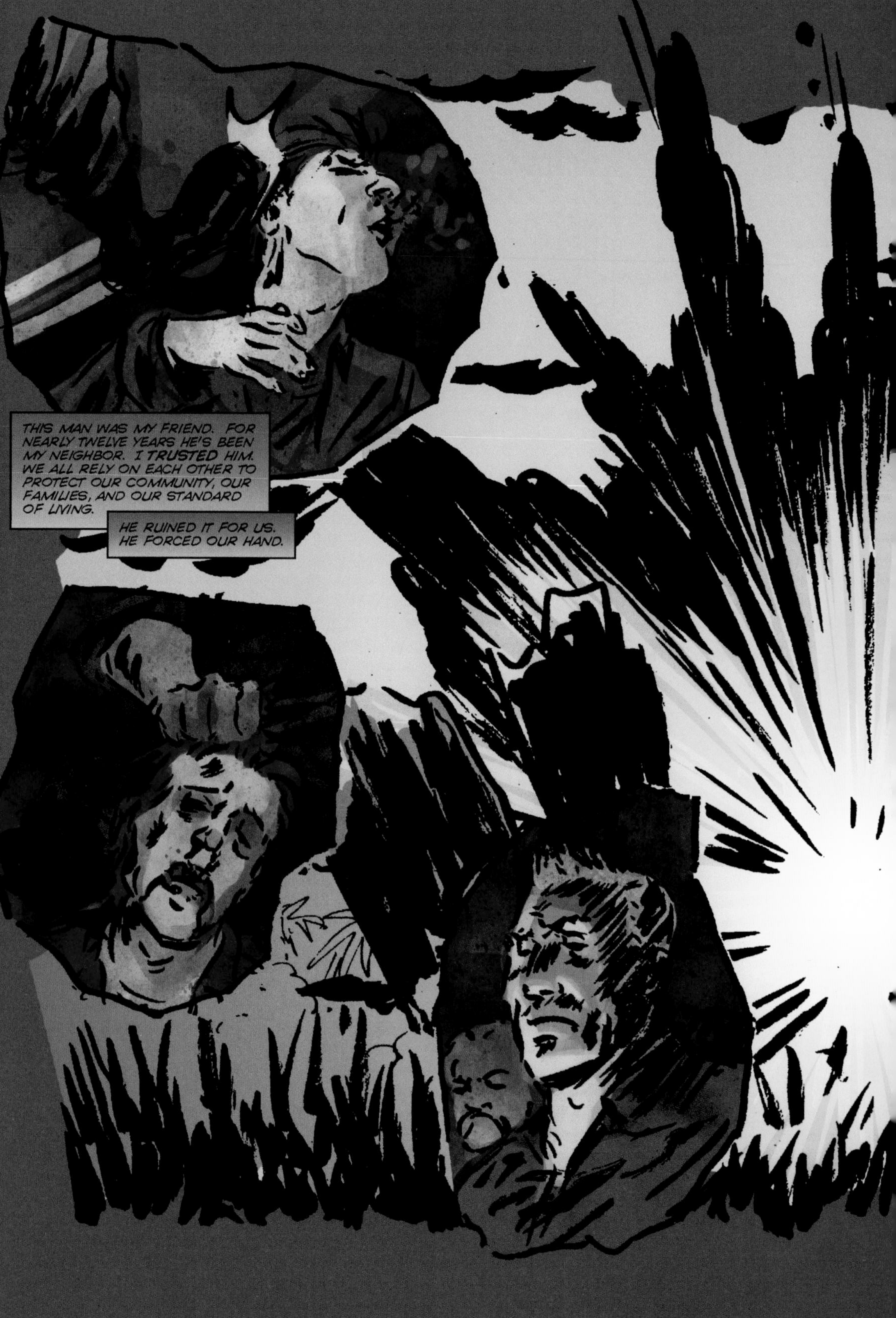
THIS MAN WAS MY FRIEND. FOR NEARLY TWELVE YEARS HE'S BEEN MY NEIGHBOR. I TRUSTED HIM. WE ALL RELY ON EACH OTHER TO PROTECT OUR COMMUNITY, OUR FAMILIES, AND OUR STANDARD OF LIVING.
HE RUINED IT FOR US. HE FORCED OUR HAND.

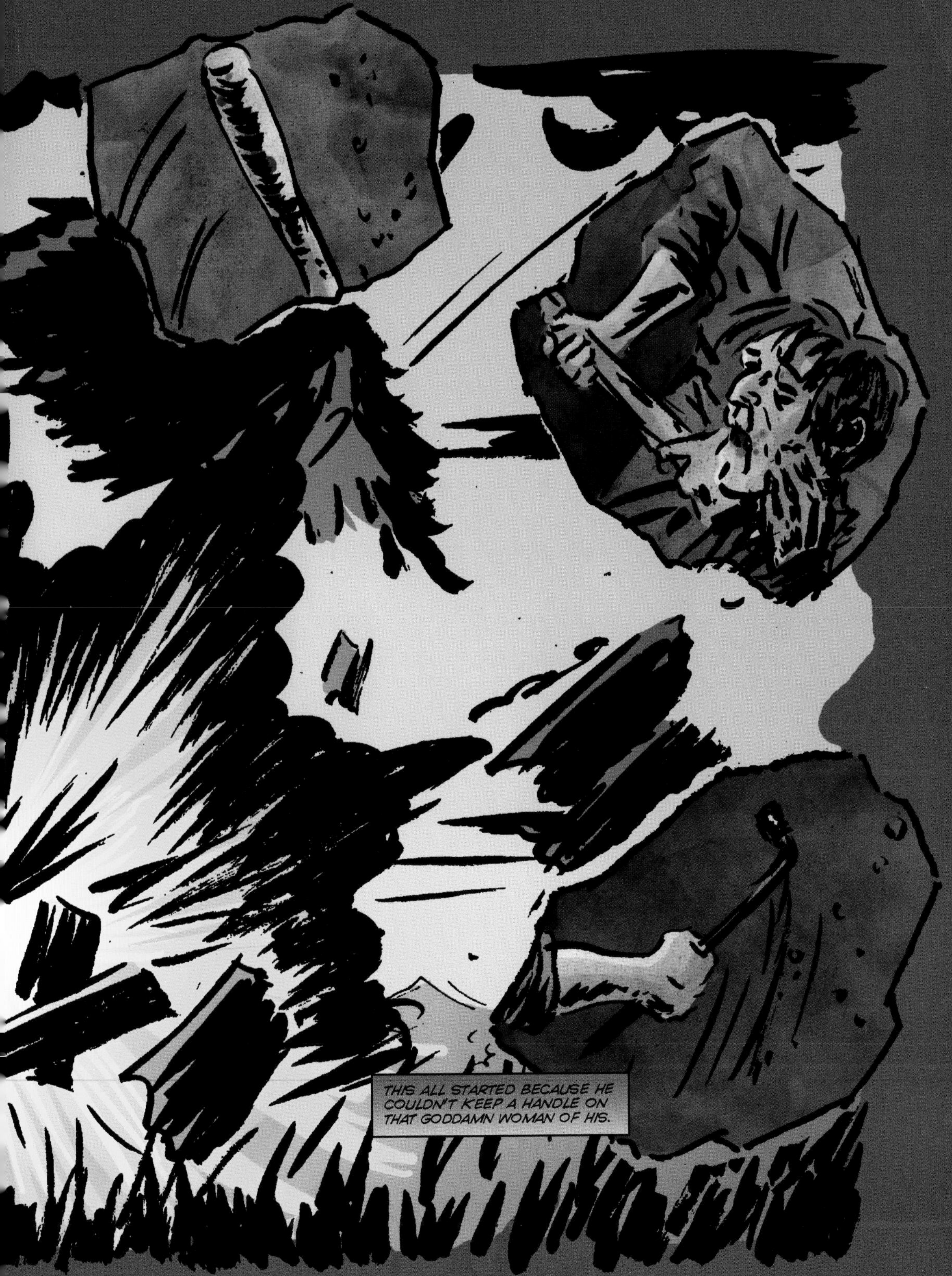
THIS ALL STARTED BECAUSE HE COULDN'T KEEP A HANDLE ON THAT GODDAMN WOMAN OF HIS.

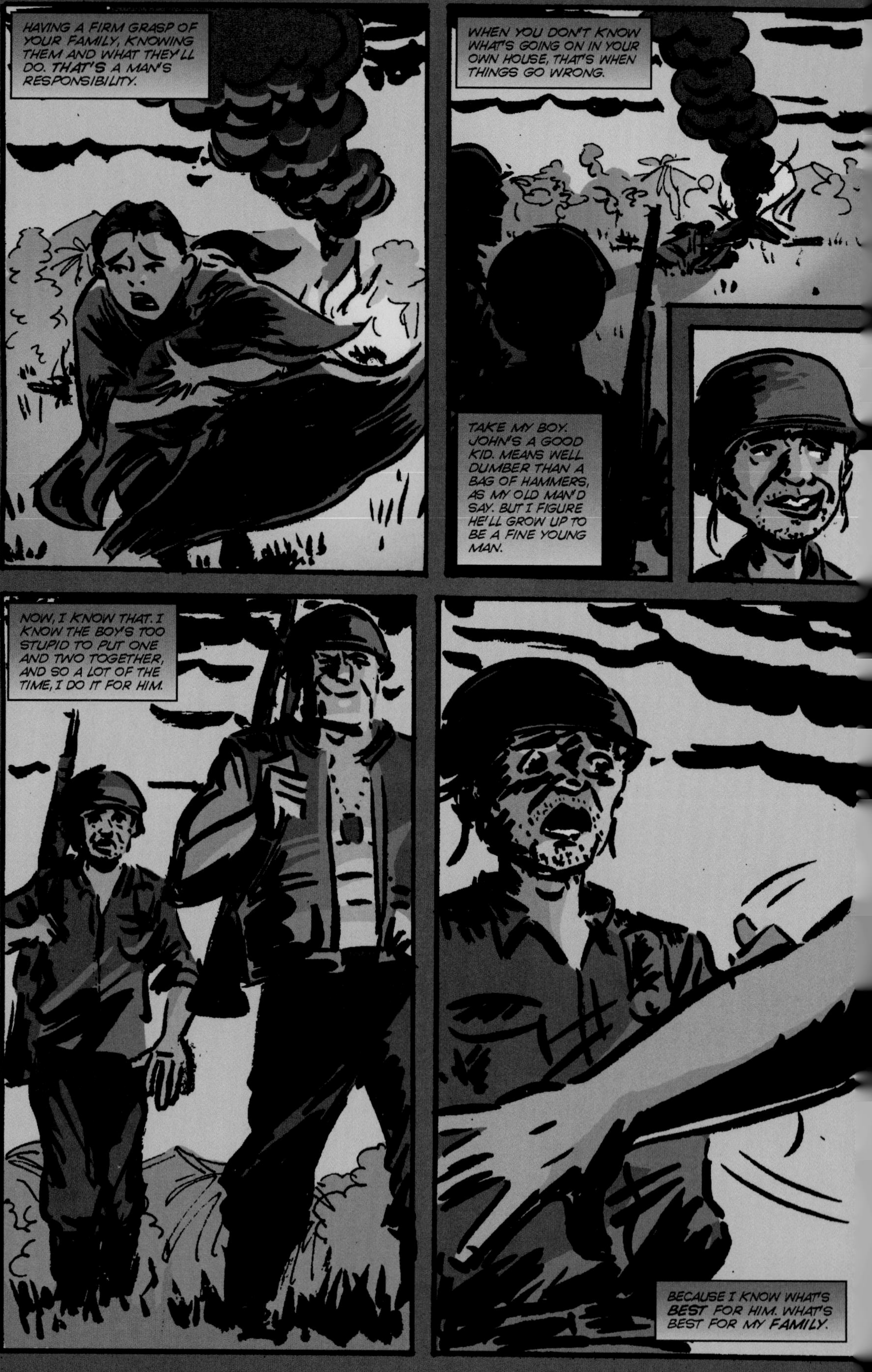
HAVING A FIRM GRASP OF YOUR FAMILY, KNOWING THEM AND WHAT THEY'LL DO. THAT'S A MAN'S RESPONSIBILITY.
WHEN YOU DON'T KNOW WHAT'S GOING ON IN YOUR OWN HOUSE, THAT'S WHEN THINGS GO WRONG.
TAKE MY BOY. JOHN'S A GOOD KID. MEANS WELL DUMBER THAN A BAG OF HAMMERS, AS MY OLD MAN'D SAY. BUT I FIGURE HE'LL GROW UP TO BE A FINE YOUNG MAN.
NOW, I KNOW THAT. I KNOW THE BOY'S TOO STUPID TO PUT ONE AND TWO TOGETHER, AND SO A LOT OF THE TIME, I DO IT FOR HIM.
BECAUSE I KNOW WHAT'S BEST FOR HIM. WHAT'S BEST FOR MY FAMILY.

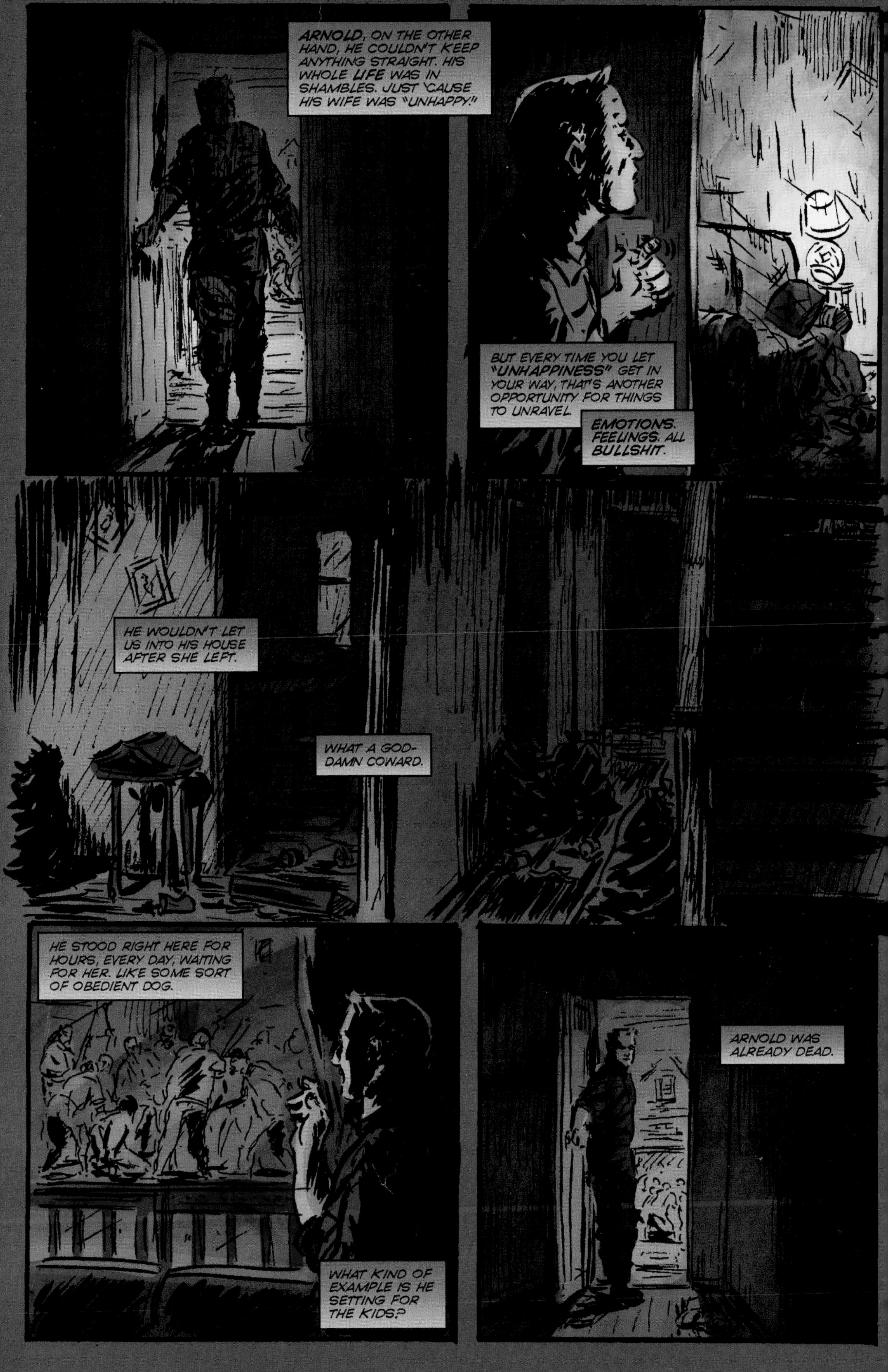
ARNOLD, ON THE OTHER HAND, HE COULDN'T KEEP ANYTHING STRAIGHT. HIS WHOLE LIFE WAS IN SHAMBLES. JUST 'CAUSE HIS WIFE WAS "UNHAPPY."
BUT EVERY TIME YOU LET "UNHAPPINESS" GET IN YOUR WAY, THAT'S ANOTHER OPPORTUNITY FOR THINGS TO UNRAVEL.
EMOTIONS. FEELINGS. ALL BULLSHIT.
HE WOULDN'T LET US INTO HIS HOUSE AFTER SHE LEFT.
WHAT A GOD-DAMN COWARD.
HE STOOD RIGHT HERE FOR HOURS, EVERY DAY, WAITING FOR HER. LIKE SOME SORT OF OBEDIENT DOG.
WHAT KIND OF EXAMPLE IS HE SETTING FOR THE KIDS?
ARNOLD WAS ALREADY DEAD.

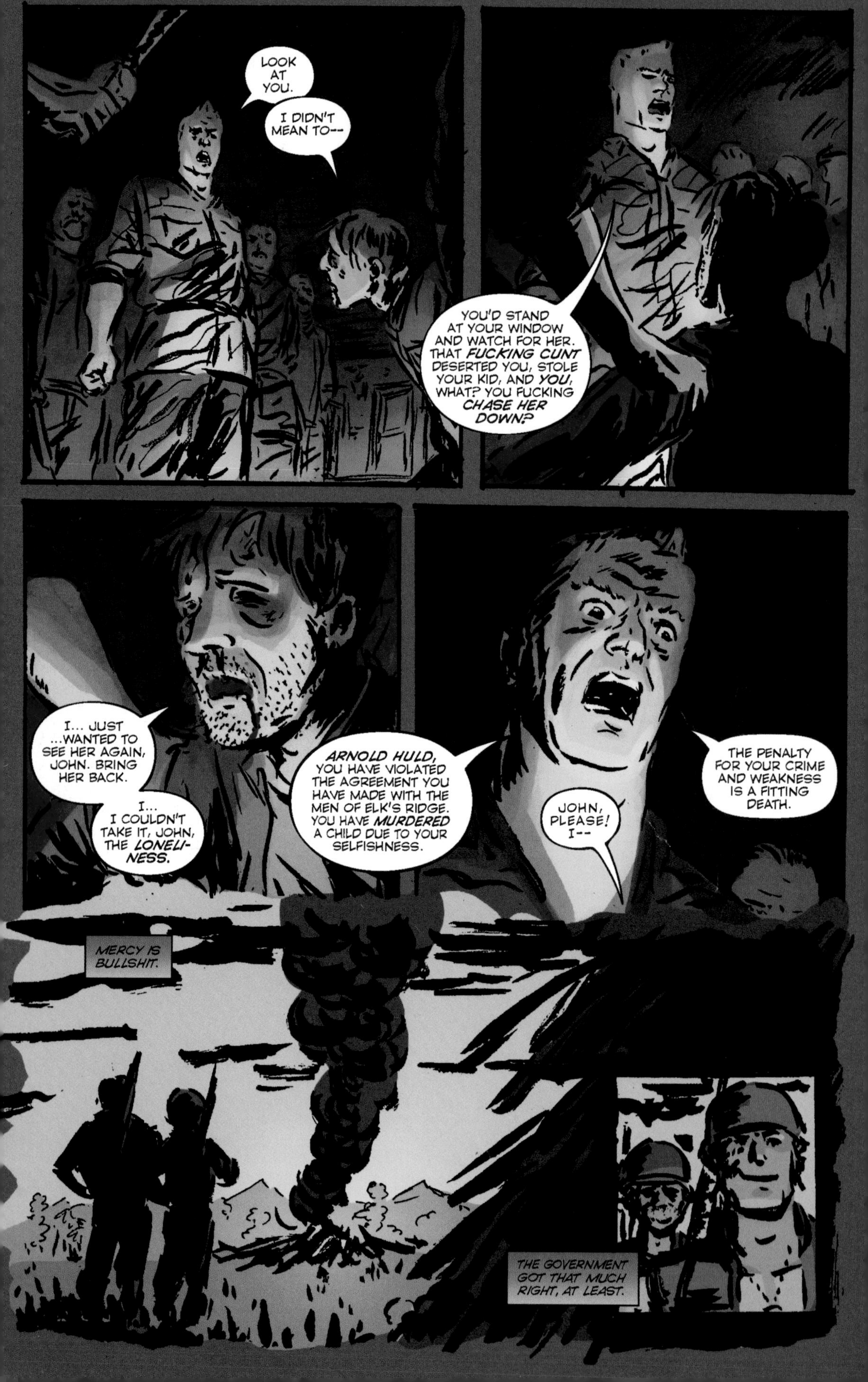
LOOK AT YOU.
I DIDN'T MEAN TO--
YOU'D STAND AT YOUR WINDOW AND WATCH FOR HER. THAT FUCKING CUNT DESERTED YOU, STOLE YOUR KID, AND YOU, WHAT? YOU FUCKING CHASE HER DOWN?
I... JUST ...WANTED TO SEE HER AGAIN, JOHN. BRING HER BACK.
I... I COULDN'T TAKE IT, JOHN, THE LONELINESS.
ARNOLD HULD, YOU HAVE VIOLATED THE AGREEMENT YOU HAVE MADE WITH THE MEN OF ELK'S RIDGE. YOU HAVE MURDERED A CHILD DUE TO YOUR SELFISHNESS.
JOHN, PLEASE! I--
THE PENALTY FOR YOUR CRIME AND WEAKNESS IS A FITTING DEATH.
MERCY IS BULLSHIT.
THE GOVERNMENT GOT THAT MUCH RIGHT, AT LEAST.

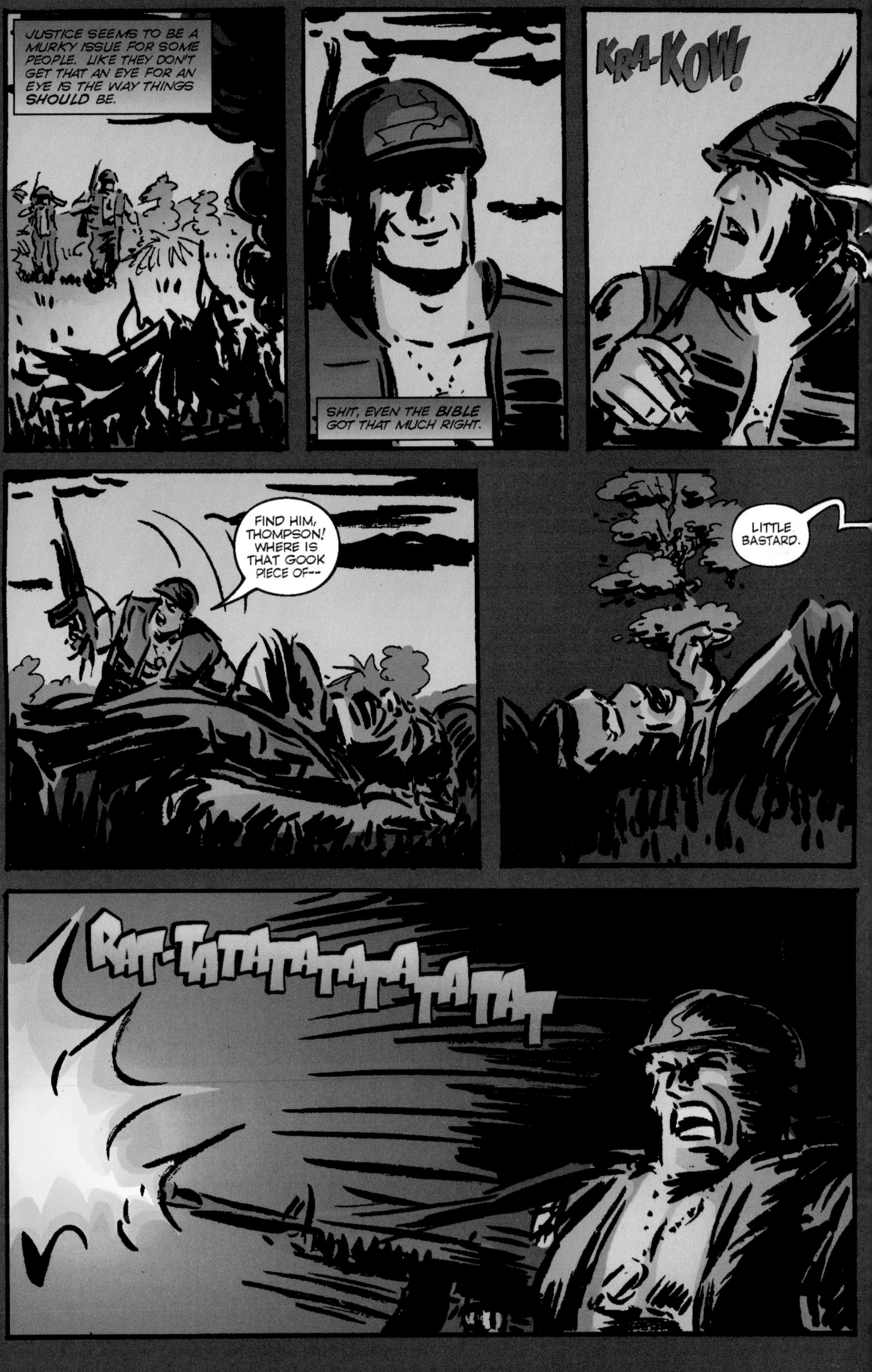
JUSTICE SEEMS TO BE A MURKY ISSUE FOR SOME PEOPLE. LIKE THEY DON'T GET THAT AN EYE FOR AN EYE IS THE WAY THINGS SHOULD BE.
SHIT, EVEN THE BIBLE GOT THAT MUCH RIGHT.
KRA-KOW!
FIND HIM, THOMPSON! WHERE IS THAT GOOK PIECE OF--
LITTLE BASTARD.
RAT-TATATATATATATATAT

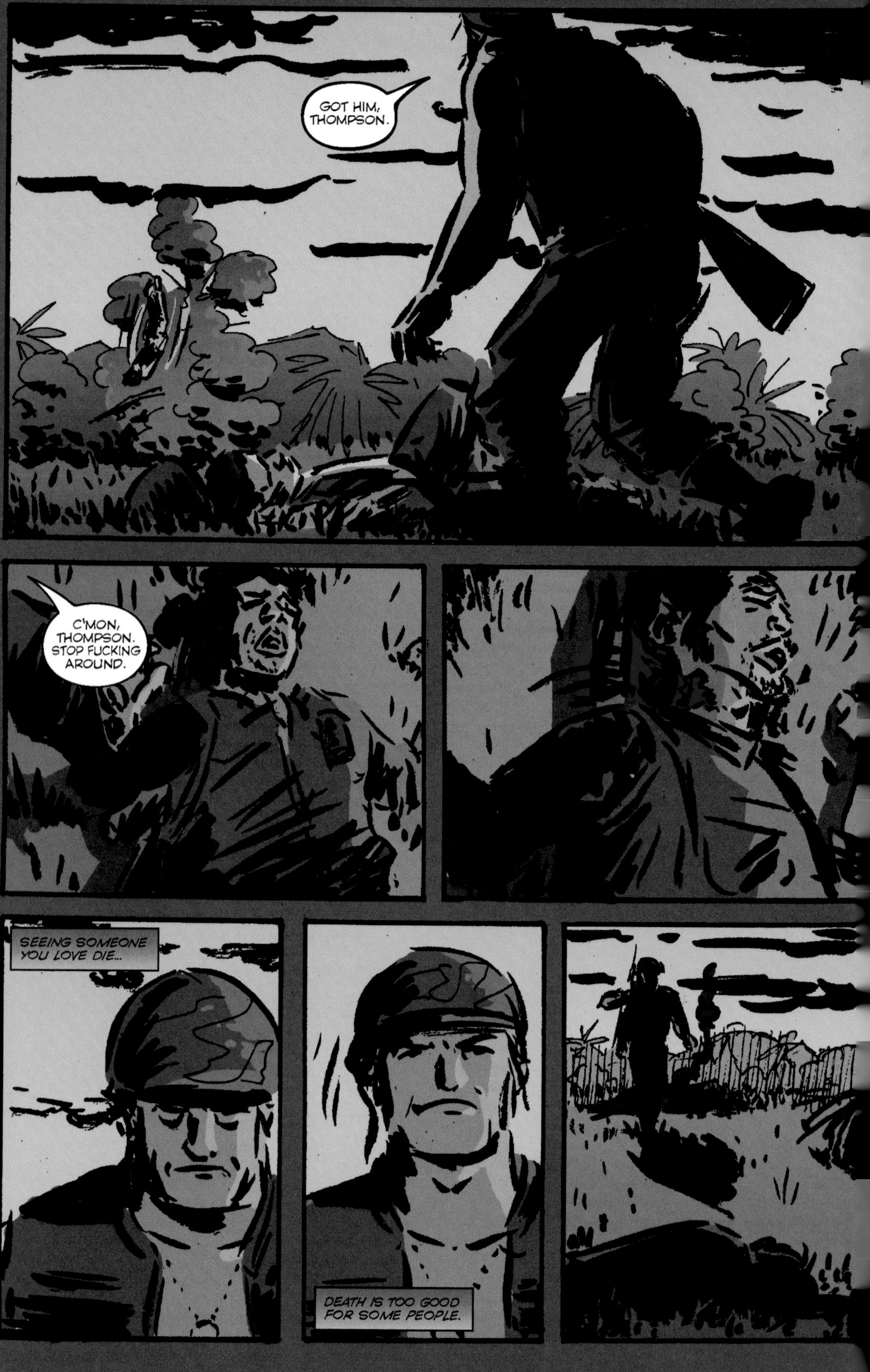
GOT HIM, THOMPSON.
C'MON, THOMPSON. STOP FUCKING AROUND.
SEEING SOMEONE YOU LOVE DIE...
DEATH IS TOO GOOD FOR SOME PEOPLE.

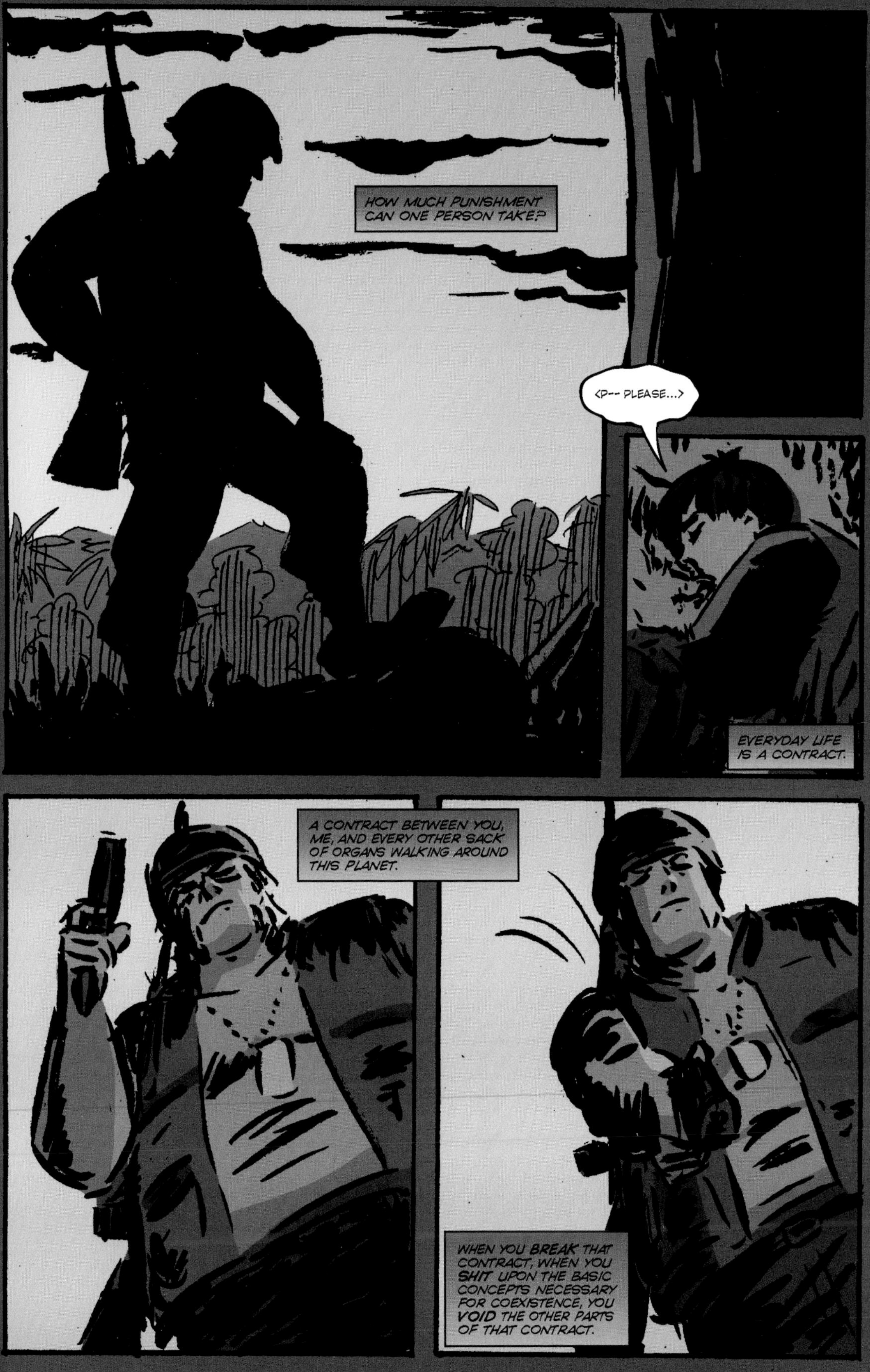
HOW MUCH PUNISHMENT CAN ONE PERSON TAKE?
<P-- PLEASE...>
EVERYDAY LIFE IS A CONTRACT.
A CONTRACT BETWEEN YOU, ME, AND EVERY OTHER SACK OF ORGANS WALKING AROUND THIS PLANET.
WHEN YOU BREAK THAT CONTRACT, WHEN YOU SHIT UPON THE BASIC CONCEPTS NECESSARY FOR COEXISTENCE, YOU VOID THE OTHER PARTS OF THAT CONTRACT.

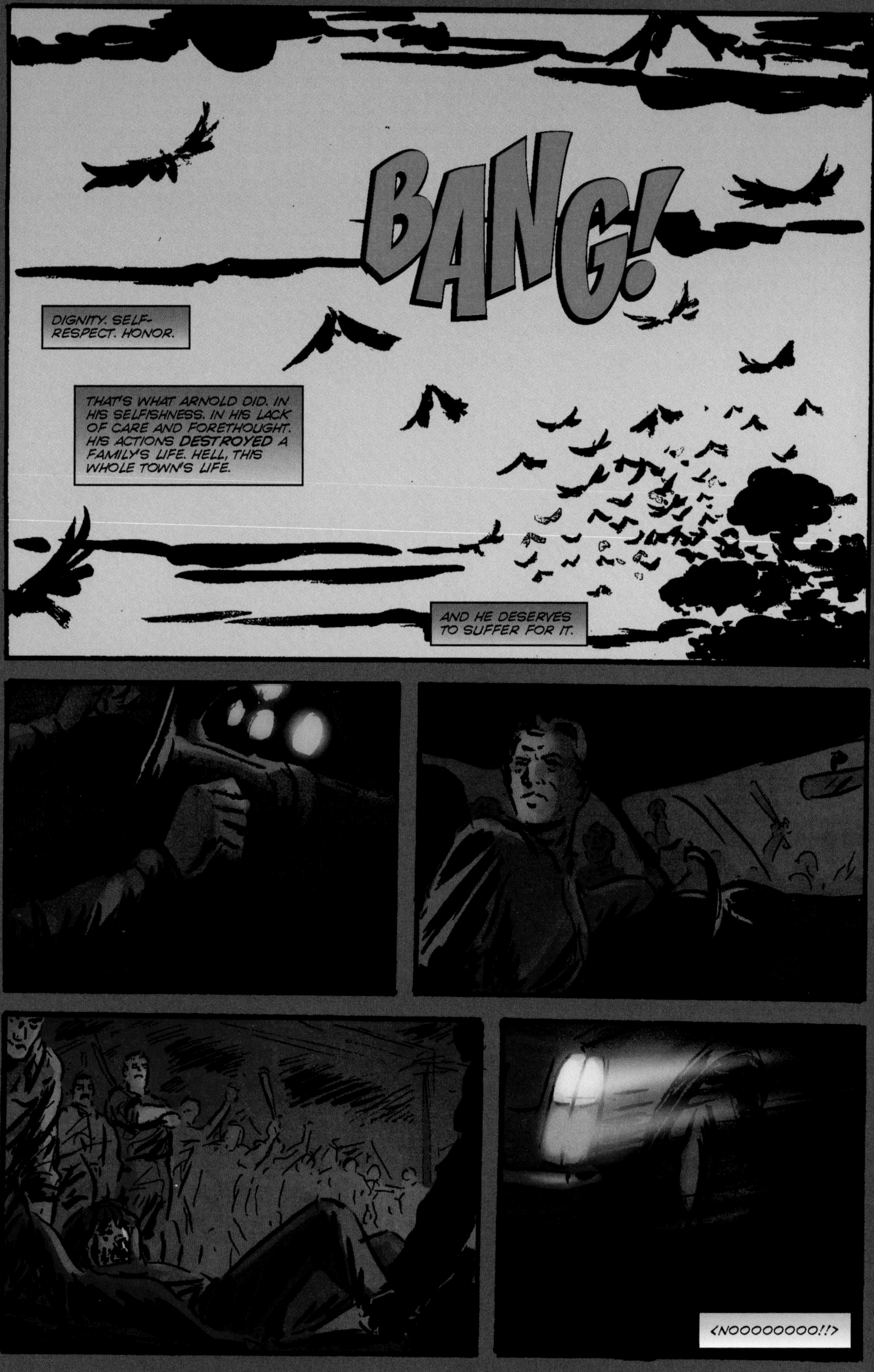
BANG!
DIGNITY. SELF-RESPECT. HONOR.
THAT'S WHAT ARNOLD DID. IN HIS SELFISHNESS. IN HIS LACK OF CARE AND FORETHOUGHT. HIS ACTIONS DESTROYED A FAMILY'S LIFE. HELL, THIS WHOLE TOWN'S LIFE.
AND HE DESERVES TO SUFFER FOR IT.
<NOOOOOOOO!!>

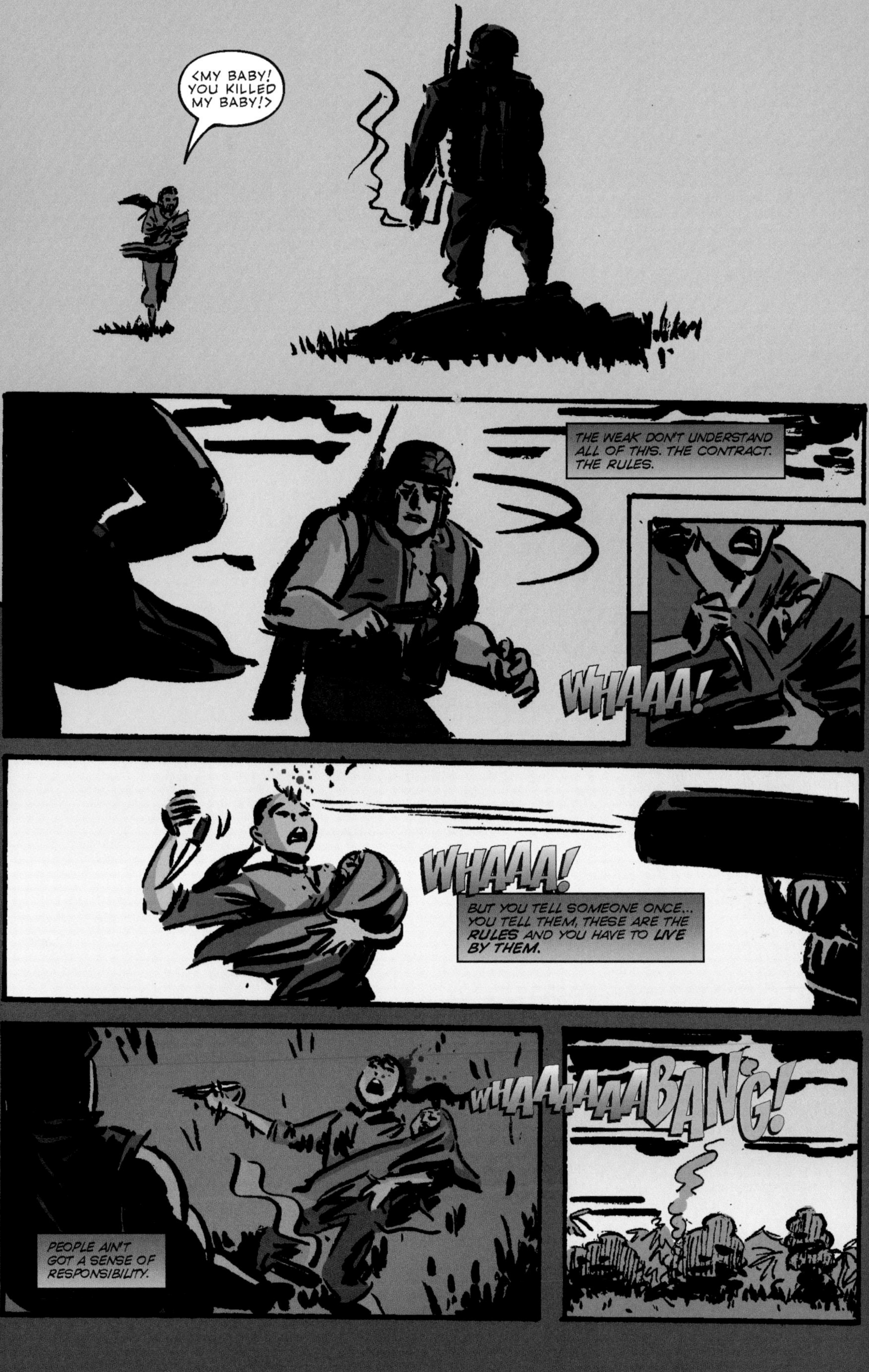
<MY BABY! YOU KILLED MY BABY!>
THE WEAK DON'T UNDERSTAND ALL OF THIS. THE CONTRACT. THE RULES.
WHAAAA!
WHAAAA!
BUT YOU TELL SOMEONE ONCE... YOU TELL THEM, THESE ARE THE RULES AND YOU HAVE TO LIVE BY THEM.
WHAAAAAAABANG!
PEOPLE AIN'T GOT A SENSE OF RESPONSIBILITY.

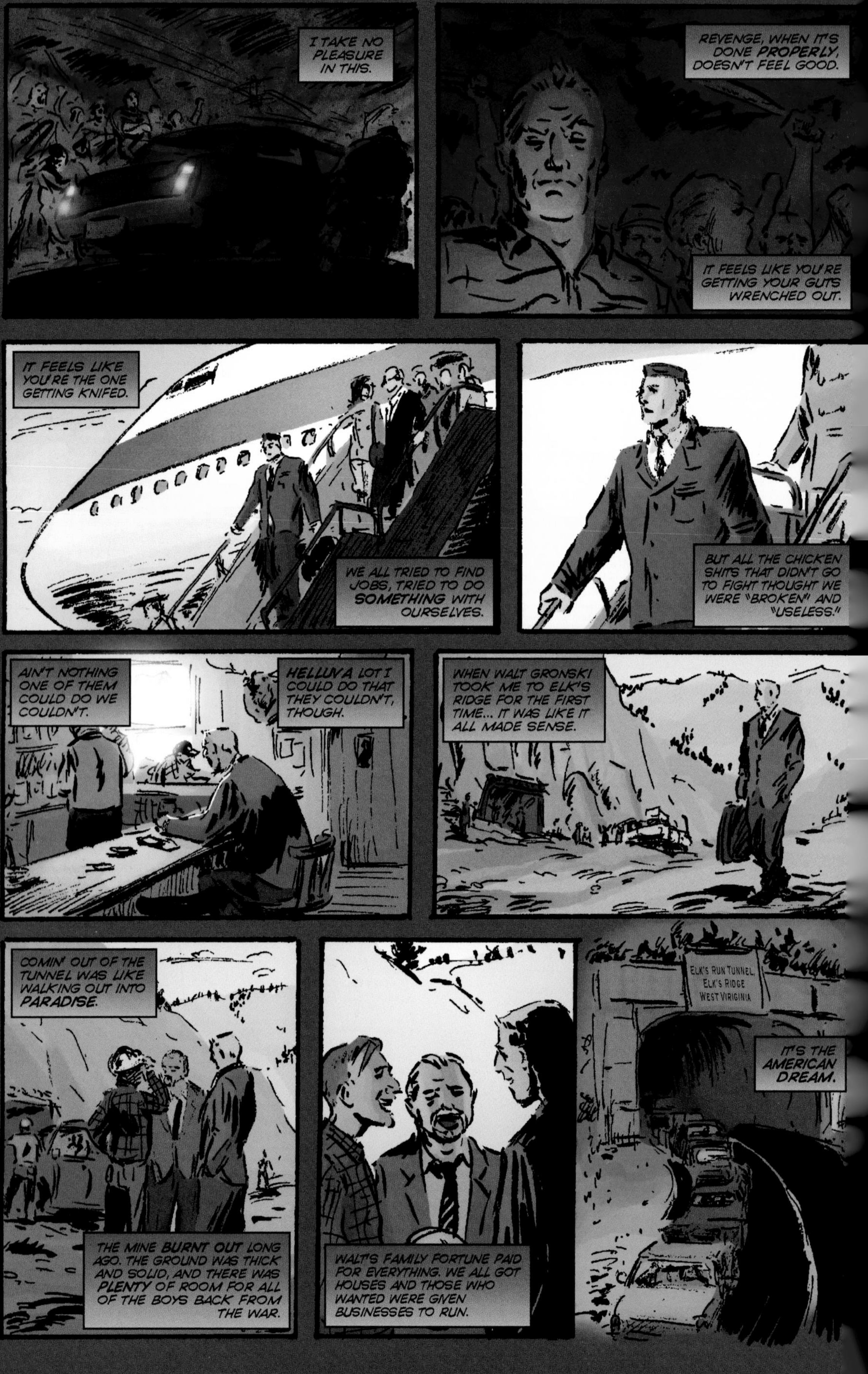
I TAKE NO PLEASURE IN THIS.
REVENGE, WHEN IT'S DONE PROPERLY, DOESN'T FEEL GOOD.
IT FEELS LIKE YOU'RE GETTING YOUR GUTS WRENCHED OUT.
IT FEELS LIKE YOU'RE THE ONE GETTING KNIFED.
WE ALL TRIED TO FIND JOBS, TRIED TO DO SOMETHING WITH OURSELVES.
BUT ALL THE CHICKEN SHITS THAT DIDN'T GO TO FIGHT THOUGHT WE WERE "BROKEN" AND "USELESS."
AIN'T NOTHING ONE OF THEM COULD DO WE COULDN'T.
HELLUVA LOT I COULD DO THAT THEY COULDN'T, THOUGH.
WHEN WALT GRONSKI TOOK ME TO ELK'S RIDGE FOR THE FIRST TIME... IT WAS LIKE IT ALL MADE SENSE.
COMIN' OUT OF THE TUNNEL WAS LIKE WALKING OUT INTO PARADISE.
THE MINE BURNT OUT LONG AGO. THE GROUND WAS THICK AND SOLID, AND THERE WAS PLENTY OF ROOM FOR ALL OF THE BOYS BACK FROM THE WAR.
WALT'S FAMILY FORTUNE PAID FOR EVERYTHING. WE ALL GOT HOUSES AND THOSE WHO WANTED WERE GIVEN BUSINESSES TO RUN.
ELK'S RUN TUNNEL
ELK'S RIDGE
WEST VIRIGINIA
IT'S THE AMERICAN DREAM.

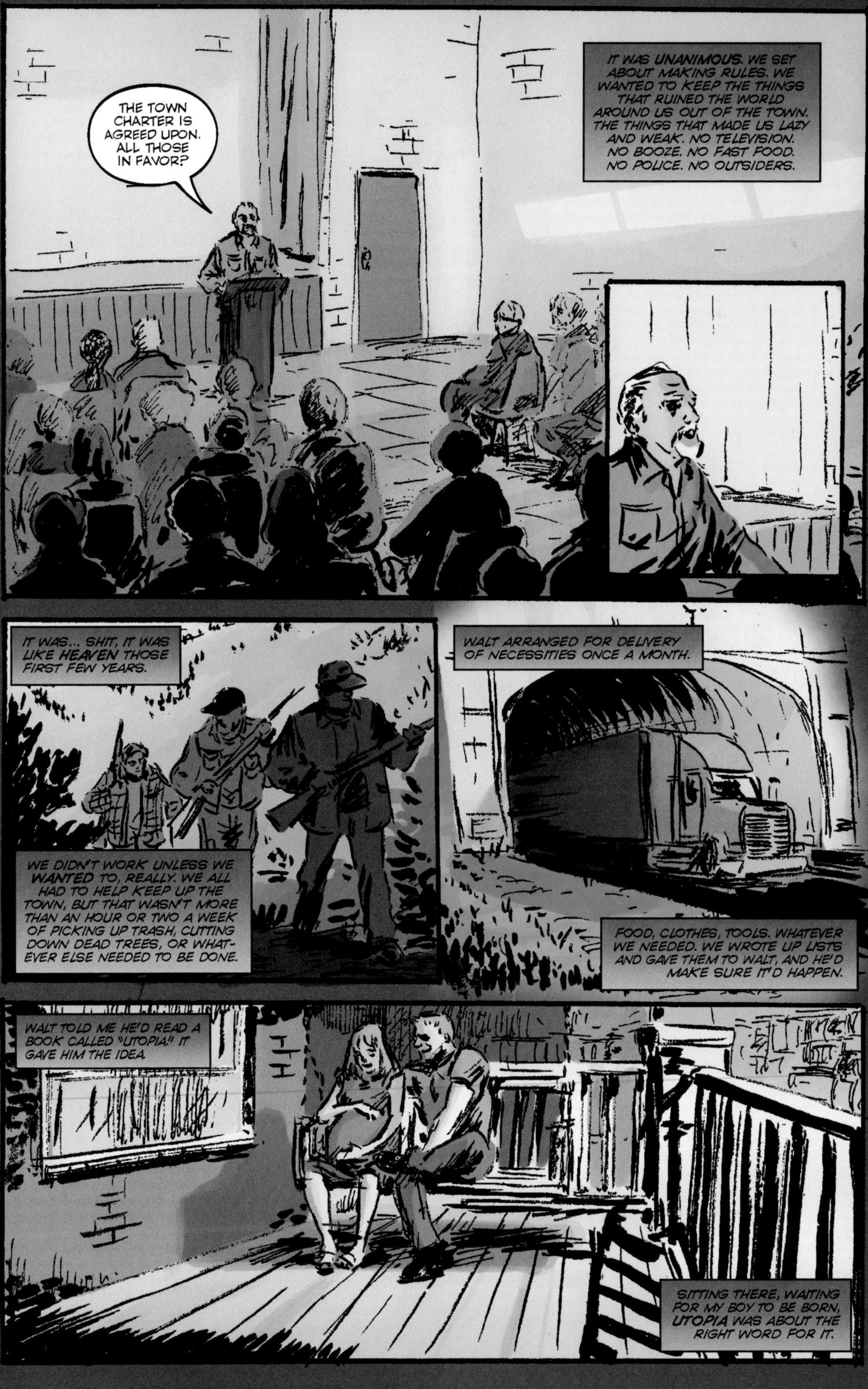
THE TOWN CHARTER IS AGREED UPON. ALL THOSE IN FAVOR?
IT WAS UNANIMOUS. WE SET ABOUT MAKING RULES. WE WANTED TO KEEP THE THINGS THAT RUINED THE WORLD AROUND US OUT OF THE TOWN. THE THINGS THAT MADE US LAZY AND WEAK. NO TELEVISION. NO BOOZE. NO FAST FOOD. NO POLICE. NO OUTSIDERS.
IT WAS... SHIT, IT WAS LIKE HEAVEN THOSE FIRST FEW YEARS.
WE DIDN'T WORK UNLESS WE WANTED TO, REALLY. WE ALL HAD TO HELP KEEP UP THE TOWN, BUT THAT WASN'T MORE THAN AN HOUR OR TWO A WEEK OF PICKING UP TRASH, CUTTING DOWN DEAD TREES, OR WHATEVER ELSE NEEDED TO BE DONE.
WALT ARRANGED FOR DELIVERY OF NECESSITIES ONCE A MONTH.
FOOD, CLOTHES, TOOLS. WHATEVER WE NEEDED. WE WROTE UP LISTS AND GAVE THEM TO WALT, AND HE'D MAKE SURE IT'D HAPPEN.
WALT TOLD ME HE'D READ A BOOK CALLED "UTOPIA." IT GAVE HIM THE IDEA.
SITTING THERE, WAITING FOR MY BOY TO BE BORN, UTOPIA WAS ABOUT THE RIGHT WORD FOR IT.

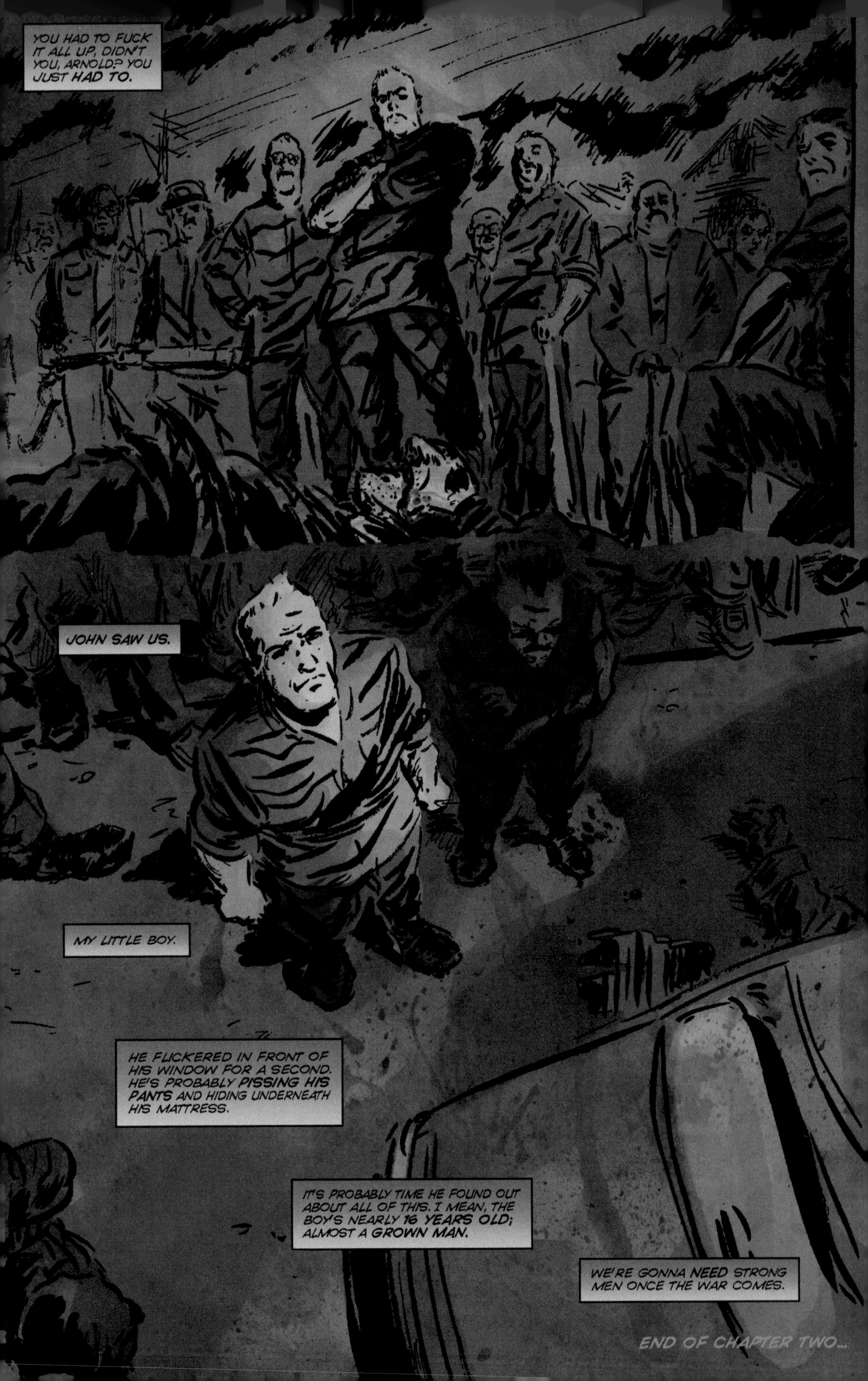
YOU HAD TO FUCK IT ALL UP, DIDN'T YOU, ARNOLD? YOU JUST HAD TO.
JOHN SAW US.
MY LITTLE BOY.
HE FLICKERED IN FRONT OF HIS WINDOW FOR A SECOND. HE'S PROBABLY PISSING HIS PANTS AND HIDING UNDERNEATH HIS MATTRESS.
IT'S PROBABLY TIME HE FOUND OUT ABOUT ALL OF THIS. I MEAN, THE BOY'S NEARLY 16 YEARS OLD; ALMOST A GROWN MAN.
WE'RE GONNA NEED STRONG MEN ONCE THE WAR COMES.
END OF CHAPTER TWO...

Chapter Three:
Mother Knows Best

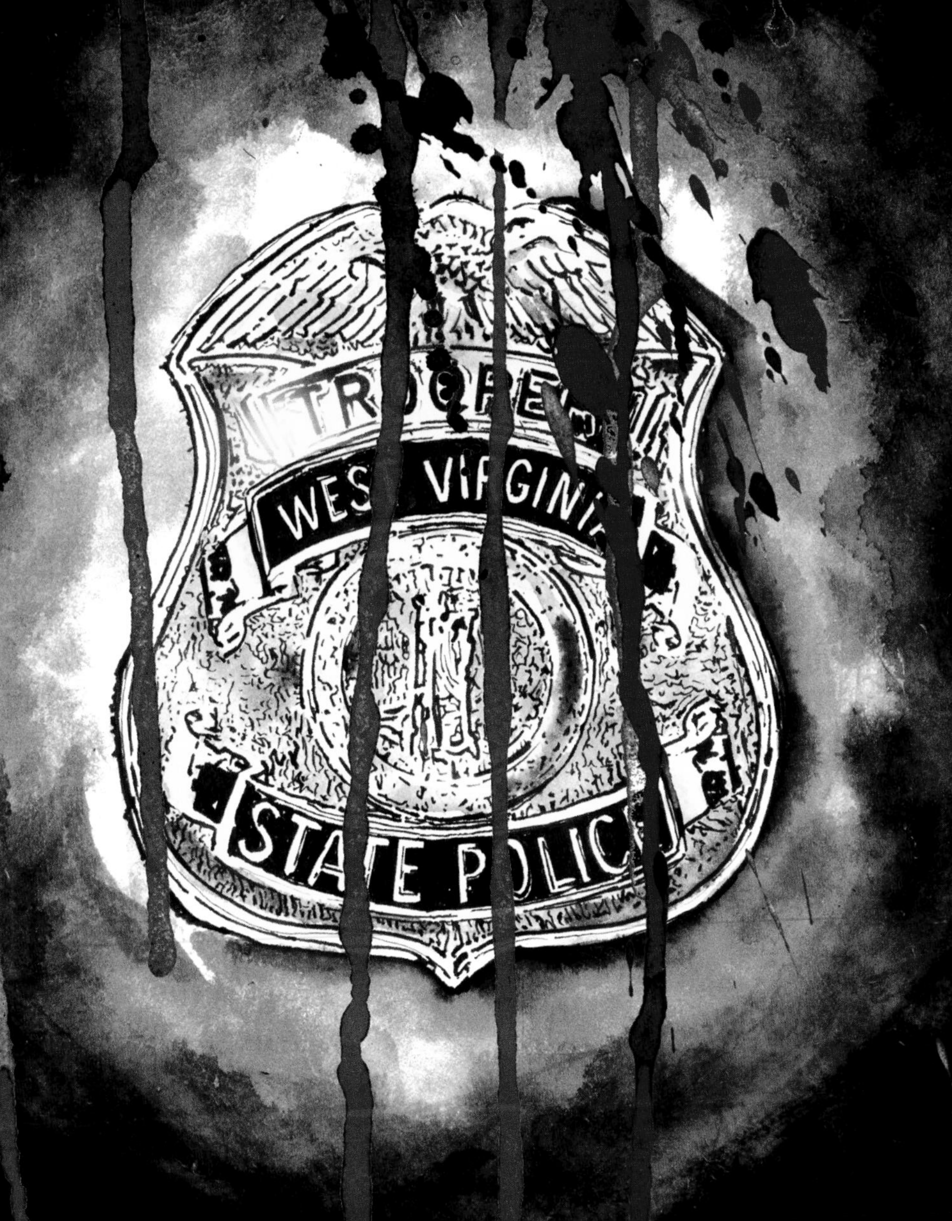

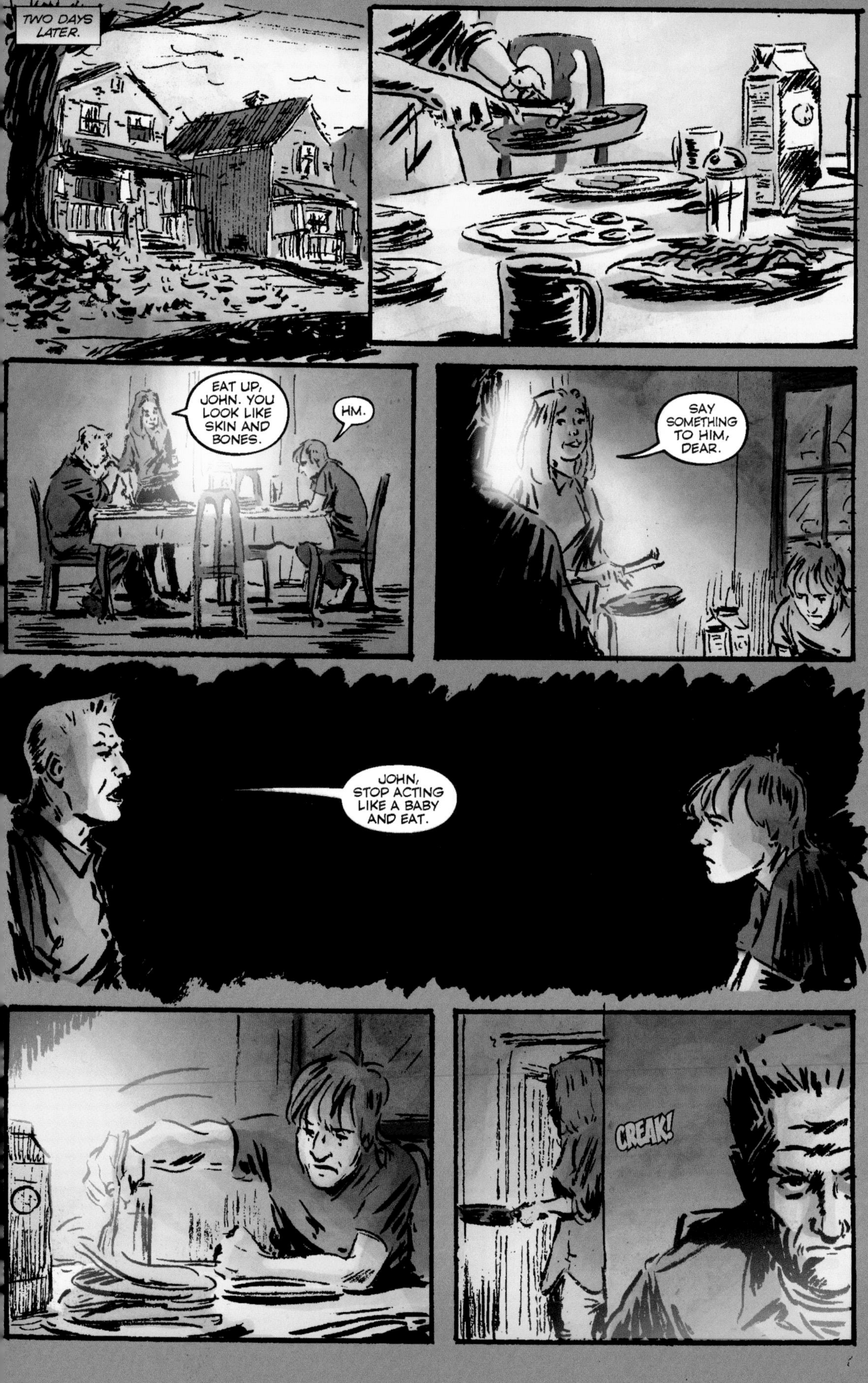
TWO DAYS LATER.
EAT UP, JOHN. YOU LOOK LIKE SKIN AND BONES.
HM.
SAY SOMETHING TO HIM, DEAR.
JOHN, STOP ACTING LIKE A BABY AND EAT.
CREAK!

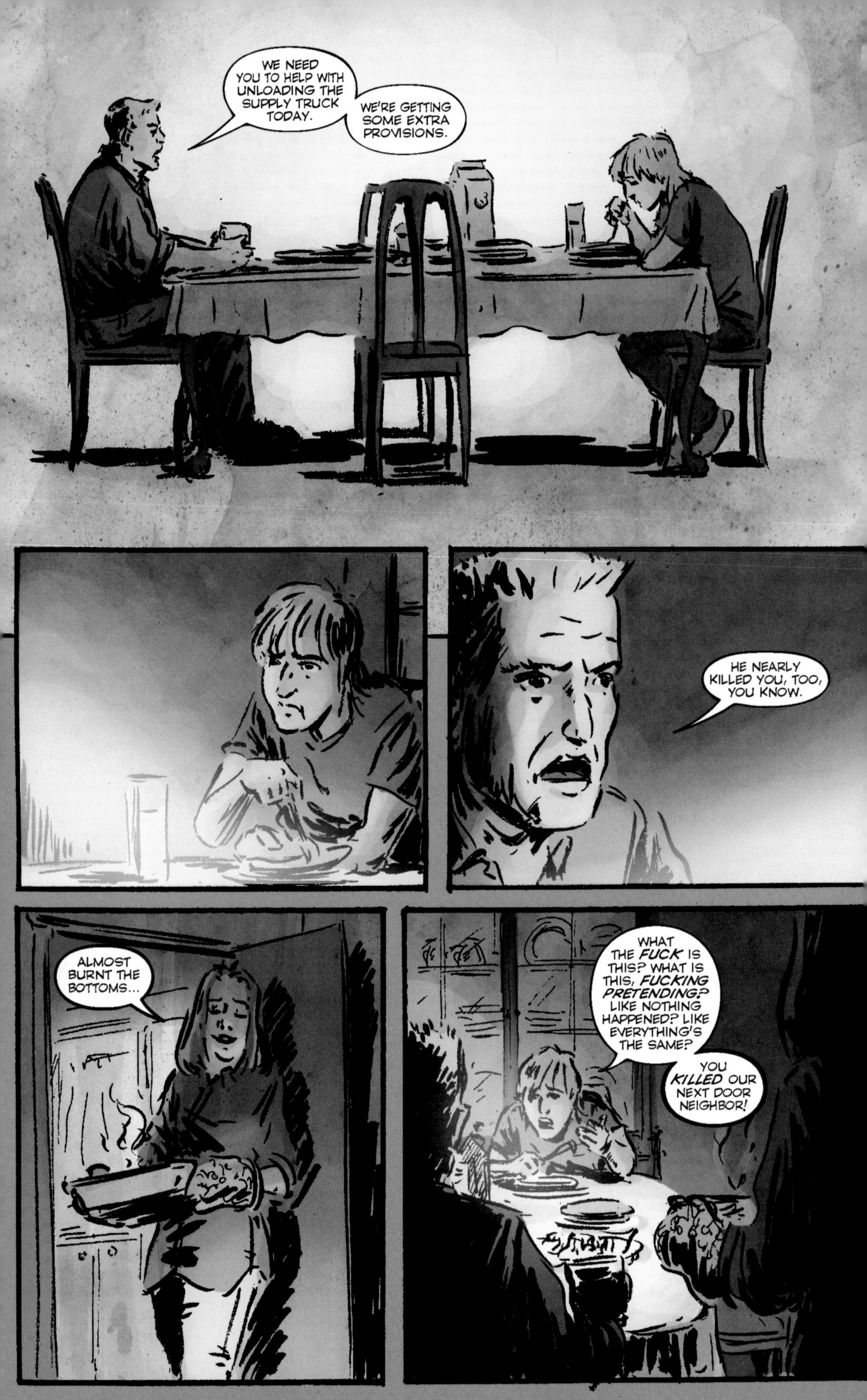
WE NEED YOU TO HELP WITH UNLOADING THE SUPPLY TRUCK TODAY.
WE'RE GETTING SOME EXTRA PROVISIONS.
HE NEARLY KILLED YOU, TOO, YOU KNOW.
ALMOST BURNT THE BOTTOMS...
WHAT THE *FUCK* IS THIS? WHAT IS THIS, *FUCKING PRETENDING?* LIKE NOTHING HAPPENED? LIKE EVERYTHING'S THE SAME?
YOU *KILLED* OUR NEXT DOOR NEIGHBOR!

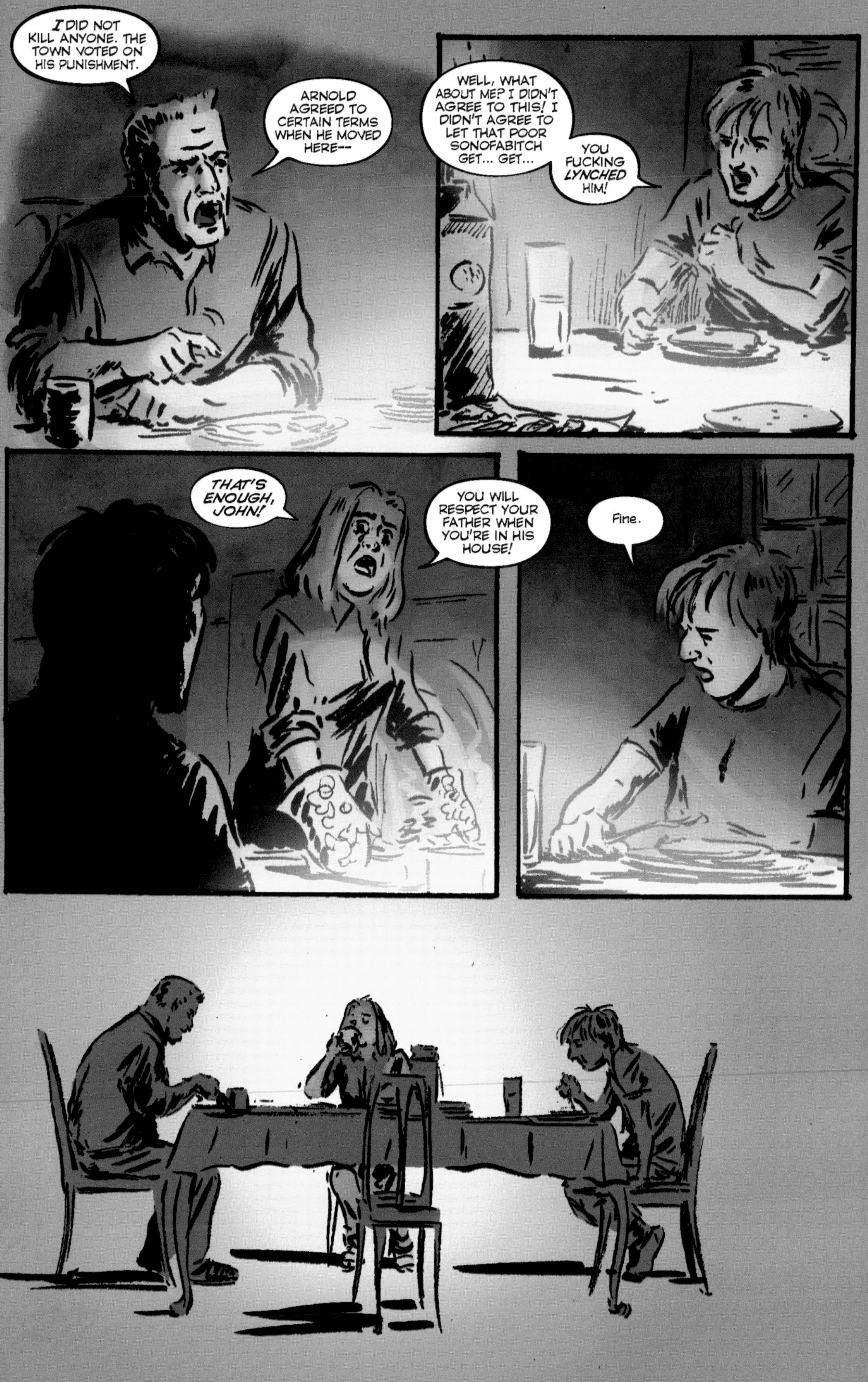
I DID NOT KILL ANYONE. THE TOWN VOTED ON HIS PUNISHMENT.
ARNOLD AGREED TO CERTAIN TERMS WHEN HE MOVED HERE--
WELL, WHAT ABOUT ME? I DIDN'T AGREE TO THIS! I DIDN'T AGREE TO LET THAT POOR SONOFABITCH GET... GET...
YOU FUCKING LYNCHED HIM!
THAT'S ENOUGH, JOHN!
YOU WILL RESPECT YOUR FATHER WHEN YOU'RE IN HIS HOUSE!
Fine.

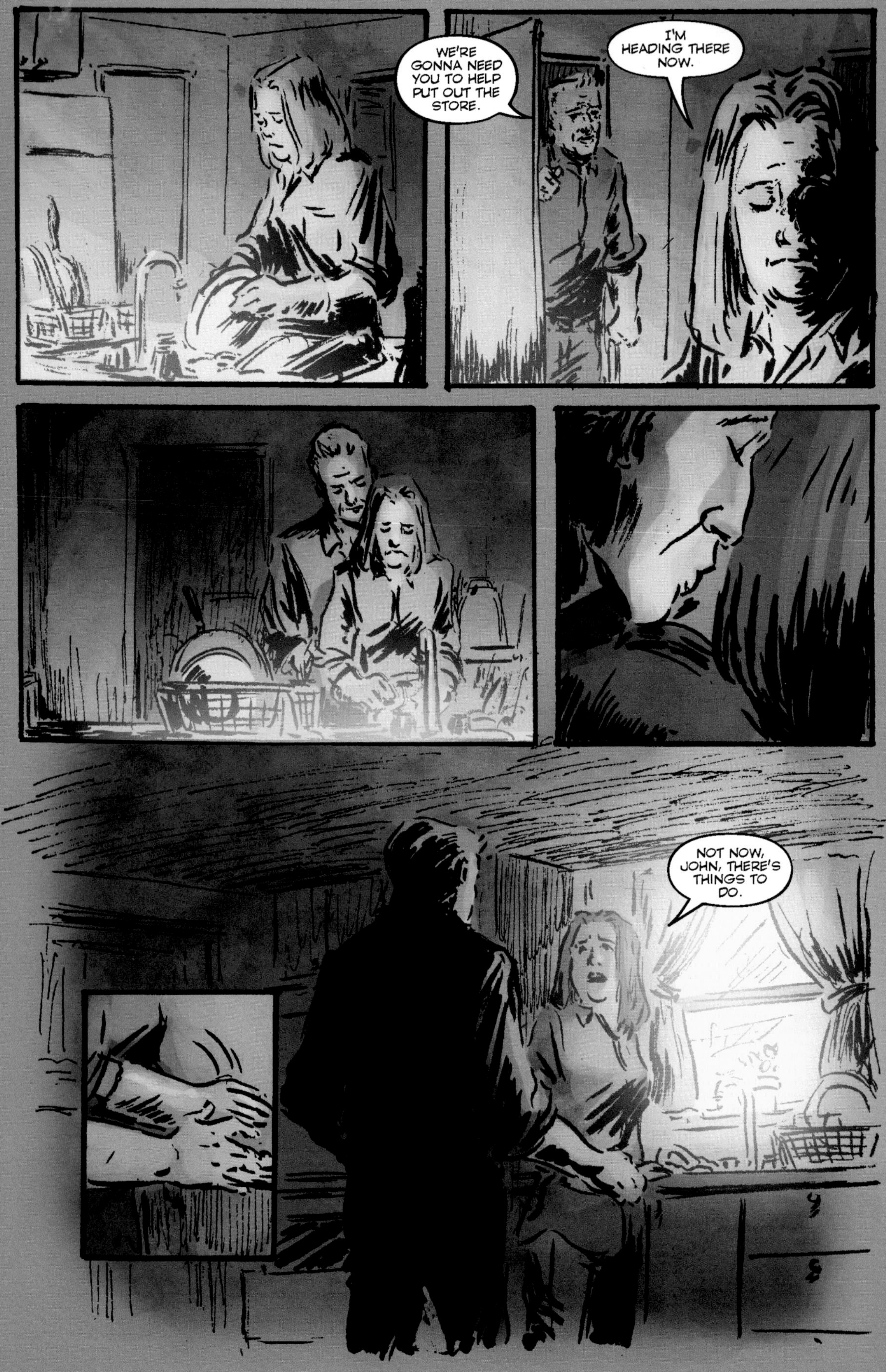

WE'RE GONNA NEED YOU TO HELP PUT OUT THE STORE.
I'M HEADING THERE NOW.
NOT NOW, JOHN, THERE'S THINGS TO DO.

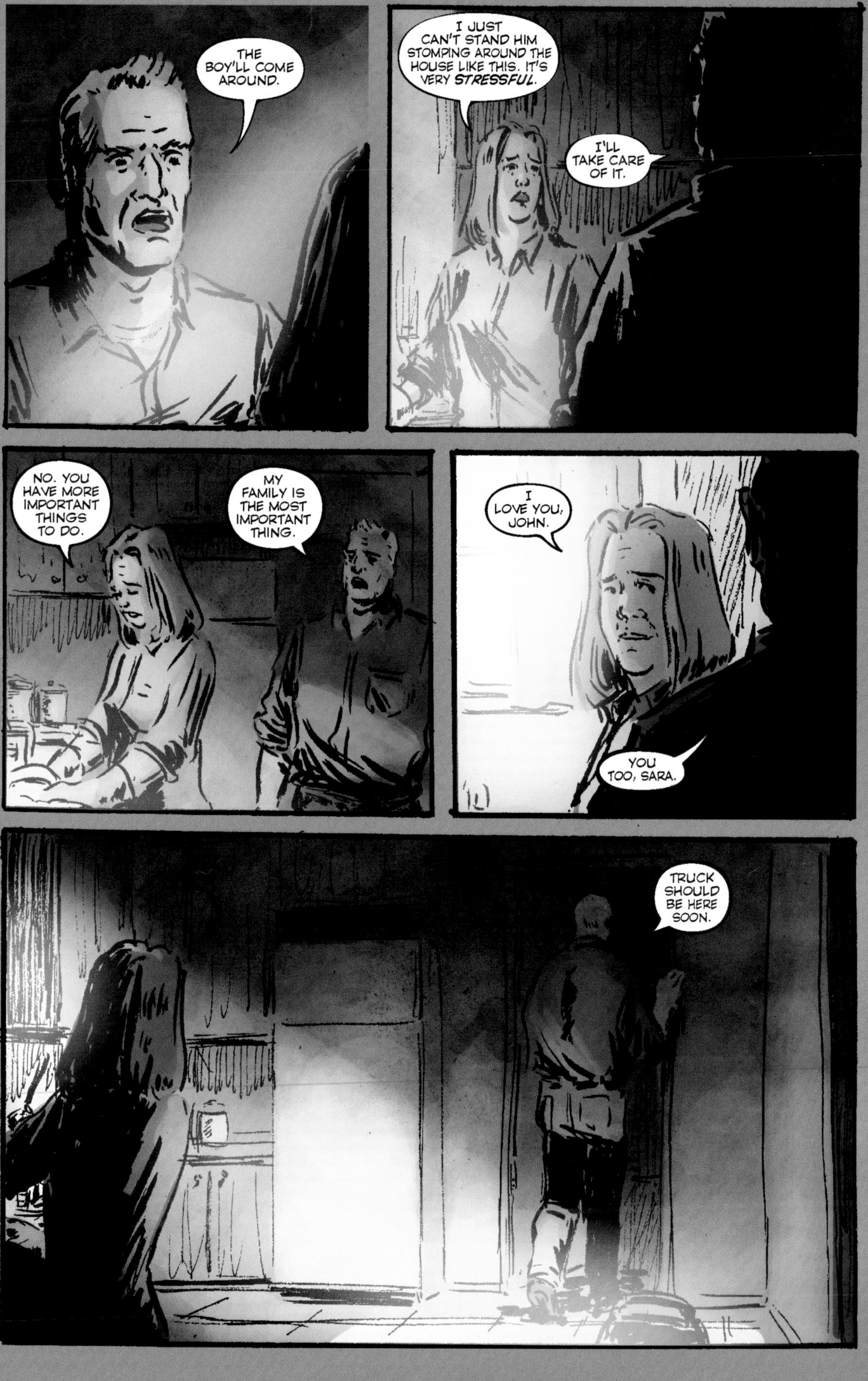
THE BOY'LL COME AROUND.
I JUST CAN'T STAND HIM STOMPING AROUND THE HOUSE LIKE THIS. IT'S VERY STRESSFUL.
I'LL TAKE CARE OF IT.
NO. YOU HAVE MORE IMPORTANT THINGS TO DO.
MY FAMILY IS THE MOST IMPORTANT THING.
I LOVE YOU, JOHN.
YOU TOO, SARA.
TRUCK SHOULD BE HERE SOON.

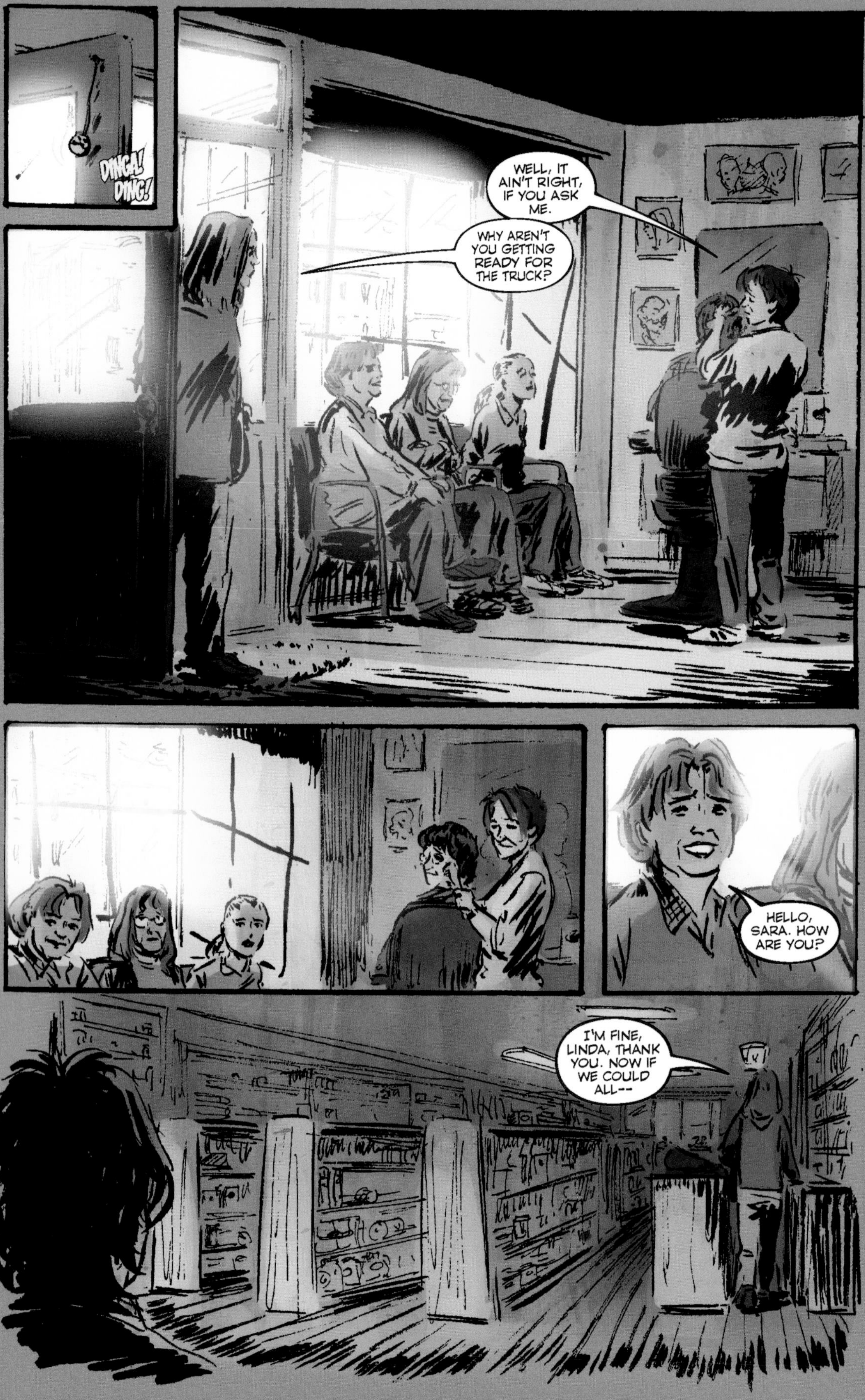
DINGA! DING!
WELL, IT AIN'T RIGHT, IF YOU ASK ME.
WHY AREN'T YOU GETTING READY FOR THE TRUCK?
HELLO, SARA. HOW ARE YOU?
I'M FINE, LINDA, THANK YOU. NOW IF WE COULD ALL--

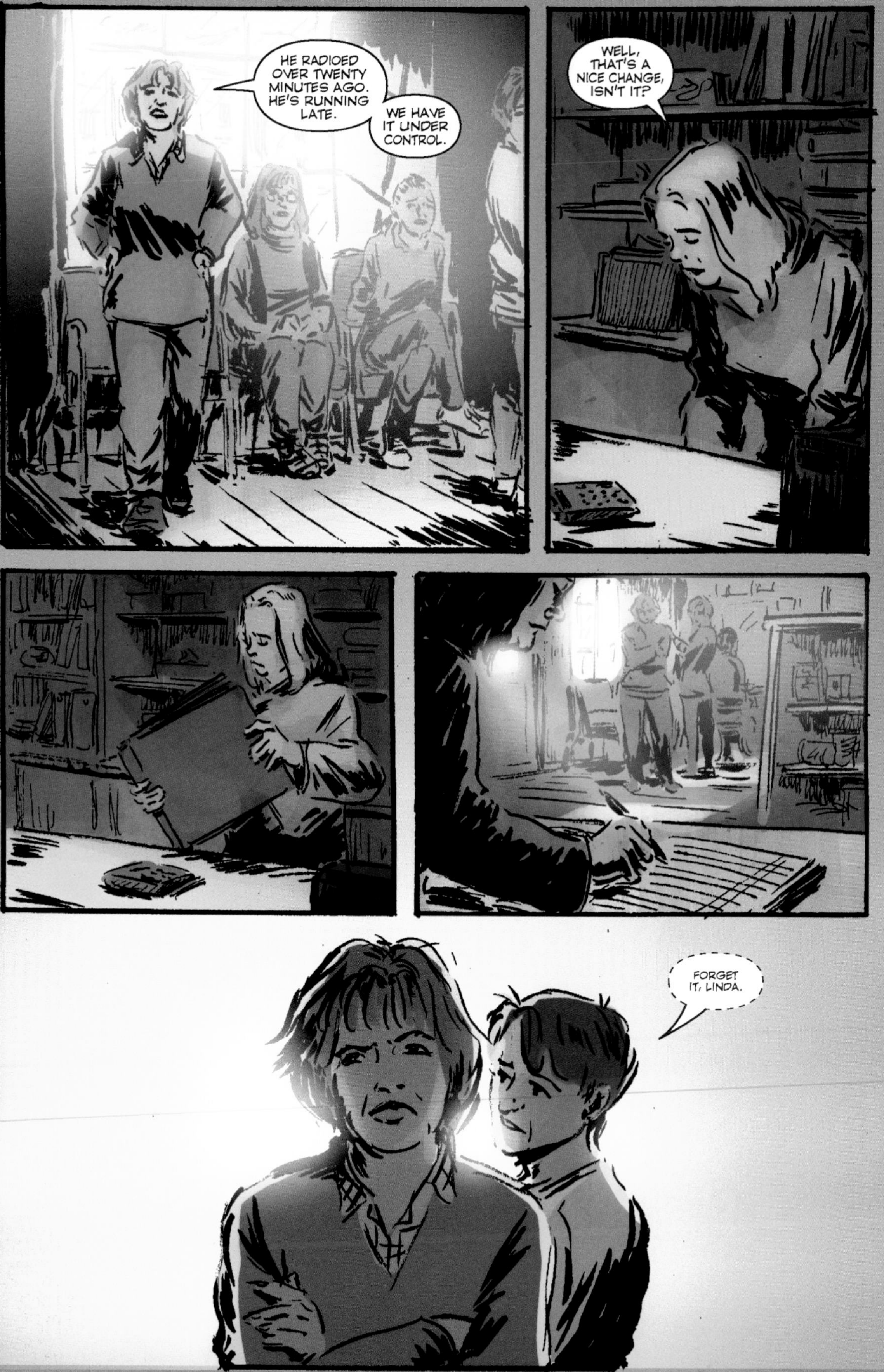
HE RADIOED OVER TWENTY MINUTES AGO. HE'S RUNNING LATE.
WE HAVE IT UNDER CONTROL.
WELL, THAT'S A NICE CHANGE, ISN'T IT?
FORGET IT, LINDA.

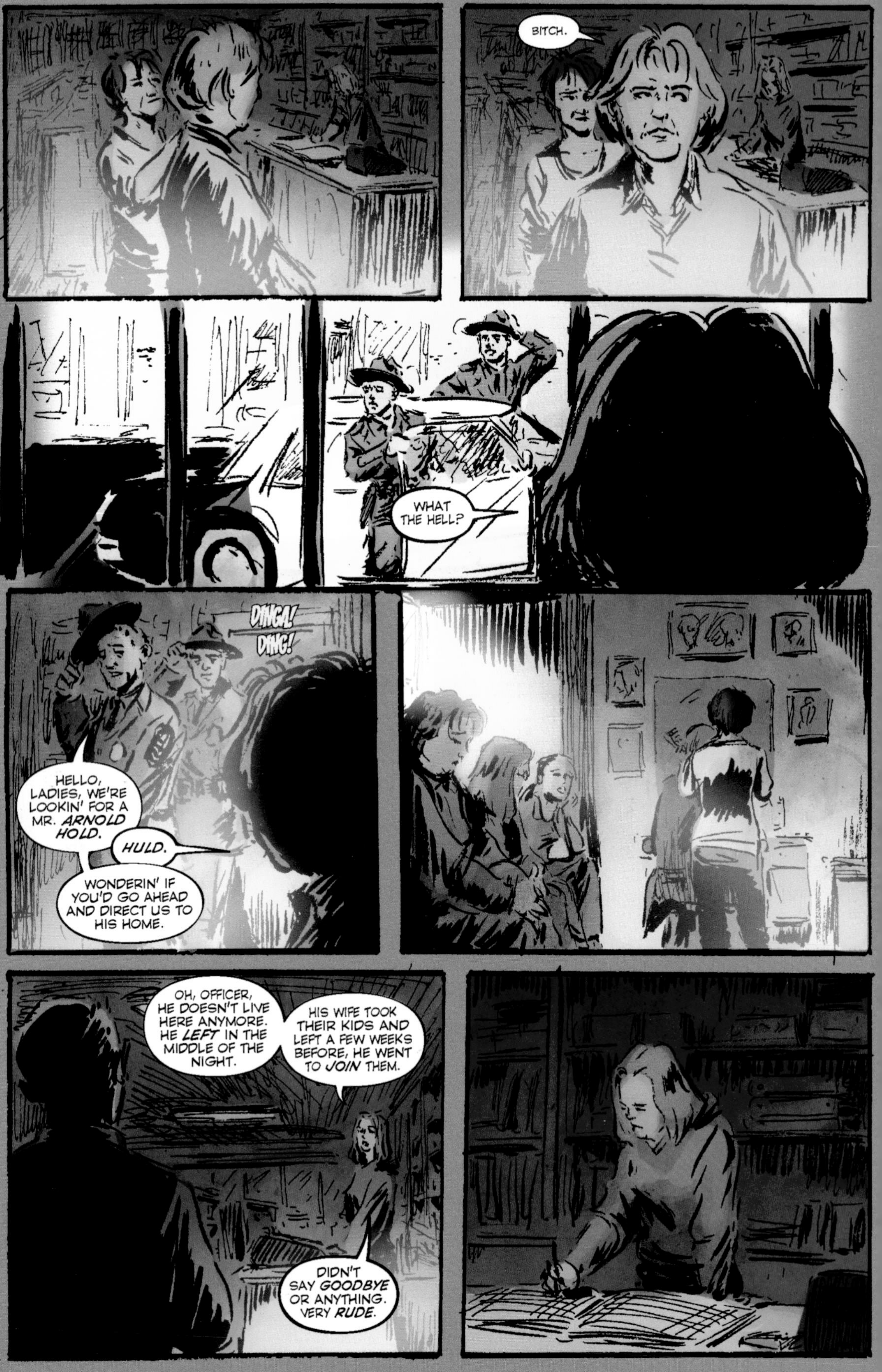
BITCH.
WHAT THE HELL?
DINGA! DING!
HELLO, LADIES, WE'RE LOOKIN' FOR A MR. ARNOLD HOLD.
HULD.
WONDERIN' IF YOU'D GO AHEAD AND DIRECT US TO HIS HOME.
OH, OFFICER, HE DOESN'T LIVE HERE ANYMORE. HE LEFT IN THE MIDDLE OF THE NIGHT.
HIS WIFE TOOK THEIR KIDS AND LEFT A FEW WEEKS BEFORE, HE WENT TO JOIN THEM.
DIDN'T SAY GOODBYE OR ANYTHING. VERY RUDE.

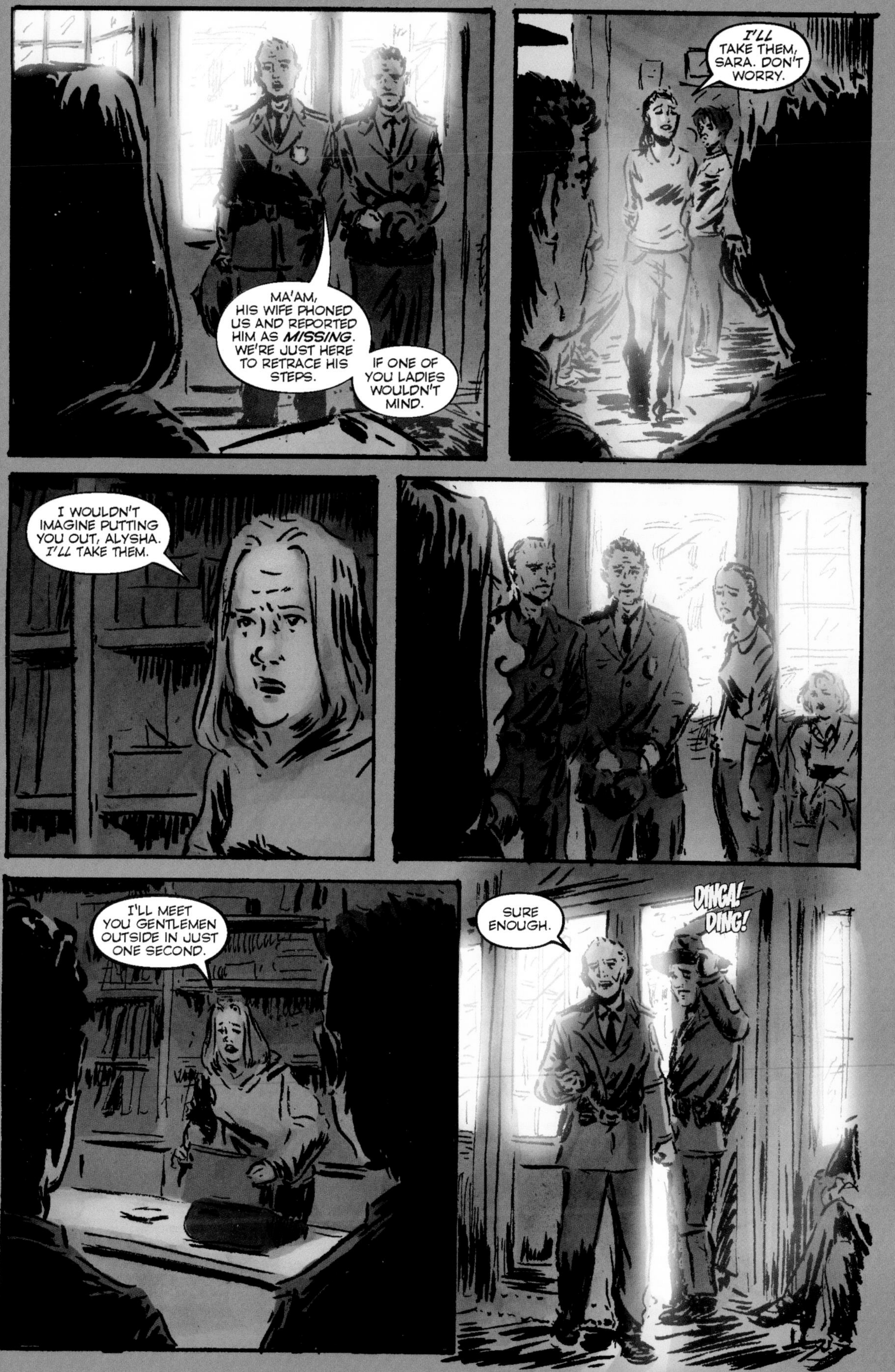
MA'AM, HIS WIFE PHONED US AND REPORTED HIM AS *MISSING*. WE'RE JUST HERE TO RETRACE HIS STEPS.
IF ONE OF YOU LADIES WOULDN'T MIND.
I'LL TAKE THEM, SARA. DON'T WORRY.
I WOULDN'T IMAGINE PUTTING YOU OUT, ALYSHA. *I'LL* TAKE THEM.
I'LL MEET YOU GENTLEMEN OUTSIDE IN JUST ONE SECOND.
SURE ENOUGH.
DINGA! DING!

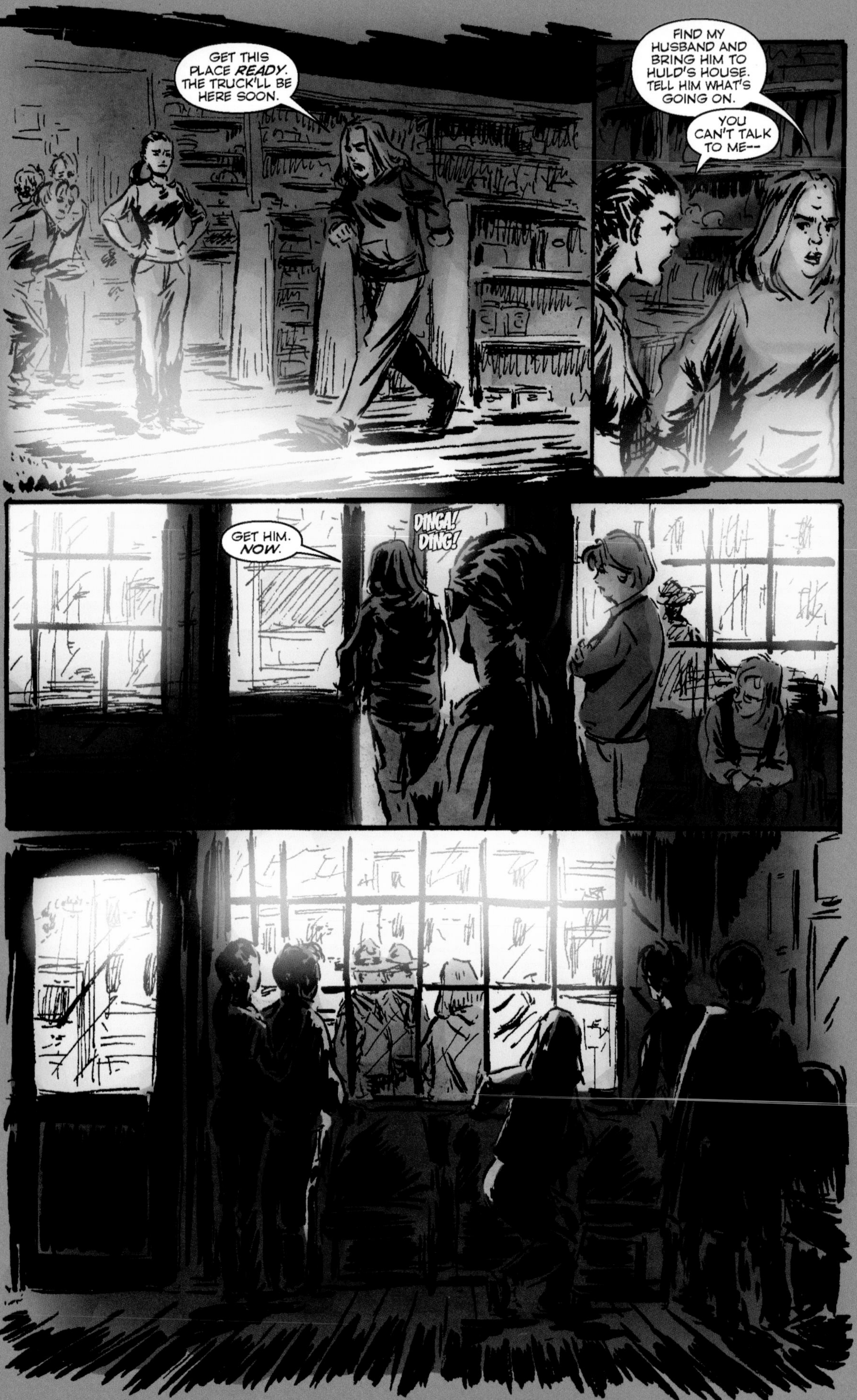
GET THIS PLACE *READY*. THE TRUCK'LL BE HERE SOON.
FIND MY HUSBAND AND BRING HIM TO HULD'S HOUSE. TELL HIM WHAT'S GOING ON.
YOU CAN'T TALK TO ME--
GET HIM. *NOW*.
DINGA! DING!

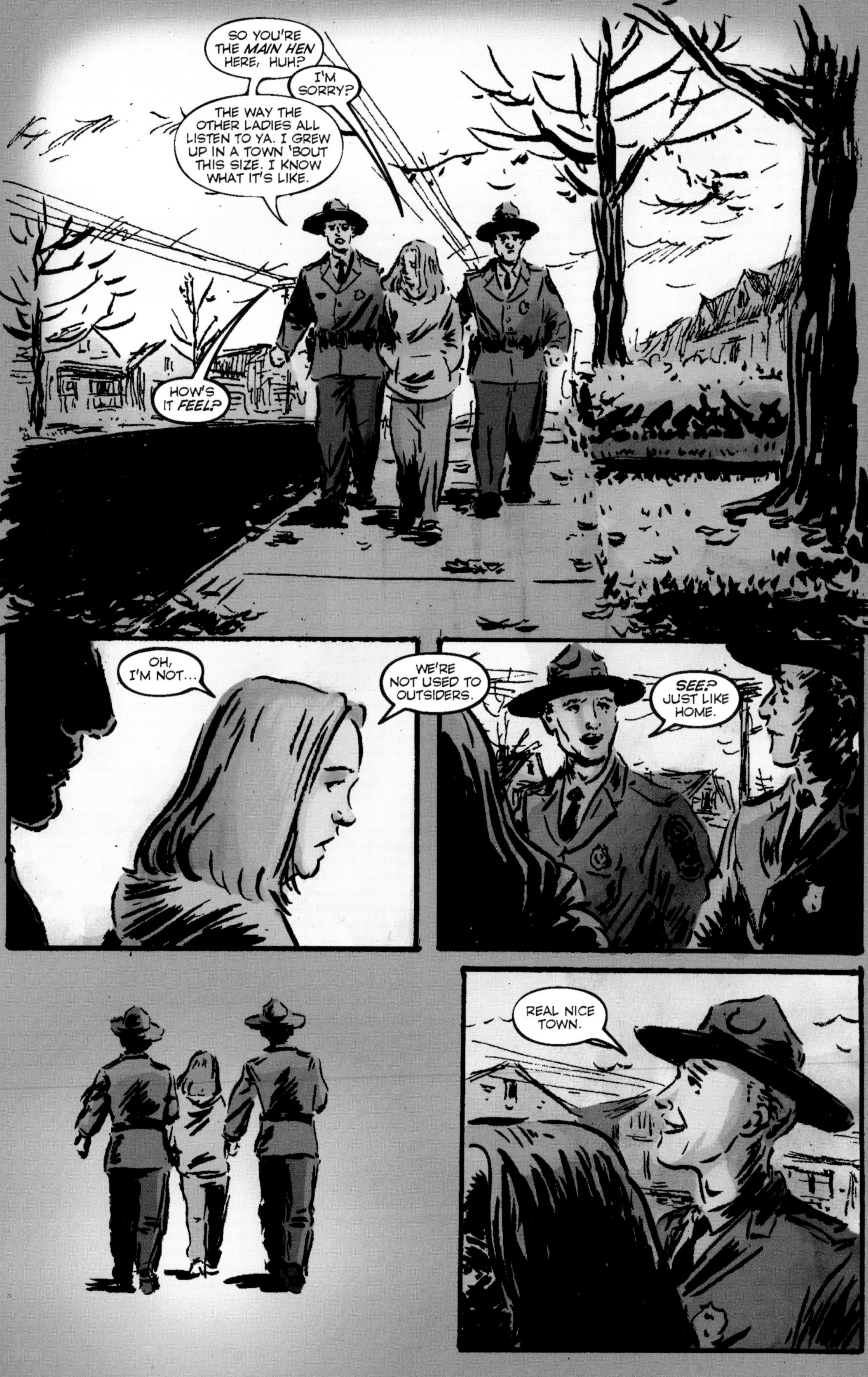

SO YOU'RE THE *MAIN HEN* HERE, HUH?
I'M SORRY?
THE WAY THE OTHER LADIES ALL LISTEN TO YA. I GREW UP IN A TOWN 'BOUT THIS SIZE. I KNOW WHAT IT'S LIKE.
HOW'S IT *FEEL?*
OH, I'M NOT...
WE'RE NOT USED TO OUTSIDERS.
SEE? JUST LIKE HOME.
REAL NICE TOWN.

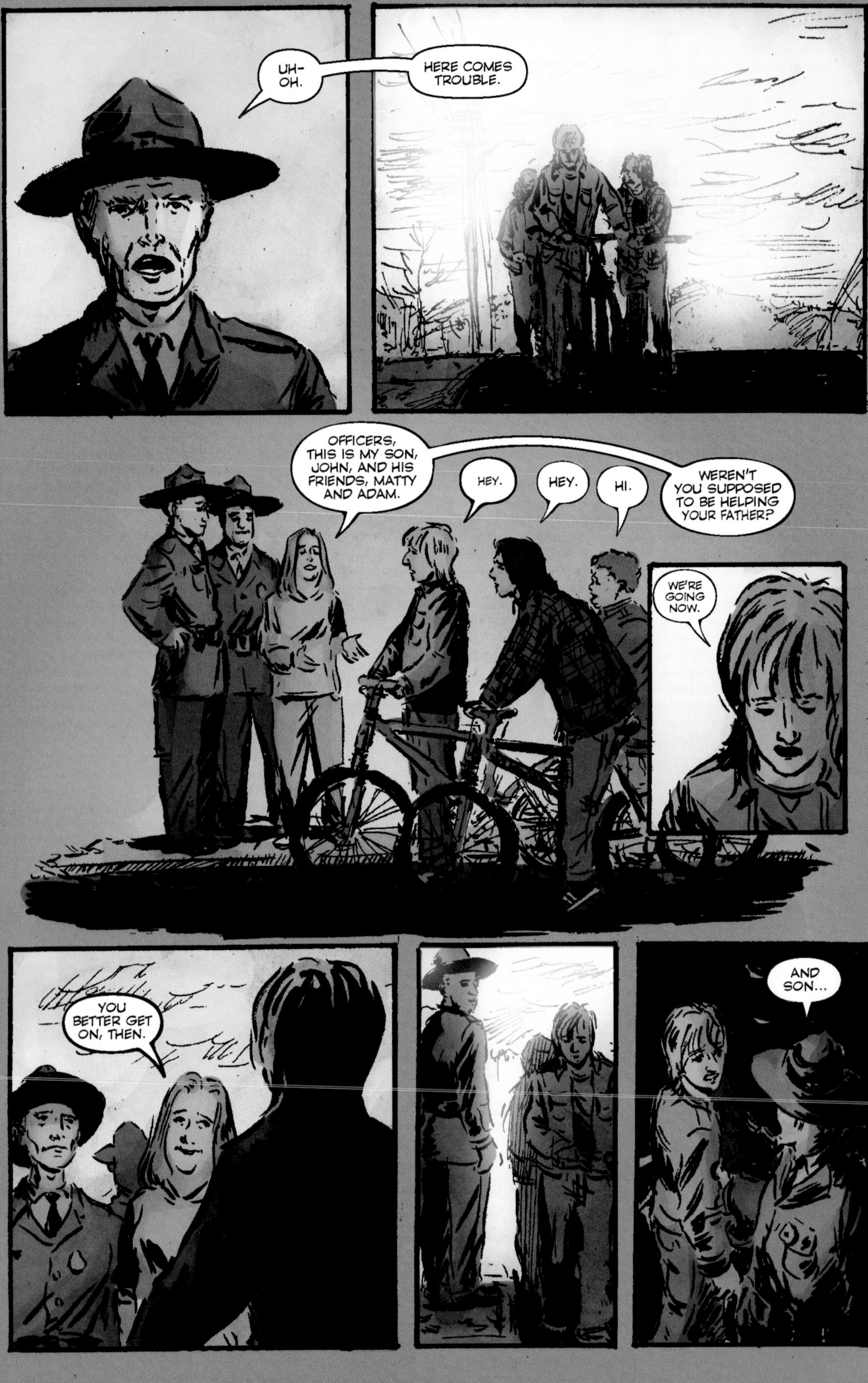
UH-OH.
HERE COMES TROUBLE.
OFFICERS, THIS IS MY SON, JOHN, AND HIS FRIENDS, MATTY AND ADAM.
HEY.
HEY.
HI.
WEREN'T YOU SUPPOSED TO BE HELPING YOUR FATHER?
WE'RE GOING NOW.
YOU BETTER GET ON, THEN.
AND SON...

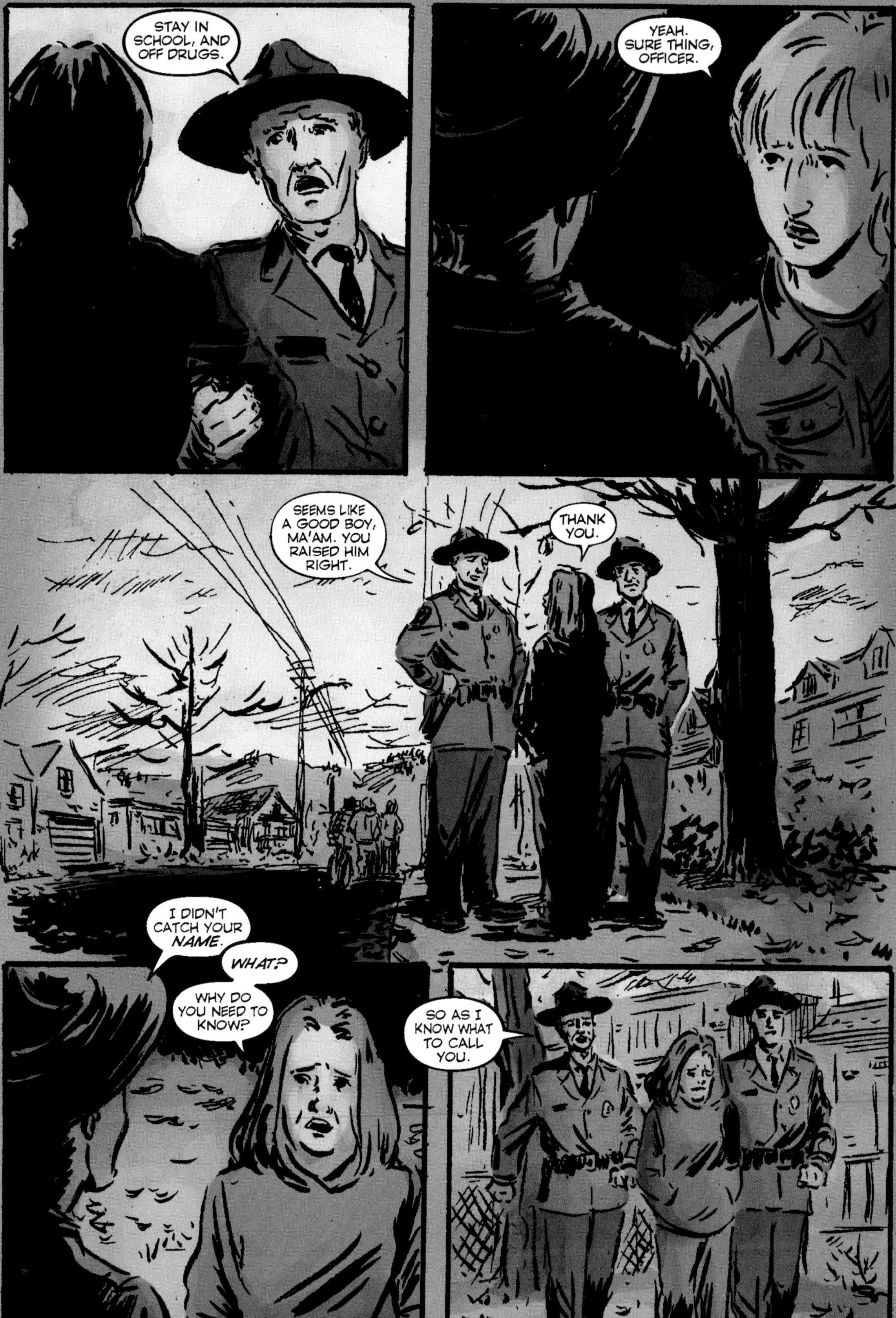
STAY IN SCHOOL, AND OFF DRUGS.
YEAH. SURE THING, OFFICER.
SEEMS LIKE A GOOD BOY, MA'AM. YOU RAISED HIM RIGHT.
THANK YOU.
I DIDN'T CATCH YOUR *NAME*.
WHAT?
WHY DO YOU NEED TO KNOW?
SO AS I KNOW WHAT TO CALL YOU.

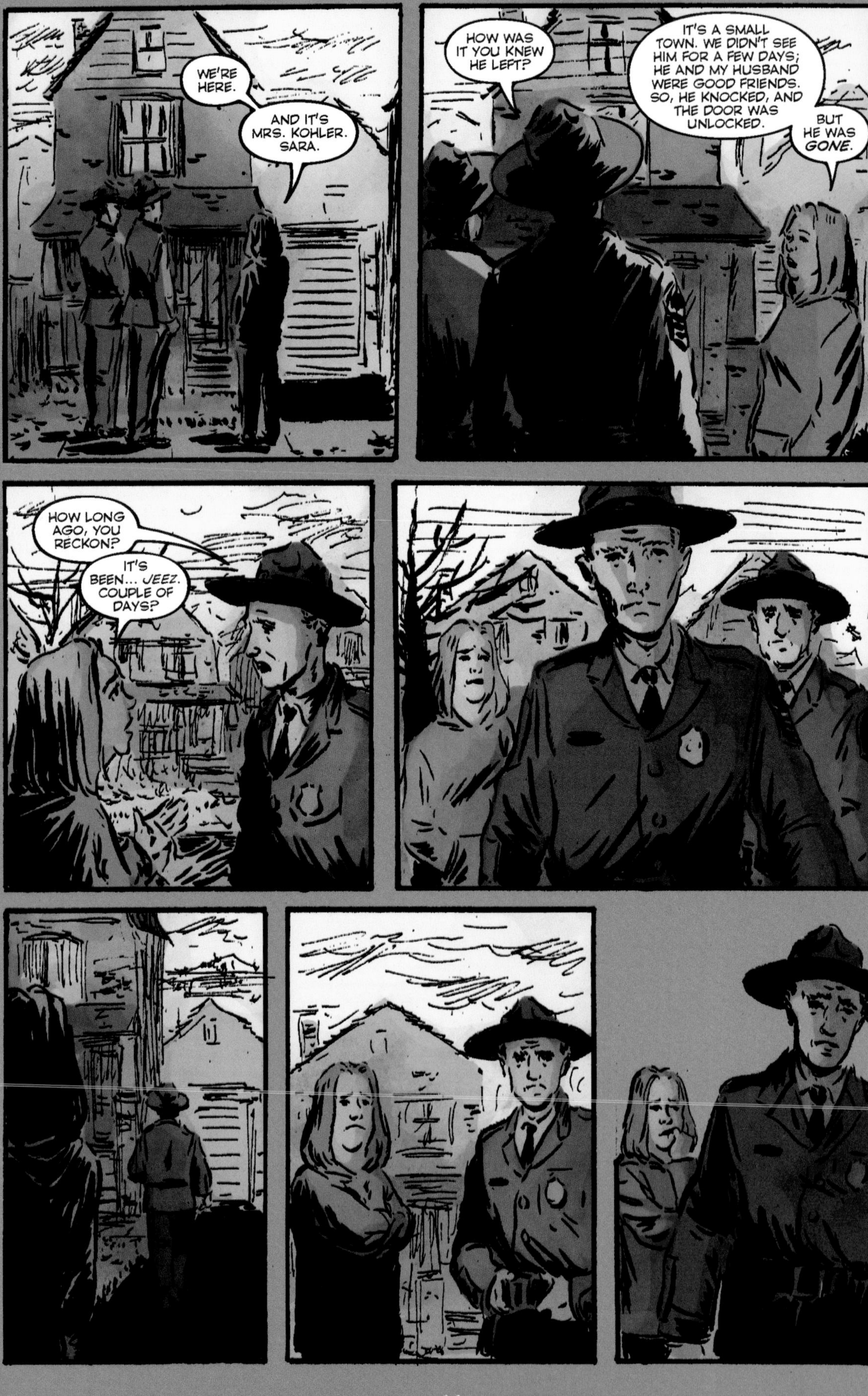
WE'RE HERE.
AND IT'S MRS. KOHLER. SARA.
HOW WAS IT YOU KNEW HE LEFT?
IT'S A SMALL TOWN. WE DIDN'T SEE HIM FOR A FEW DAYS; HE AND MY HUSBAND WERE GOOD FRIENDS. SO, HE KNOCKED, AND THE DOOR WAS UNLOCKED.
BUT HE WAS *GONE*.
HOW LONG AGO, YOU RECKON?
IT'S BEEN... *JEEZ*. COUPLE OF DAYS?

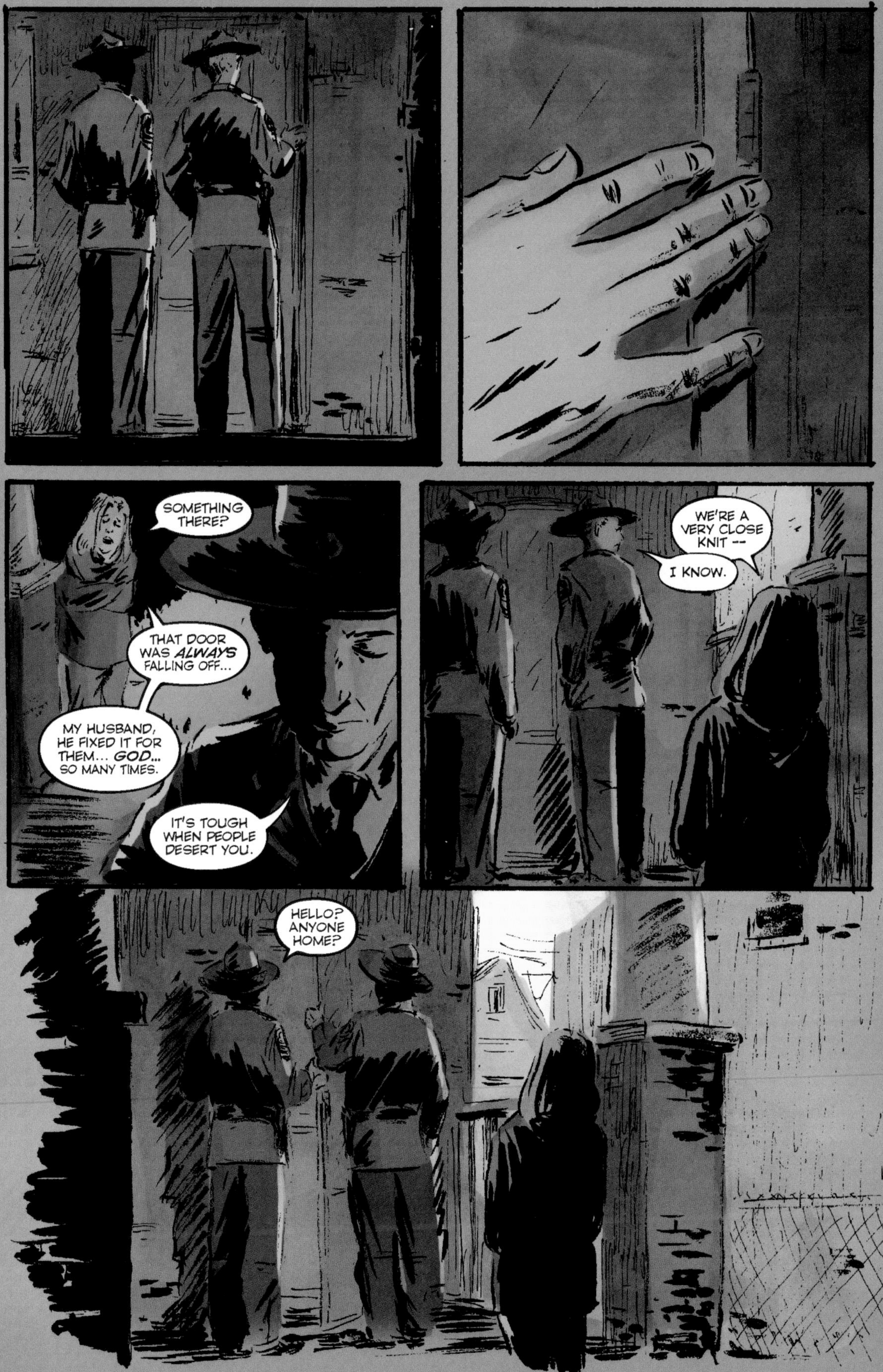
SOMETHING THERE?
THAT DOOR WAS *ALWAYS* FALLING OFF...
MY HUSBAND, HE FIXED IT FOR THEM... *GOD...* SO MANY TIMES.
IT'S TOUGH WHEN PEOPLE DESERT YOU.
WE'RE A VERY CLOSE KNIT --
I KNOW.
HELLO? ANYONE HOME?

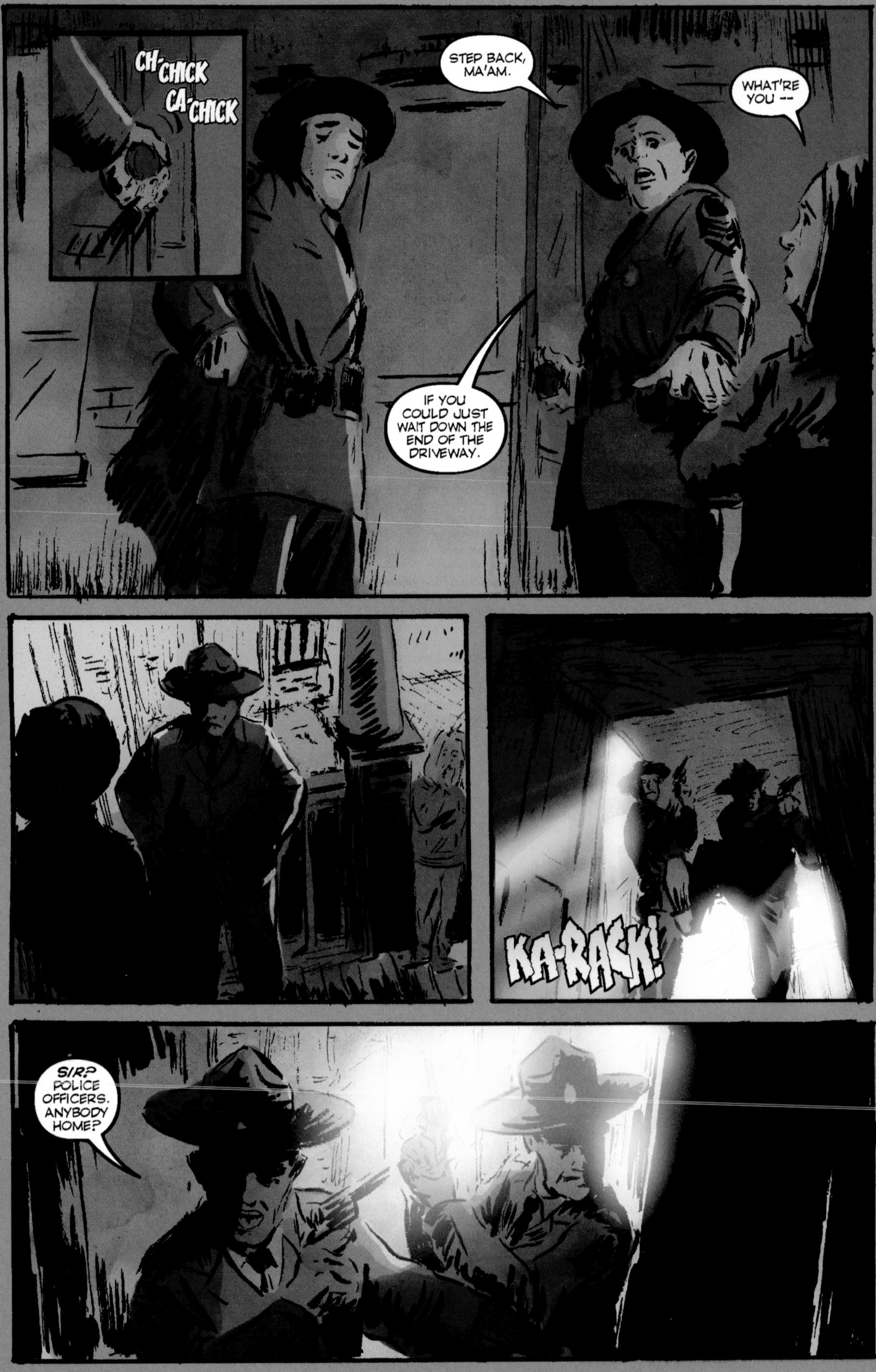
CH-CHICK
CA-CHICK
STEP BACK, MA'AM.
WHAT'RE YOU --
IF YOU COULD JUST WAIT DOWN THE END OF THE DRIVEWAY.
KA-RACK!
SIR? POLICE OFFICERS. ANYBODY HOME?

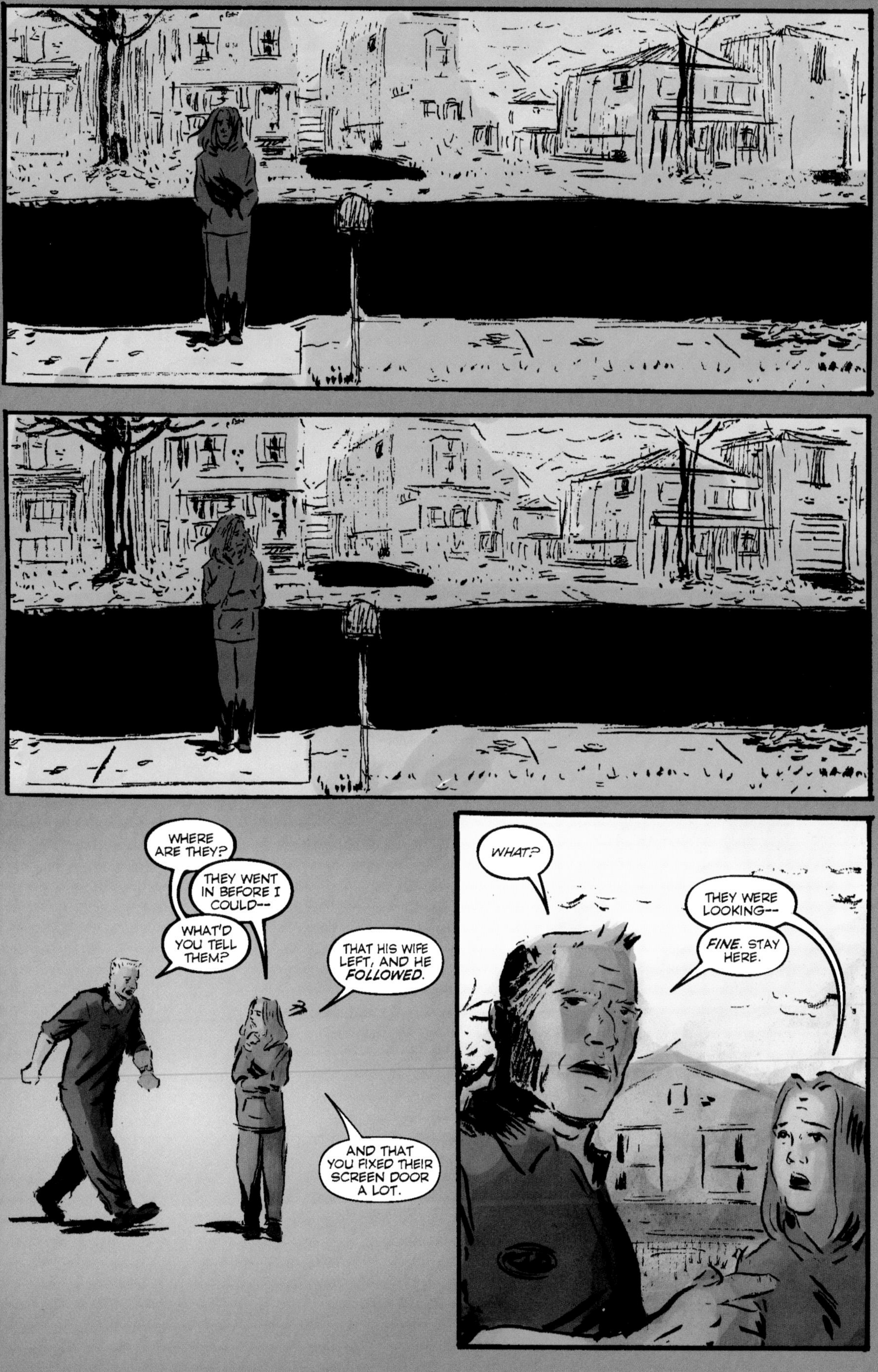
WHERE ARE THEY?
THEY WENT IN BEFORE I COULD--
WHAT'D YOU TELL THEM?
THAT HIS WIFE LEFT, AND HE *FOLLOWED*.
AND THAT YOU FIXED THEIR SCREEN DOOR A LOT.
WHAT?
THEY WERE LOOKING--
FINE. STAY HERE.

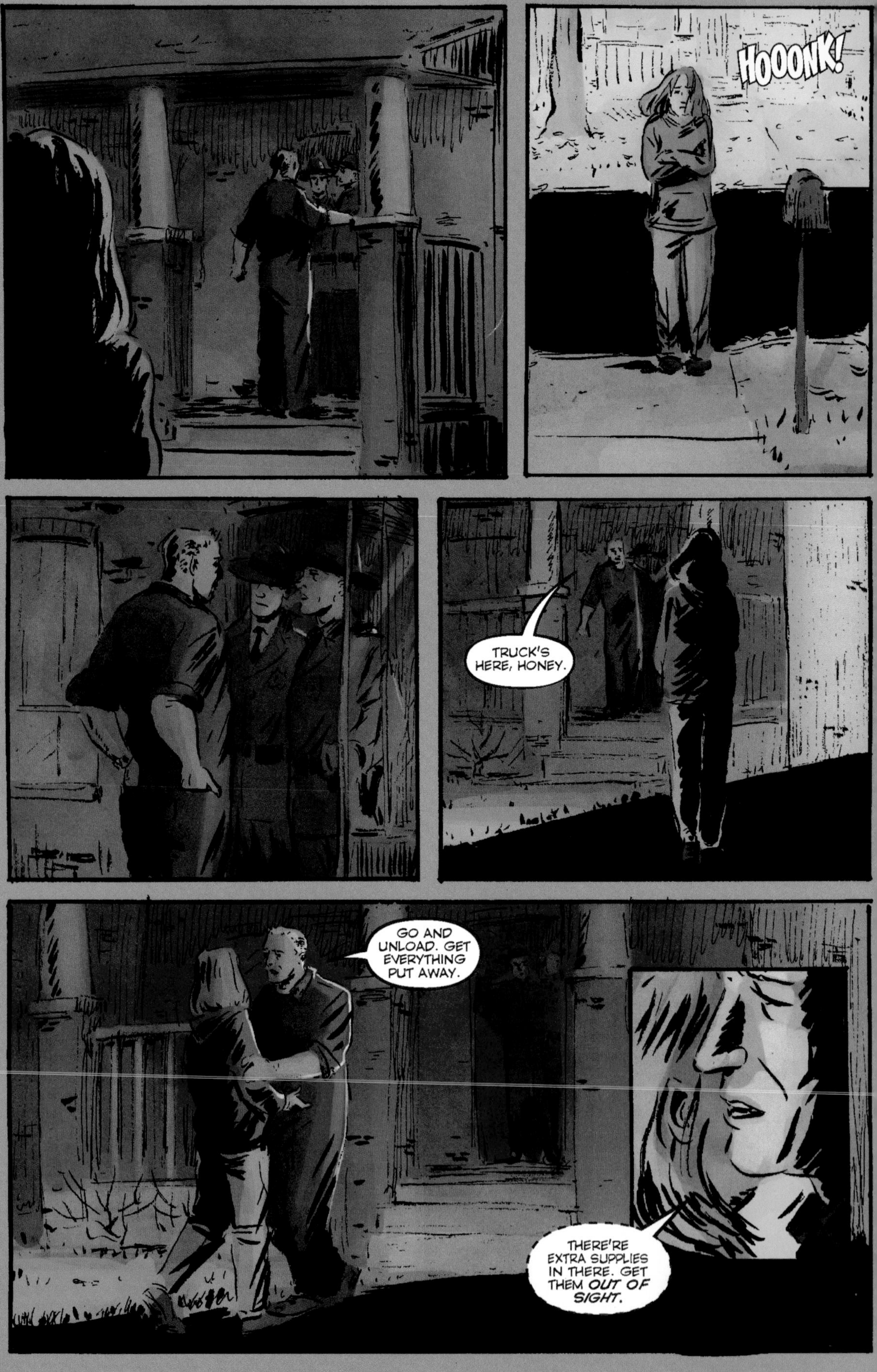
HOOONK!
TRUCK'S HERE, HONEY.
GO AND UNLOAD. GET EVERYTHING PUT AWAY.
THERE'RE EXTRA SUPPLIES IN THERE. GET THEM *OUT OF SIGHT*.

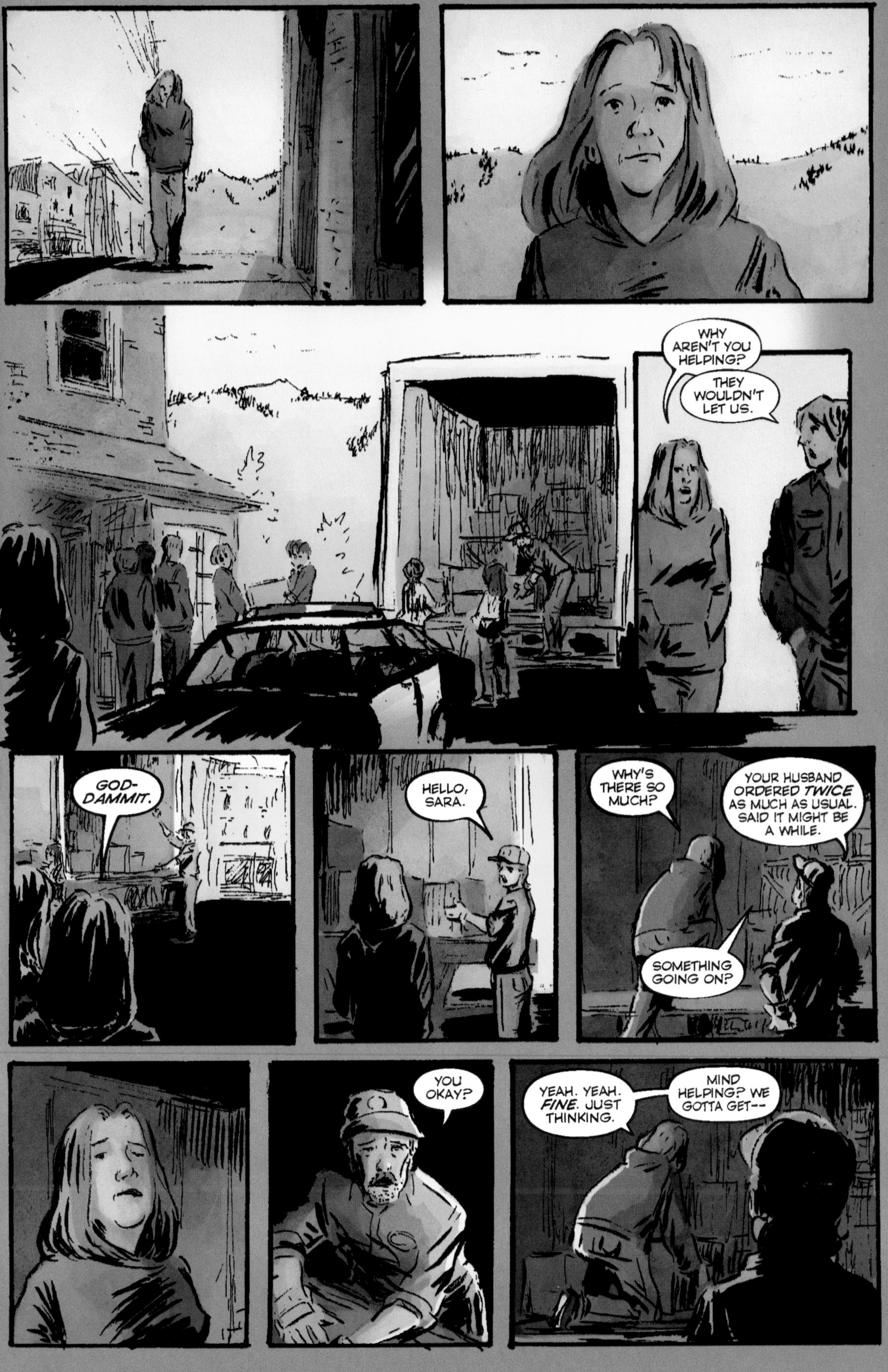
WHY AREN'T YOU HELPING?
THEY WOULDN'T LET US.
GOD-DAMMIT.
HELLO, SARA.
WHY'S THERE SO MUCH?
YOUR HUSBAND ORDERED TWICE AS MUCH AS USUAL. SAID IT MIGHT BE A WHILE.
SOMETHING GOING ON?
YOU OKAY?
YEAH. YEAH. FINE. JUST THINKING.
MIND HELPING? WE GOTTA GET--

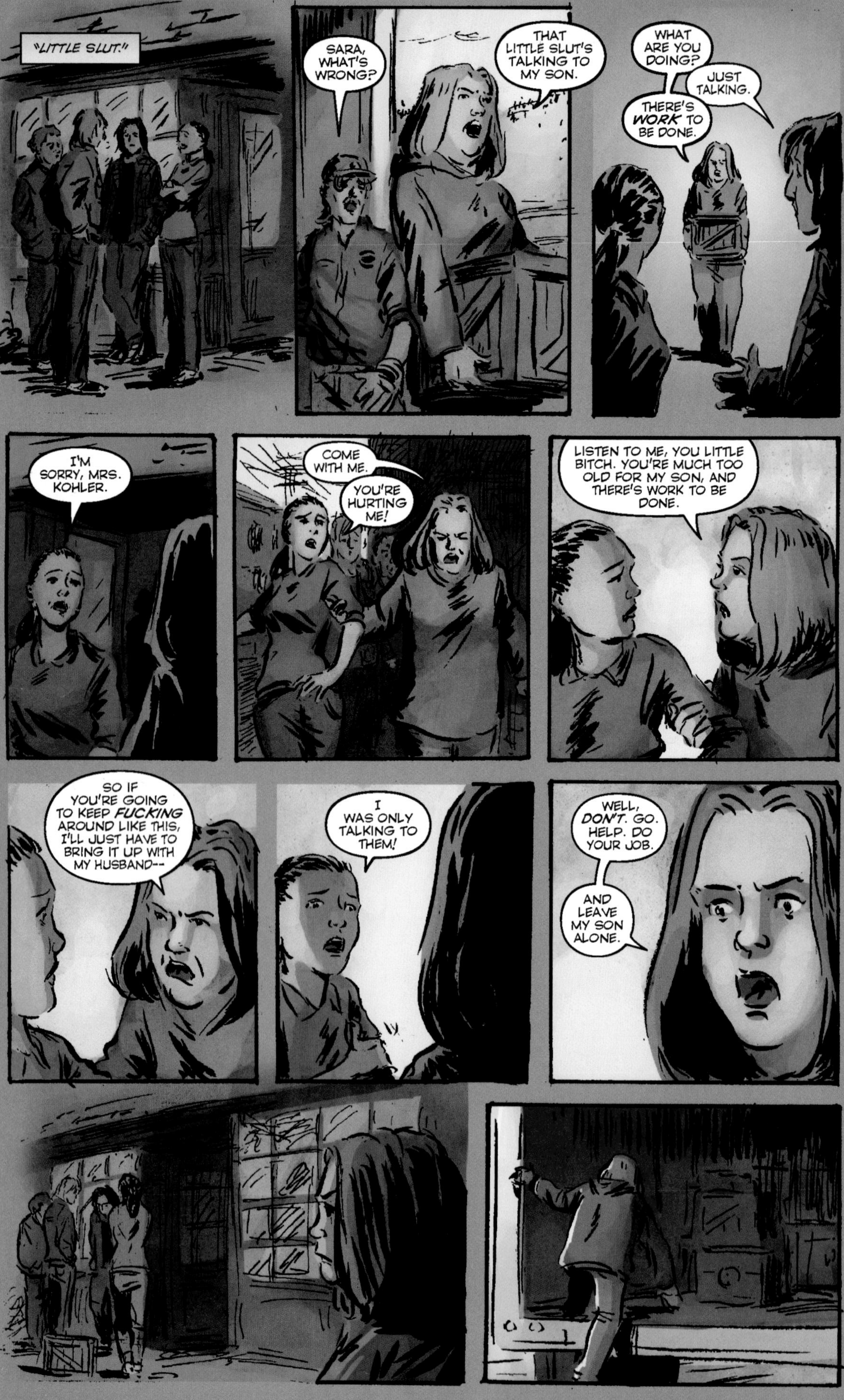
"LITTLE SLUT."
SARA, WHAT'S WRONG?
THAT LITTLE SLUT'S TALKING TO MY SON.
WHAT ARE YOU DOING?
JUST TALKING.
THERE'S WORK TO BE DONE.
I'M SORRY, MRS. KOHLER.
COME WITH ME.
YOU'RE HURTING ME!
LISTEN TO ME, YOU LITTLE BITCH. YOU'RE MUCH TOO OLD FOR MY SON, AND THERE'S WORK TO BE DONE.
SO IF YOU'RE GOING TO KEEP FUCKING AROUND LIKE THIS, I'LL JUST HAVE TO BRING IT UP WITH MY HUSBAND--
I WAS ONLY TALKING TO THEM!
WELL, DON'T. GO. HELP. DO YOUR JOB.
AND LEAVE MY SON ALONE.

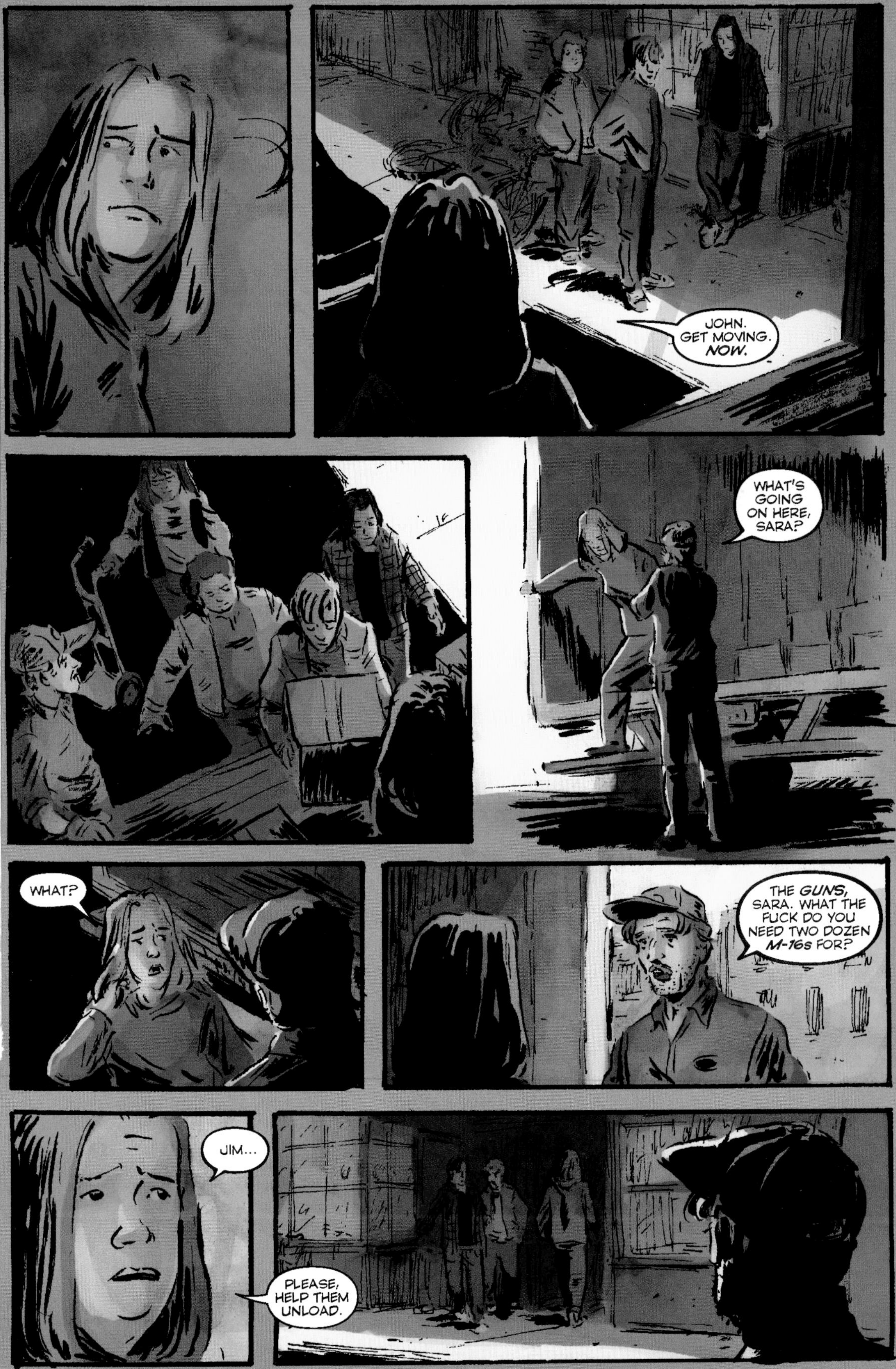
JOHN. GET MOVING. *NOW.*
WHAT'S GOING ON HERE, SARA?
WHAT?
THE *GUNS,* SARA. WHAT THE FUCK DO YOU NEED TWO DOZEN *M-16s* FOR?
JIM...
PLEASE, HELP THEM UNLOAD.

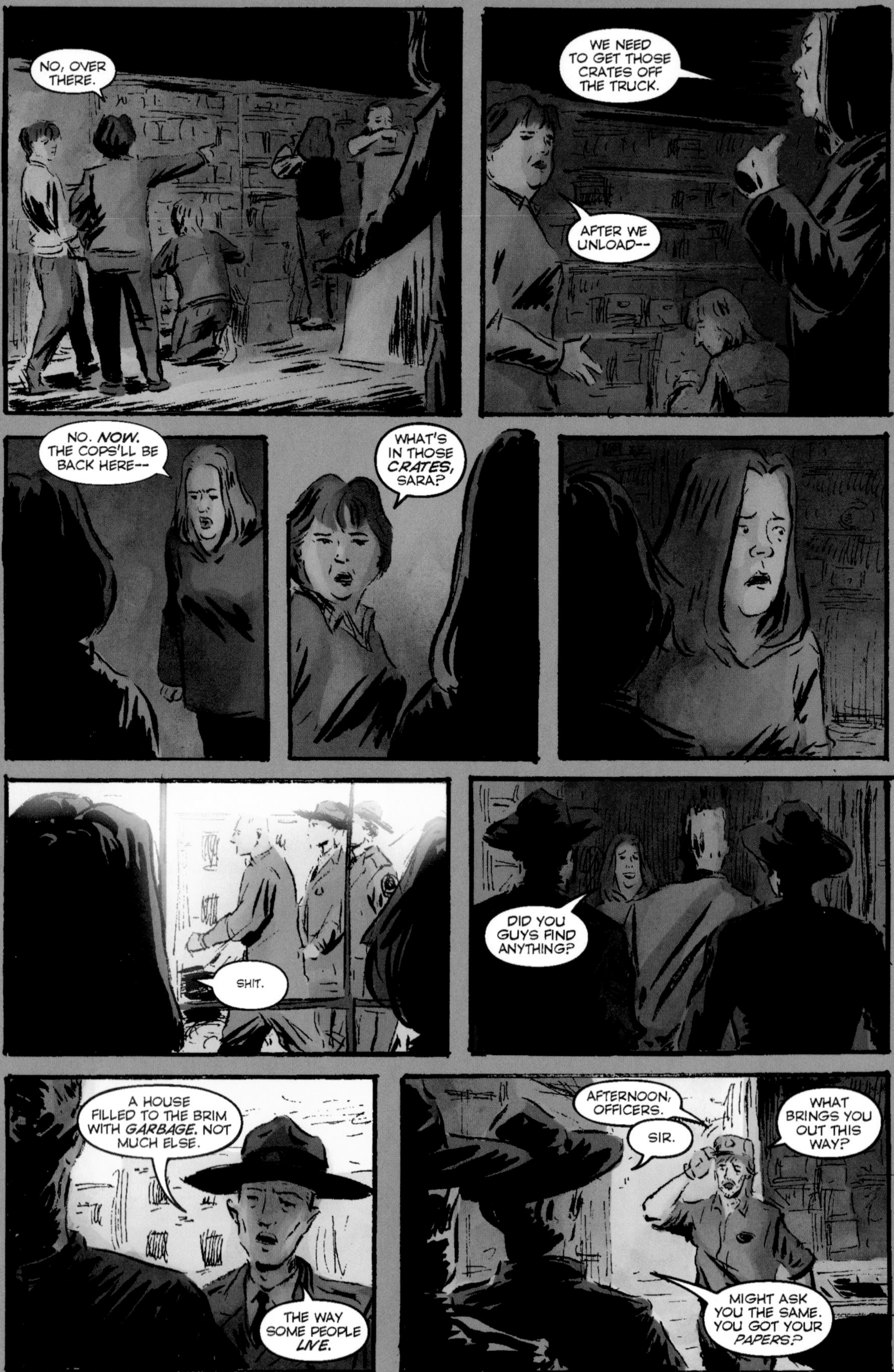
NO, OVER THERE.
WE NEED TO GET THOSE CRATES OFF THE TRUCK.
AFTER WE UNLOAD--
NO. NOW. THE COPS'LL BE BACK HERE--
WHAT'S IN THOSE CRATES, SARA?
SHIT.
DID YOU GUYS FIND ANYTHING?
A HOUSE FILLED TO THE BRIM WITH GARBAGE. NOT MUCH ELSE.
THE WAY SOME PEOPLE LIVE.
AFTERNOON, OFFICERS.
SIR.
WHAT BRINGS YOU OUT THIS WAY?
MIGHT ASK YOU THE SAME. YOU GOT YOUR PAPERS?

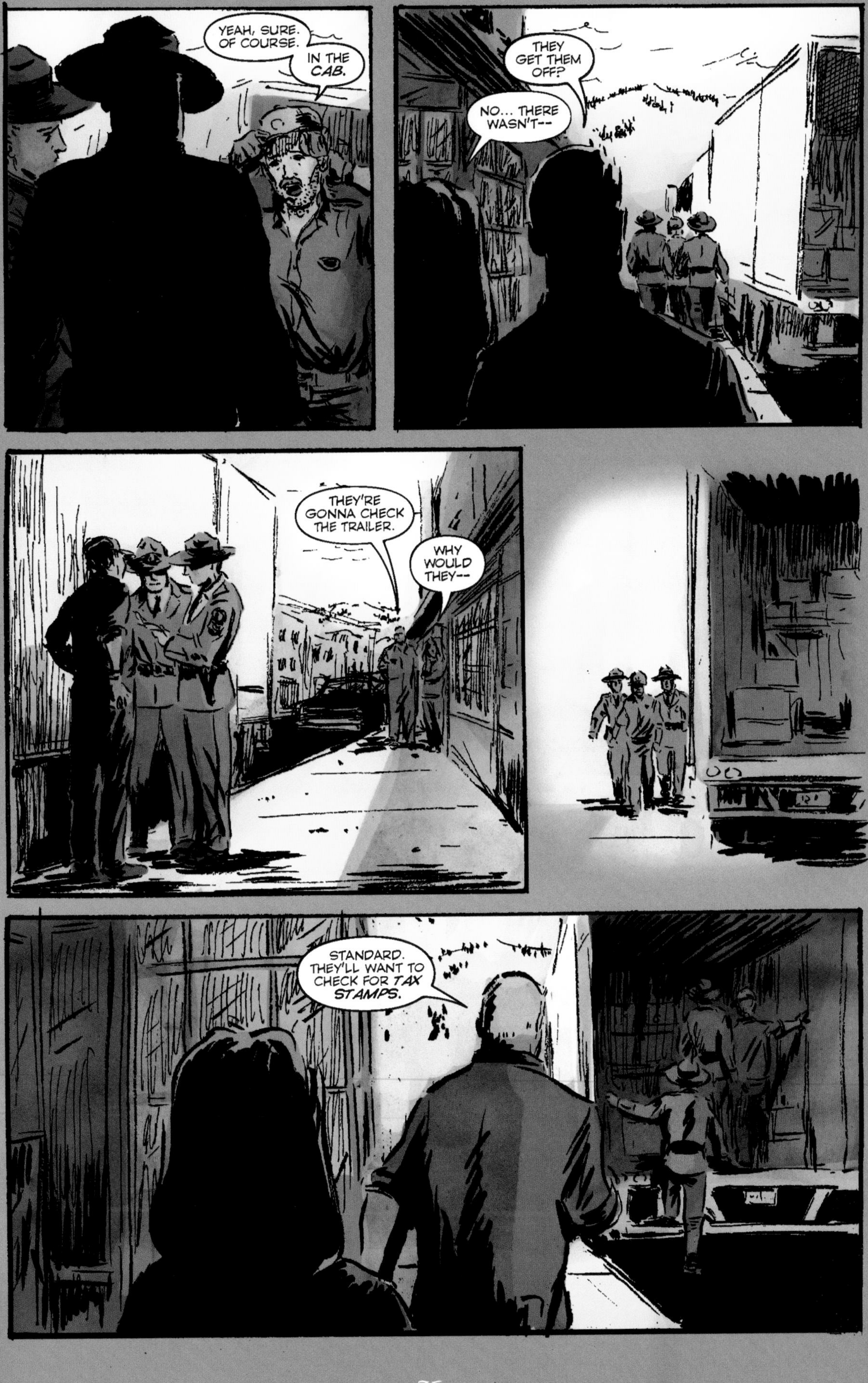
YEAH, SURE. OF COURSE.
IN THE CAB.
THEY GET THEM OFF?
NO... THERE WASN'T--
THEY'RE GONNA CHECK THE TRAILER.
WHY WOULD THEY--
STANDARD. THEY'LL WANT TO CHECK FOR TAX STAMPS.

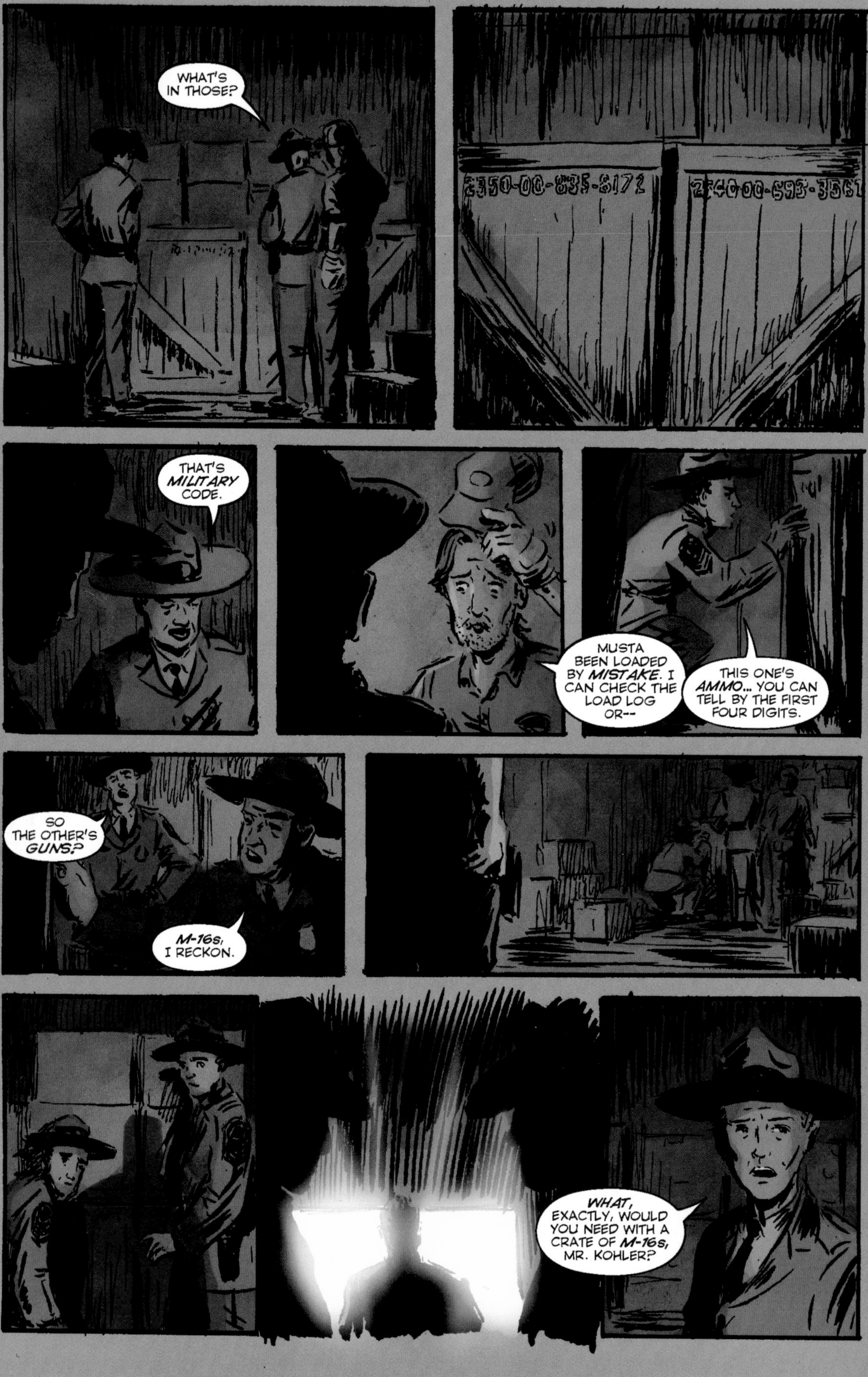
WHAT'S IN THOSE?
2350-00-835-8172
2340-00-693-3561
THAT'S MILITARY CODE.
MUSTA BEEN LOADED BY MISTAKE. I CAN CHECK THE LOAD LOG OR--
THIS ONE'S AMMO... YOU CAN TELL BY THE FIRST FOUR DIGITS.
SO THE OTHER'S GUNS?
M-16s, I RECKON.
WHAT, EXACTLY, WOULD YOU NEED WITH A CRATE OF M-16s, MR. KOHLER?

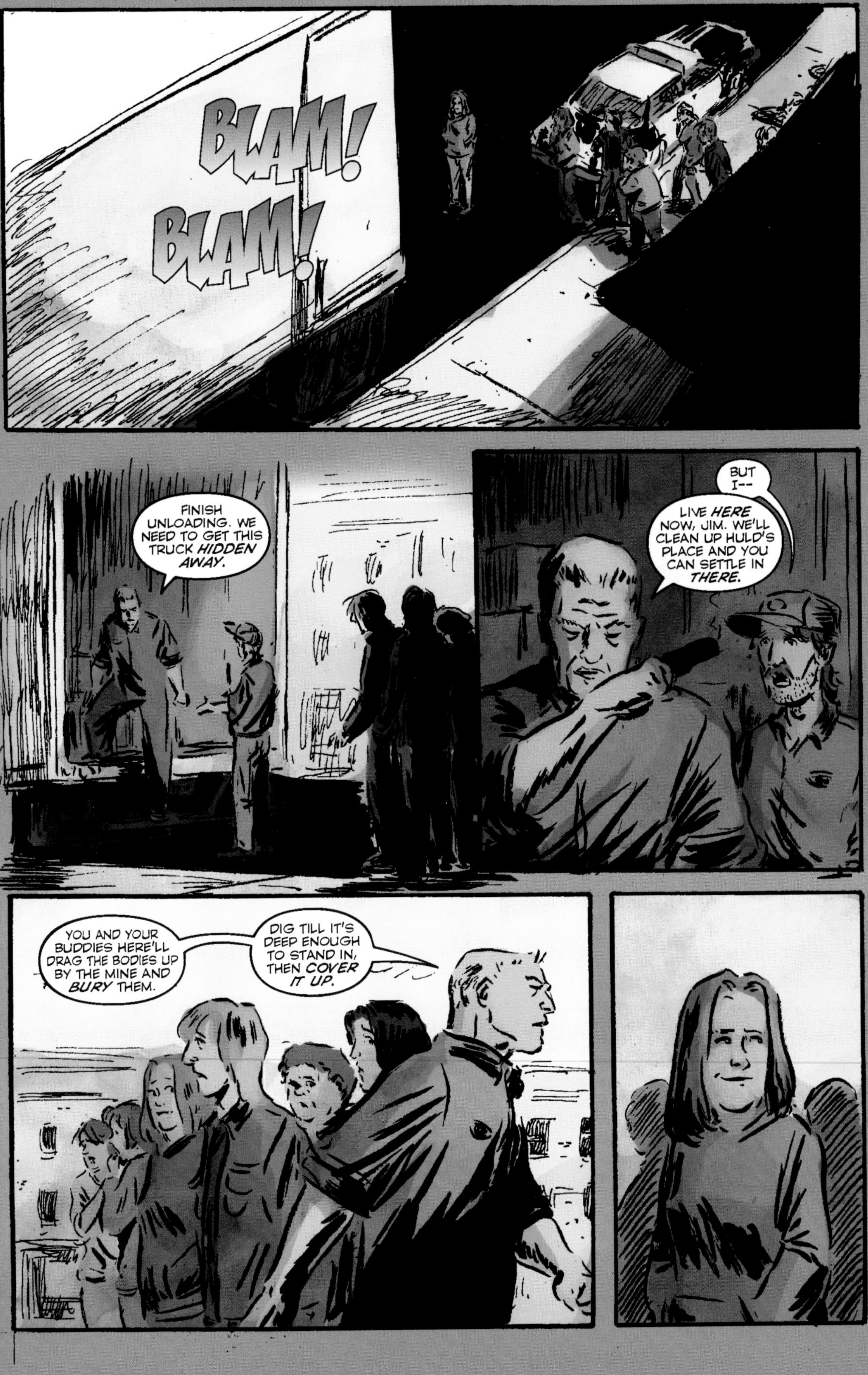
BLAM!
BLAM!
FINISH UNLOADING. WE NEED TO GET THIS TRUCK HIDDEN AWAY.
BUT I--
LIVE HERE NOW, JIM. WE'LL CLEAN UP HULD'S PLACE AND YOU CAN SETTLE IN THERE.
YOU AND YOUR BUDDIES HERE'LL DRAG THE BODIES UP BY THE MINE AND BURY THEM.
DIG TILL IT'S DEEP ENOUGH TO STAND IN, THEN COVER IT UP.

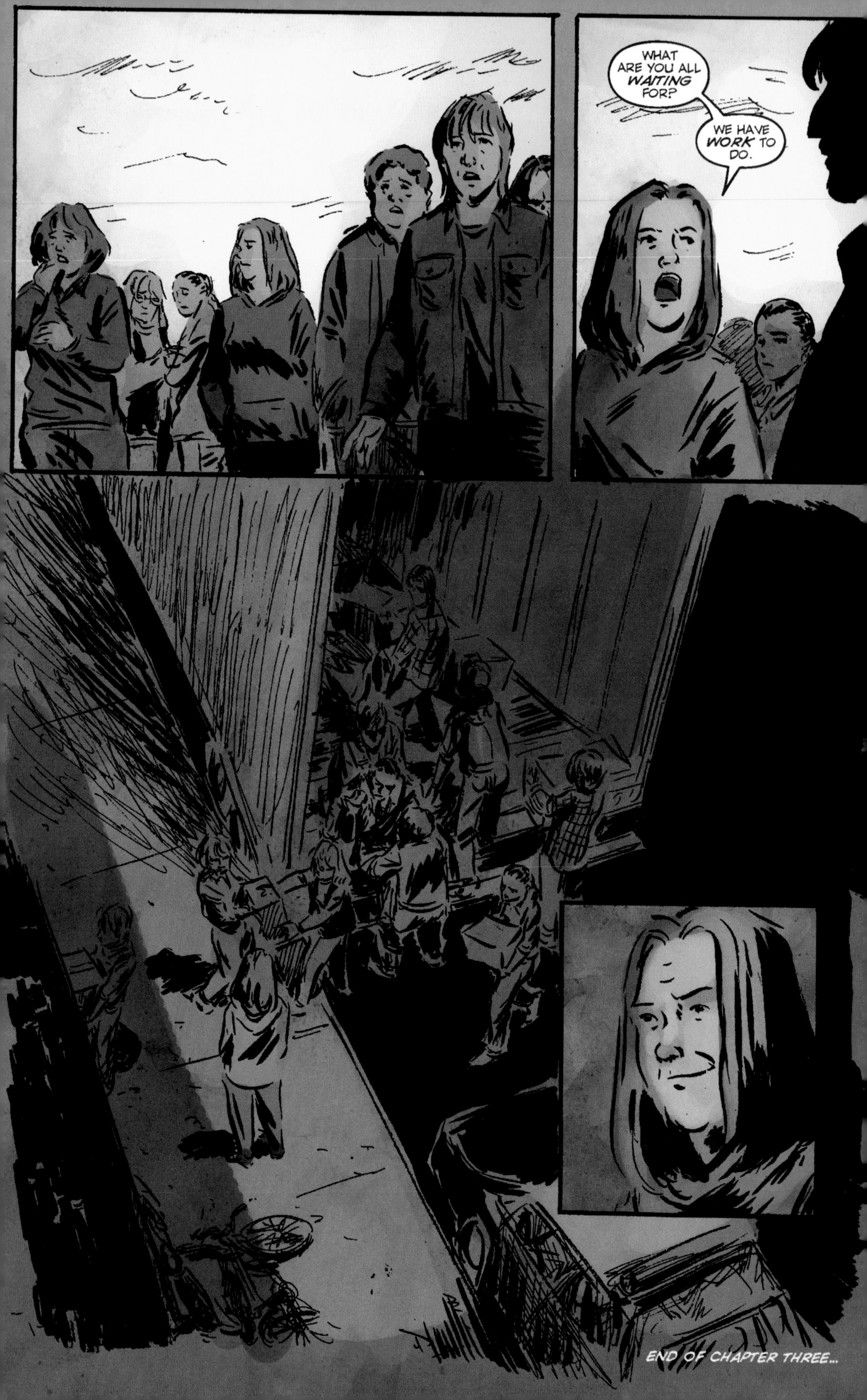
WHAT ARE YOU ALL *WAITING* FOR?
WE HAVE *WORK* TO DO.
END OF CHAPTER THREE...

Chapter Four:
The Hunter and the Hunted

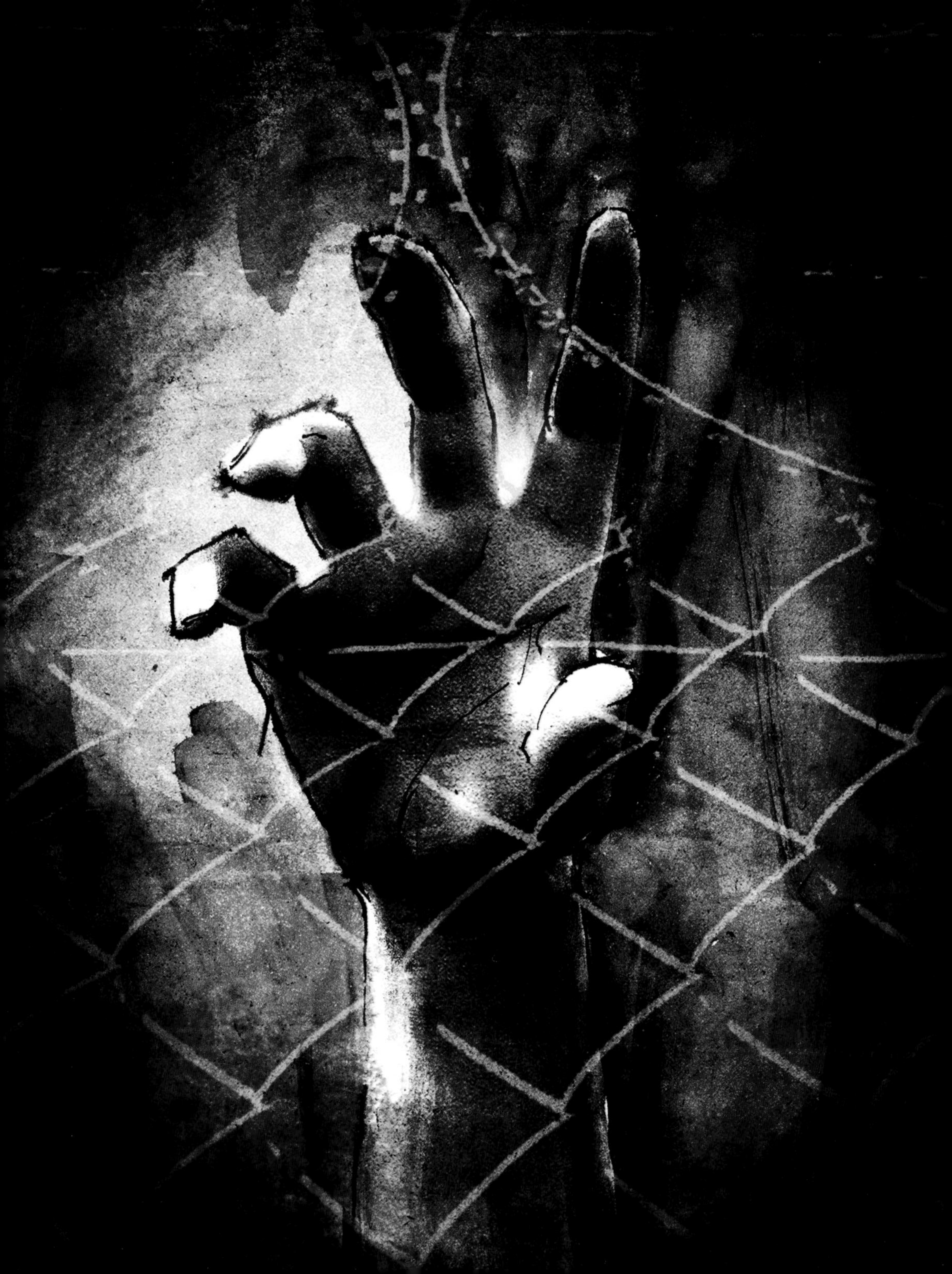

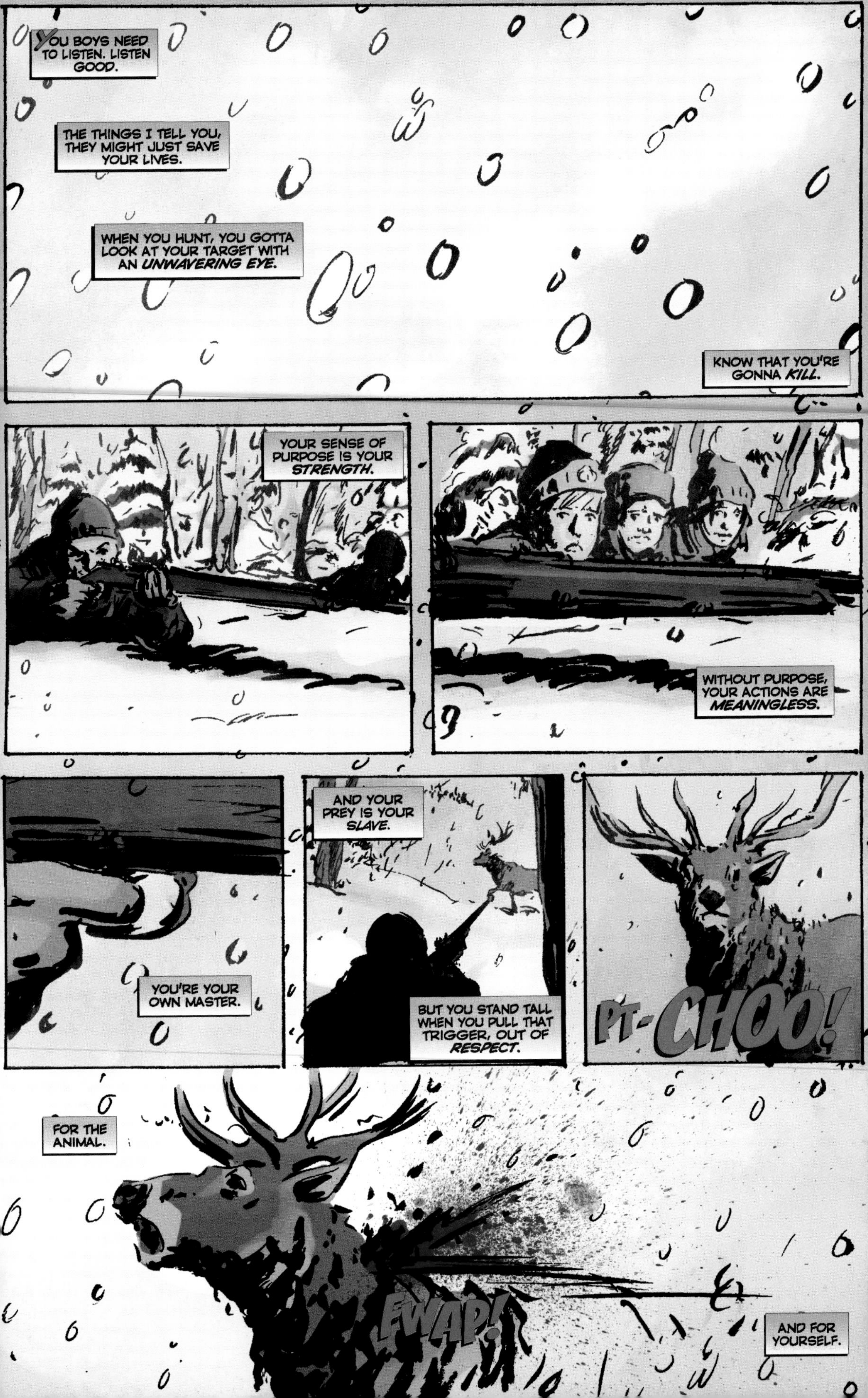

YOU BOYS NEED TO LISTEN. LISTEN GOOD.
THE THINGS I TELL YOU, THEY MIGHT JUST SAVE YOUR LIVES.
WHEN YOU HUNT, YOU GOTTA LOOK AT YOUR TARGET WITH AN UNWAVERING EYE.
KNOW THAT YOU'RE GONNA KILL.
YOUR SENSE OF PURPOSE IS YOUR STRENGTH.
WITHOUT PURPOSE, YOUR ACTIONS ARE MEANINGLESS.
YOU'RE YOUR OWN MASTER.
AND YOUR PREY IS YOUR SLAVE.
BUT YOU STAND TALL WHEN YOU PULL THAT TRIGGER, OUT OF RESPECT.
PT-CHOO!
FOR THE ANIMAL.
FWAP!
AND FOR YOURSELF.

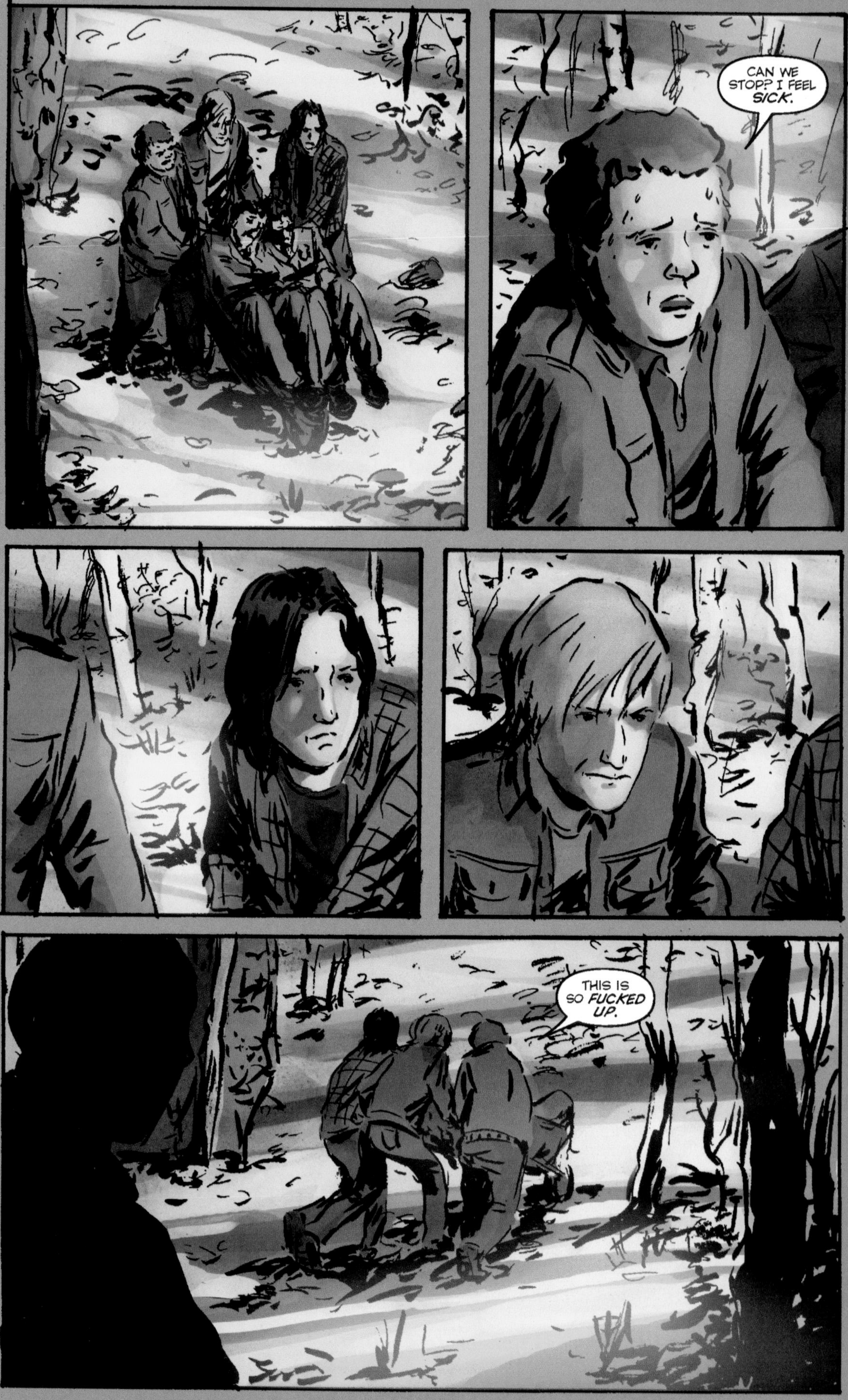
CAN WE STOP? I FEEL SICK.
THIS IS SO FUCKED UP.

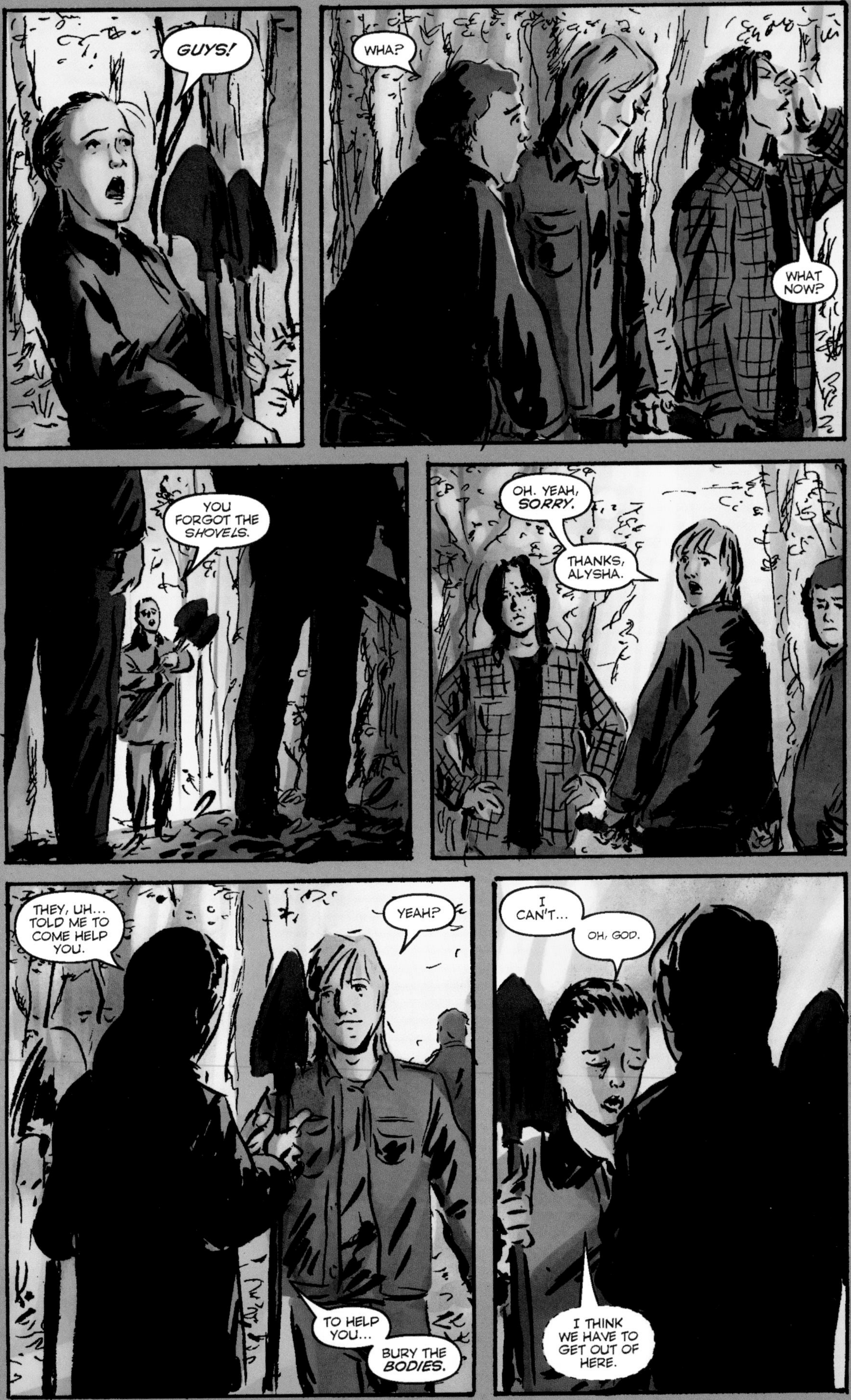
GUYS!
WHA?
WHAT NOW?
YOU FORGOT THE SHOVELS.
OH. YEAH, SORRY.
THANKS, ALYSHA.
THEY, UH... TOLD ME TO COME HELP YOU.
YEAH?
TO HELP YOU...
BURY THE BODIES.
I CAN'T...
OH, GOD.
I THINK WE HAVE TO GET OUT OF HERE.

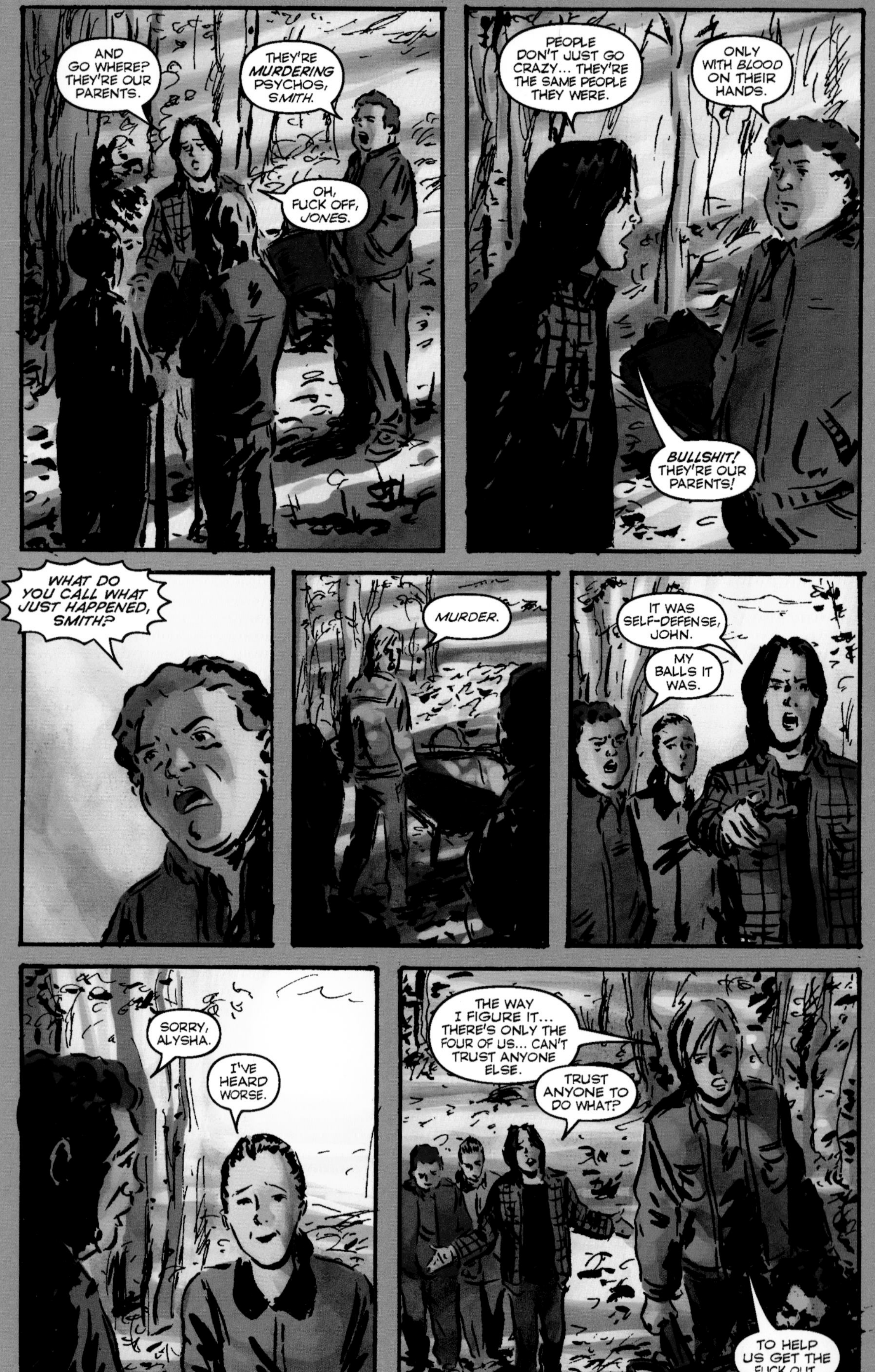
AND GO WHERE? THEY'RE OUR PARENTS.
THEY'RE *MURDERING* PSYCHOS, *SMITH.*
OH, FUCK OFF, *JONES.*
PEOPLE DON'T JUST GO CRAZY... THEY'RE THE SAME PEOPLE THEY WERE.
ONLY WITH *BLOOD* ON THEIR HANDS.
BULLSHIT! THEY'RE OUR PARENTS!
WHAT DO YOU CALL WHAT JUST HAPPENED, SMITH?
MURDER.
IT WAS SELF-DEFENSE, JOHN.
MY BALLS IT WAS.
SORRY, ALYSHA.
I'VE HEARD WORSE.
THE WAY I FIGURE IT... THERE'S ONLY THE FOUR OF US... CAN'T TRUST ANYONE ELSE.
TRUST ANYONE TO DO WHAT?
TO HELP US GET THE FUCK OUT.

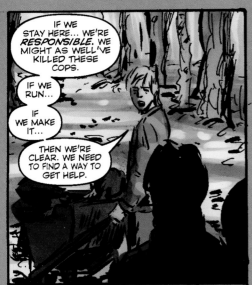

IF WE STAY HERE... WE'RE *RESPONSIBLE*. WE MIGHT AS WELL'VE KILLED THESE COPS.

IF WE RUN...

IF WE MAKE IT...

THEN WE'RE CLEAR. WE NEED TO FIND A WAY TO GET HELP.

WE DON'T NEED HELP, JOHN. WE'RE FINE. WE JUST NEED TO DO WHAT WE'RE TOLD, AND EVERYTHING'S FINE.

WHY CAN'T WE JUST RUN THROUGH THE TUNNEL?

THEY'LL BE *WATCHING* IT. WE'LL HAVE TO GO OVER THE FENCES.

THIS IS FUCKING RIDICULOUS.

THEY KILLED A COUPLE OF *COPS*... WHO WERE SNOOPING AROUND.

THEY KILLED MR. HULD TOO, MAN.

ALL IN THE NAME OF "JUSTICE," RIGHT?

WHO KNOWS WHAT ELSE THEY'VE DONE...

FUCK THIS. I'M GOING TO BURY THE BODIES.

DID YOU HEAR WHAT YOU JUST *SAID?*

IS THIS WHAT *SANE* PEOPLE DO?

IS THIS WHAT NORMAL PARENTS MAKE THEIR KIDS DO?

REALLY?

THIS WHOLE TOWN IS FUCKED UP, SMITH.

WE'RE LEAVING.

YOU COMING OR WHAT?

WHAT THE FUCK *ELSE* AM I SUPPOSED TO DO?

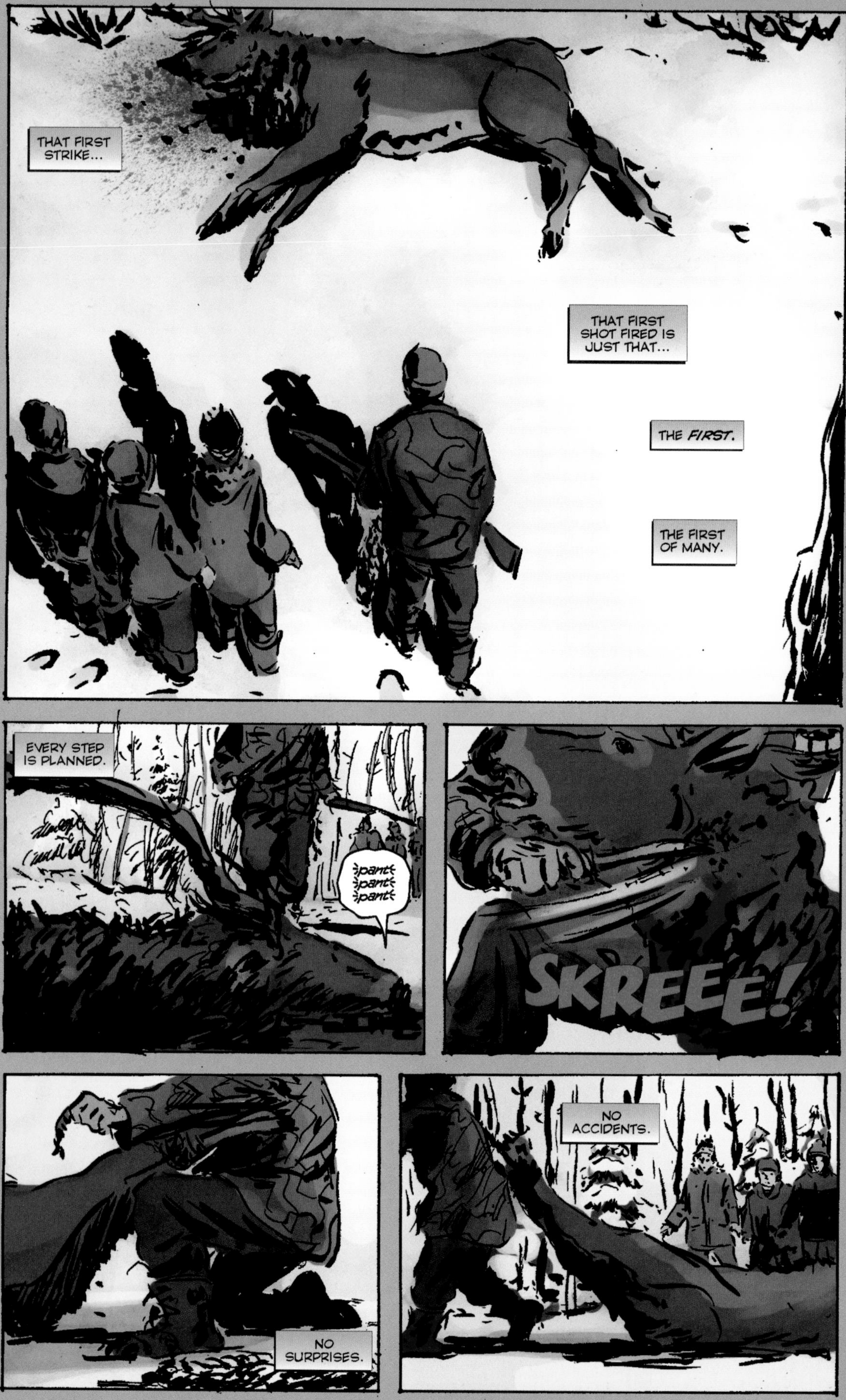
THAT FIRST STRIKE...
THAT FIRST SHOT FIRED IS JUST THAT...
THE *FIRST*.
THE FIRST OF MANY.
EVERY STEP IS PLANNED.
pant pant pant
SKREEE!
NO SURPRISES.
NO ACCIDENTS.

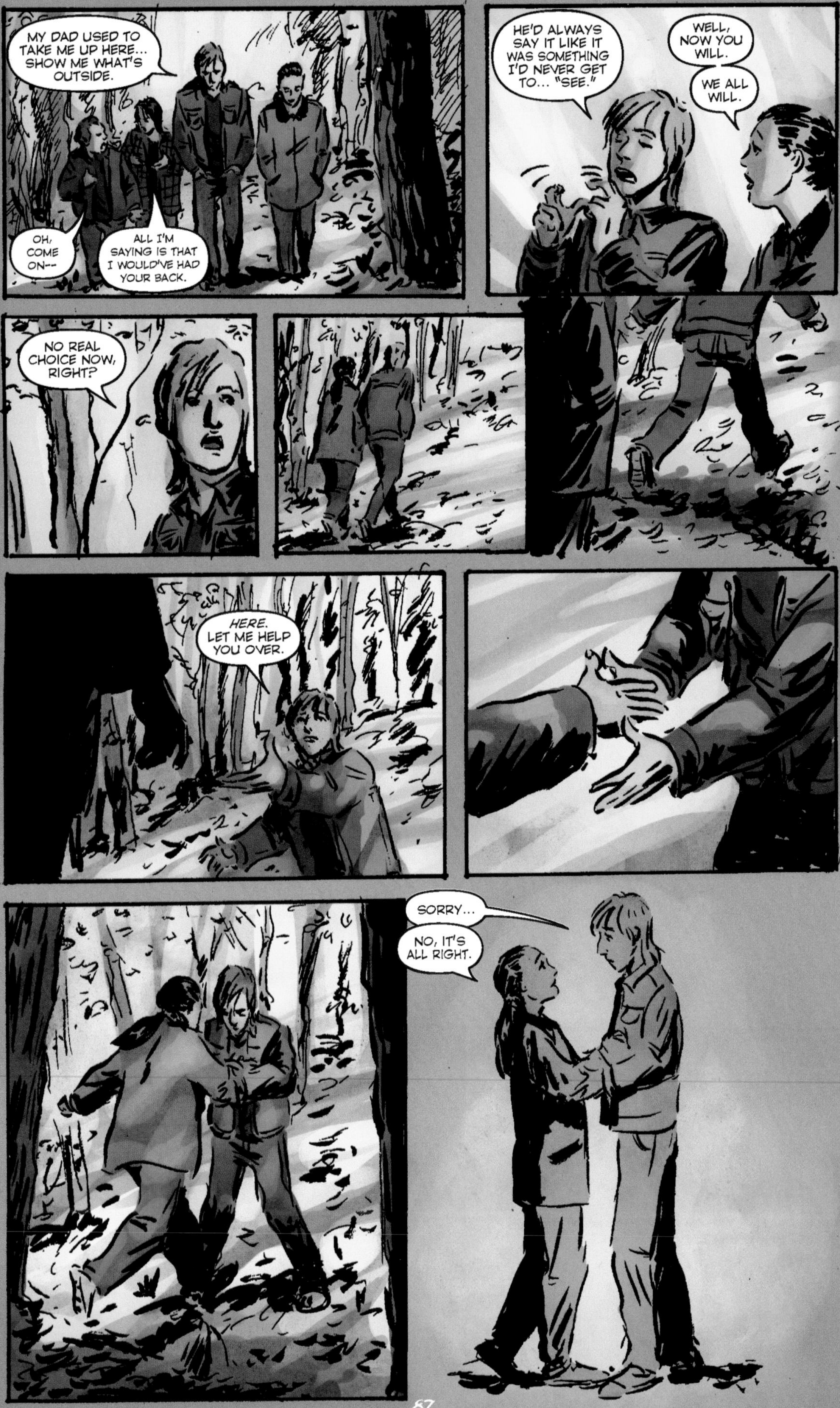
MY DAD USED TO TAKE ME UP HERE... SHOW ME WHAT'S OUTSIDE.
OH, COME ON--
ALL I'M SAYING IS THAT I WOULD'VE HAD YOUR BACK.
HE'D ALWAYS SAY IT LIKE IT WAS SOMETHING I'D NEVER GET TO... "SEE."
WELL, NOW YOU WILL.
WE ALL WILL.
NO REAL CHOICE NOW, RIGHT?
HERE. LET ME HELP YOU OVER.
SORRY...
NO, IT'S ALL RIGHT.

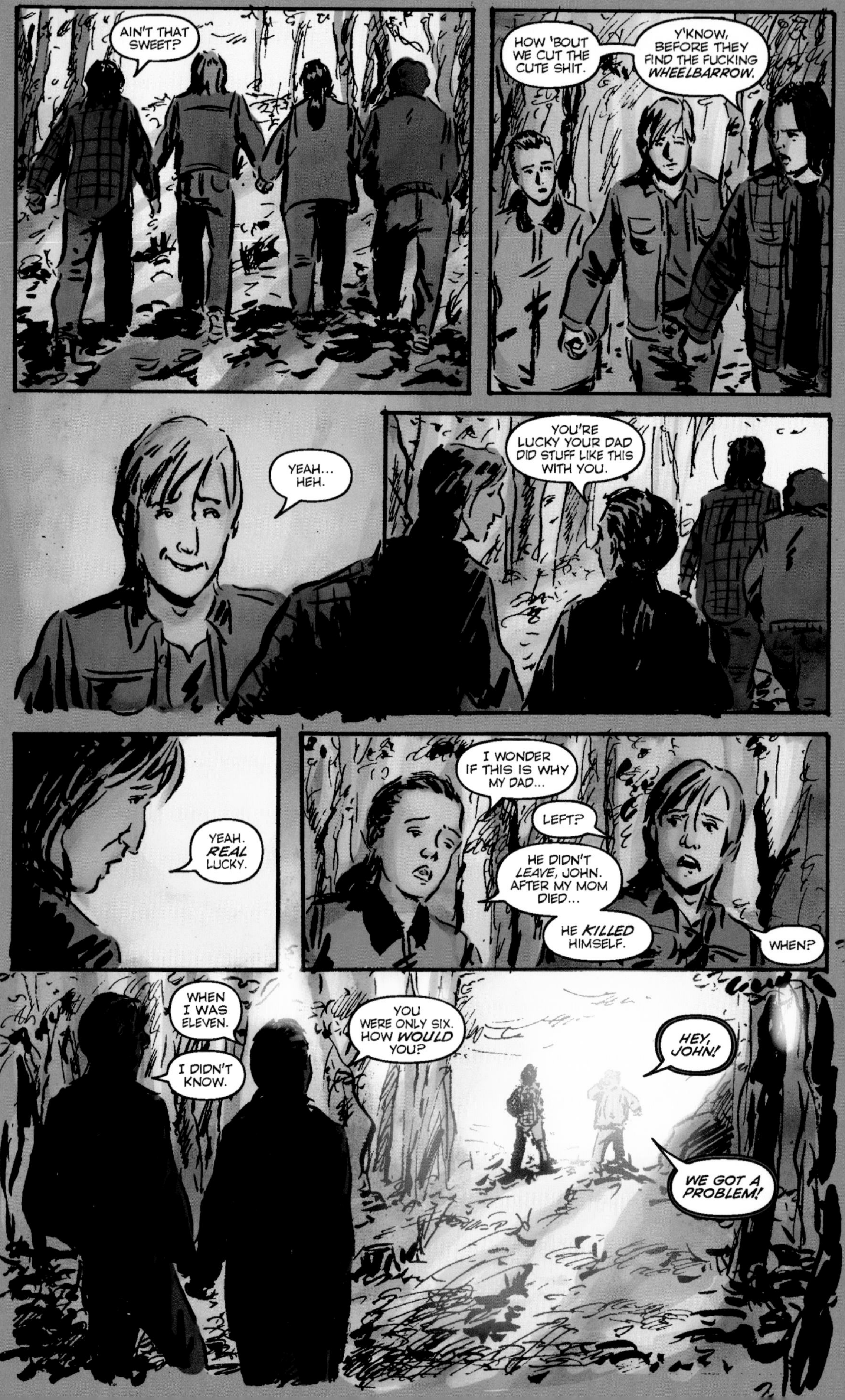
AIN'T THAT SWEET?
HOW 'BOUT WE CUT THE CUTE SHIT.
Y'KNOW, BEFORE THEY FIND THE FUCKING *WHEELBARROW.*
YEAH... HEH.
YOU'RE LUCKY YOUR DAD DID STUFF LIKE THIS WITH YOU.
YEAH. *REAL* LUCKY.
I WONDER IF THIS IS WHY MY DAD...
LEFT?
HE DIDN'T *LEAVE*, JOHN. AFTER MY MOM DIED...
HE *KILLED* HIMSELF.
WHEN?
WHEN I WAS ELEVEN.
I DIDN'T KNOW.
YOU WERE ONLY SIX. HOW *WOULD* YOU?
HEY, JOHN!
WE GOT A PROBLEM!

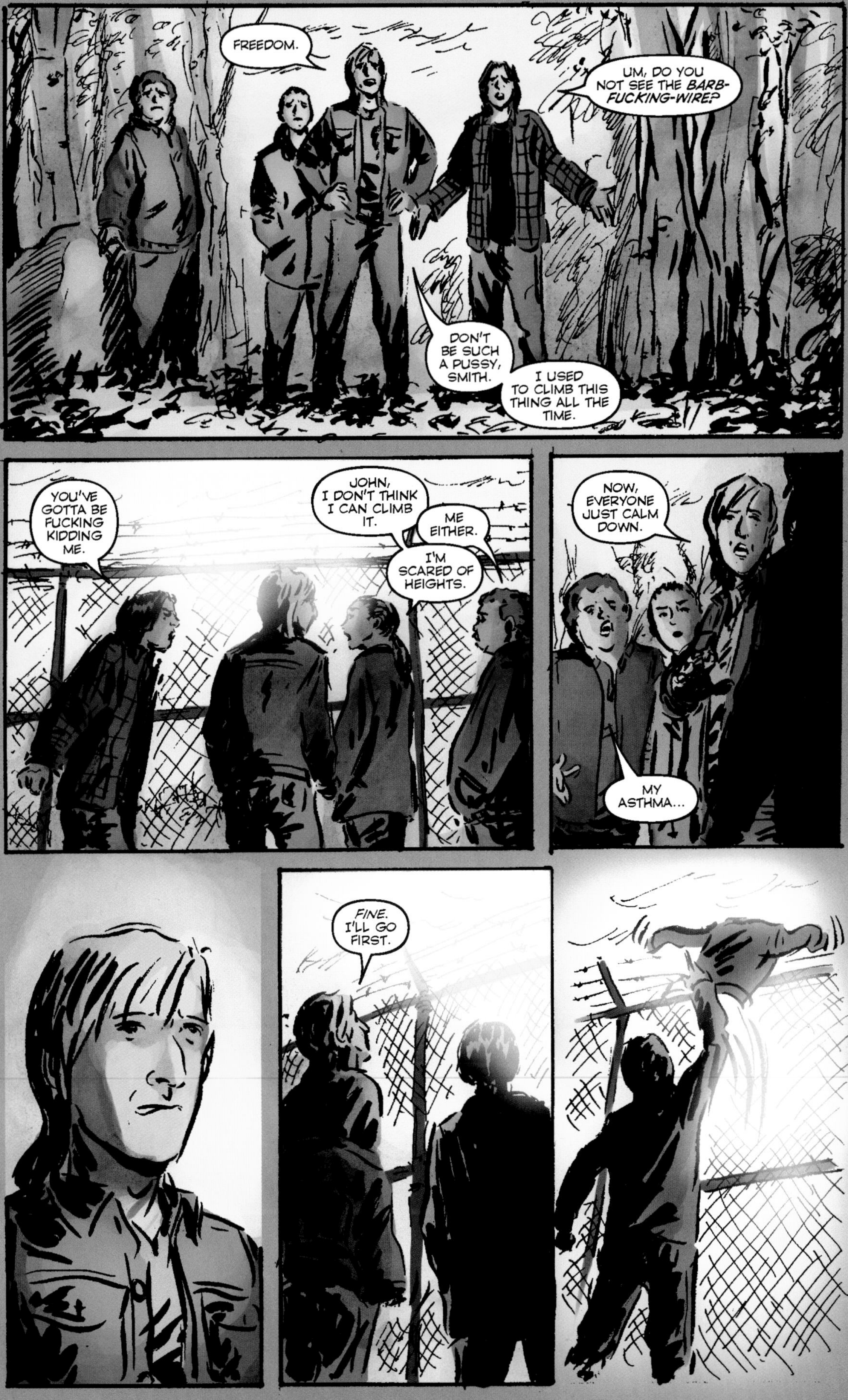
FREEDOM.
UM, DO YOU NOT SEE THE *BARB-FUCKING-WIRE?*
DON'T BE SUCH A PUSSY, SMITH.
I USED TO CLIMB THIS THING ALL THE TIME.
YOU'VE GOTTA BE FUCKING KIDDING ME.
JOHN, I DON'T THINK I CAN CLIMB IT.
ME EITHER.
I'M SCARED OF HEIGHTS.
NOW, EVERYONE JUST CALM DOWN.
MY ASTHMA...
FINE. I'LL GO FIRST.

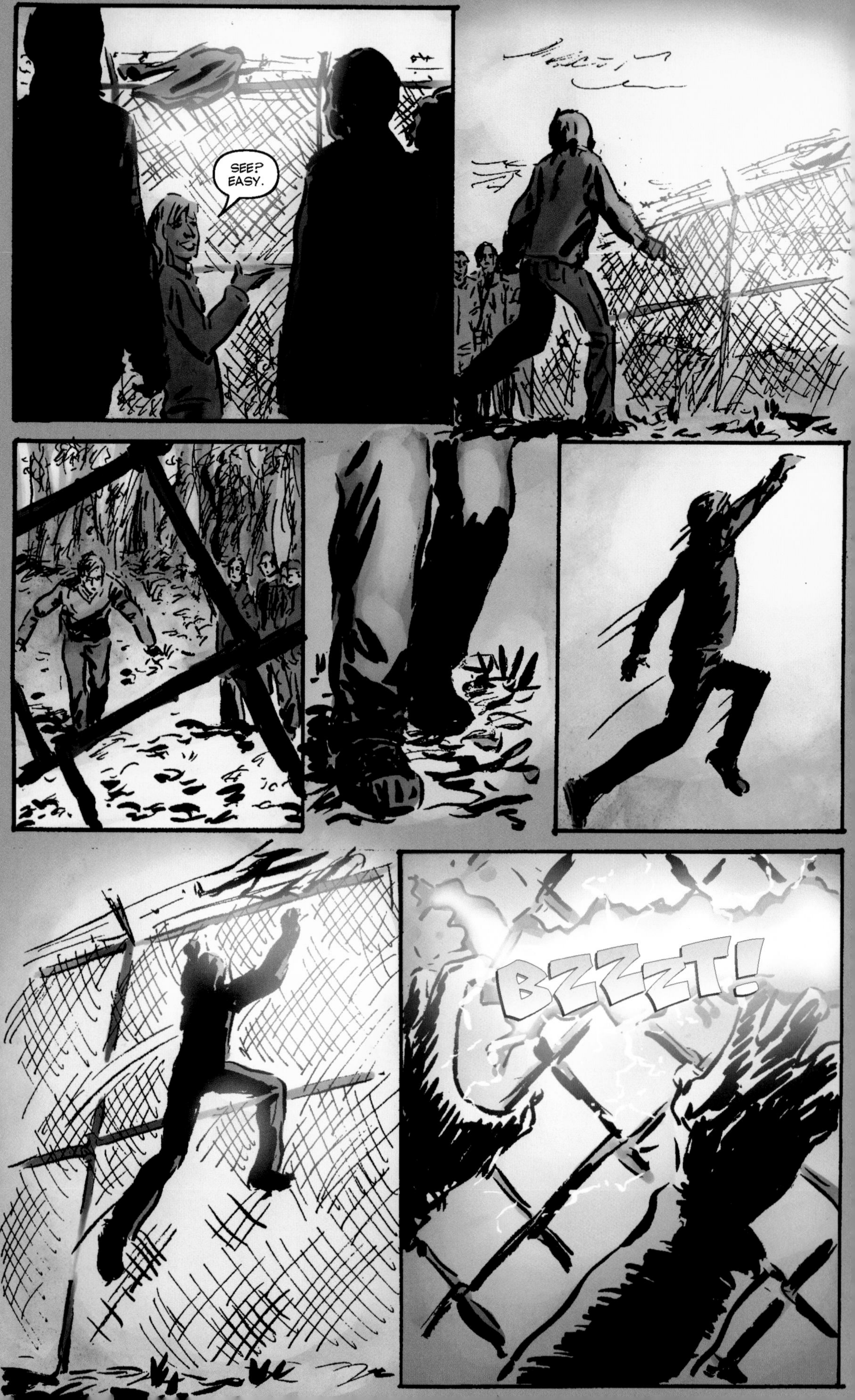
SEE? EASY.
BZZZT!

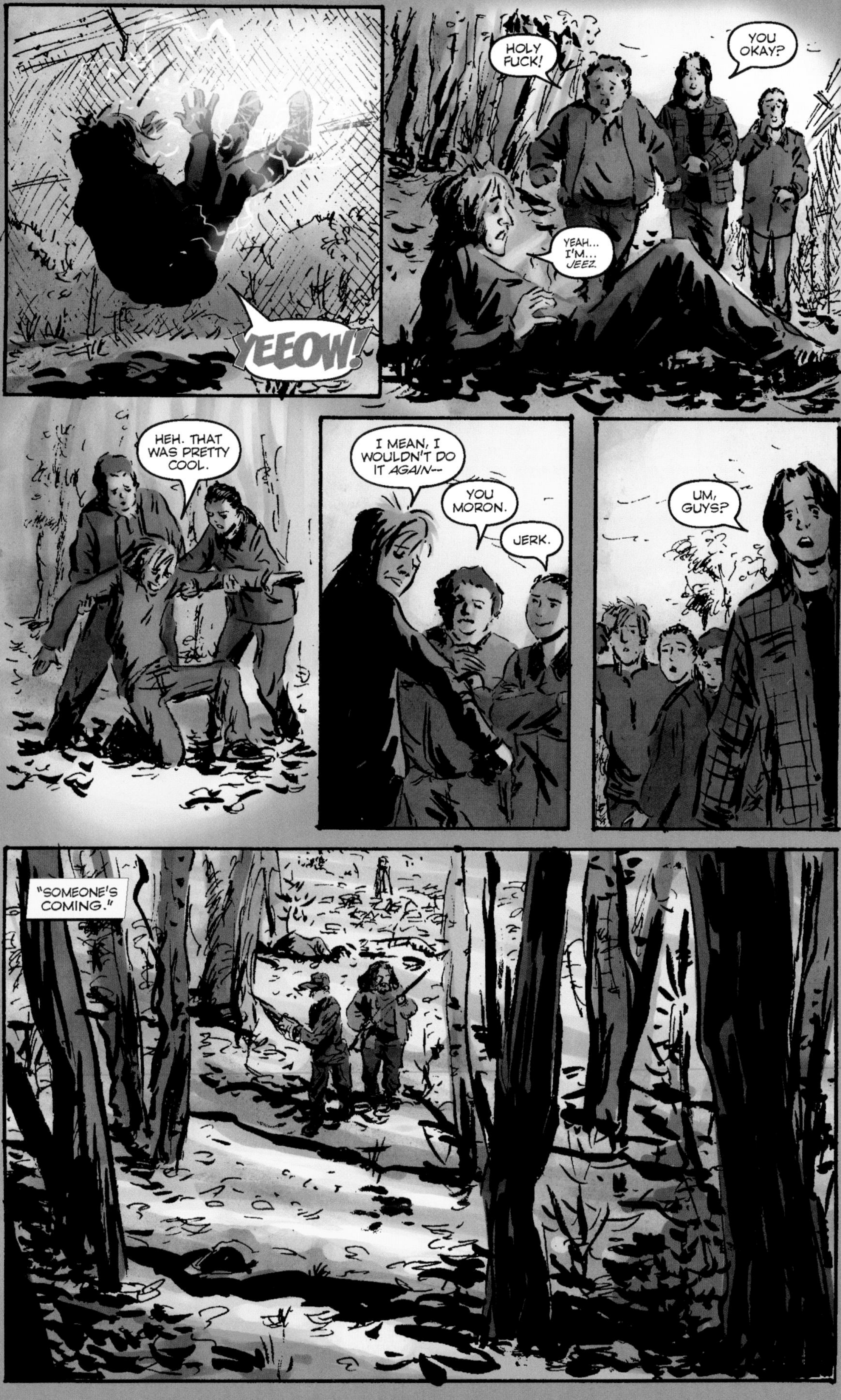
YEEOW!
HOLY FUCK!
YOU OKAY?
YEAH... I'M... JEEZ.
HEH. THAT WAS PRETTY COOL.
I MEAN, I WOULDN'T DO IT *AGAIN*--
YOU MORON.
JERK.
UM, GUYS?
"SOMEONE'S COMING."

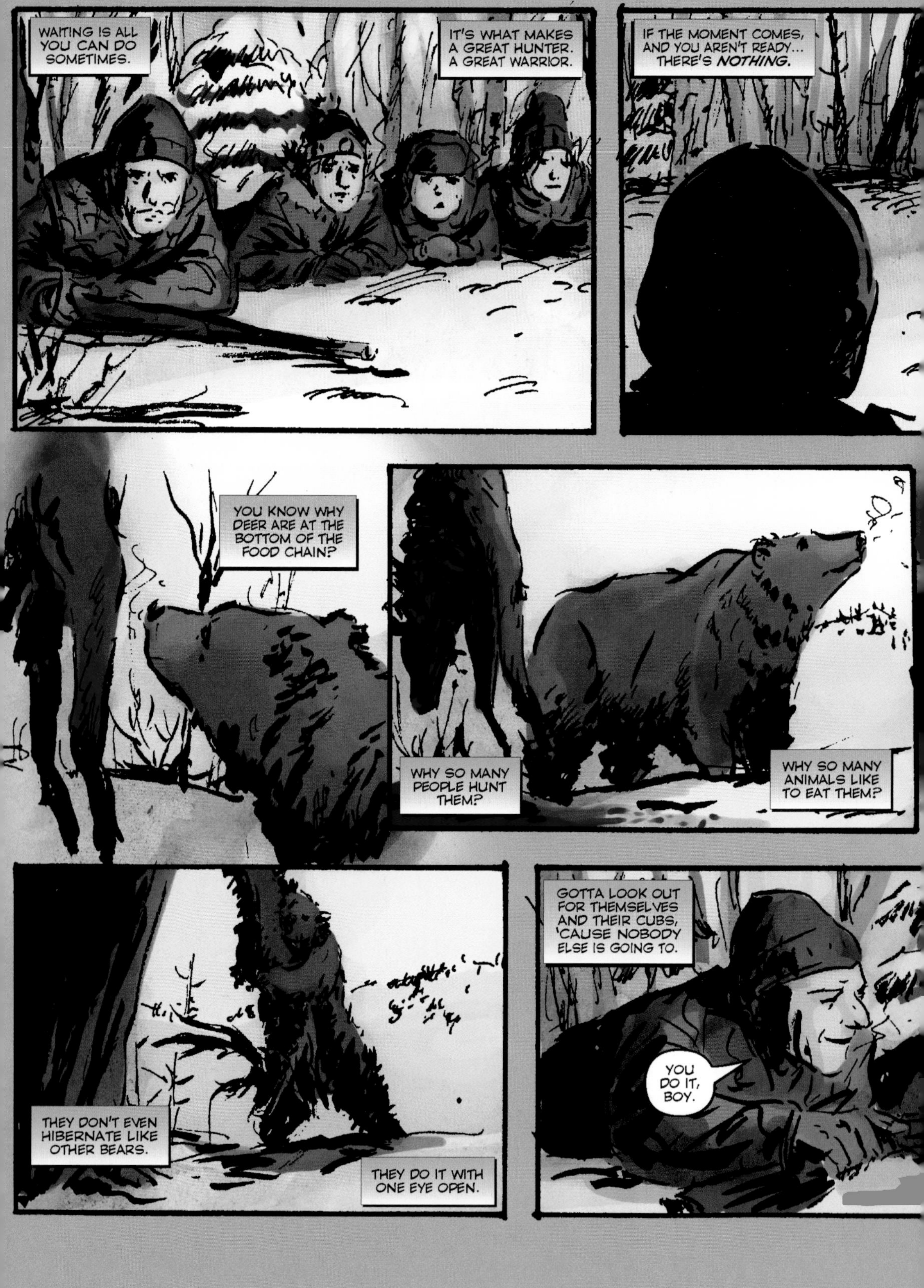
WAITING IS ALL YOU CAN DO SOMETIMES.
IT'S WHAT MAKES A GREAT HUNTER. A GREAT WARRIOR.
IF THE MOMENT COMES, AND YOU AREN'T READY... THERE'S *NOTHING.*
YOU KNOW WHY DEER ARE AT THE BOTTOM OF THE FOOD CHAIN?
WHY SO MANY PEOPLE HUNT THEM?
WHY SO MANY ANIMALS LIKE TO EAT THEM?
THEY DON'T EVEN HIBERNATE LIKE OTHER BEARS.
THEY DO IT WITH ONE EYE OPEN.
GOTTA LOOK OUT FOR THEMSELVES AND THEIR CUBS, 'CAUSE NOBODY ELSE IS GOING TO.
YOU DO IT, BOY.

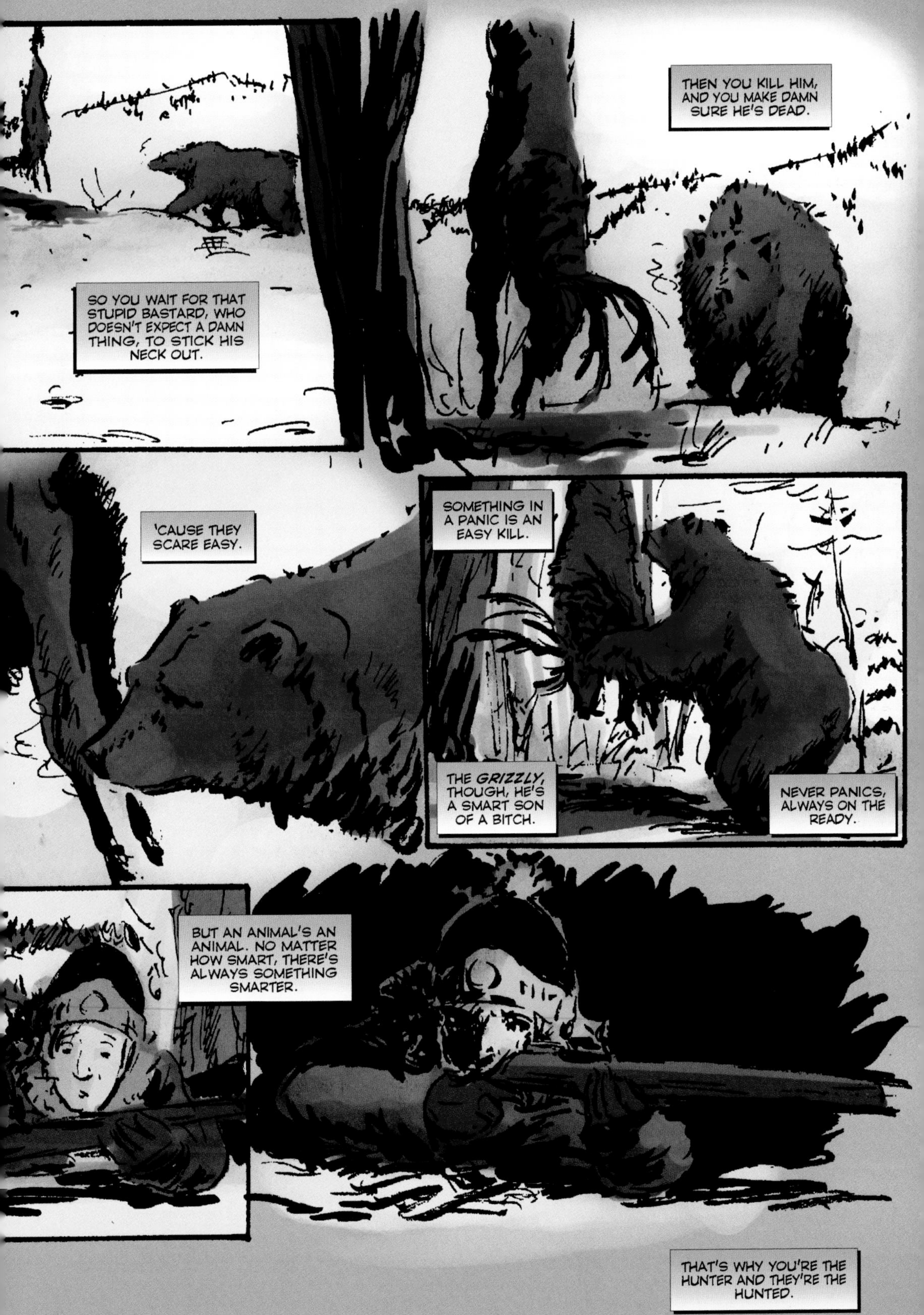
SO YOU WAIT FOR THAT STUPID BASTARD, WHO DOESN'T EXPECT A DAMN THING, TO STICK HIS NECK OUT.
THEN YOU KILL HIM, AND YOU MAKE DAMN SURE HE'S DEAD.
'CAUSE THEY SCARE EASY.
SOMETHING IN A PANIC IS AN EASY KILL.
THE *GRIZZLY*, THOUGH, HE'S A SMART SON OF A BITCH.
NEVER PANICS, ALWAYS ON THE READY.
BUT AN ANIMAL'S AN ANIMAL. NO MATTER HOW SMART, THERE'S ALWAYS SOMETHING SMARTER.
THAT'S WHY YOU'RE THE HUNTER AND THEY'RE THE HUNTED.

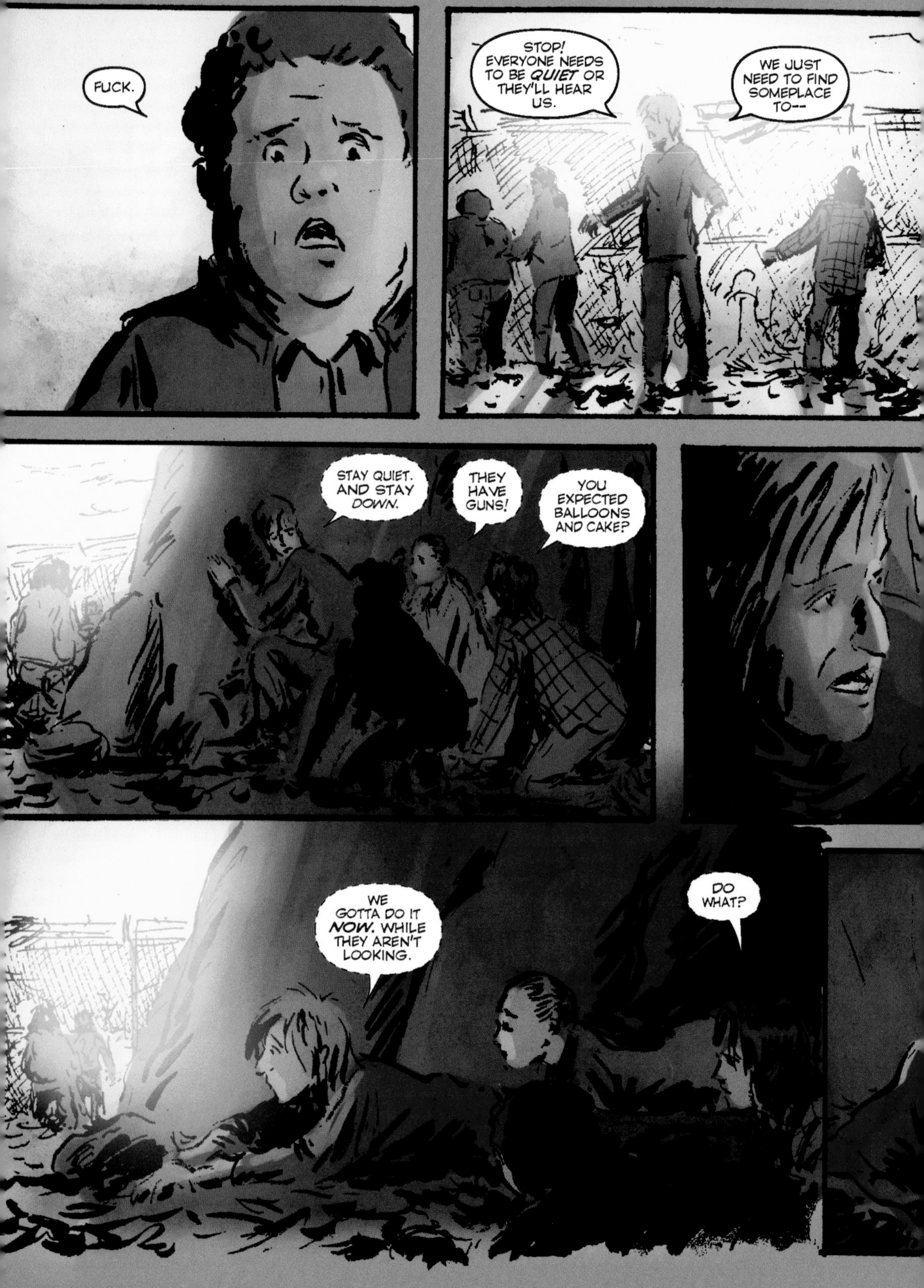
FUCK.
STOP! EVERYONE NEEDS TO BE *QUIET* OR THEY'LL HEAR US.
WE JUST NEED TO FIND SOMEPLACE TO--
STAY QUIET. AND STAY *DOWN*.
THEY HAVE GUNS!
YOU EXPECTED BALLOONS AND CAKE?
WE GOTTA DO IT ***NOW***. WHILE THEY AREN'T LOOKING.
DO WHAT?

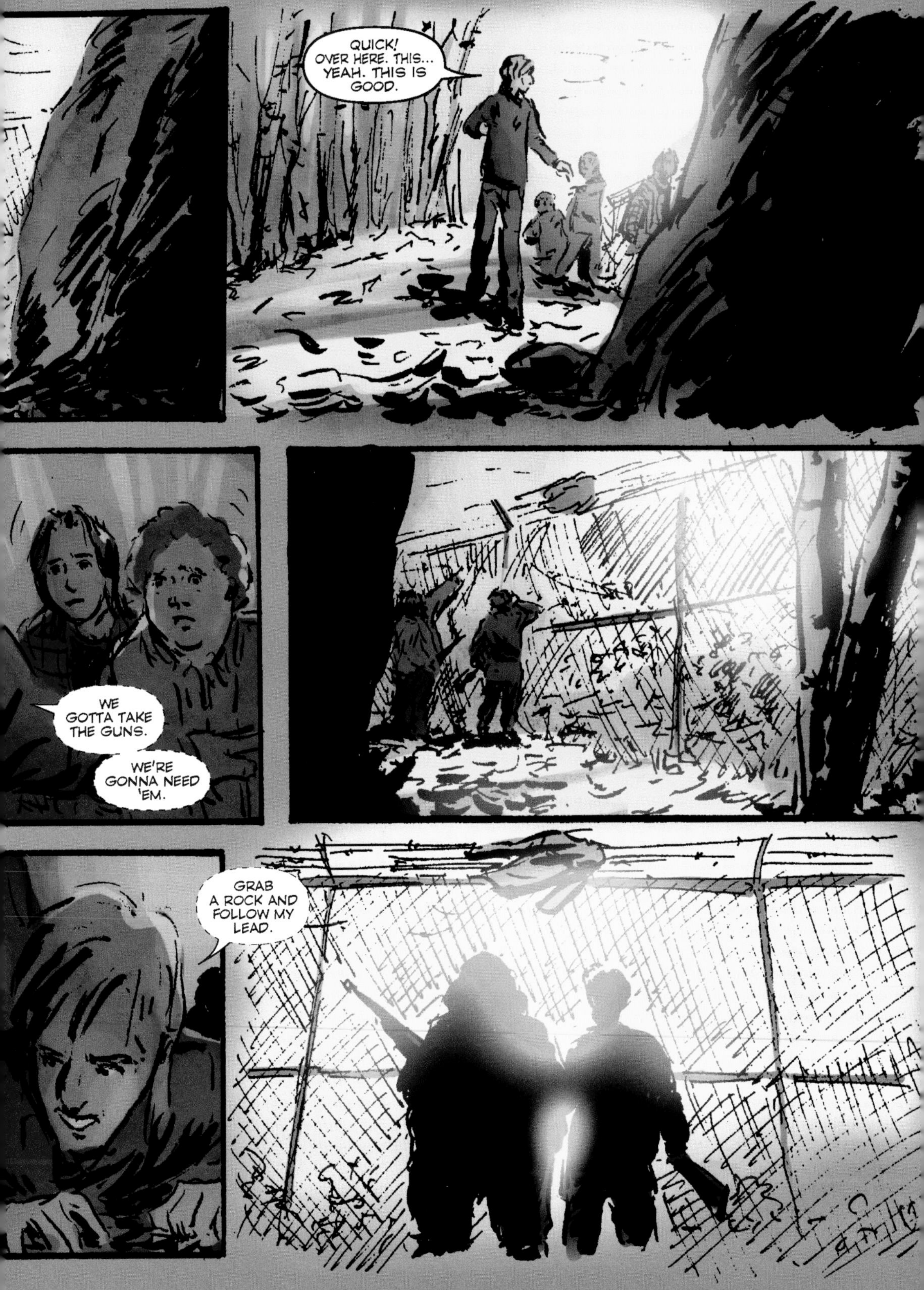
QUICK! OVER HERE. THIS... YEAH. THIS IS GOOD.
WE GOTTA TAKE THE GUNS.
WE'RE GONNA NEED 'EM.
GRAB A ROCK AND FOLLOW MY LEAD.

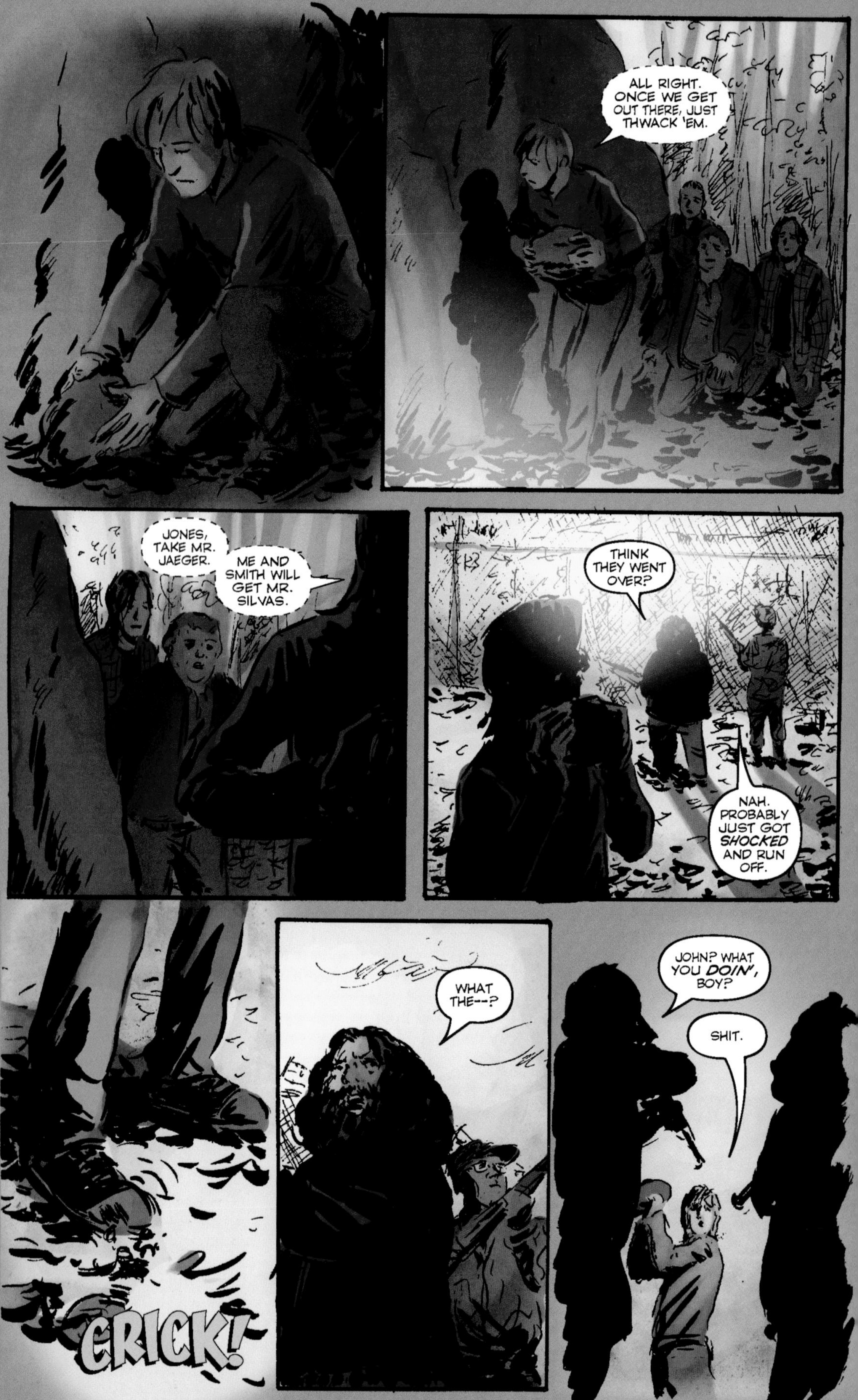
ALL RIGHT. ONCE WE GET OUT THERE, JUST THWACK 'EM.
JONES, TAKE MR. JAEGER.
ME AND SMITH WILL GET MR. SILVAS.
THINK THEY WENT OVER?
NAH. PROBABLY JUST GOT SHOCKED AND RUN OFF.
CRICK!
WHAT THE--?
JOHN? WHAT YOU DOIN', BOY?
SHIT.

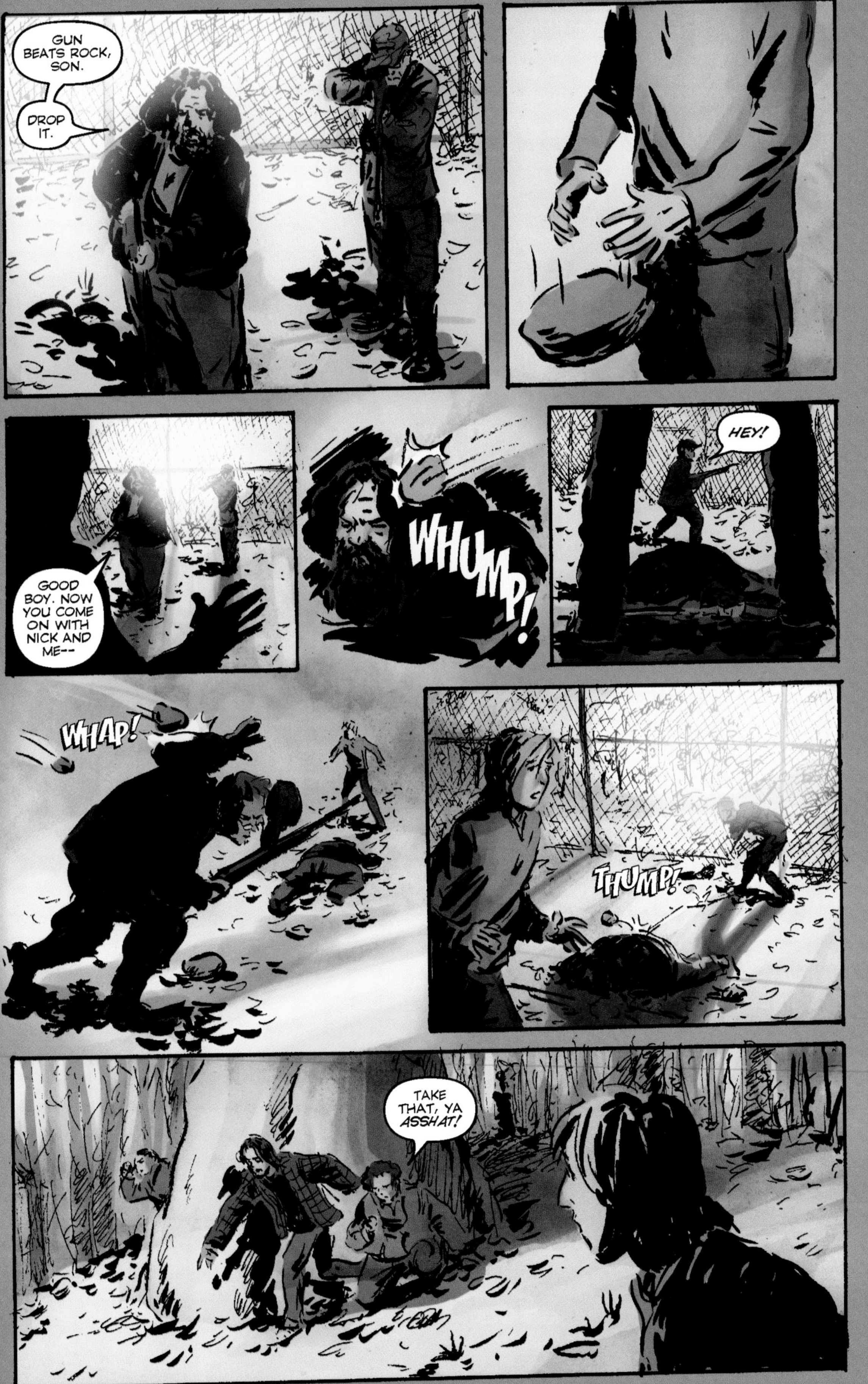

GUN BEATS ROCK, SON.
DROP IT.
GOOD BOY. NOW YOU COME ON WITH NICK AND ME--
WHUMP!
HEY!
WHAP!
THUMP!
TAKE THAT, YA *ASSHAT!*

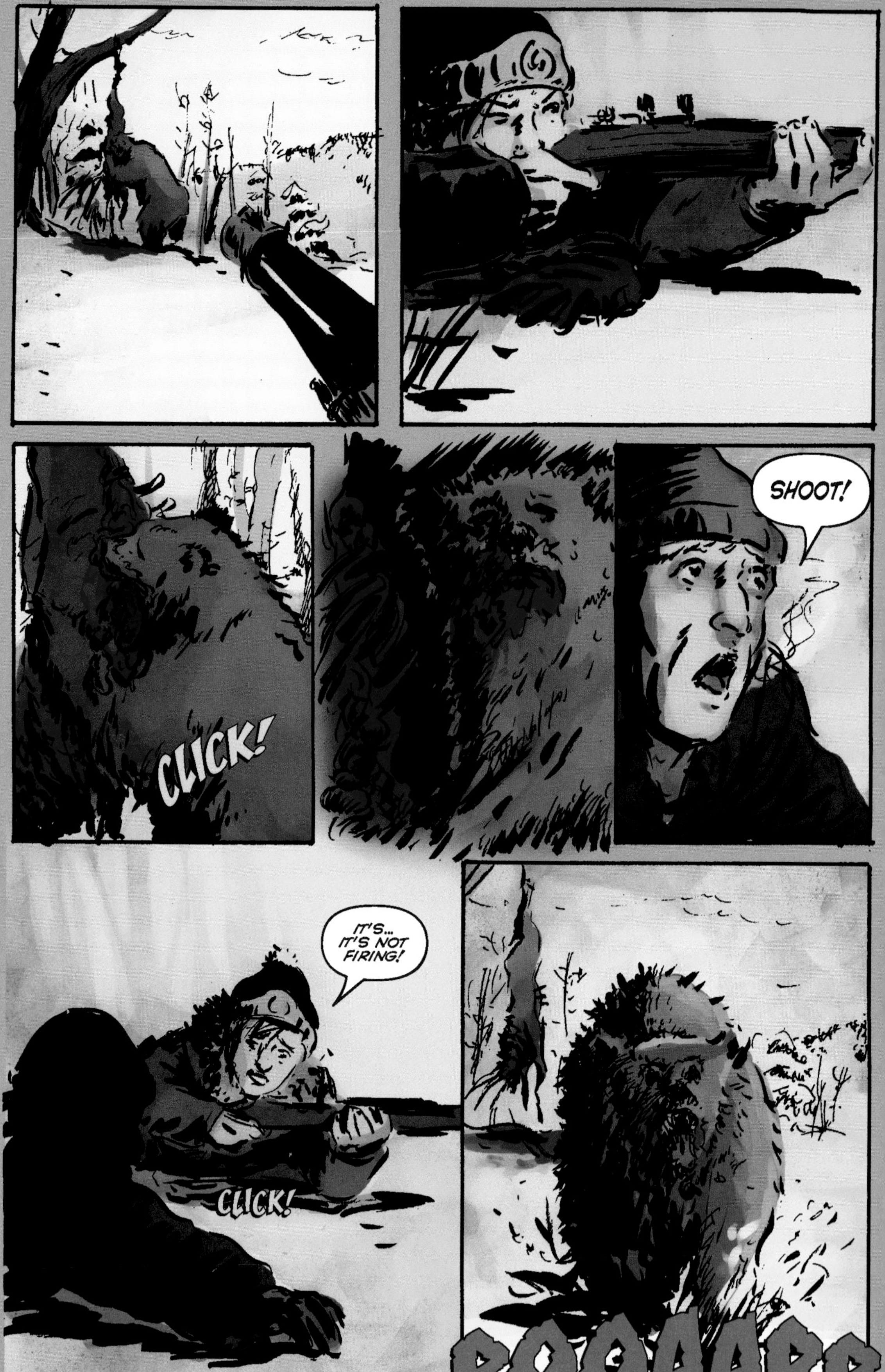
CLICK!
SHOOT!
IT'S... IT'S NOT FIRING!
CLICK!
ROOAARR

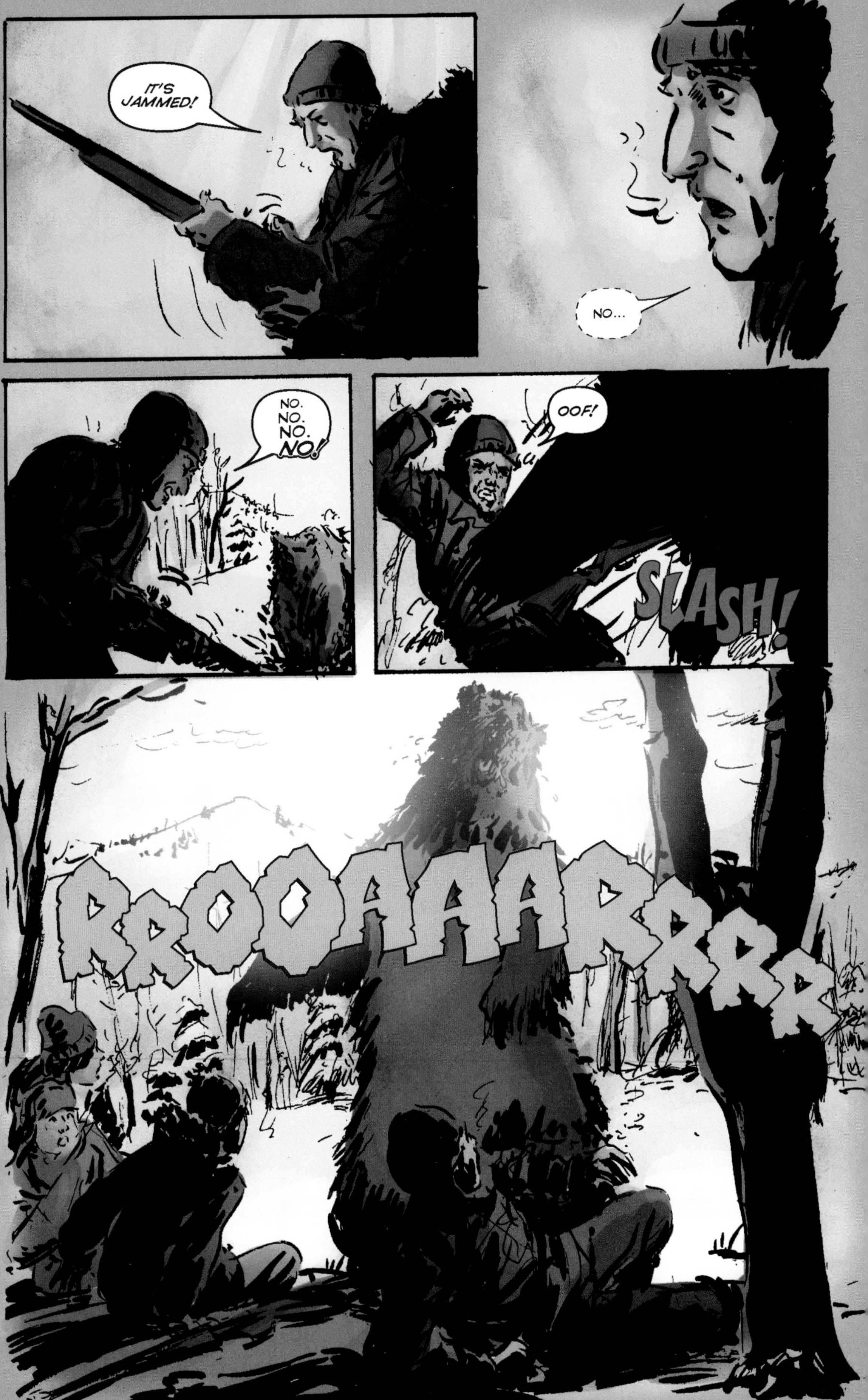
IT'S JAMMED!
NO...
NO. NO. NO. NO!
OOF!
SLASH!
RROOAAARRRR

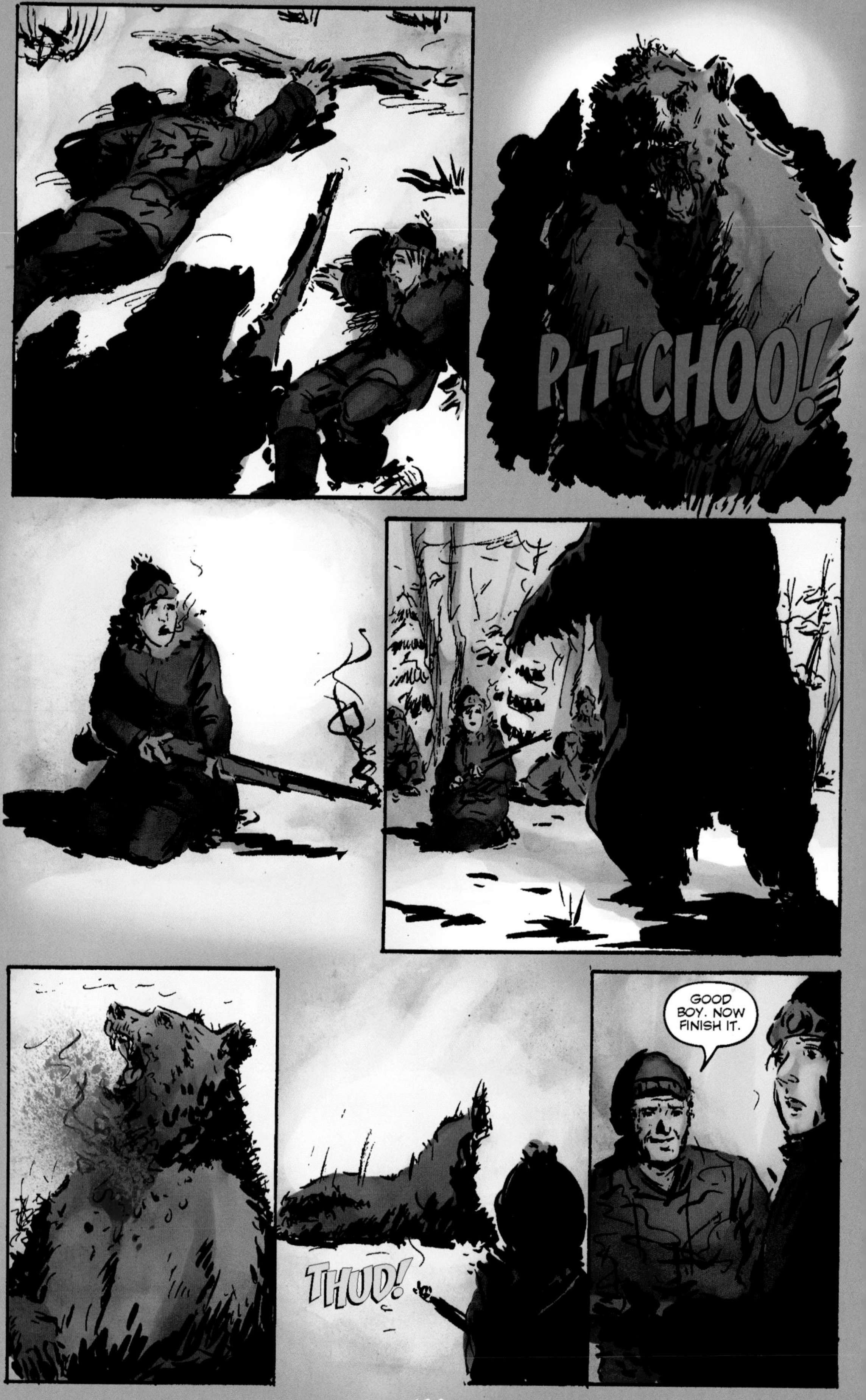
PIT-CHOO!
THUD!
GOOD BOY. NOW FINISH IT.

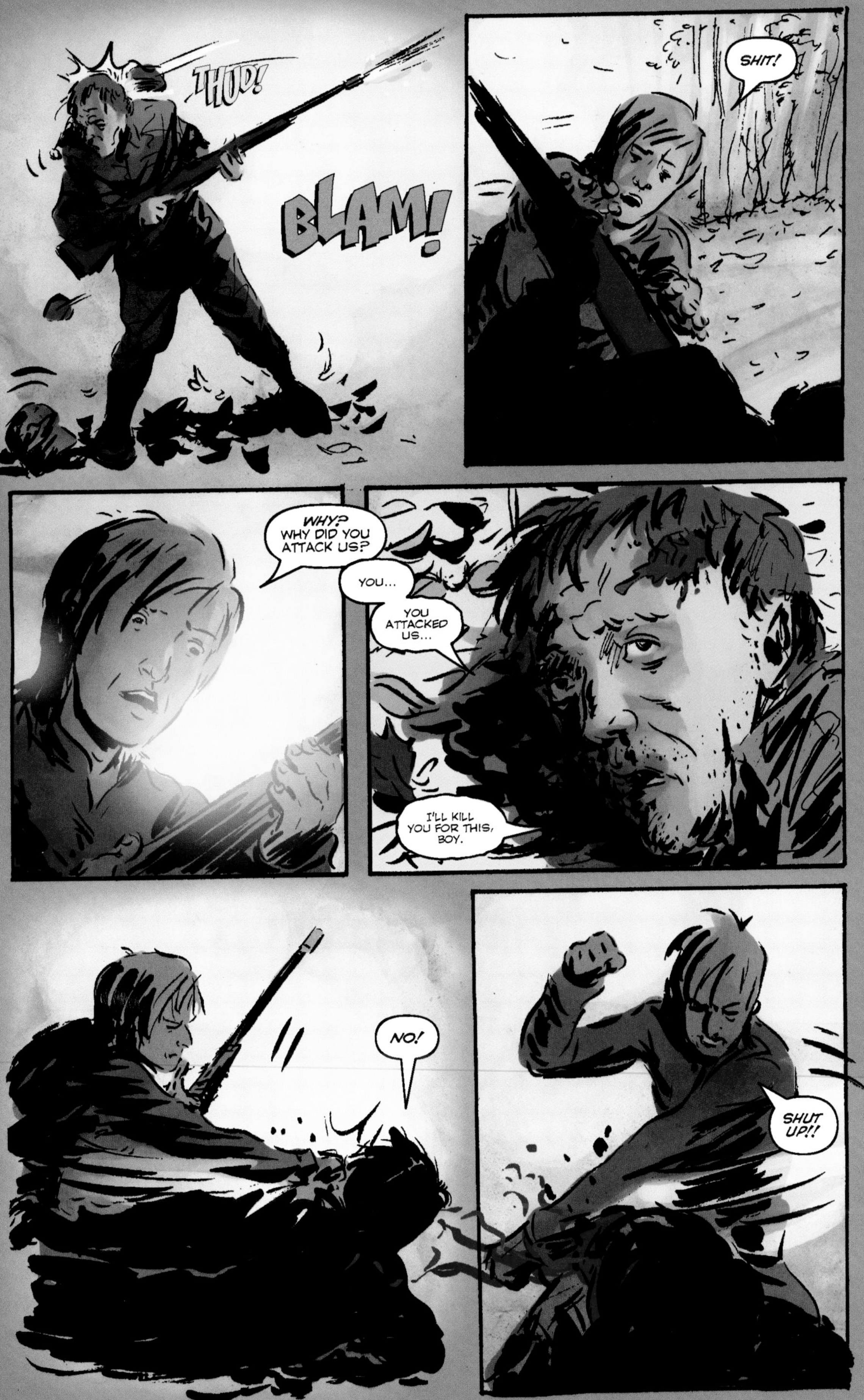
THUD!
BLAM!
SHIT!
WHY? WHY DID YOU ATTACK US?
YOU...
YOU ATTACKED US...
I'LL KILL YOU FOR THIS, BOY.
NO!
SHUT UP!!

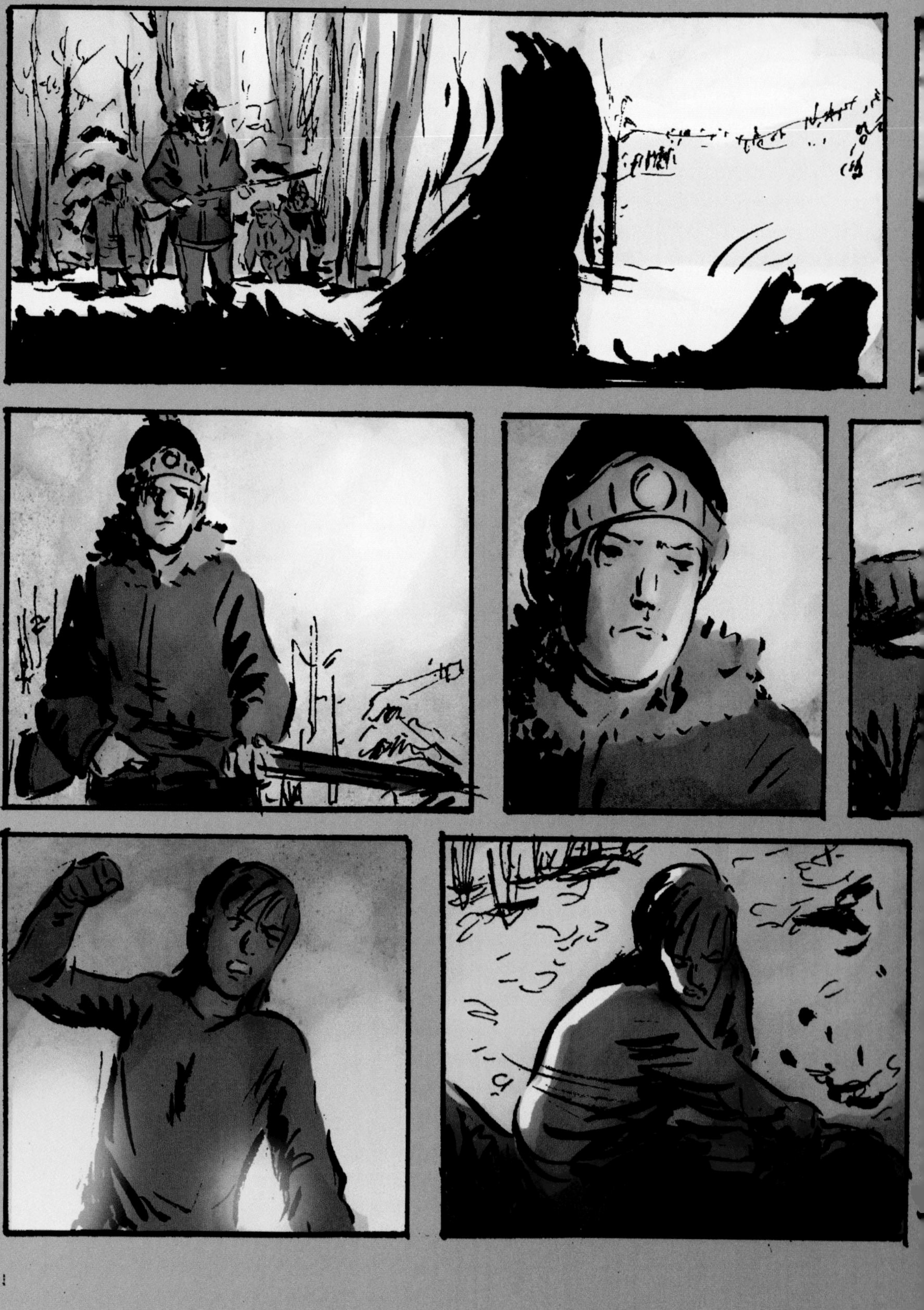

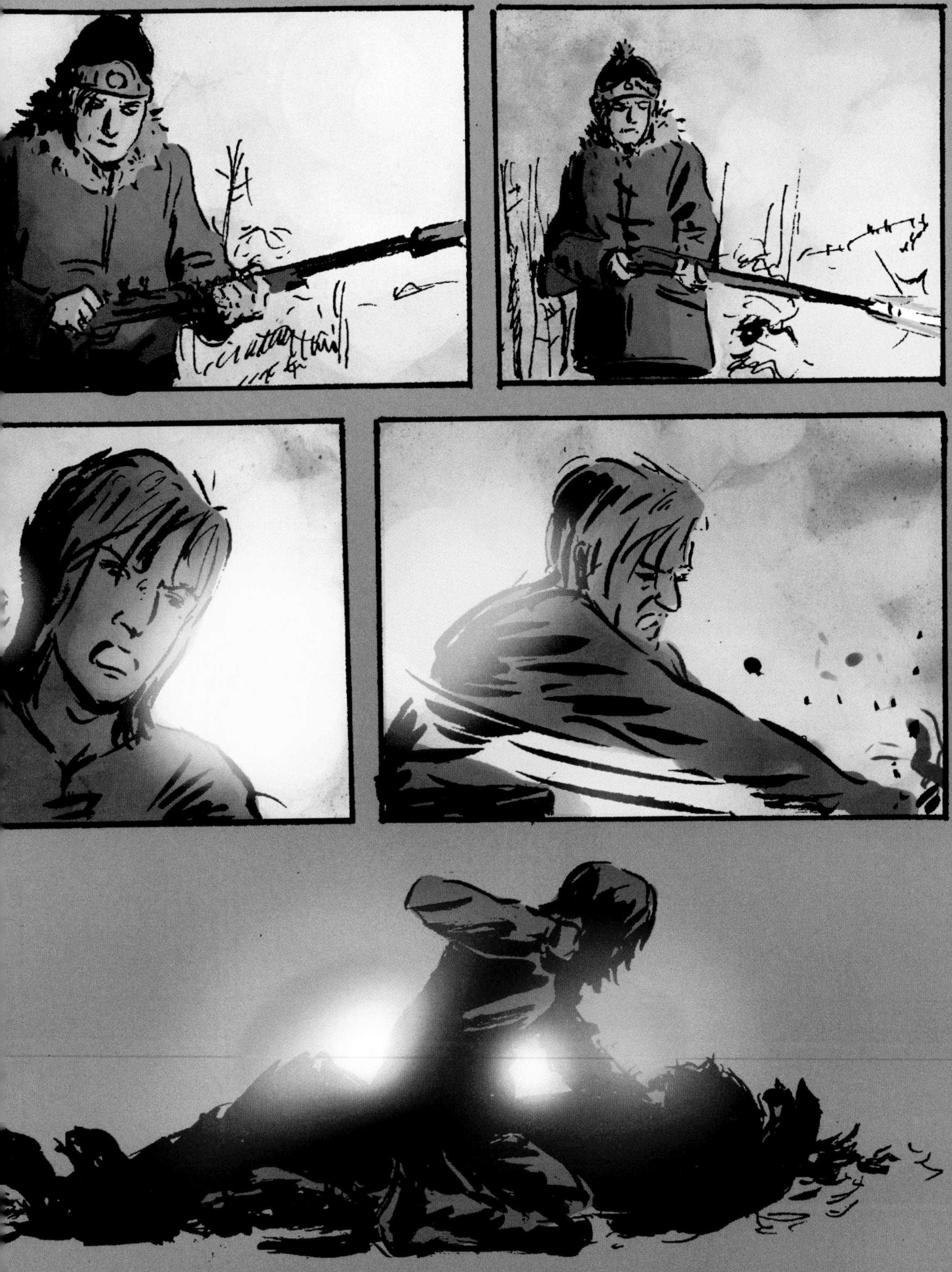

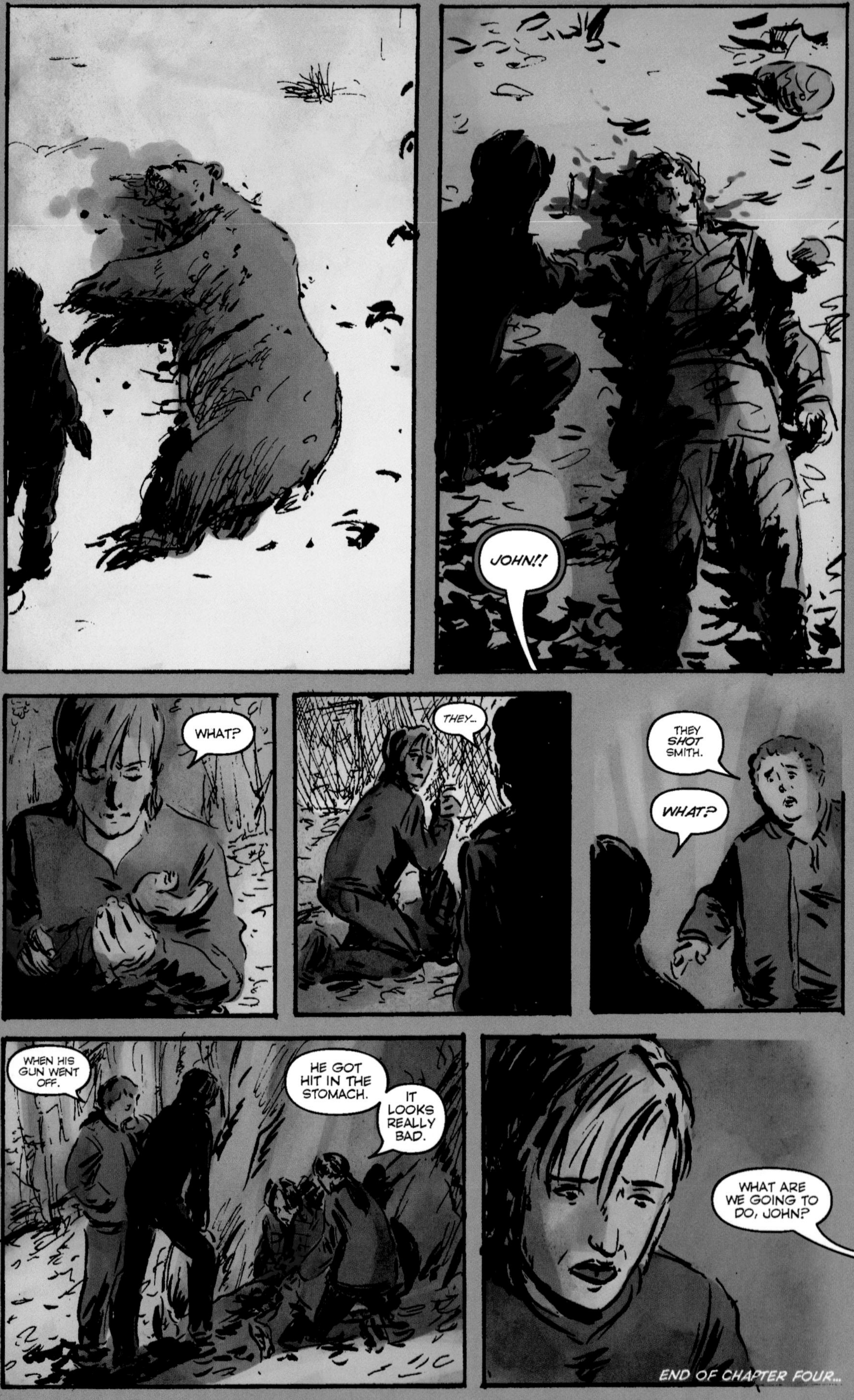
JOHN!!
WHAT?
THEY...
THEY SHOT SMITH.
WHAT?
WHEN HIS GUN WENT OFF.
HE GOT HIT IN THE STOMACH.
IT LOOKS REALLY BAD.
WHAT ARE WE GOING TO DO, JOHN?
END OF CHAPTER FOUR...

Chapter Five: Trio

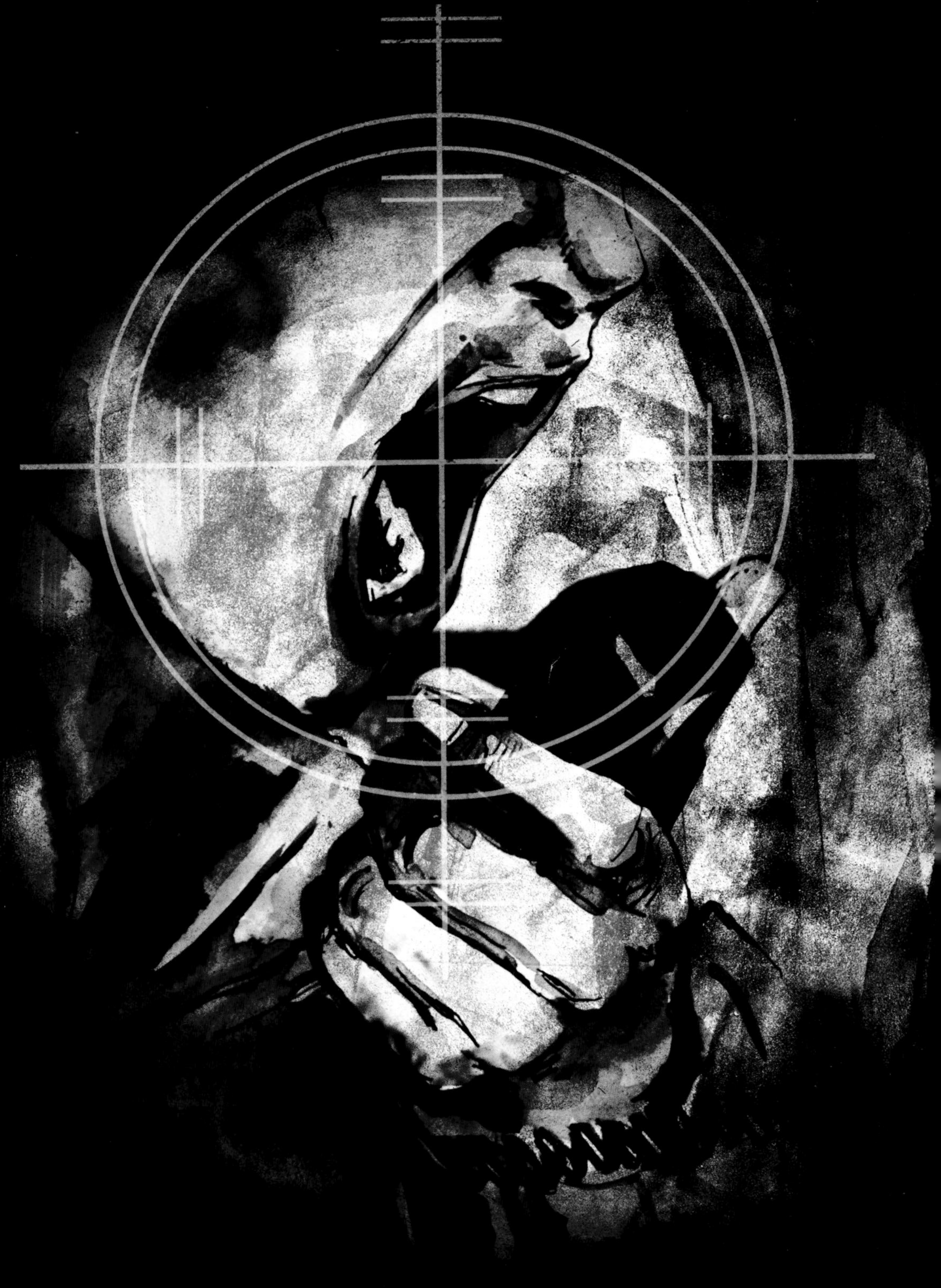

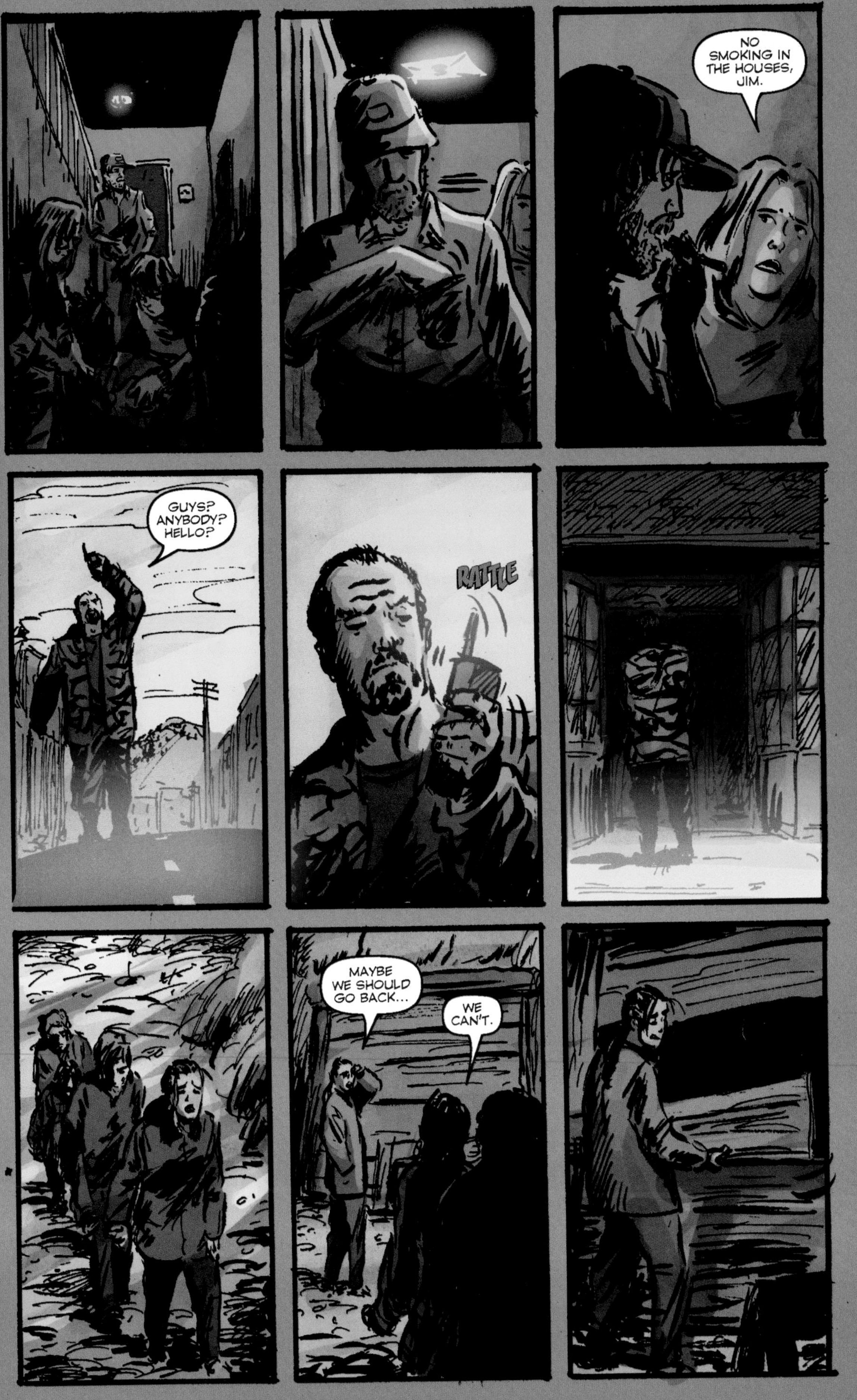
NO SMOKING IN THE HOUSES, JIM.
GUYS? ANYBODY? HELLO?
RATTLE
MAYBE WE SHOULD GO BACK...
WE CAN'T.

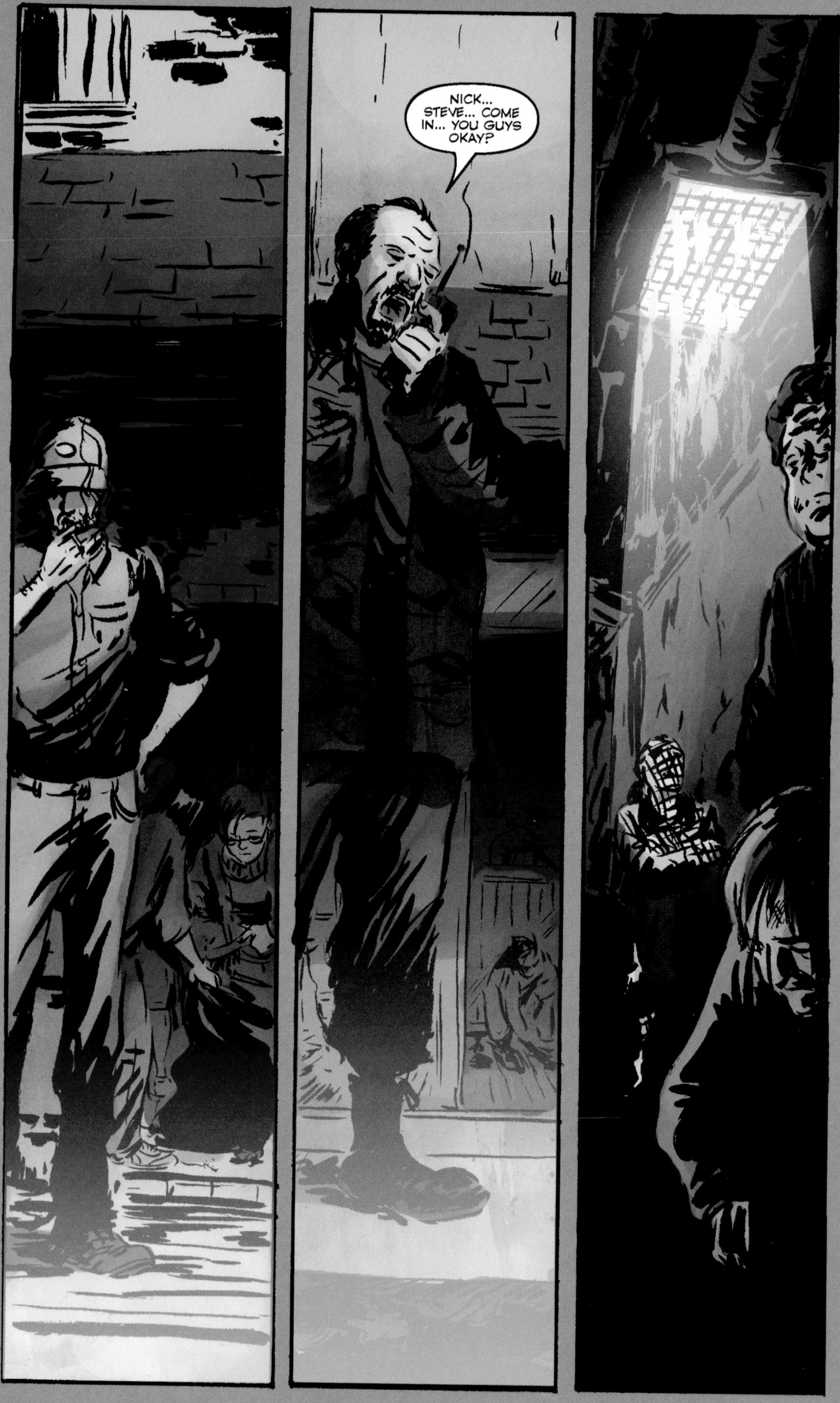
NICK... STEVE... COME IN... YOU GUYS OKAY?

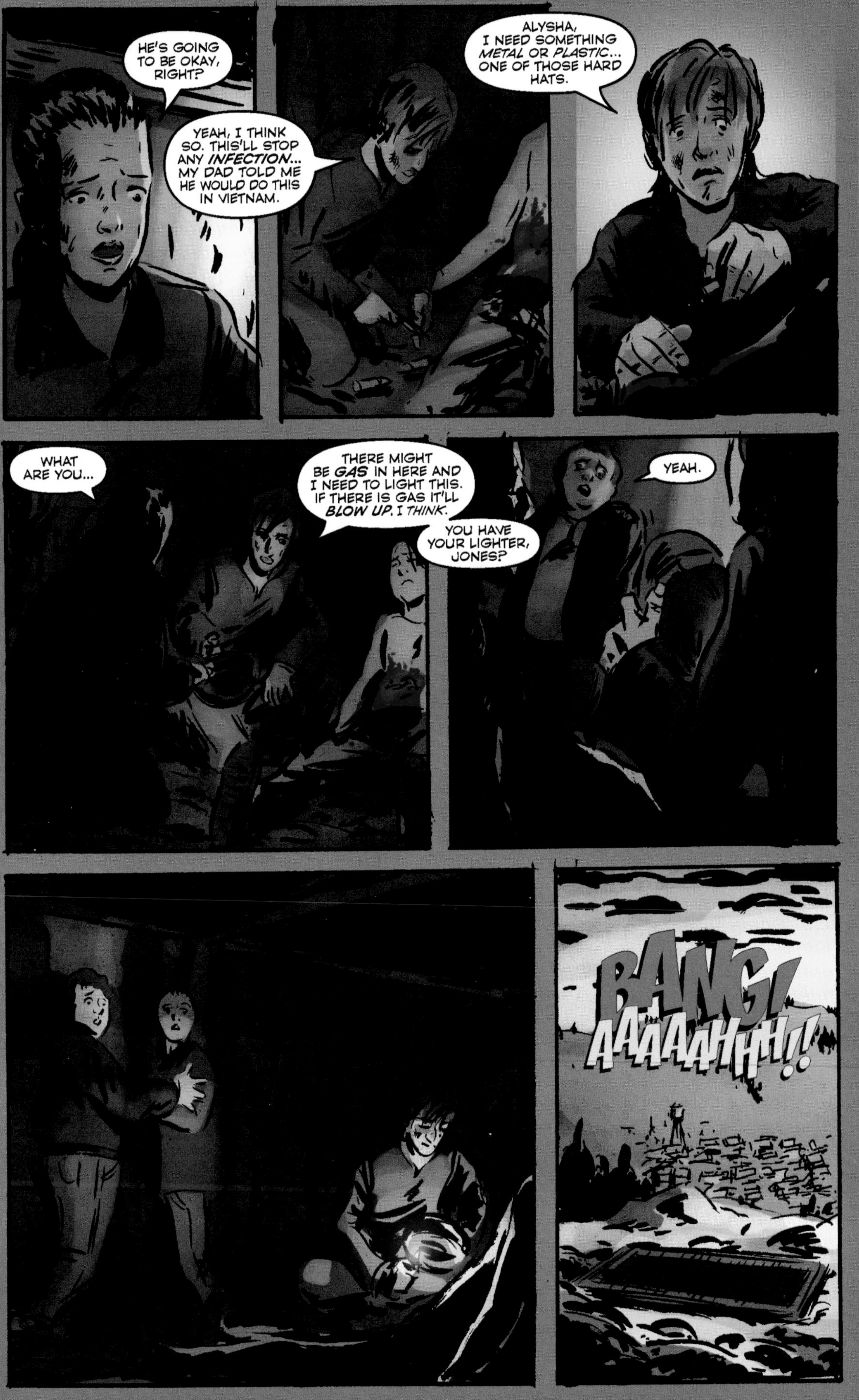
HE'S GOING TO BE OKAY, RIGHT?
YEAH, I THINK SO. THIS'LL STOP ANY *INFECTION*... MY DAD TOLD ME HE WOULD DO THIS IN VIETNAM.
ALYSHA, I NEED SOMETHING *METAL* OR *PLASTIC*... ONE OF THOSE HARD HATS.
WHAT ARE YOU...
THERE MIGHT BE *GAS* IN HERE AND I NEED TO LIGHT THIS. IF THERE IS GAS IT'LL *BLOW UP*. I *THINK*.
YOU HAVE YOUR LIGHTER, JONES?
YEAH.
BANG!
AAAAAHHH!!

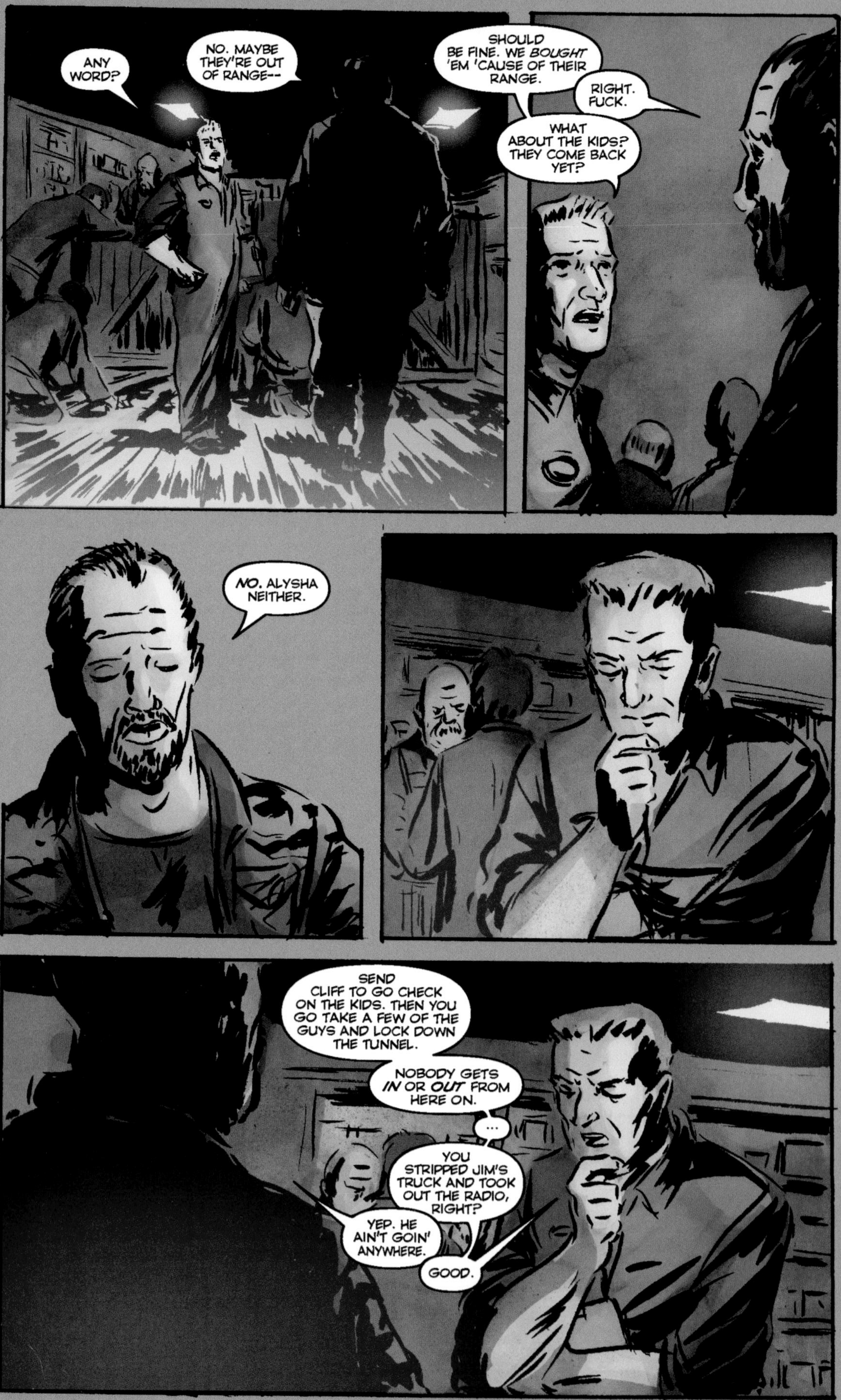
ANY WORD?
NO. MAYBE THEY'RE OUT OF RANGE--
SHOULD BE FINE. WE *BOUGHT* 'EM 'CAUSE OF THEIR RANGE.
RIGHT. FUCK.
WHAT ABOUT THE KIDS? THEY COME BACK YET?
NO. ALYSHA NEITHER.
SEND CLIFF TO GO CHECK ON THE KIDS. THEN YOU GO TAKE A FEW OF THE GUYS AND LOCK DOWN THE TUNNEL.
NOBODY GETS *IN* OR *OUT* FROM HERE ON.
...
YOU STRIPPED JIM'S TRUCK AND TOOK OUT THE RADIO, RIGHT?
YEP. HE AIN'T GOIN' ANYWHERE.
GOOD.

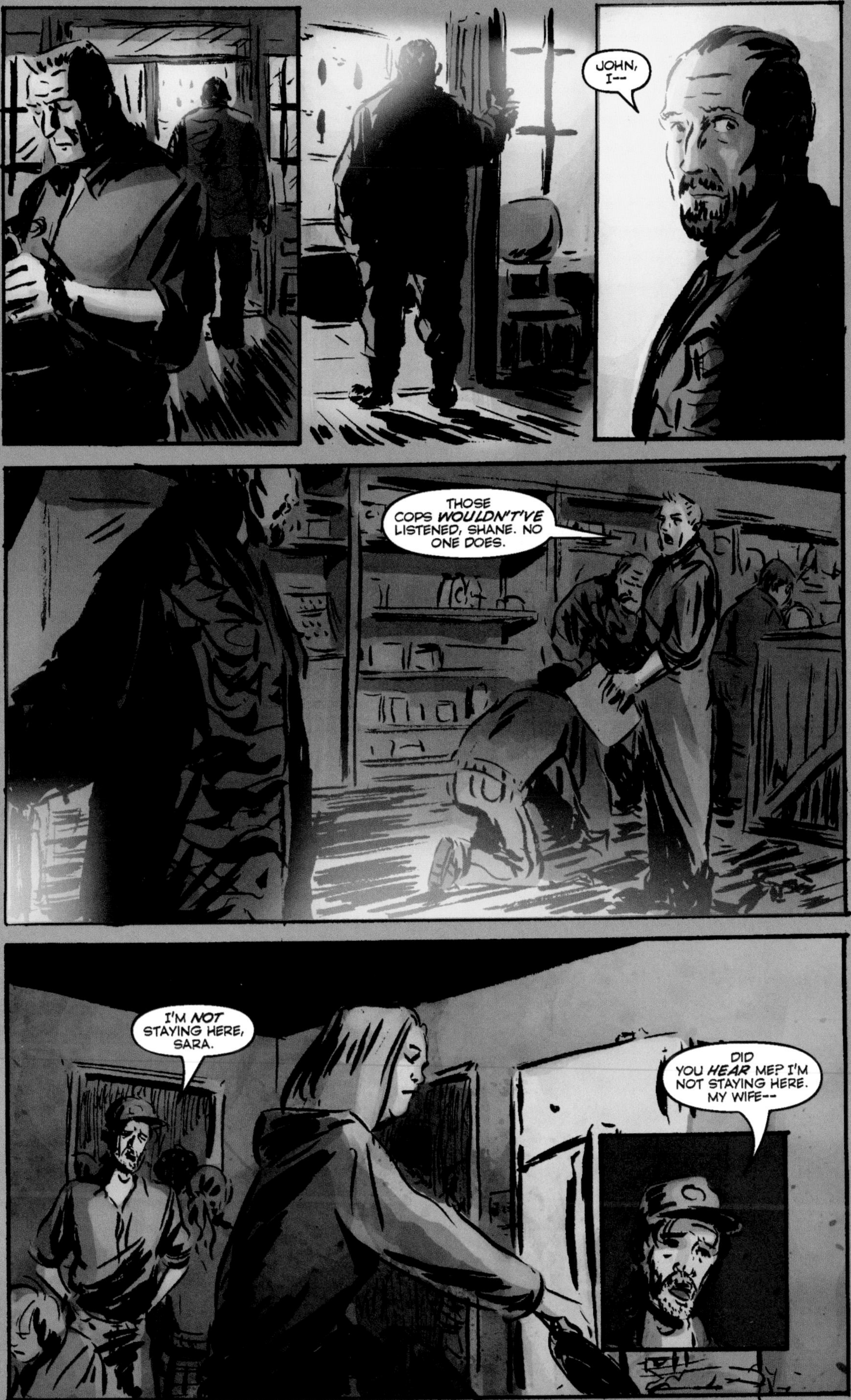
JOHN, I--
THOSE COPS WOULDN'T'VE LISTENED, SHANE. NO ONE DOES.
I'M NOT STAYING HERE, SARA.
DID YOU HEAR ME? I'M NOT STAYING HERE. MY WIFE--

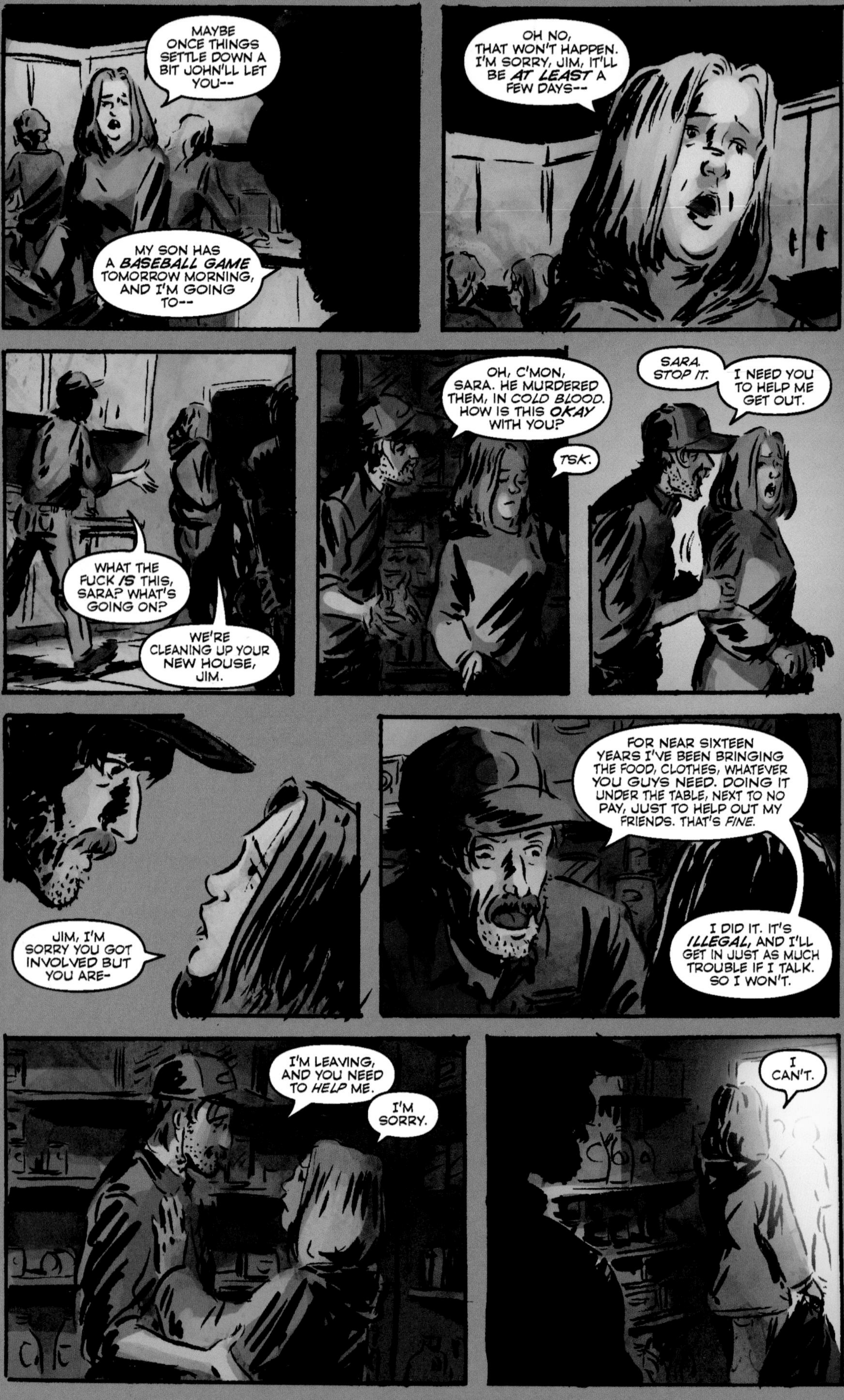
MAYBE ONCE THINGS SETTLE DOWN A BIT JOHN'LL LET YOU--
MY SON HAS A *BASEBALL GAME* TOMORROW MORNING, AND I'M GOING TO--
OH NO, THAT WON'T HAPPEN. I'M SORRY, JIM, IT'LL BE *AT LEAST* A FEW DAYS--
WHAT THE FUCK *IS* THIS, SARA? WHAT'S GOING ON?
WE'RE CLEANING UP YOUR NEW HOUSE, JIM.
OH, C'MON, SARA. HE MURDERED THEM, IN *COLD BLOOD*. HOW IS THIS *OKAY* WITH YOU?
TSK.
SARA. STOP IT.
I NEED YOU TO HELP ME GET OUT.
JIM, I'M SORRY YOU GOT INVOLVED BUT YOU ARE-
FOR NEAR SIXTEEN YEARS I'VE BEEN BRINGING THE FOOD, CLOTHES, WHATEVER YOU GUYS NEED. DOING IT UNDER THE TABLE, NEXT TO NO PAY, JUST TO HELP OUT MY FRIENDS. THAT'S *FINE*.
I DID IT. IT'S *ILLEGAL*, AND I'LL GET IN JUST AS MUCH TROUBLE IF I TALK. SO I WON'T.
I'M LEAVING, AND YOU NEED TO *HELP* ME.
I'M SORRY.
I CAN'T.

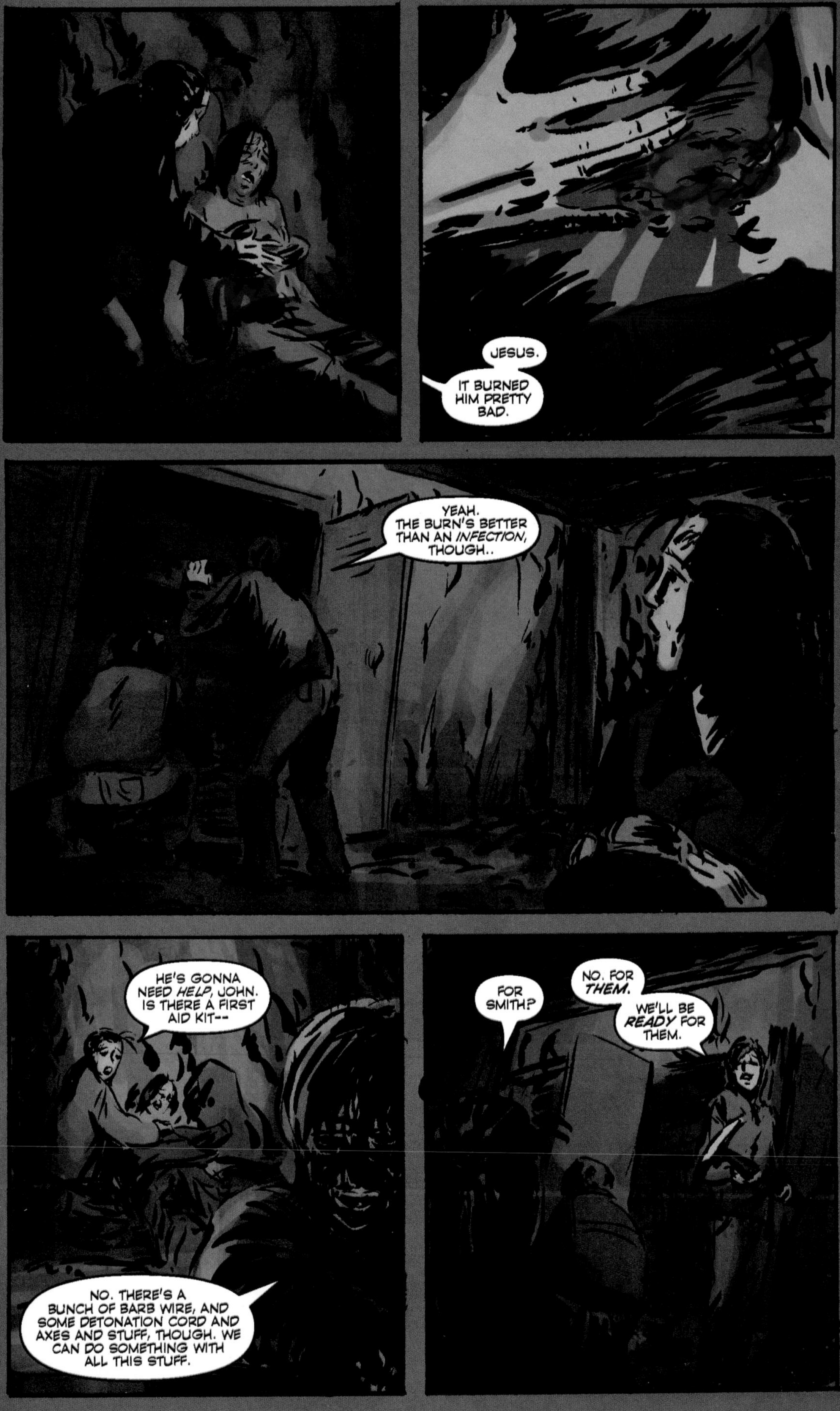
JESUS.
IT BURNED HIM PRETTY BAD.
YEAH. THE BURN'S BETTER THAN AN *INFECTION*, THOUGH..
HE'S GONNA NEED *HELP*, JOHN. IS THERE A FIRST AID KIT--
NO. THERE'S A BUNCH OF BARB WIRE, AND SOME DETONATION CORD AND AXES AND STUFF, THOUGH. WE CAN DO SOMETHING WITH ALL THIS STUFF.
FOR SMITH?
NO. FOR *THEM*.
WE'LL BE *READY* FOR THEM.

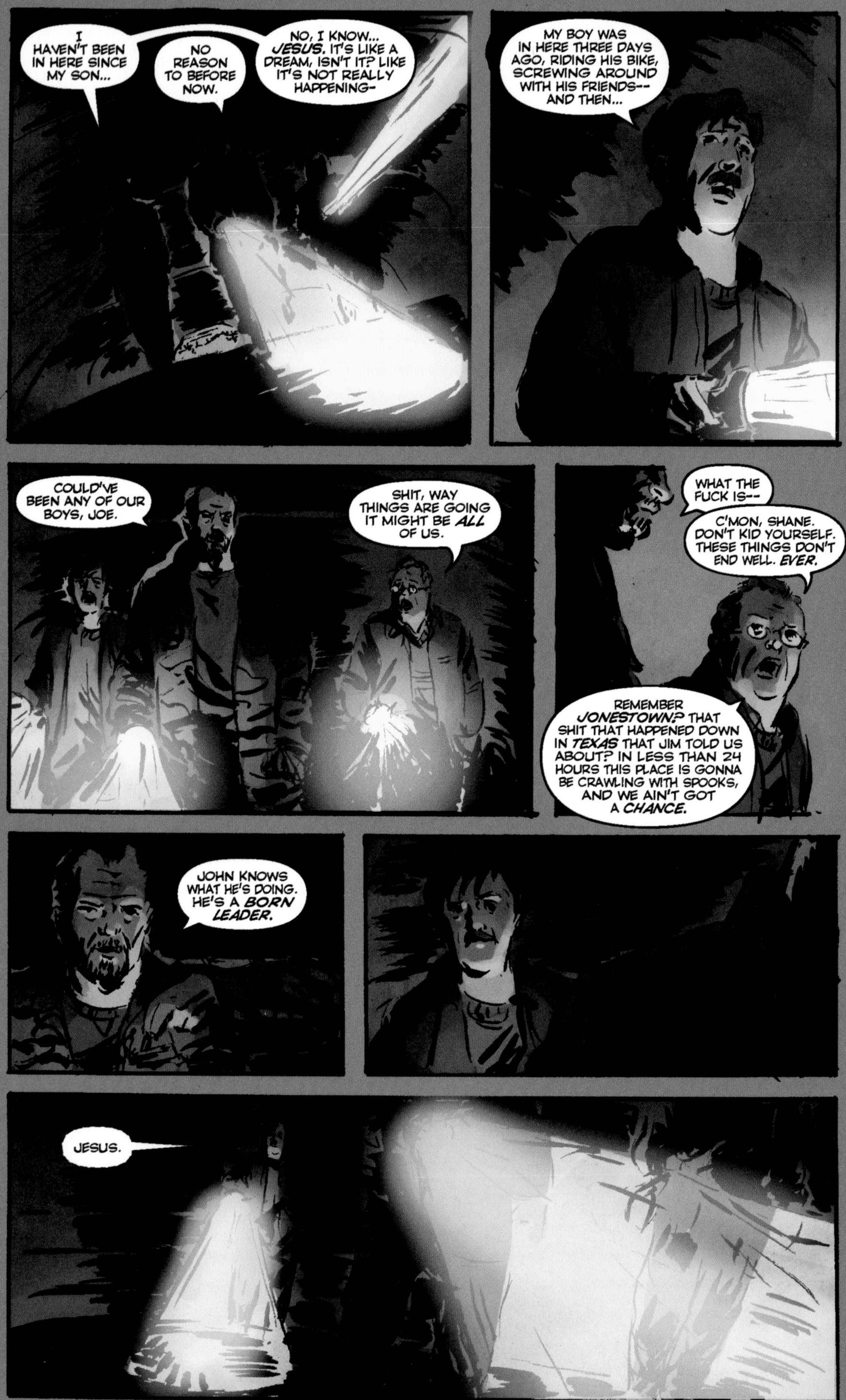
I HAVEN'T BEEN IN HERE SINCE MY SON...
NO REASON TO BEFORE NOW.
NO, I KNOW... *JESUS.* IT'S LIKE A DREAM, ISN'T IT? LIKE IT'S NOT REALLY HAPPENING-
MY BOY WAS IN HERE THREE DAYS AGO, RIDING HIS BIKE, SCREWING AROUND WITH HIS FRIENDS-- AND THEN...
COULD'VE BEEN ANY OF OUR BOYS, JOE.
SHIT, WAY THINGS ARE GOING IT MIGHT BE *ALL* OF US.
WHAT THE FUCK IS--
C'MON, SHANE. DON'T KID YOURSELF. THESE THINGS DON'T END WELL. *EVER.*
REMEMBER *JONESTOWN?* THAT SHIT THAT HAPPENED DOWN IN *TEXAS* THAT JIM TOLD US ABOUT? IN LESS THAN 24 HOURS THIS PLACE IS GONNA BE CRAWLING WITH SPOOKS, AND WE AIN'T GOT A *CHANCE.*
JOHN KNOWS WHAT HE'S DOING. HE'S A *BORN LEADER.*
JESUS.

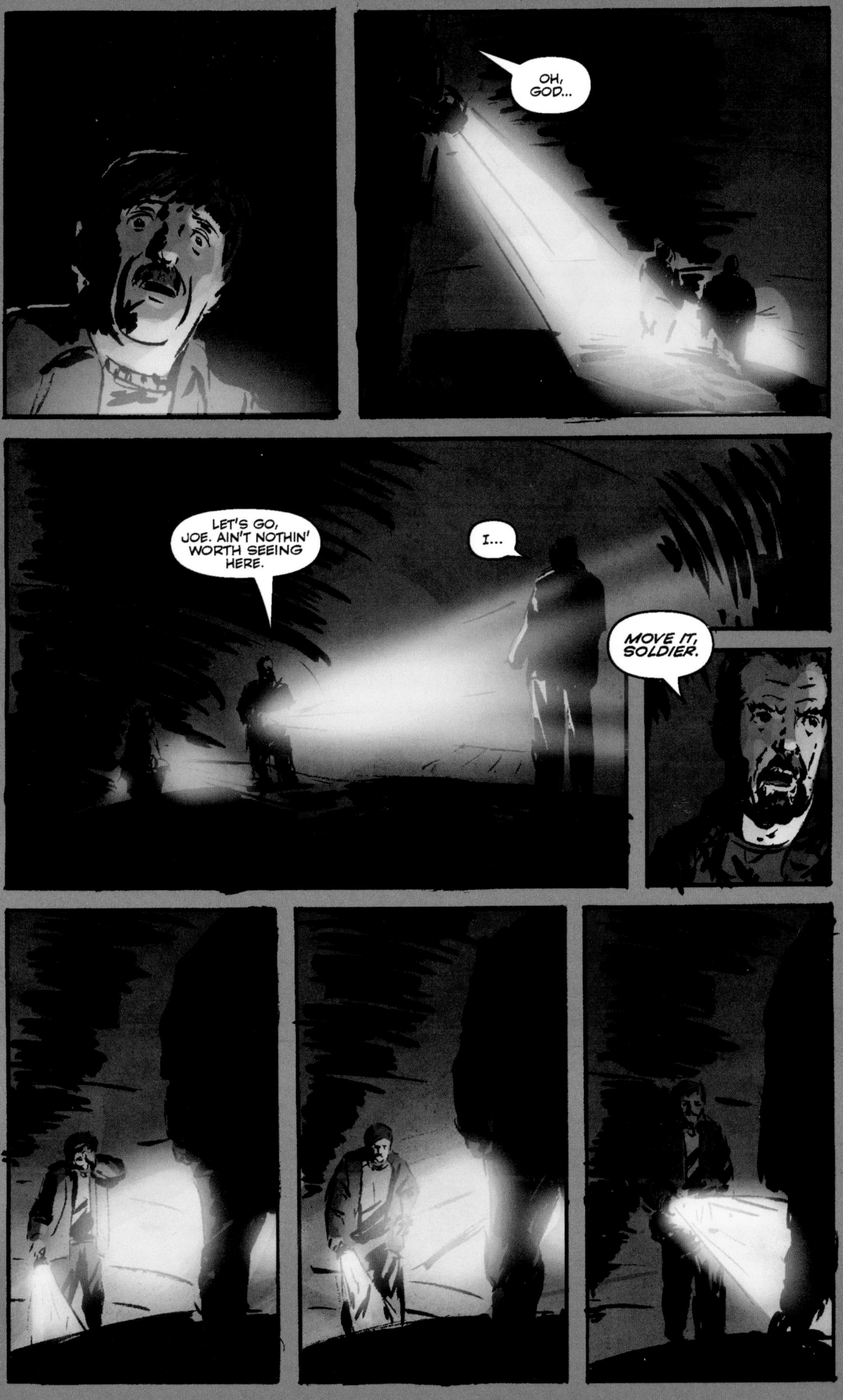
OH, GOD...
LET'S GO, JOE. AIN'T NOTHIN' WORTH SEEING HERE.
I...
MOVE IT, SOLDIER.

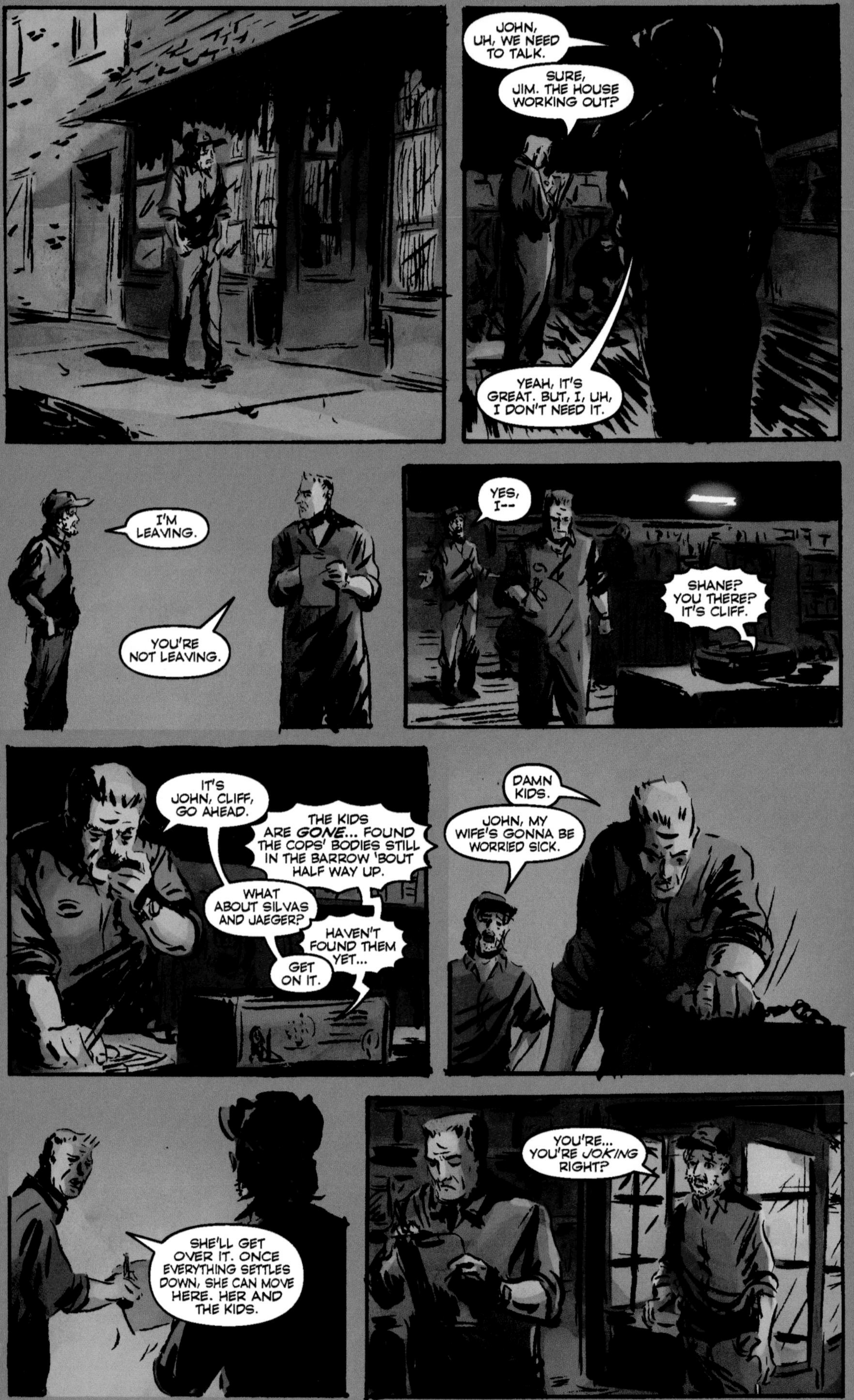
JOHN, UH, WE NEED TO TALK.
SURE, JIM. THE HOUSE WORKING OUT?
YEAH, IT'S GREAT. BUT, I, UH, I DON'T NEED IT.
I'M LEAVING.
YOU'RE NOT LEAVING.
YES, I--
SHANE? YOU THERE? IT'S CLIFF.
IT'S JOHN, CLIFF, GO AHEAD.
THE KIDS ARE *GONE*... FOUND THE COPS' BODIES STILL IN THE BARROW 'BOUT HALF WAY UP.
WHAT ABOUT SILVAS AND JAEGER?
HAVEN'T FOUND THEM YET...
GET ON IT.
DAMN KIDS.
JOHN, MY WIFE'S GONNA BE WORRIED SICK.
SHE'LL GET OVER IT. ONCE EVERYTHING SETTLES DOWN, SHE CAN MOVE HERE. HER AND THE KIDS.
YOU'RE... YOU'RE *JOKING* RIGHT?

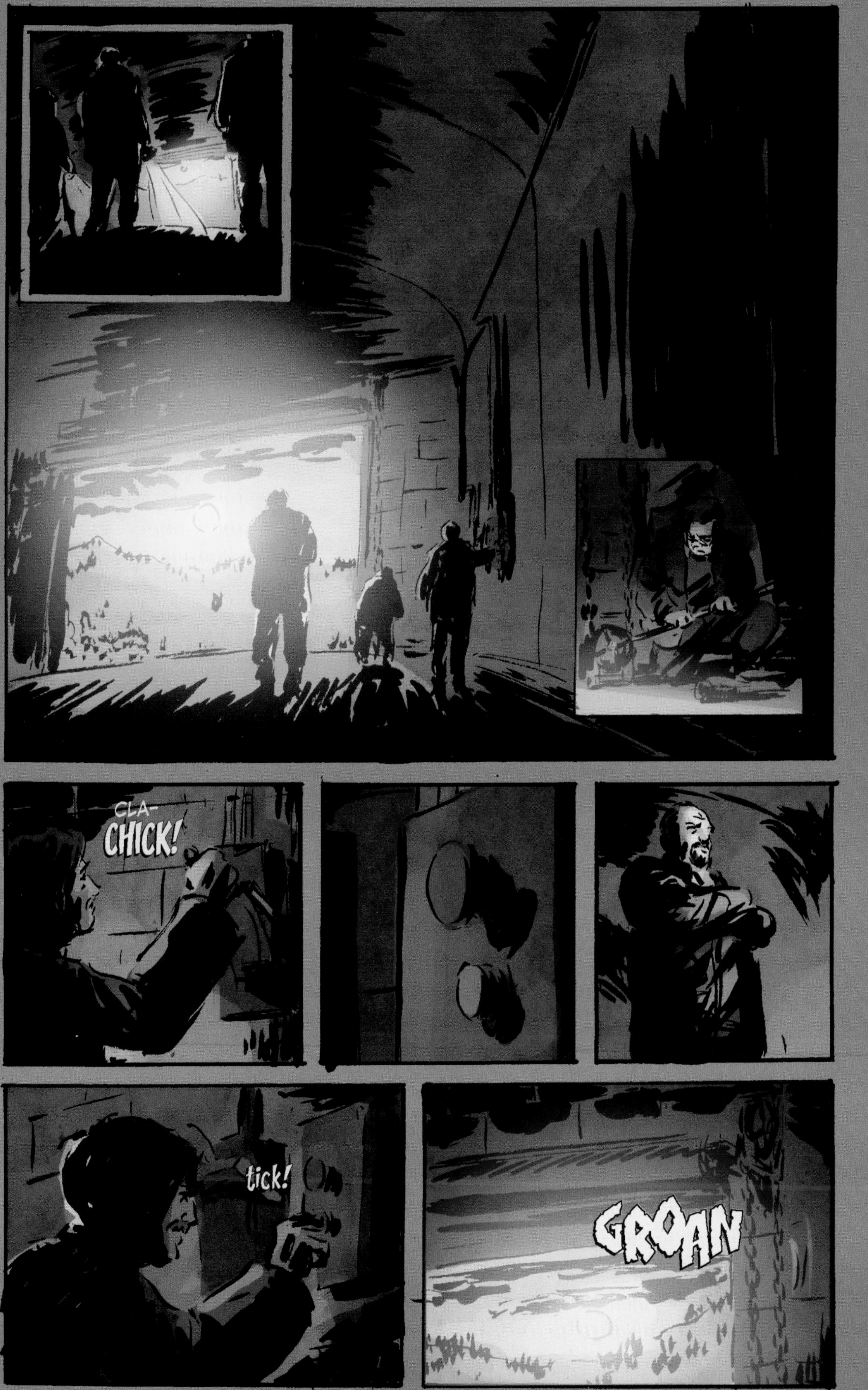
CLA-
CHICK!
tick!
GROAN

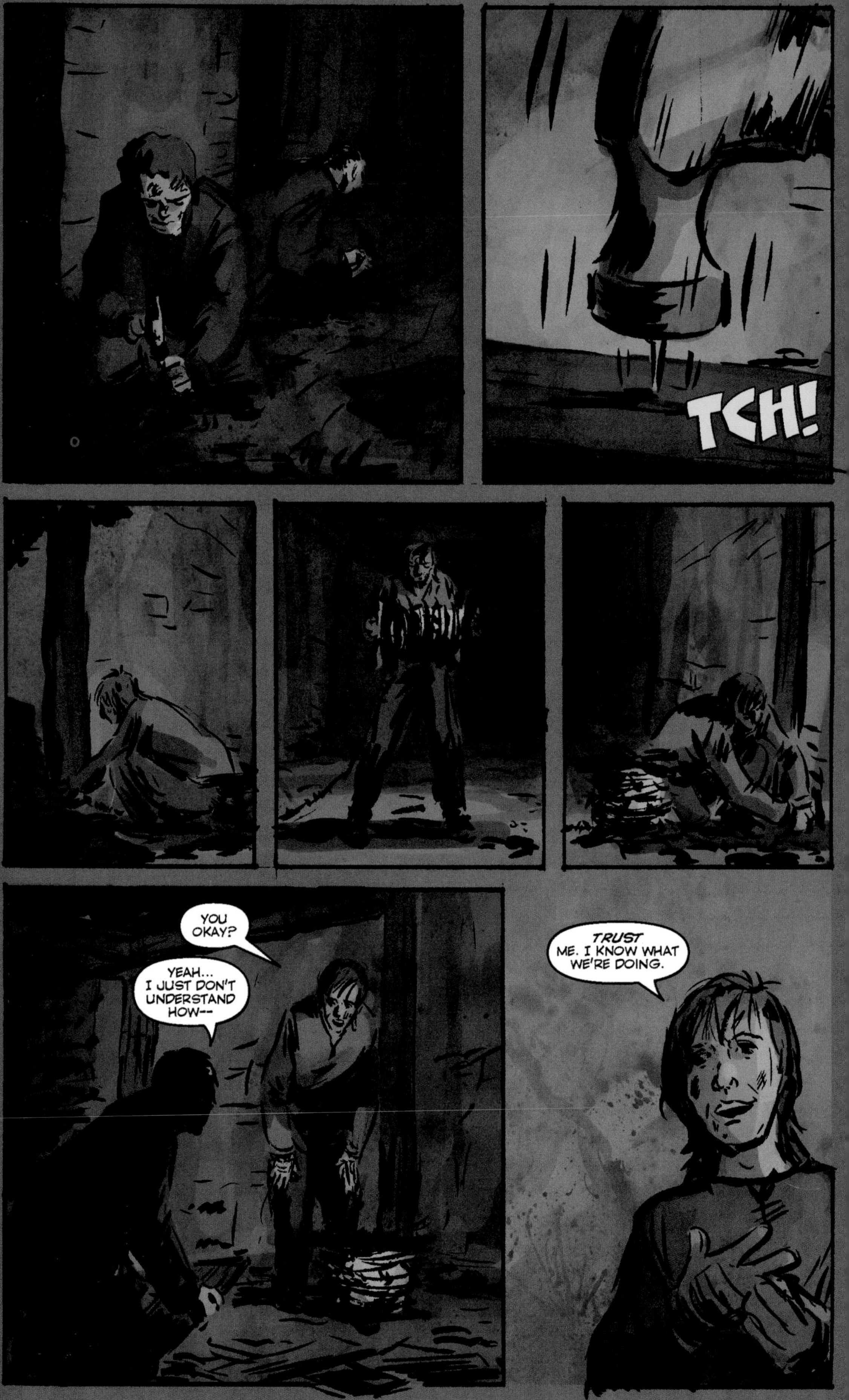
TCH!
YOU OKAY?
YEAH... I JUST DON'T UNDERSTAND HOW--
TRUST ME. I KNOW WHAT WE'RE DOING.

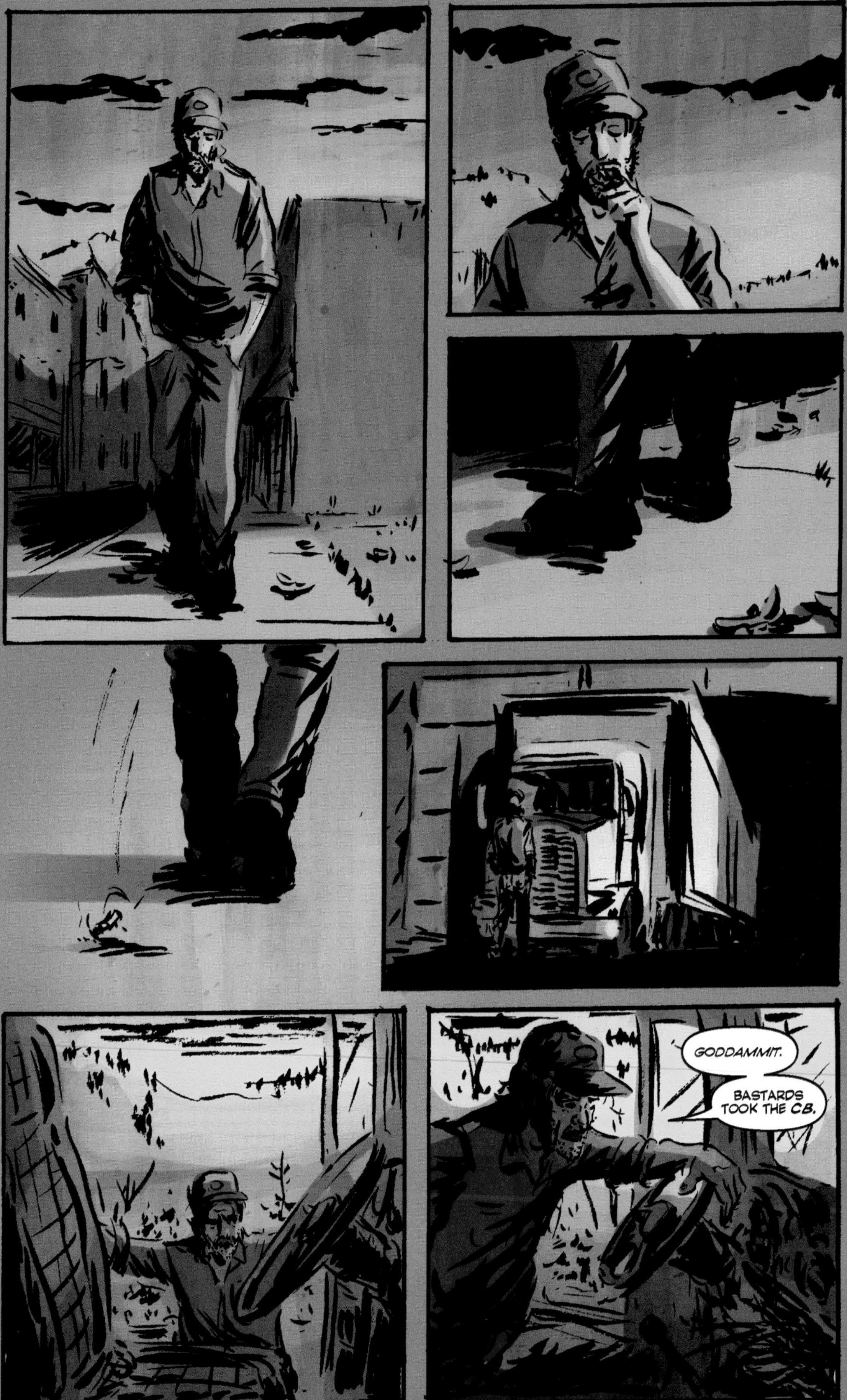
GODDAMMIT.
BASTARDS TOOK THE CB.

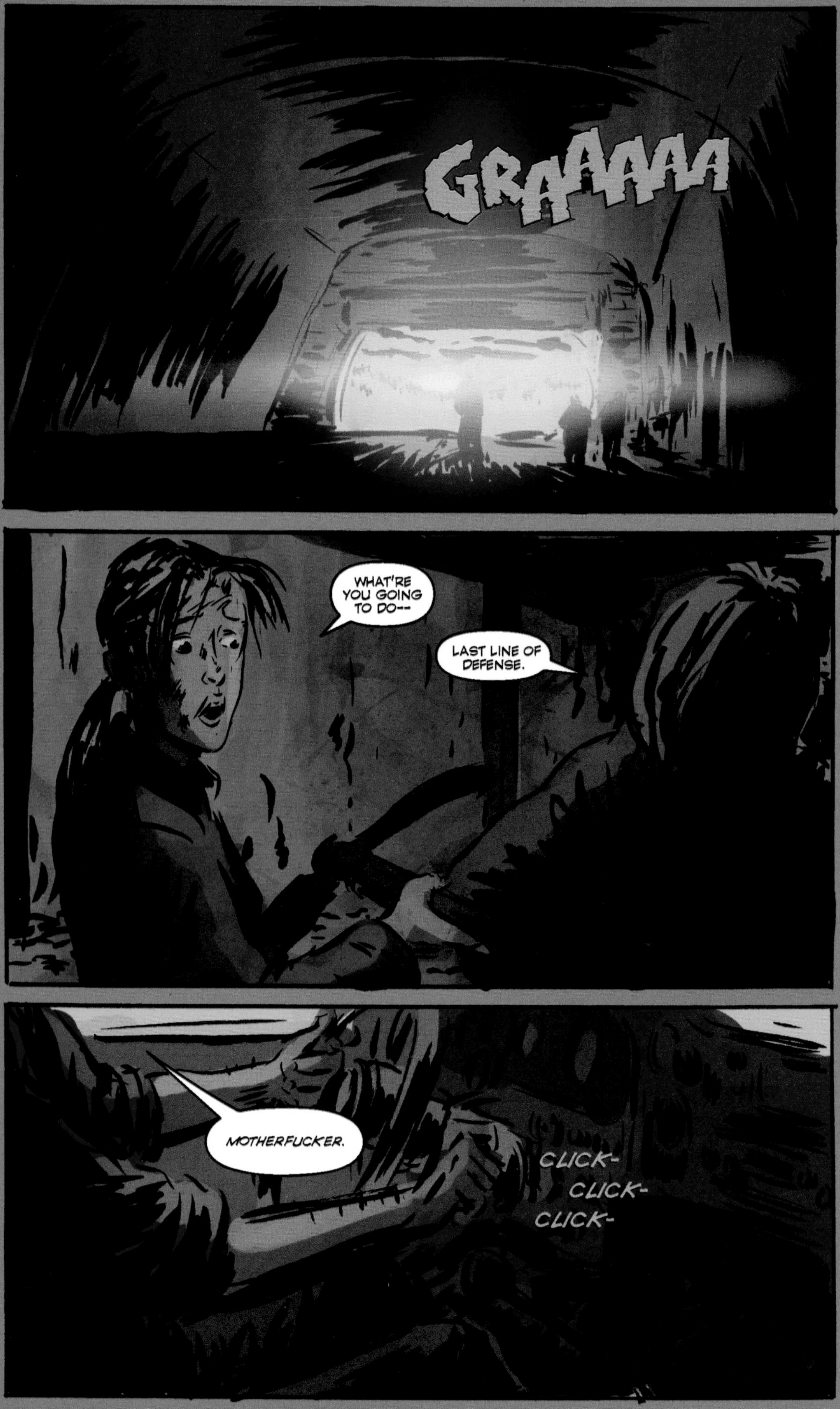
GRAAAAA
WHAT'RE YOU GOING TO DO--
LAST LINE OF DEFENSE.
MOTHERFUCKER.
CLICK-
CLICK-
CLICK-

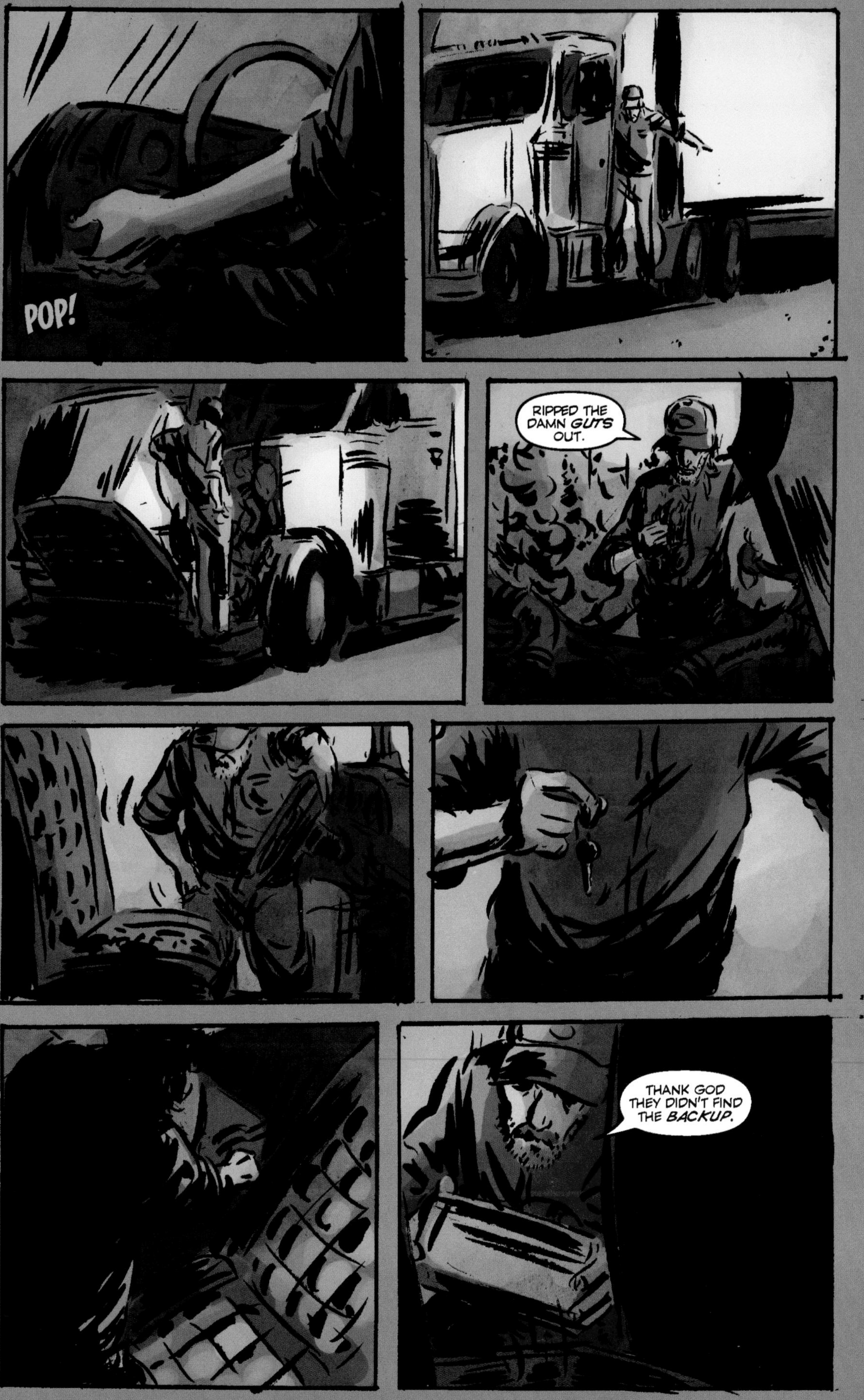
POP!
RIPPED THE DAMN GUTS OUT.
THANK GOD THEY DIDN'T FIND THE BACKUP.

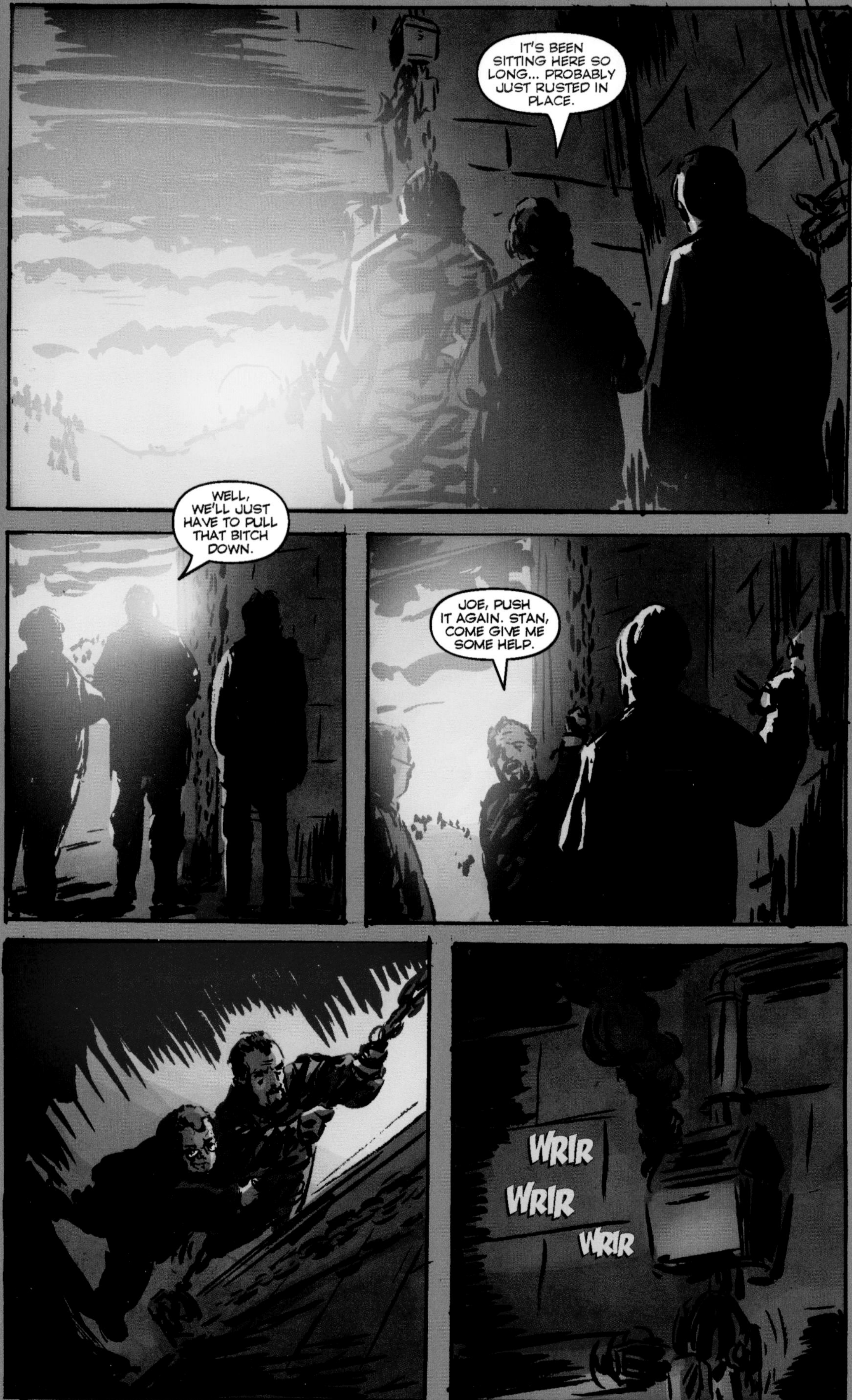
IT'S BEEN SITTING HERE SO LONG... PROBABLY JUST RUSTED IN PLACE.
WELL, WE'LL JUST HAVE TO PULL THAT BITCH DOWN.
JOE, PUSH IT AGAIN. STAN, COME GIVE ME SOME HELP.
WRIR
WRIR
WRIR

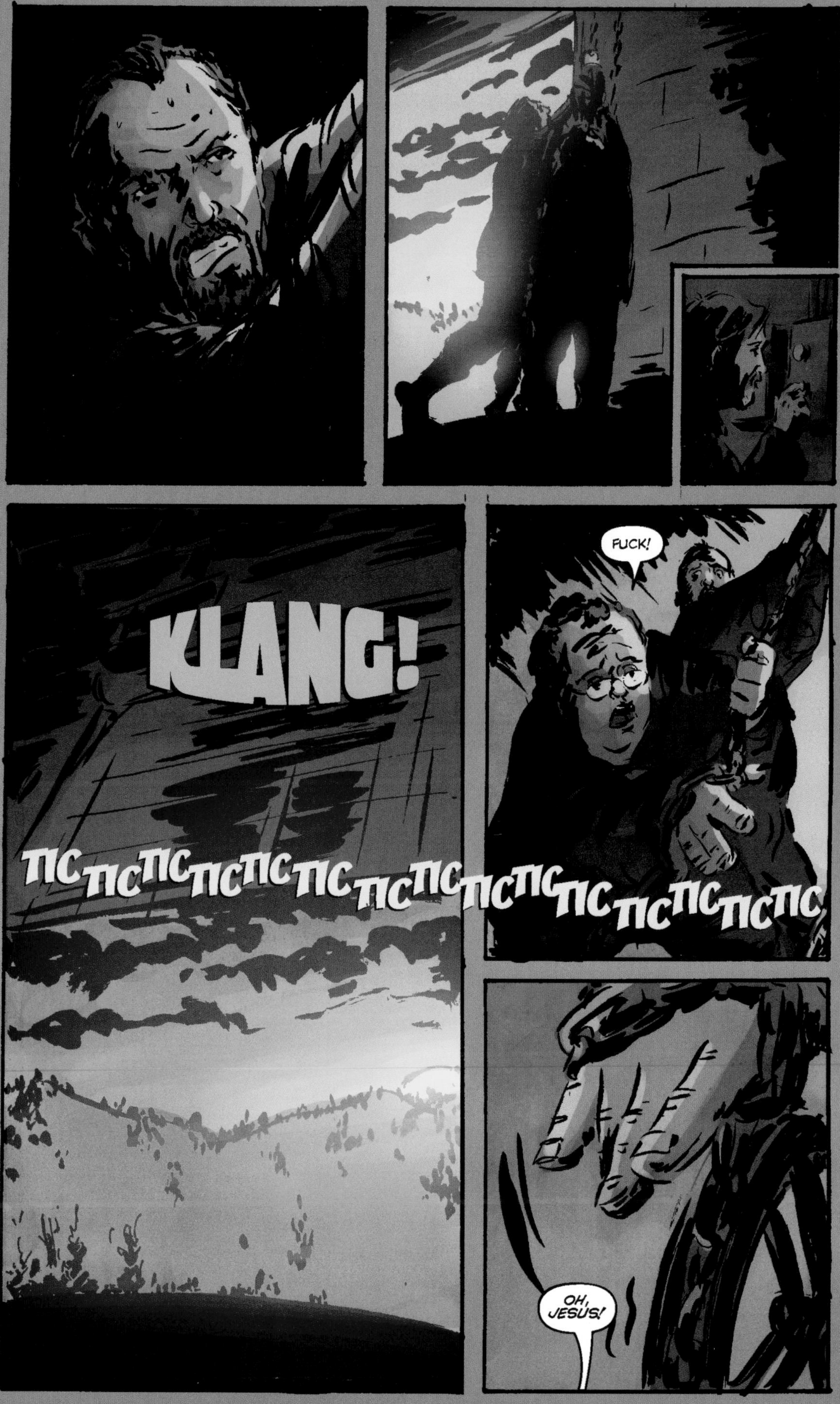
KLANG!
TIC TIC TIC TIC TIC TIC TIC TIC TIC TIC TIC TIC TIC TIC TIC TIC TIC
FUCK!
OH, JESUS!

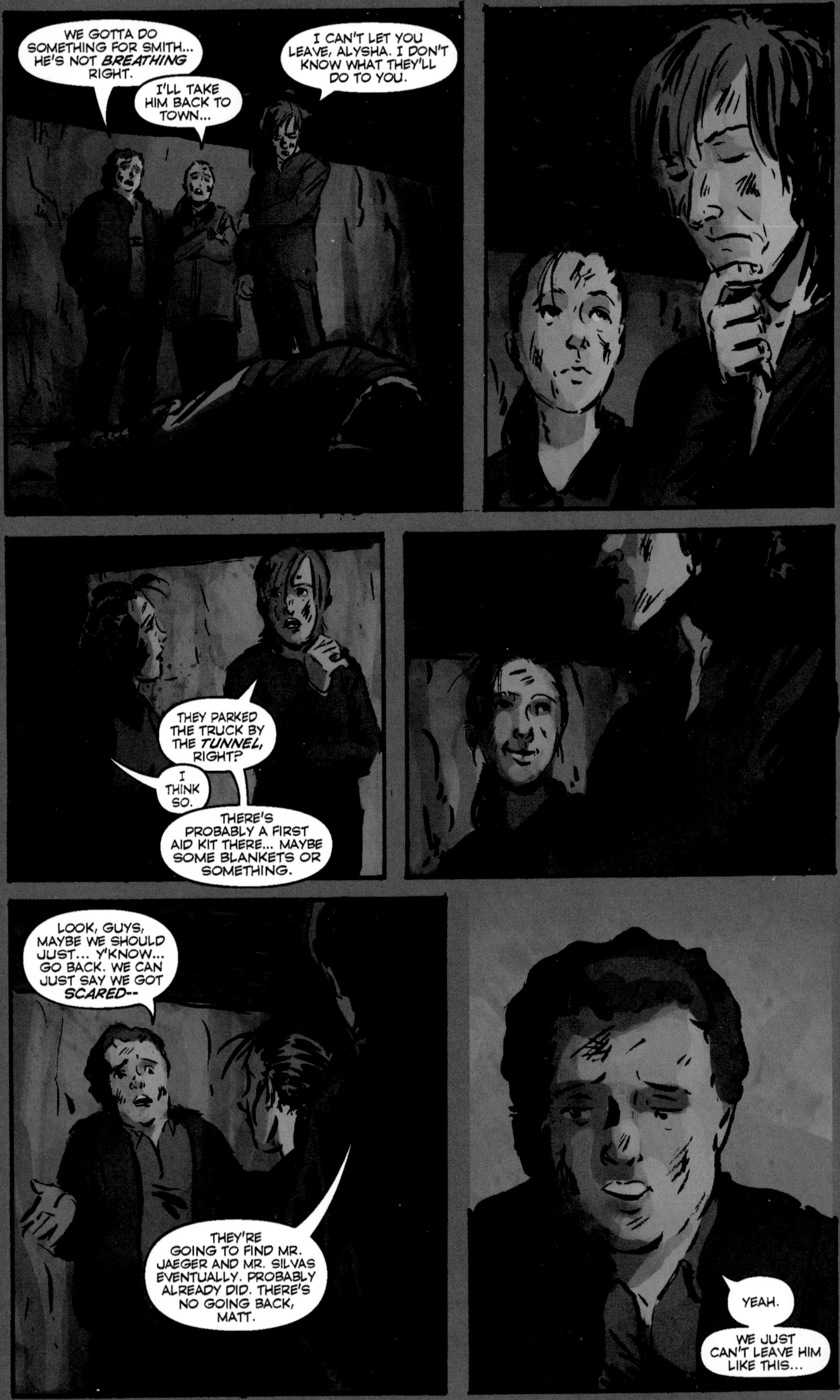
WE GOTTA DO SOMETHING FOR SMITH... HE'S NOT *BREATHING* RIGHT.
I'LL TAKE HIM BACK TO TOWN...
I CAN'T LET YOU LEAVE, ALYSHA. I DON'T KNOW WHAT THEY'LL DO TO YOU.
THEY PARKED THE TRUCK BY THE *TUNNEL*, RIGHT?
I THINK SO.
THERE'S PROBABLY A FIRST AID KIT THERE... MAYBE SOME BLANKETS OR SOMETHING.
LOOK, GUYS, MAYBE WE SHOULD JUST... Y'KNOW... GO BACK. WE CAN JUST SAY WE GOT *SCARED*--
THEY'RE GOING TO FIND MR. JAEGER AND MR. SILVAS EVENTUALLY. PROBABLY ALREADY DID. THERE'S NO GOING BACK, MATT.
YEAH.
WE JUST CAN'T LEAVE HIM LIKE THIS...

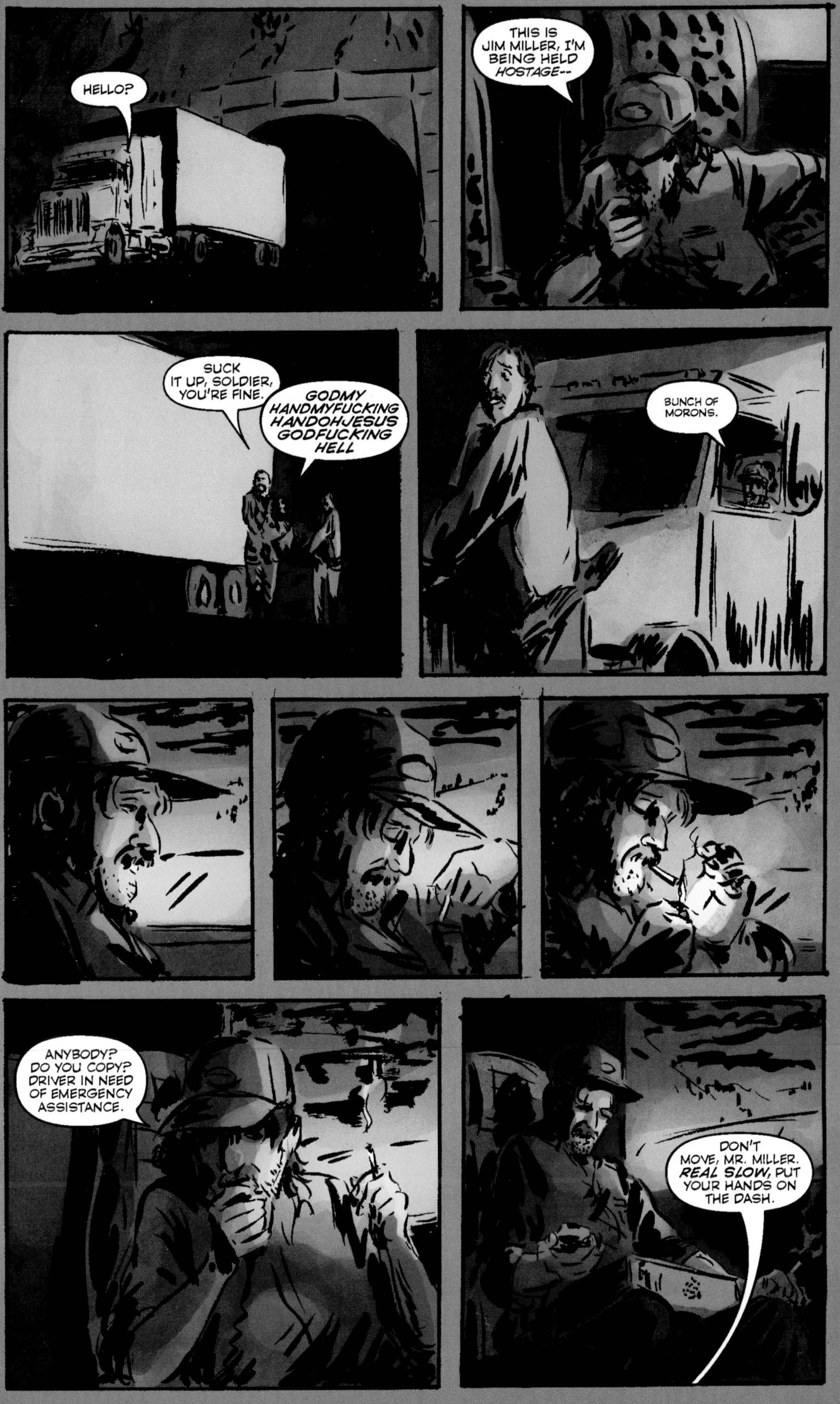
HELLO?
THIS IS JIM MILLER, I'M BEING HELD HOSTAGE--
SUCK IT UP, SOLDIER, YOU'RE FINE.
GODMY HANDMYFUCKING HANDOHJESUS GODFUCKING HELL
BUNCH OF MORONS.
ANYBODY? DO YOU COPY? DRIVER IN NEED OF EMERGENCY ASSISTANCE.
DON'T MOVE, MR. MILLER. REAL SLOW, PUT YOUR HANDS ON THE DASH.

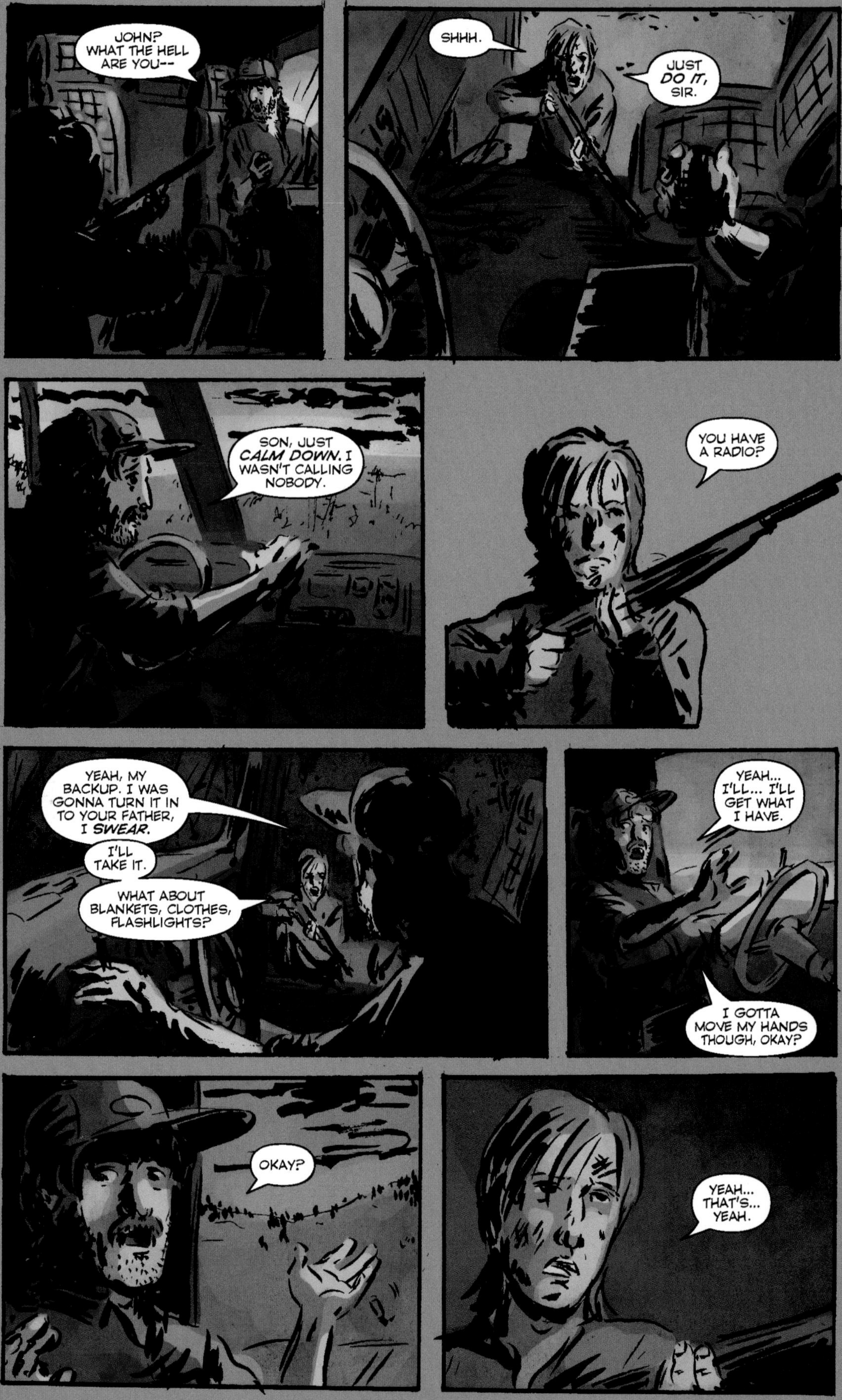
JOHN? WHAT THE HELL ARE YOU--
SHHH.
JUST DO IT, SIR.
SON, JUST CALM DOWN. I WASN'T CALLING NOBODY.
YOU HAVE A RADIO?
YEAH, MY BACKUP. I WAS GONNA TURN IT IN TO YOUR FATHER, I SWEAR.
I'LL TAKE IT.
WHAT ABOUT BLANKETS, CLOTHES, FLASHLIGHTS?
YEAH... I'LL... I'LL GET WHAT I HAVE.
I GOTTA MOVE MY HANDS THOUGH, OKAY?
OKAY?
YEAH... THAT'S... YEAH.

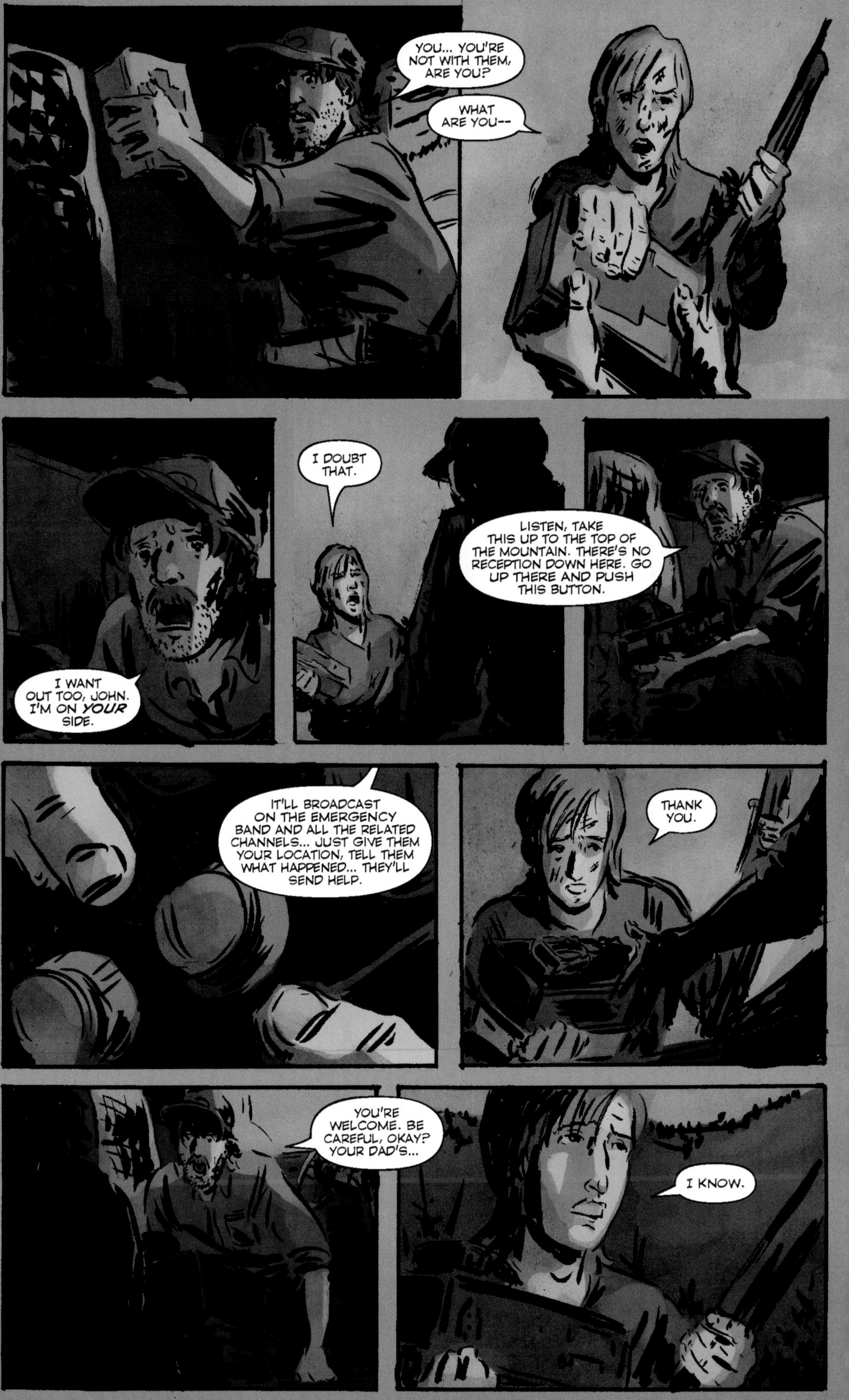
YOU... YOU'RE NOT WITH THEM, ARE YOU?
WHAT ARE YOU--
I WANT OUT TOO, JOHN. I'M ON *YOUR* SIDE.
I DOUBT THAT.
LISTEN, TAKE THIS UP TO THE TOP OF THE MOUNTAIN. THERE'S NO RECEPTION DOWN HERE. GO UP THERE AND PUSH THIS BUTTON.
IT'LL BROADCAST ON THE EMERGENCY BAND AND ALL THE RELATED CHANNELS... JUST GIVE THEM YOUR LOCATION, TELL THEM WHAT HAPPENED... THEY'LL SEND HELP.
THANK YOU.
YOU'RE WELCOME. BE CAREFUL, OKAY? YOUR DAD'S...
I KNOW.

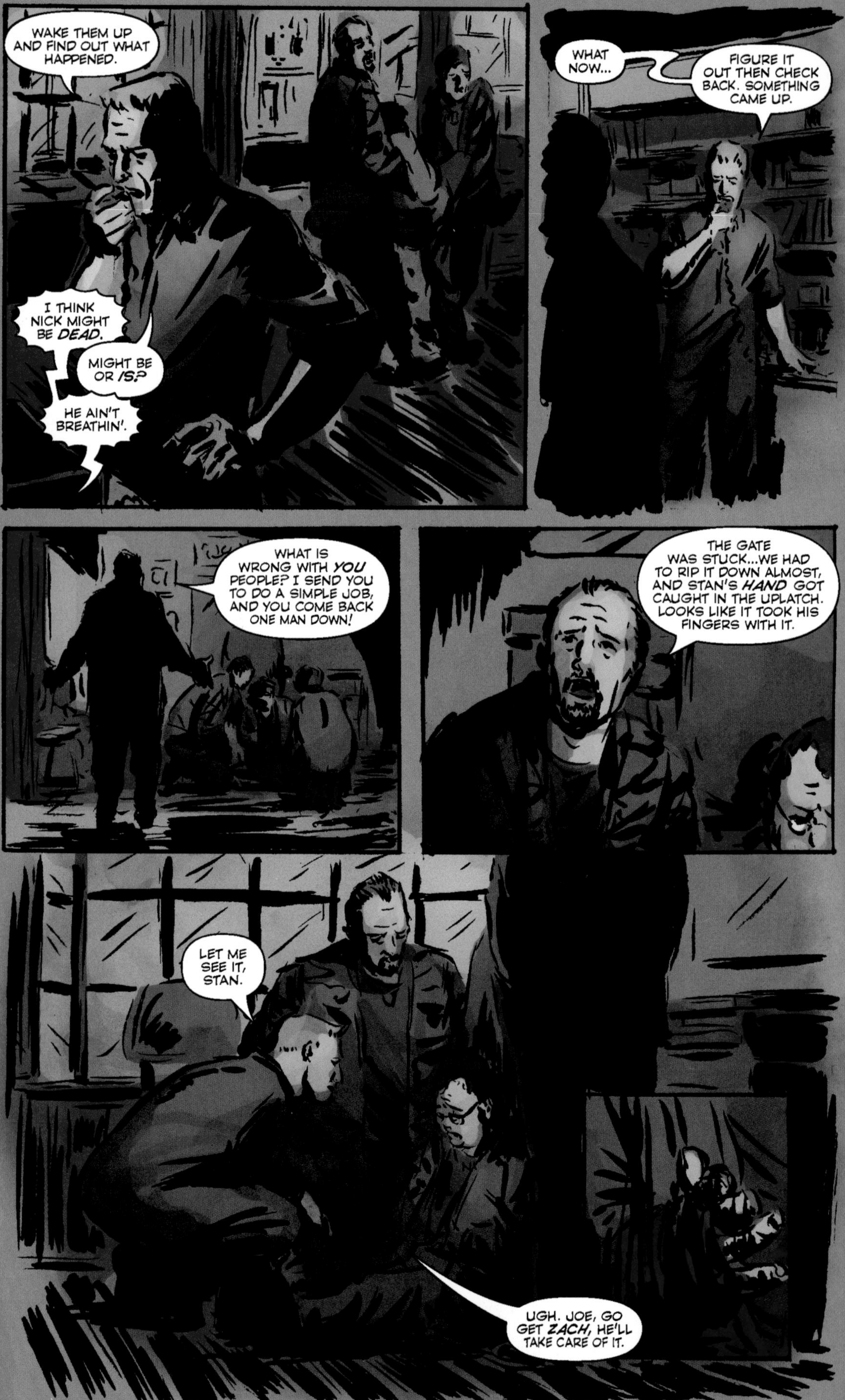
WAKE THEM UP AND FIND OUT WHAT HAPPENED.
I THINK NICK MIGHT BE *DEAD*.
MIGHT BE OR *IS?*
HE AIN'T BREATHIN'.
WHAT NOW...
FIGURE IT OUT THEN CHECK BACK. SOMETHING CAME UP.
WHAT IS WRONG WITH *YOU* PEOPLE? I SEND YOU TO DO A SIMPLE JOB, AND YOU COME BACK ONE MAN DOWN!
THE GATE WAS STUCK...WE HAD TO RIP IT DOWN ALMOST, AND STAN'S *HAND* GOT CAUGHT IN THE UPLATCH. LOOKS LIKE IT TOOK HIS FINGERS WITH IT.
LET ME SEE IT, STAN.
UGH. JOE, GO GET *ZACH*, HE'LL TAKE CARE OF IT.

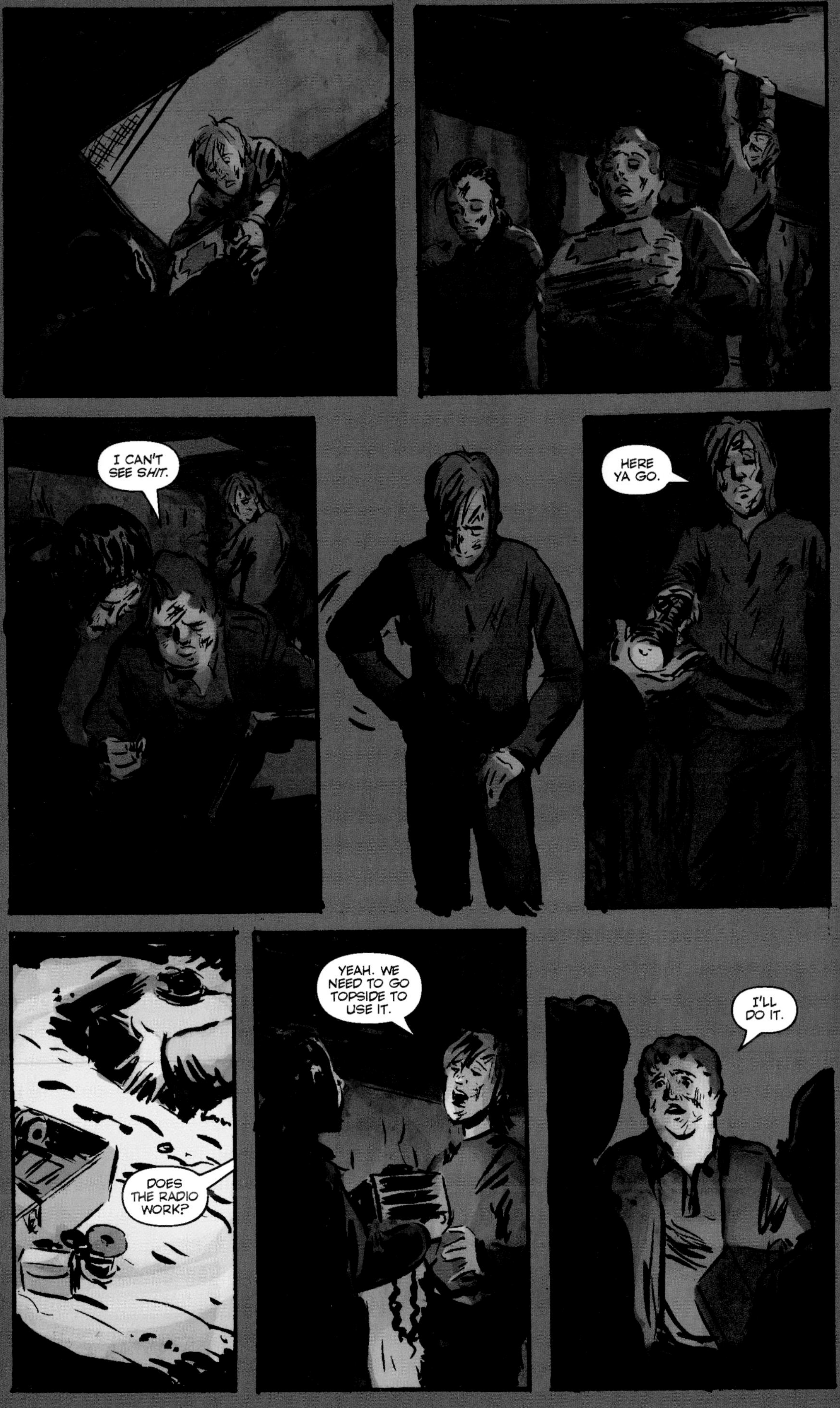
I CAN'T SEE *SHIT*.
HERE YA GO.
DOES THE RADIO WORK?
YEAH. WE NEED TO GO TOPSIDE TO USE IT.
I'LL DO IT.

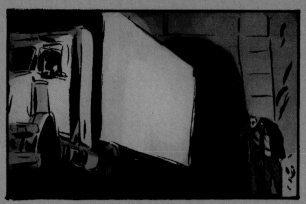

WHAT THE FUCK ARE YOU DOING?

SMOKING AND WAITING.

GIVE ME A HAND WITH HIM, HE'S PRETTY OUT OF IT.

HE'S GONNA BE OKAY, RIGHT, ZACH?

I FIGURE SO. LOST A LOT OF BLOOD. GRAB ME ONE OF THOSE BOTTLES OF JUICE. HE NEEDS *GLUCOSE.*

SO HE RECKONS THE KIDS *KILLED* NICK?

STEVE SAID THAT THEY THREW ROCKS AT 'EM, AND STARTED POUNDING ON THEM.

MY BOY BEAT NICK TO DEATH WITH HIS *BARE HANDS.*

JESUS.

CHIP OFF THE OLD BLOCK, RIGHT?

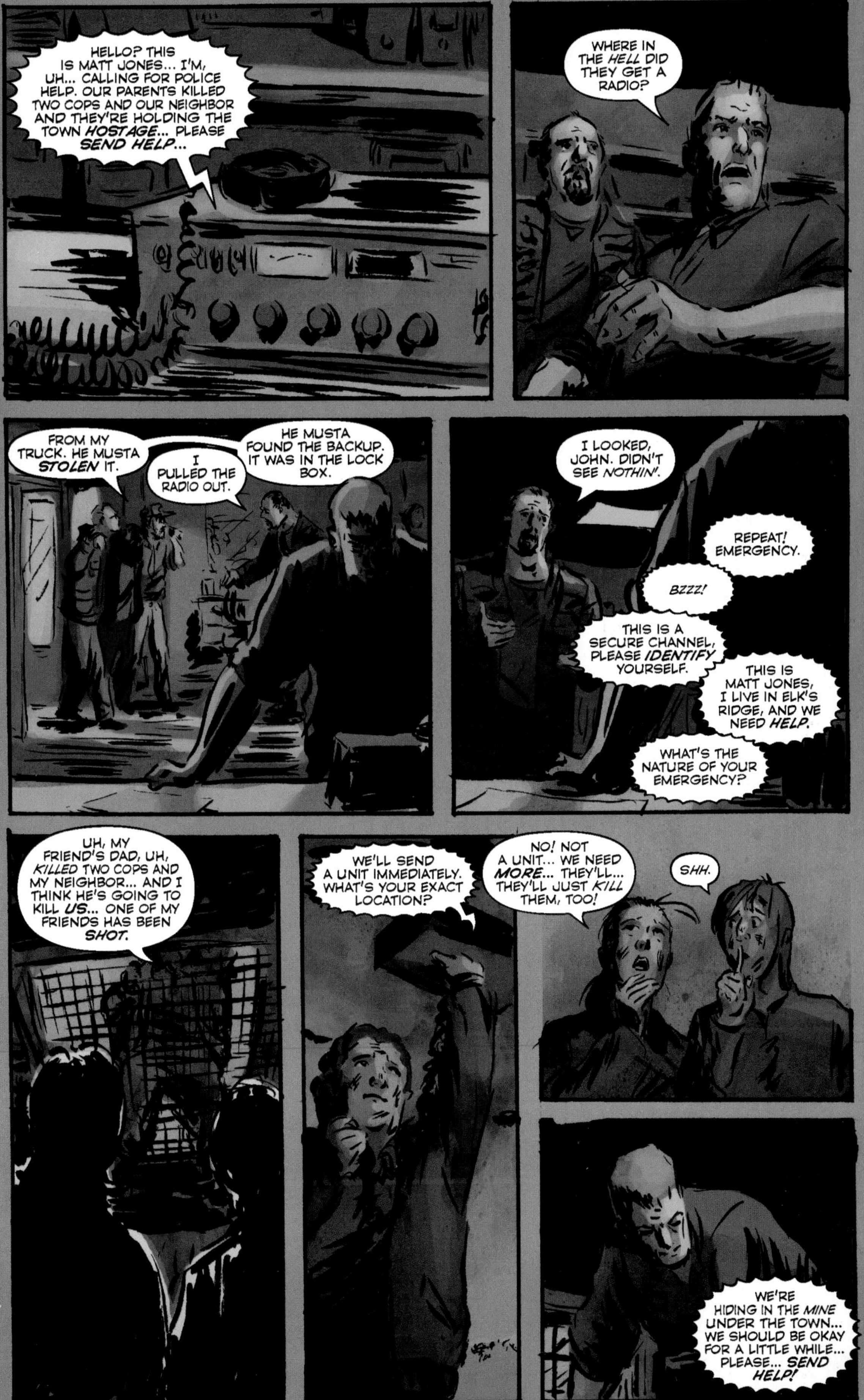
HELLO? THIS IS MATT JONES... I'M, UH... CALLING FOR POLICE HELP. OUR PARENTS KILLED TWO COPS AND OUR NEIGHBOR AND THEY'RE HOLDING THE TOWN HOSTAGE... PLEASE SEND HELP...
WHERE IN THE HELL DID THEY GET A RADIO?
FROM MY TRUCK. HE MUSTA STOLEN IT.
I PULLED THE RADIO OUT.
HE MUSTA FOUND THE BACKUP. IT WAS IN THE LOCK BOX.
I LOOKED, JOHN. DIDN'T SEE NOTHIN'.
REPEAT! EMERGENCY.
BZZZ!
THIS IS A SECURE CHANNEL, PLEASE IDENTIFY YOURSELF.
THIS IS MATT JONES, I LIVE IN ELK'S RIDGE, AND WE NEED HELP.
WHAT'S THE NATURE OF YOUR EMERGENCY?
UH, MY FRIEND'S DAD, UH, KILLED TWO COPS AND MY NEIGHBOR... AND I THINK HE'S GOING TO KILL US... ONE OF MY FRIENDS HAS BEEN SHOT.
WE'LL SEND A UNIT IMMEDIATELY. WHAT'S YOUR EXACT LOCATION?
NO! NOT A UNIT... WE NEED MORE... THEY'LL... THEY'LL JUST KILL THEM, TOO!
SHH.
WE'RE HIDING IN THE MINE UNDER THE TOWN... WE SHOULD BE OKAY FOR A LITTLE WHILE... PLEASE... SEND HELP!

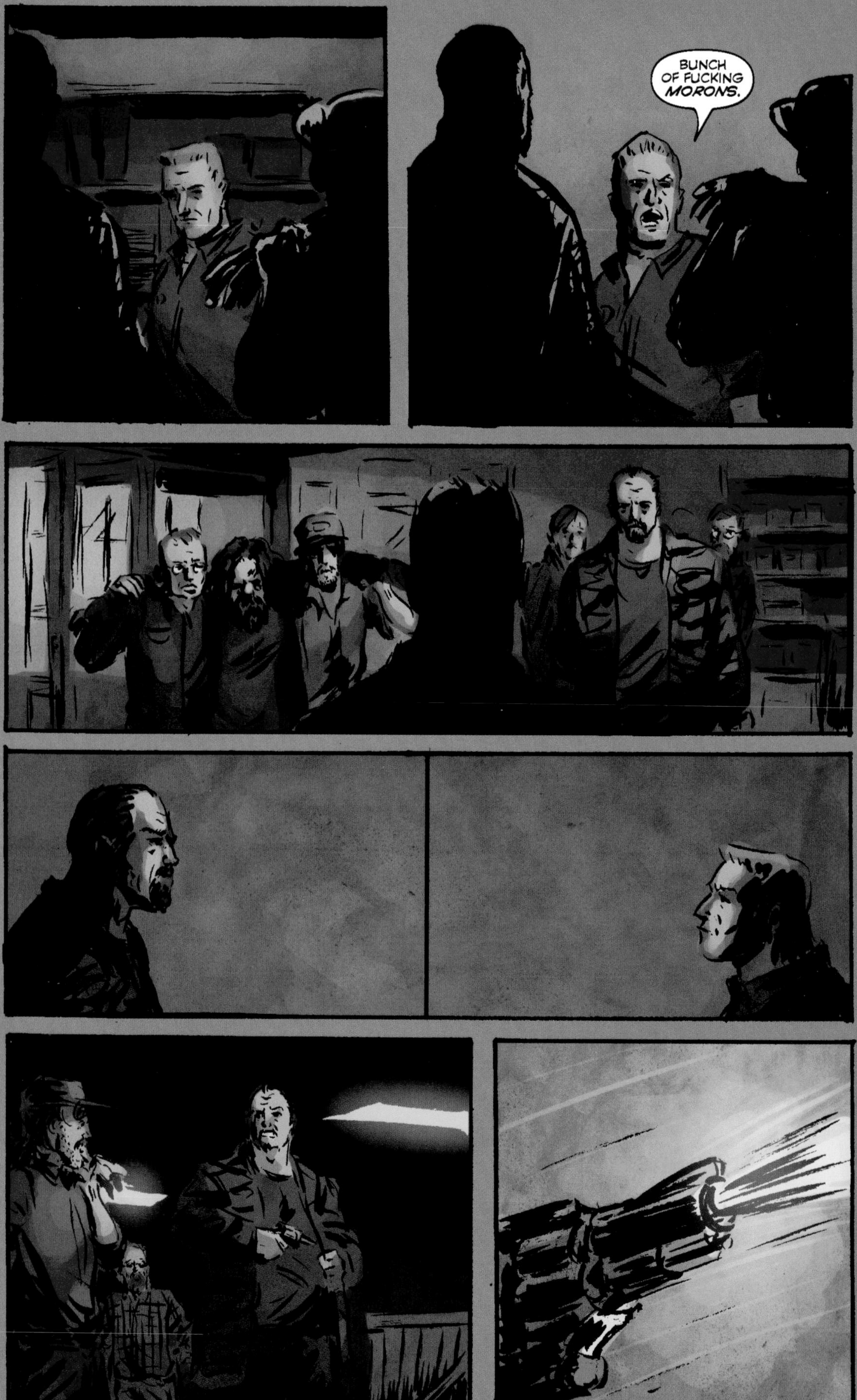
BUNCH OF FUCKING MORONS.

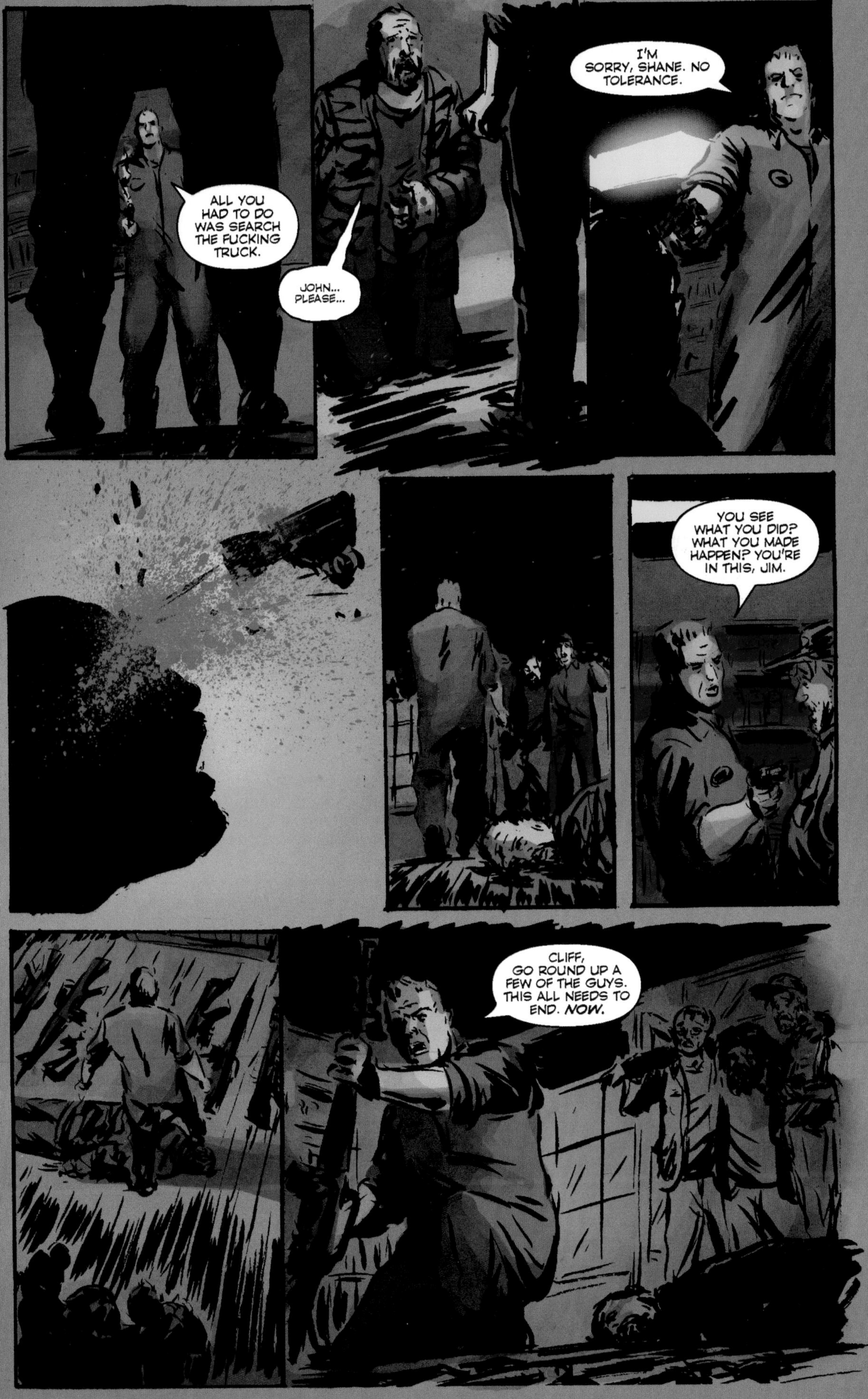
ALL YOU HAD TO DO WAS SEARCH THE FUCKING TRUCK.
JOHN... PLEASE...
I'M SORRY, SHANE. NO TOLERANCE.
YOU SEE WHAT YOU DID? WHAT YOU MADE HAPPEN? YOU'RE IN THIS, JIM.
CLIFF, GO ROUND UP A FEW OF THE GUYS. THIS ALL NEEDS TO END. *NOW.*

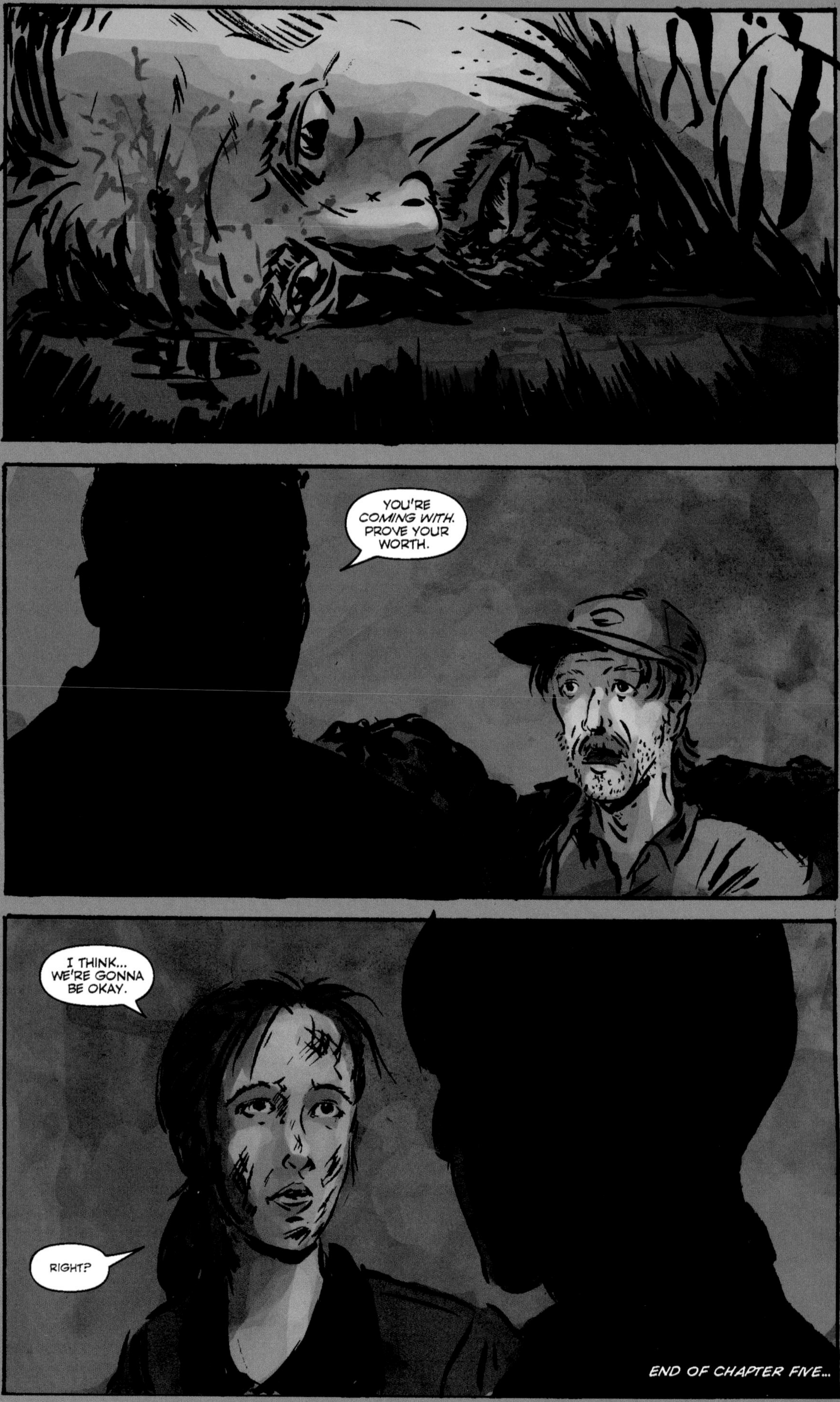
YOU'RE COMING WITH. PROVE YOUR WORTH.
I THINK... WE'RE GONNA BE OKAY.
RIGHT?
END OF CHAPTER FIVE...

Chapter Six: Memories

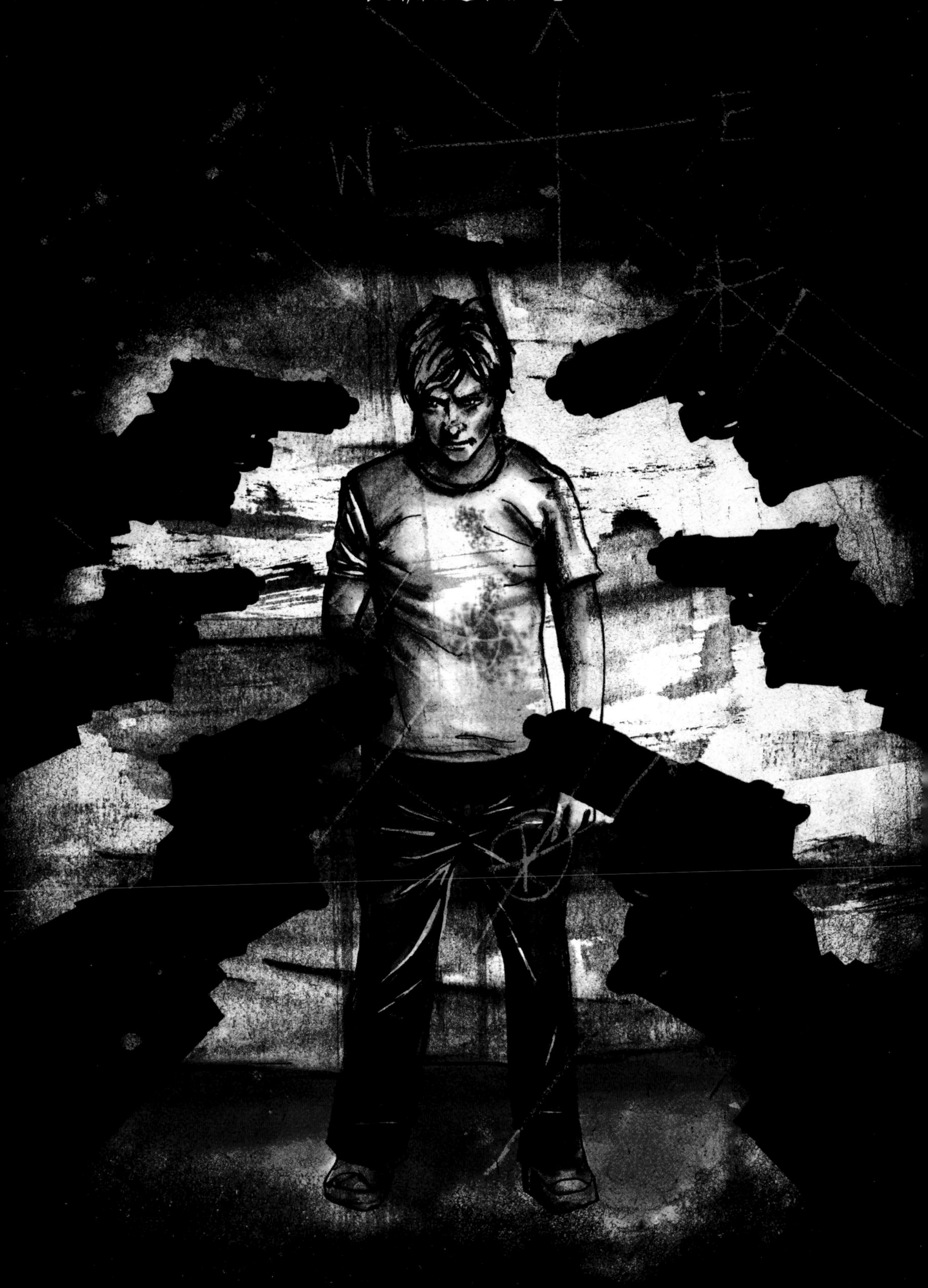

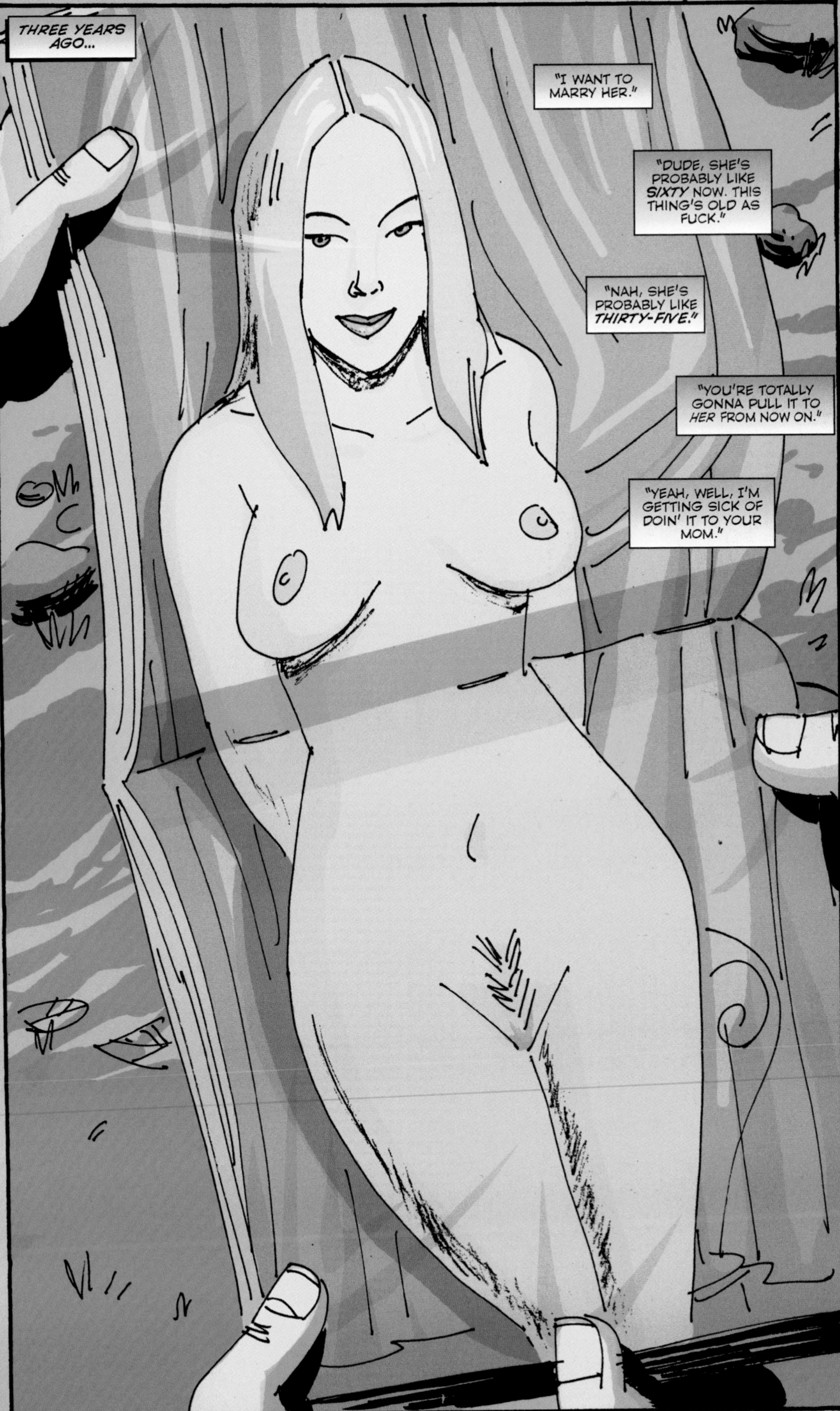
THREE YEARS AGO...
"I WANT TO MARRY HER."
"DUDE, SHE'S PROBABLY LIKE SIXTY NOW. THIS THING'S OLD AS FUCK."
"NAH, SHE'S PROBABLY LIKE THIRTY-FIVE."
"YOU'RE TOTALLY GONNA PULL IT TO HER FROM NOW ON."
"YEAH, WELL, I'M GETTING SICK OF DOIN' IT TO YOUR MOM."

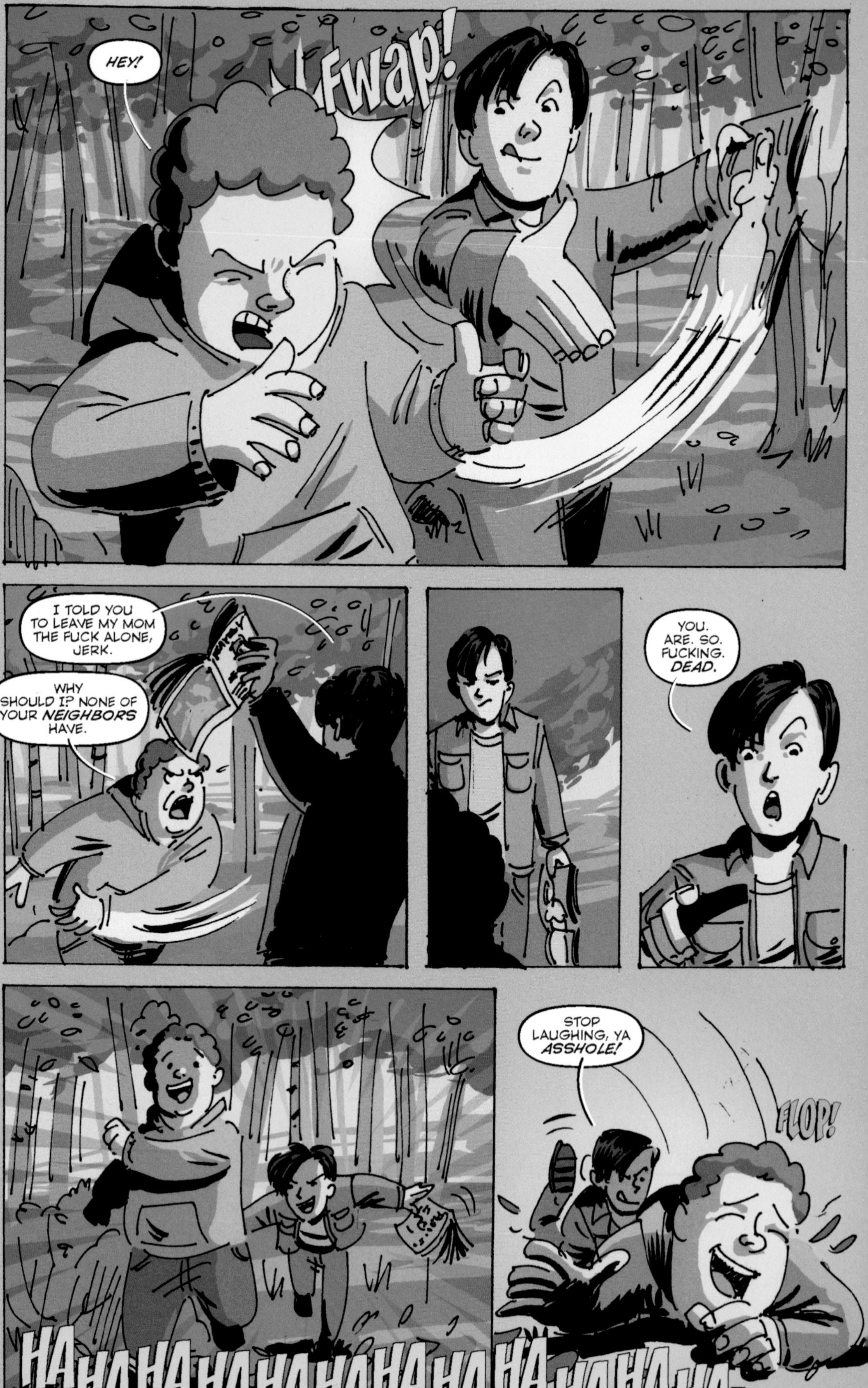
HEY!
Fwap!
I TOLD YOU TO LEAVE MY MOM THE FUCK ALONE, JERK.
WHY SHOULD I? NONE OF YOUR NEIGHBORS HAVE.
YOU. ARE. SO. FUCKING. DEAD.
STOP LAUGHING, YA ASSHOLE!
FLOP!
HAHAHAHAHAHAHAHAHAHAHAHAHAHAHA

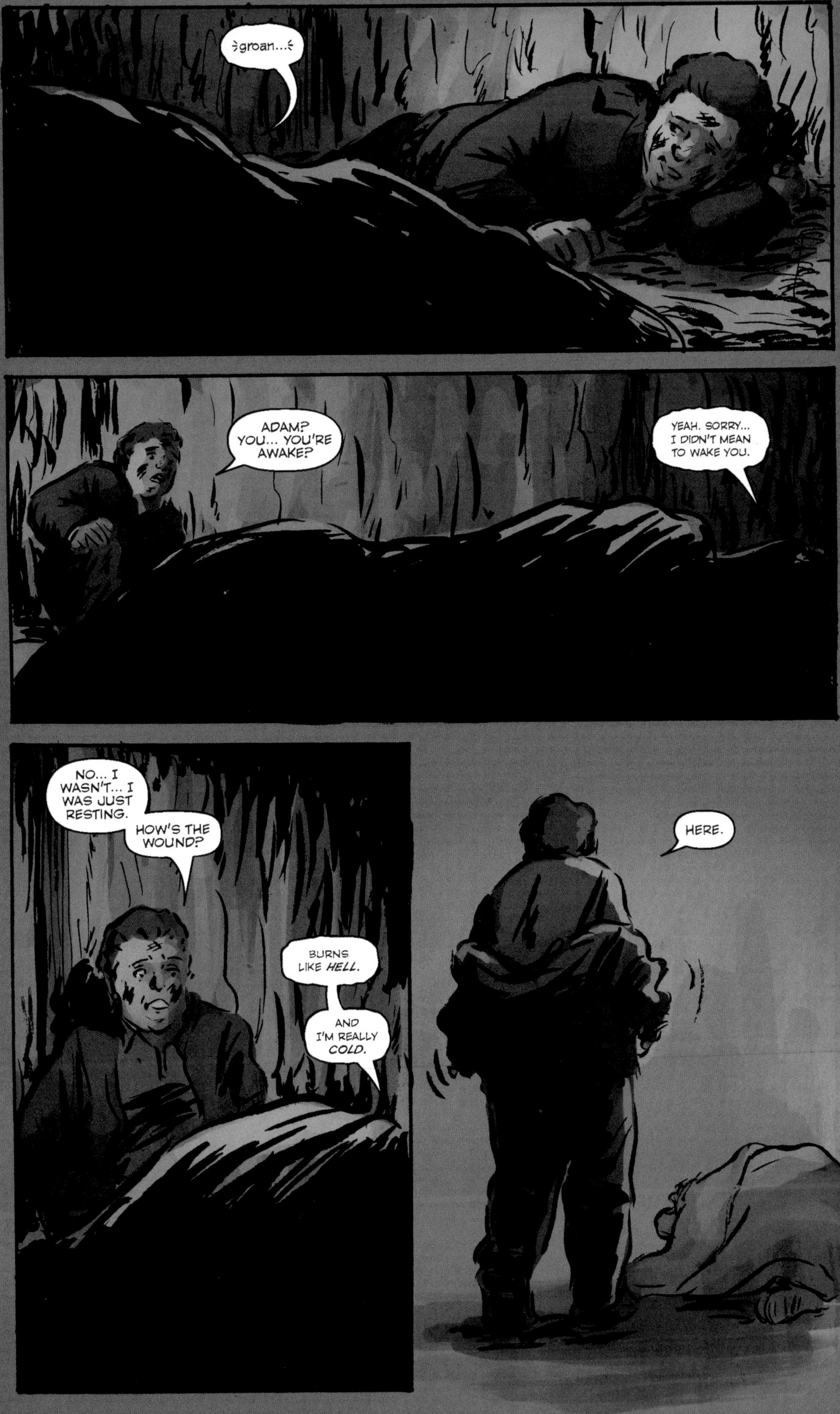
groan...
ADAM? YOU... YOU'RE AWAKE?
YEAH. SORRY... I DIDN'T MEAN TO WAKE YOU.
NO... I WASN'T... I WAS JUST RESTING.
HOW'S THE WOUND?
BURNS LIKE *HELL*.
AND I'M REALLY *COLD*.
HERE.

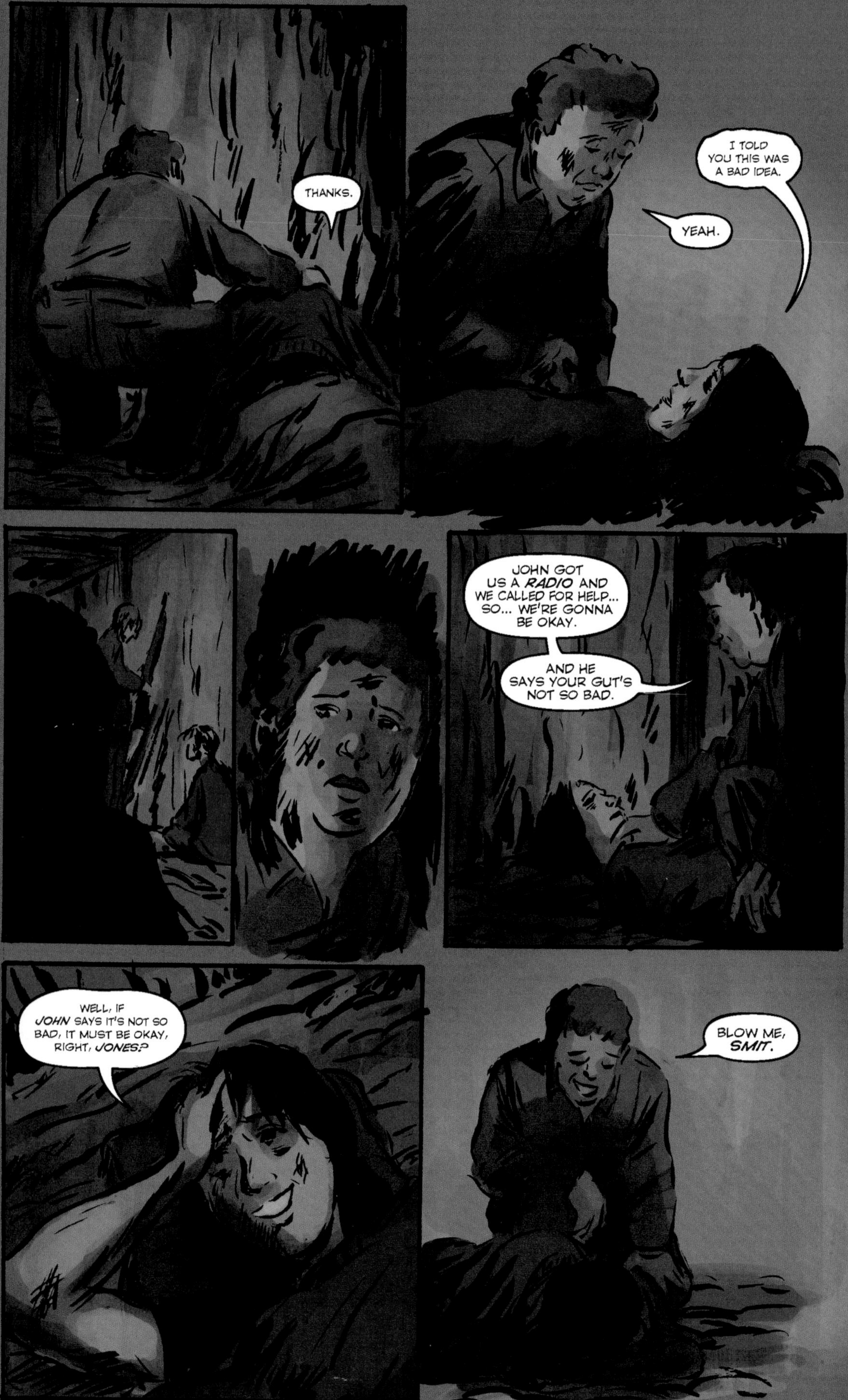
THANKS.
I TOLD YOU THIS WAS A BAD IDEA.
YEAH.
JOHN GOT US A *RADIO* AND WE CALLED FOR HELP... SO... WE'RE GONNA BE OKAY.
AND HE SAYS YOUR GUT'S NOT SO BAD.
WELL, IF *JOHN* SAYS IT'S NOT SO BAD, IT MUST BE OKAY, RIGHT, *JONES*?
BLOW ME, **SMIT**.

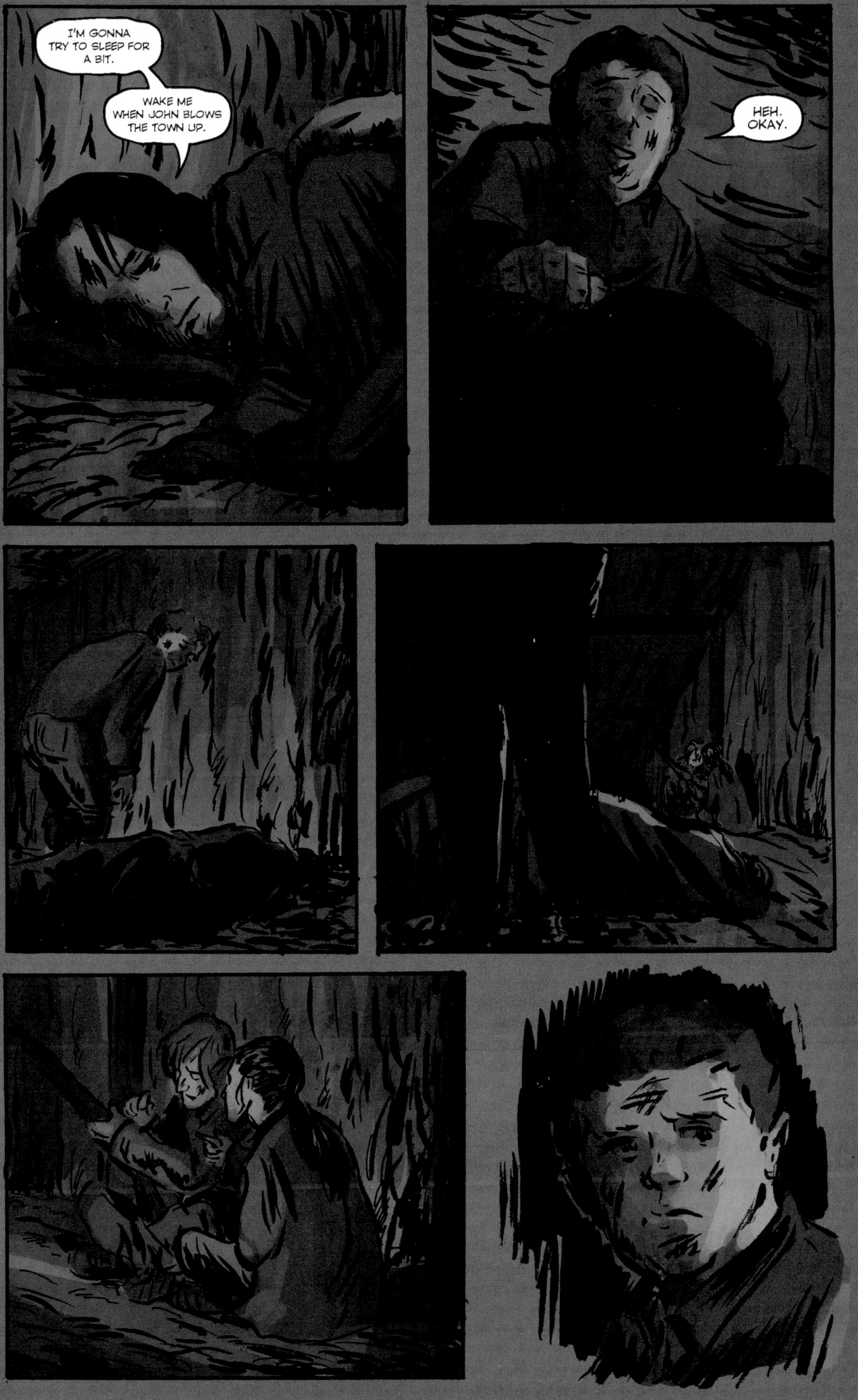
I'M GONNA TRY TO SLEEP FOR A BIT.
WAKE ME WHEN JOHN BLOWS THE TOWN UP.
HEH. OKAY.

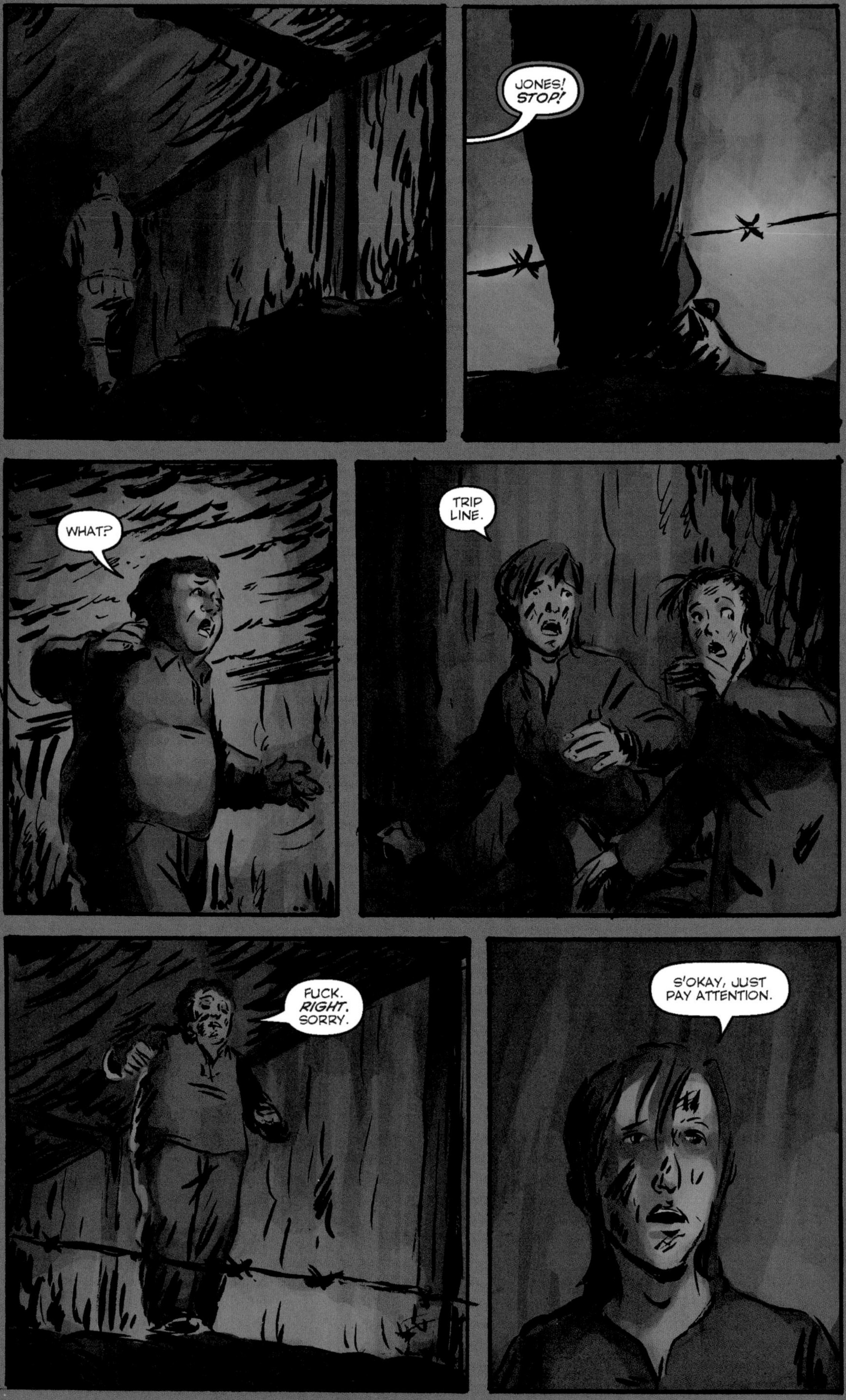
JONES! STOP!
WHAT?
TRIP LINE.
FUCK. RIGHT. SORRY.
S'OKAY, JUST PAY ATTENTION.

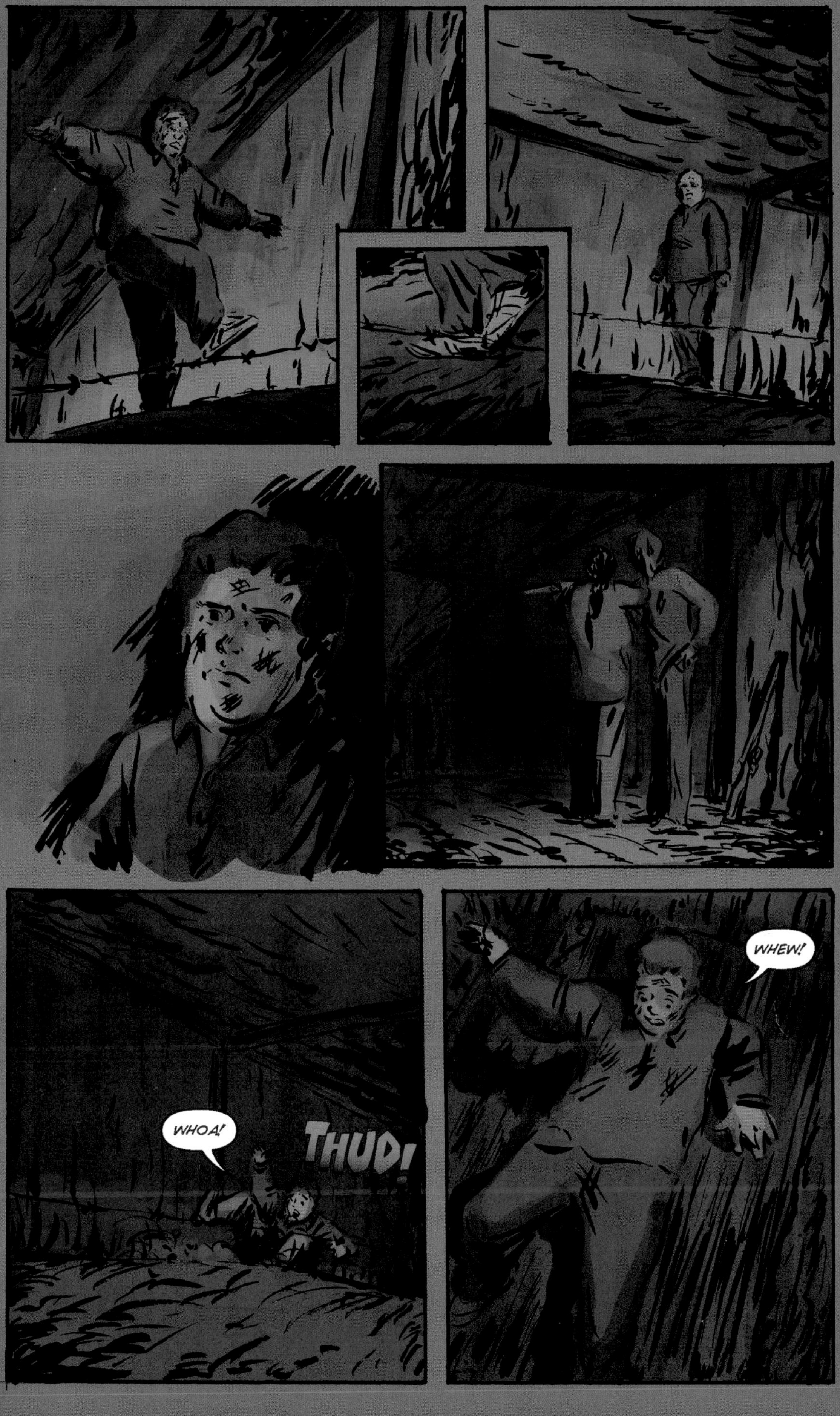
WHOA!
THUD!
WHEW!

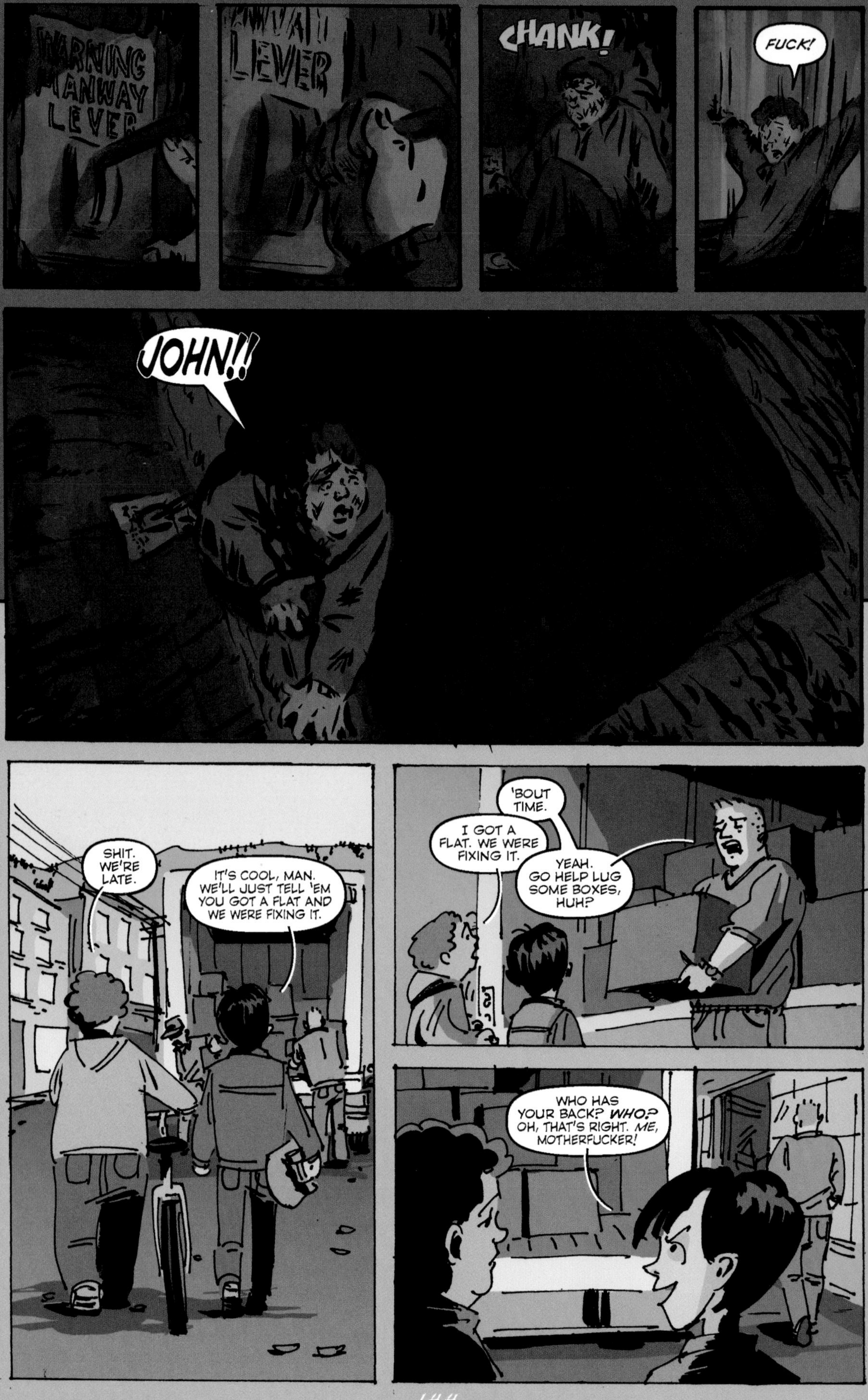
WARNING MANWAY LEVER
LEVER
CHANK!
FUCK!
JOHN!!
SHIT. WE'RE LATE.
IT'S COOL, MAN. WE'LL JUST TELL 'EM YOU GOT A FLAT AND WE WERE FIXING IT.
'BOUT TIME.
I GOT A FLAT. WE WERE FIXING IT.
YEAH. GO HELP LUG SOME BOXES, HUH?
WHO HAS YOUR BACK? WHO? OH, THAT'S RIGHT. ME, MOTHERFUCKER!

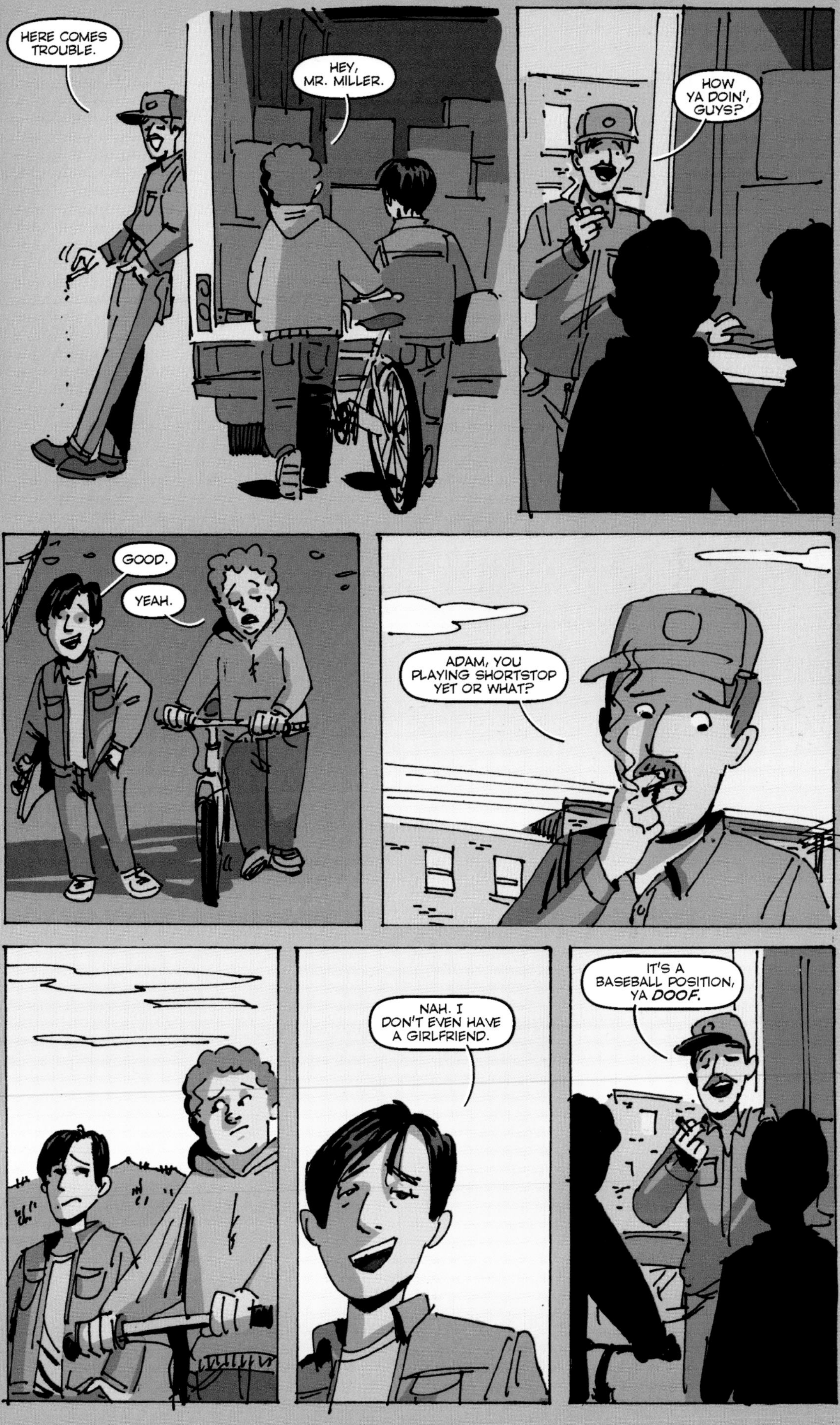
HERE COMES TROUBLE.
HEY, MR. MILLER.
HOW YA DOIN', GUYS?
GOOD.
YEAH.
ADAM, YOU PLAYING SHORTSTOP YET OR WHAT?
NAH. I DON'T EVEN HAVE A GIRLFRIEND.
IT'S A BASEBALL POSITION, YA *DOOF*.

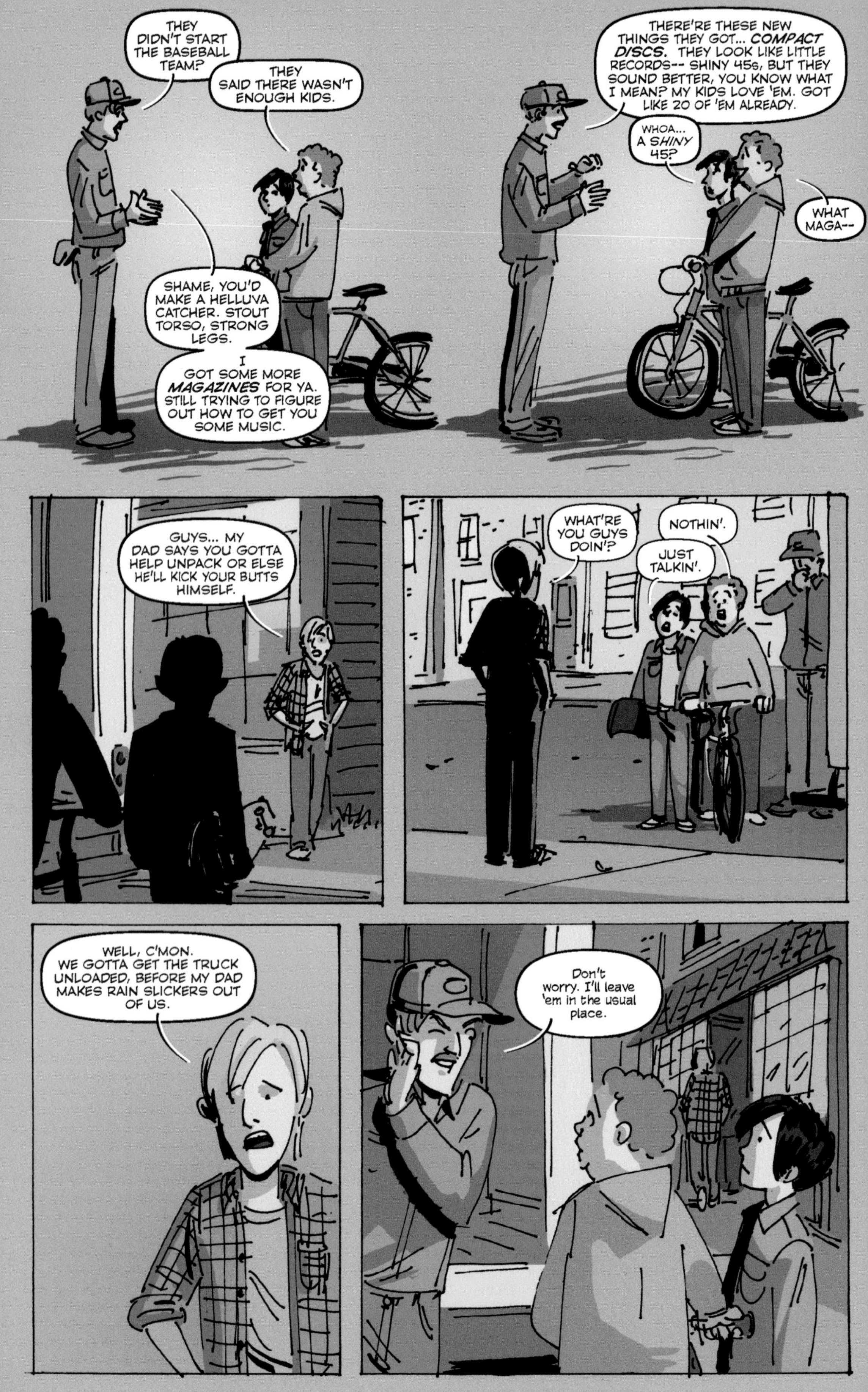
THEY DIDN'T START THE BASEBALL TEAM?
THEY SAID THERE WASN'T ENOUGH KIDS.
SHAME, YOU'D MAKE A HELLUVA CATCHER. STOUT TORSO, STRONG LEGS.
I GOT SOME MORE MAGAZINES FOR YA. STILL TRYING TO FIGURE OUT HOW TO GET YOU SOME MUSIC.
THERE'RE THESE NEW THINGS THEY GOT... COMPACT DISCS. THEY LOOK LIKE LITTLE RECORDS-- SHINY 45s, BUT THEY SOUND BETTER, YOU KNOW WHAT I MEAN? MY KIDS LOVE 'EM. GOT LIKE 20 OF 'EM ALREADY.
WHOA... A SHINY 45?
WHAT MAGA--
GUYS... MY DAD SAYS YOU GOTTA HELP UNPACK OR ELSE HE'LL KICK YOUR BUTTS HIMSELF.
WHAT'RE YOU GUYS DOIN'?
NOTHIN'.
JUST TALKIN'.
WELL, C'MON. WE GOTTA GET THE TRUCK UNLOADED, BEFORE MY DAD MAKES RAIN SLICKERS OUT OF US.
Don't worry. I'll leave 'em in the usual place.

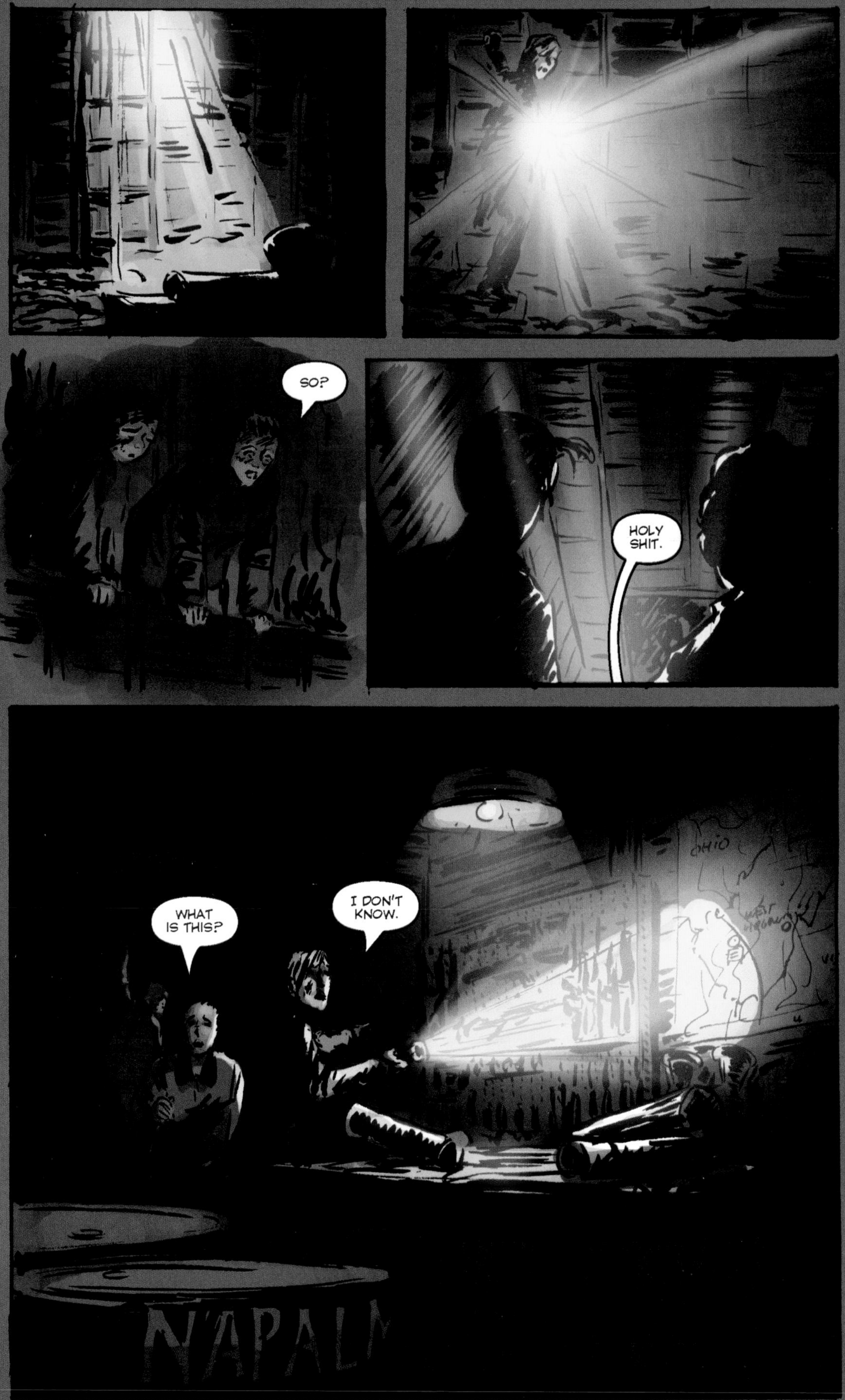
SO?
HOLY SHIT.
WHAT IS THIS?
I DON'T KNOW.
OHIO
NAPAL

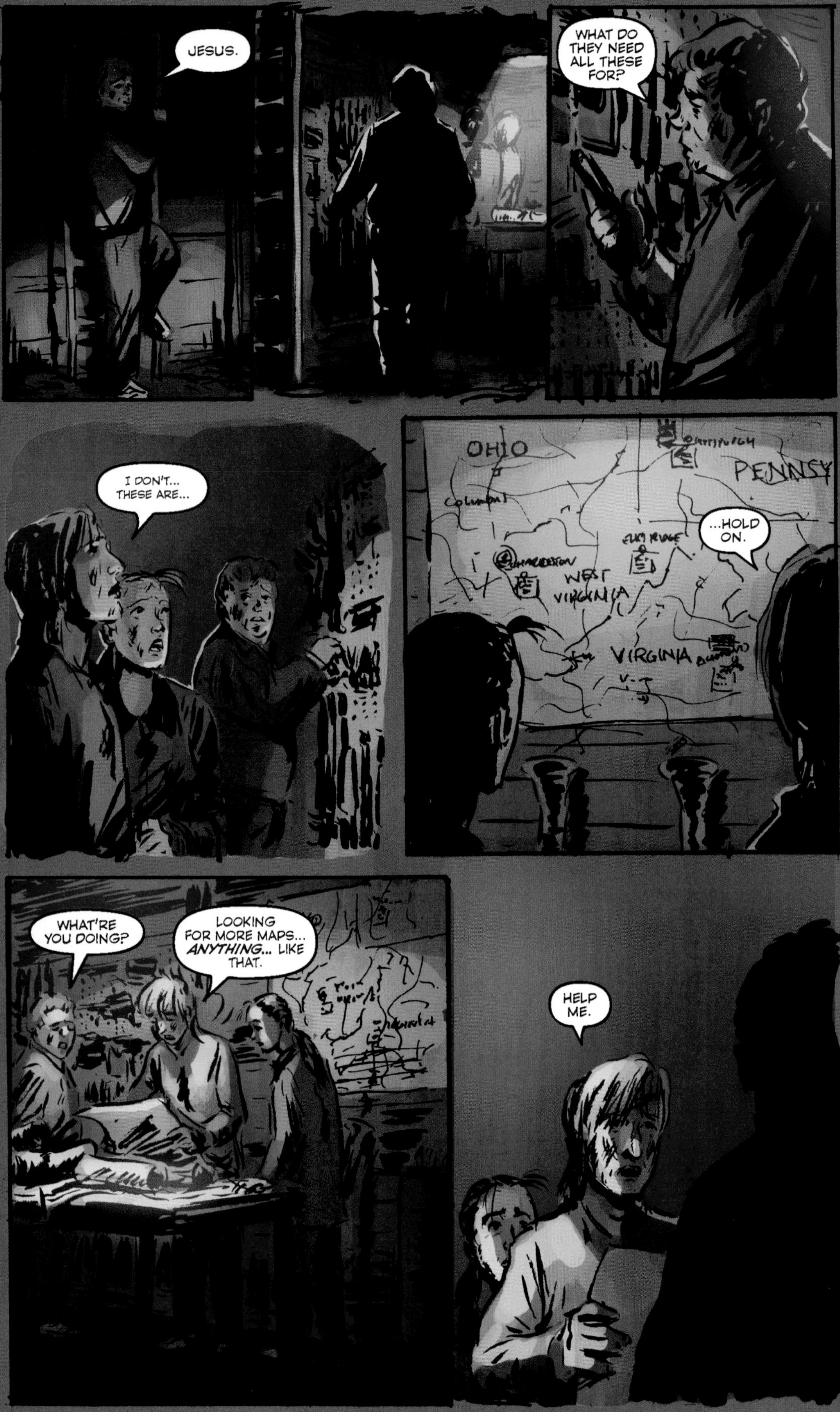
JESUS.
WHAT DO THEY NEED ALL THESE FOR?
I DON'T... THESE ARE...
OHIO
PENNSY
WEST VIRGINIA
VIRGINIA
...HOLD ON.
WHAT'RE YOU DOING?
LOOKING FOR MORE MAPS... *ANYTHING*... LIKE THAT.
HELP ME.

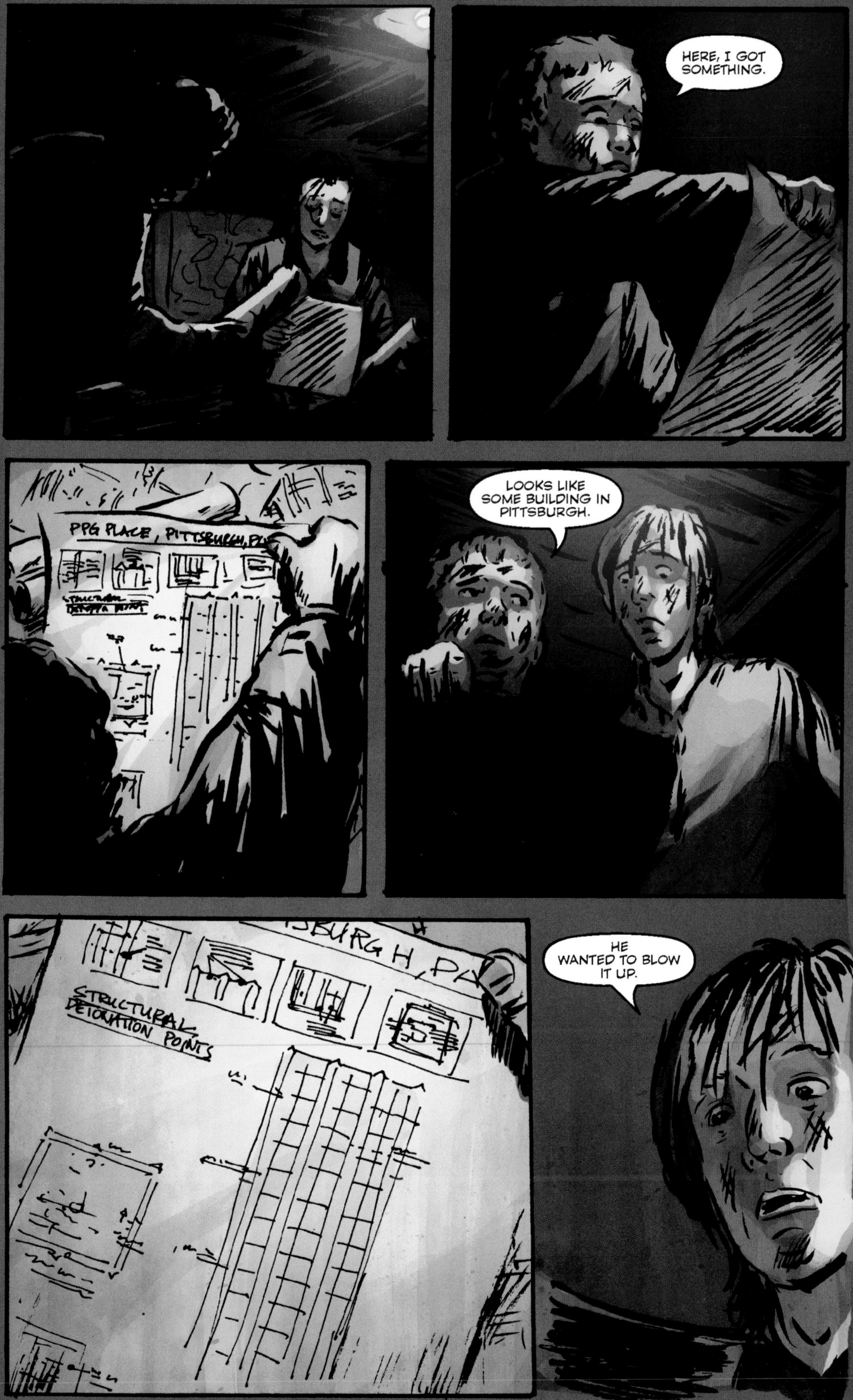
HERE, I GOT SOMETHING.
PPG PLACE, PITTSBURGH,
LOOKS LIKE SOME BUILDING IN PITTSBURGH.
STRUCTURAL DETONATION POINTS
HE WANTED TO BLOW IT UP.

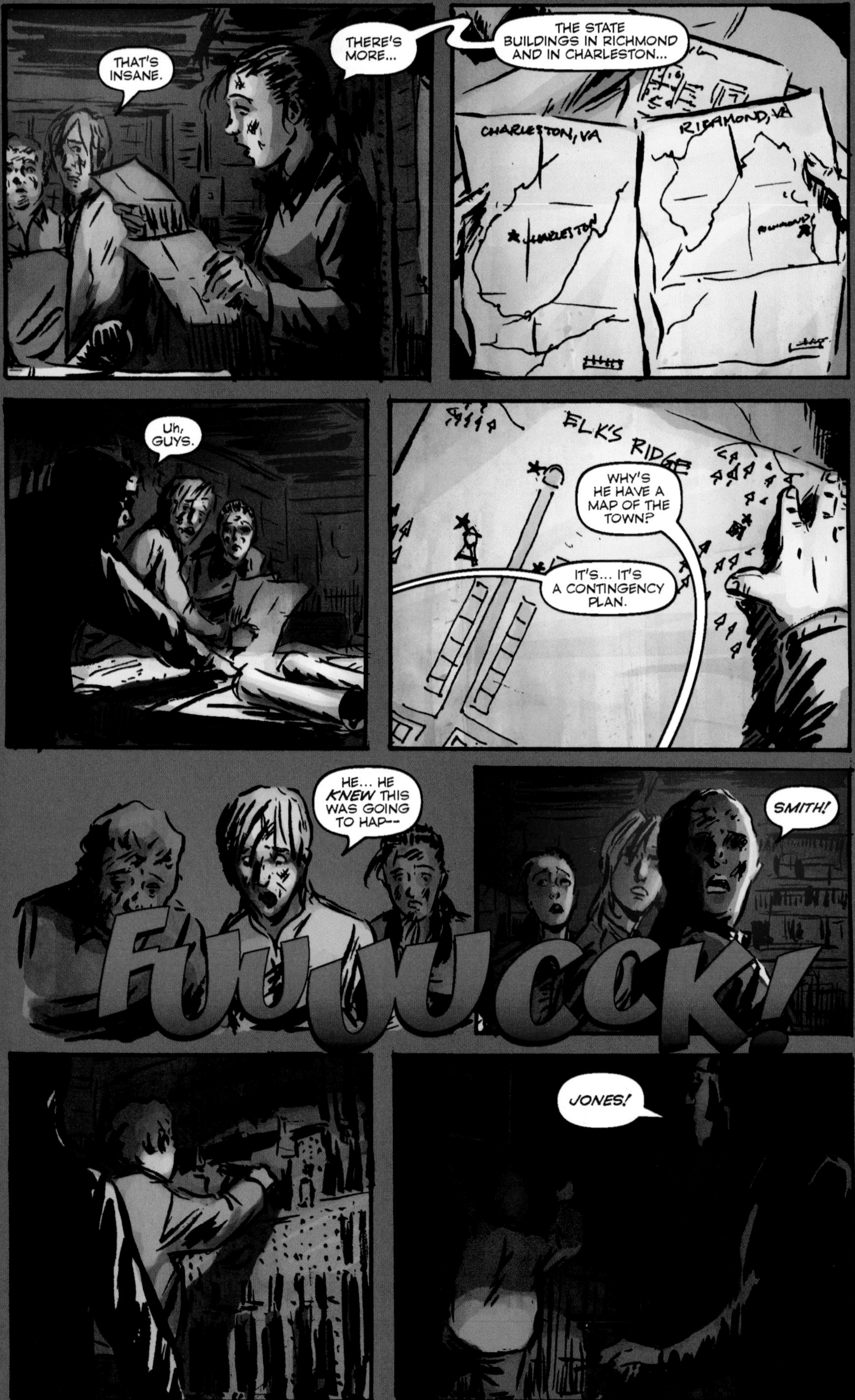
THAT'S INSANE.
THERE'S MORE...
THE STATE BUILDINGS IN RICHMOND AND IN CHARLESTON...
CHARLESTON, VA
RICHMOND, VA
CHARLESTON
Uh, GUYS.
ELK'S RIDGE
WHY'S HE HAVE A MAP OF THE TOWN?
IT'S... IT'S A CONTINGENCY PLAN.
HE... HE *KNEW* THIS WAS GOING TO HAP--
FUUUUCCK!
SMITH!
JONES!

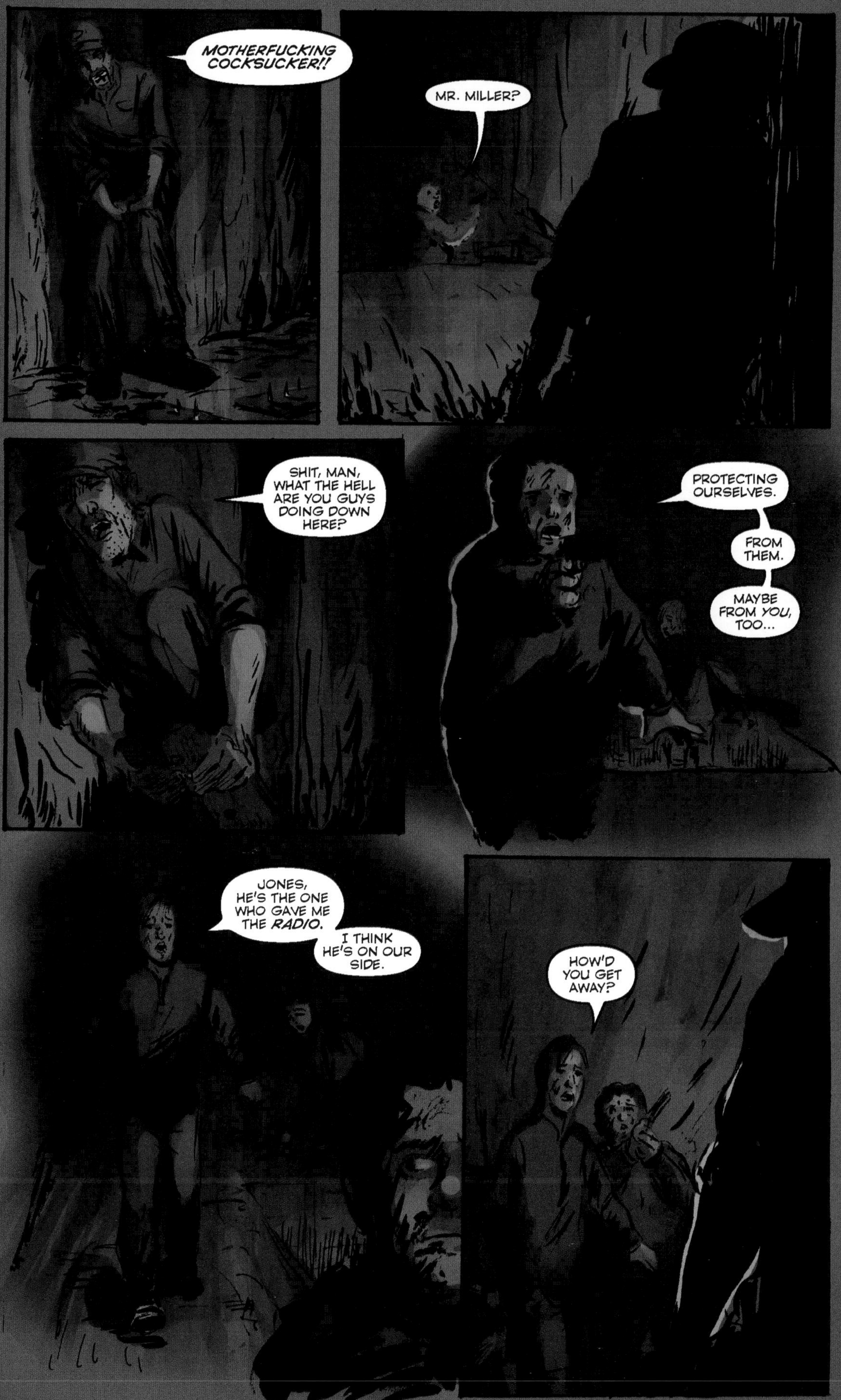
MOTHERFUCKING COCKSUCKER!!
MR. MILLER?
SHIT, MAN, WHAT THE HELL ARE YOU GUYS DOING DOWN HERE?
PROTECTING OURSELVES.
FROM THEM.
MAYBE FROM YOU, TOO...
JONES, HE'S THE ONE WHO GAVE ME THE RADIO.
I THINK HE'S ON OUR SIDE.
HOW'D YOU GET AWAY?

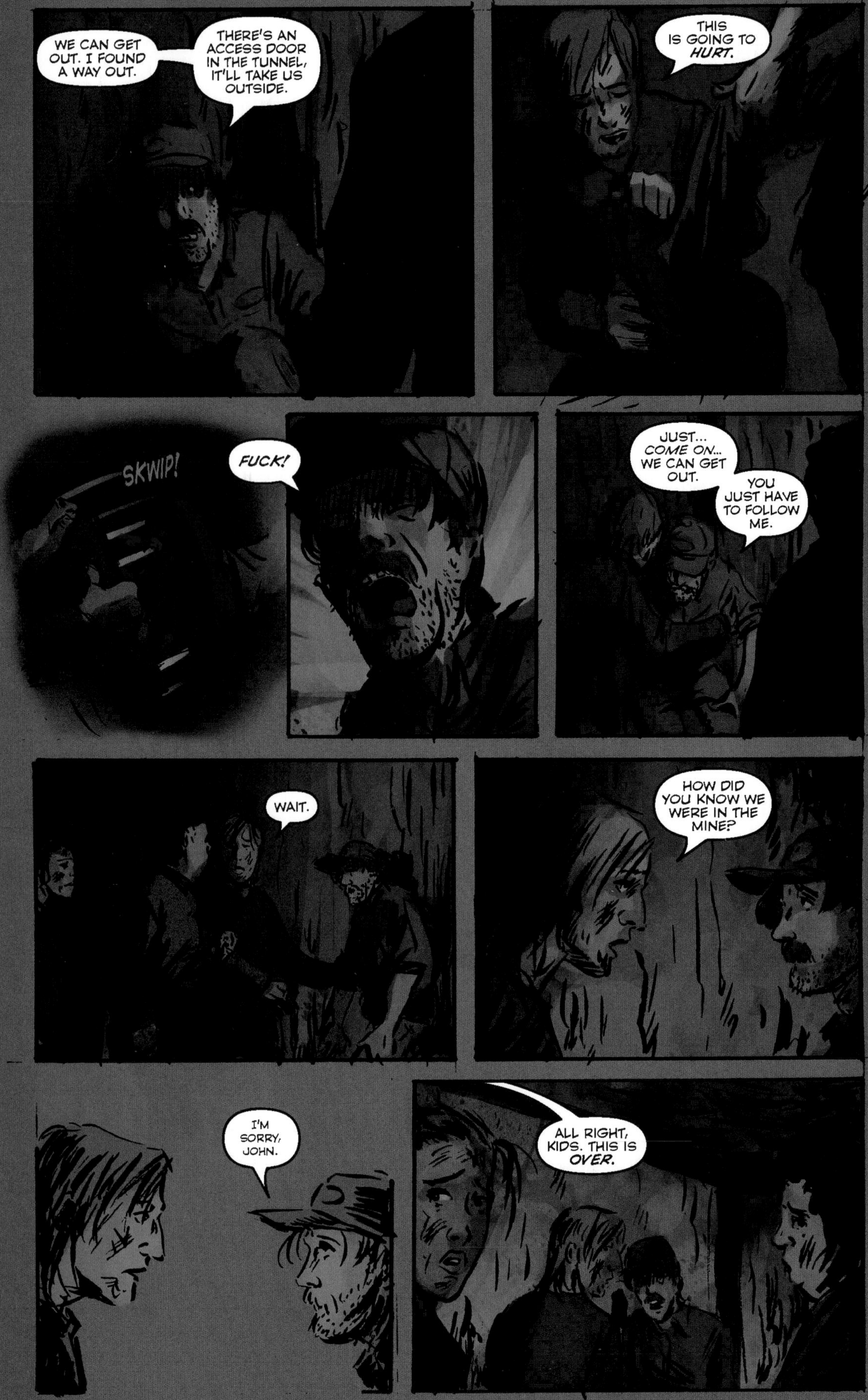
WE CAN GET OUT. I FOUND A WAY OUT.
THERE'S AN ACCESS DOOR IN THE TUNNEL, IT'LL TAKE US OUTSIDE.
THIS IS GOING TO HURT.
SKWIP!
FUCK!
JUST... COME ON... WE CAN GET OUT.
YOU JUST HAVE TO FOLLOW ME.
WAIT.
HOW DID YOU KNOW WE WERE IN THE MINE?
I'M SORRY, JOHN.
ALL RIGHT, KIDS. THIS IS OVER.

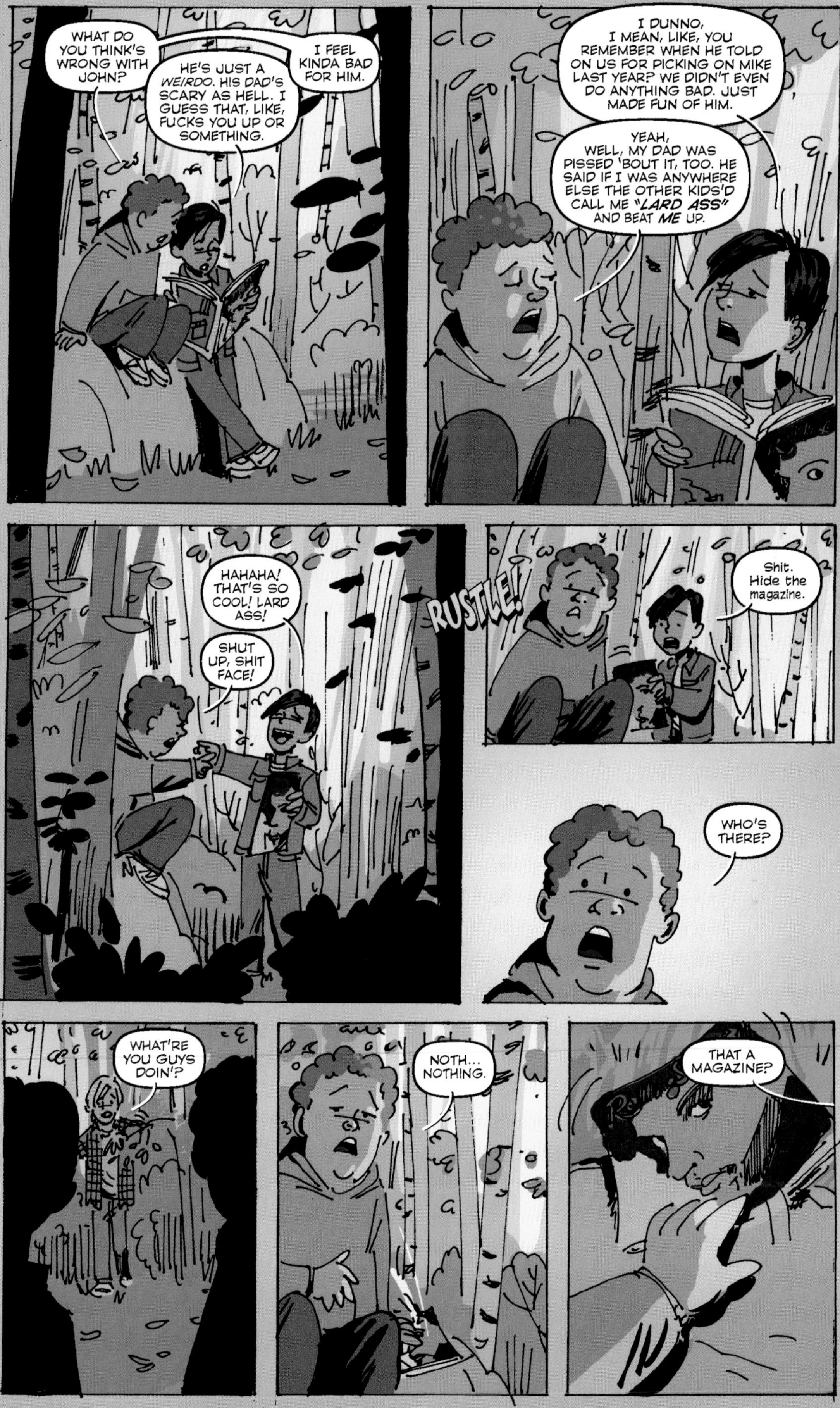

WHAT DO YOU THINK'S WRONG WITH JOHN?
I FEEL KINDA BAD FOR HIM.
HE'S JUST A WEIRDO. HIS DAD'S SCARY AS HELL. I GUESS THAT, LIKE, FUCKS YOU UP OR SOMETHING.
I DUNNO, I MEAN, LIKE, YOU REMEMBER WHEN HE TOLD ON US FOR PICKING ON MIKE LAST YEAR? WE DIDN'T EVEN DO ANYTHING BAD. JUST MADE FUN OF HIM.
YEAH, WELL, MY DAD WAS PISSED 'BOUT IT, TOO. HE SAID IF I WAS ANYWHERE ELSE THE OTHER KIDS'D CALL ME "LARD ASS" AND BEAT ME UP.
HAHAHA! THAT'S SO COOL! LARD ASS!
SHUT UP, SHIT FACE!
RUSTLE!
Shit. Hide the magazine.
WHO'S THERE?
WHAT'RE YOU GUYS DOIN'?
NOTH... NOTHING.
THAT A MAGAZINE?

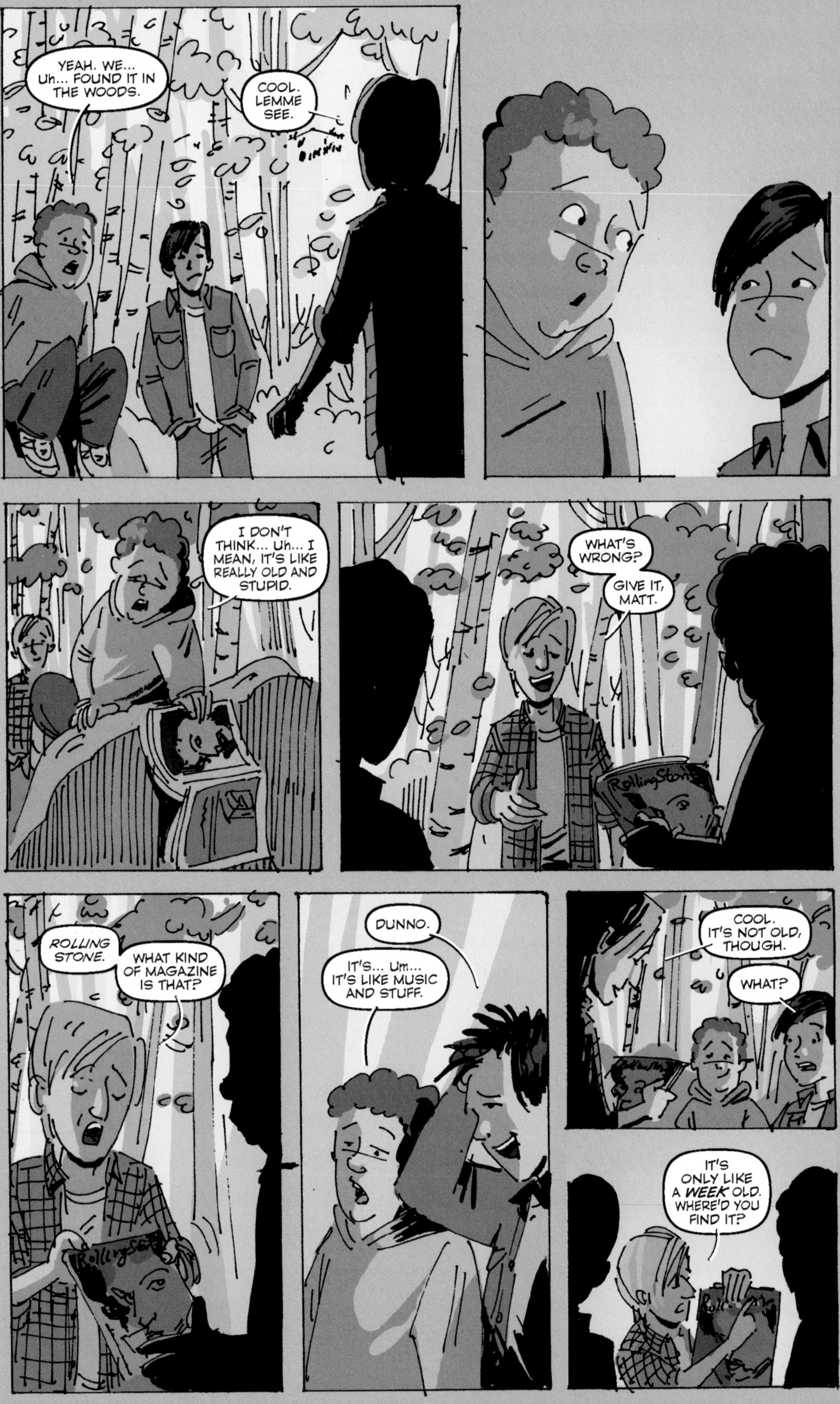
YEAH. WE... Uh... FOUND IT IN THE WOODS.
COOL. LEMME SEE.
I DON'T THINK... Uh... I MEAN, IT'S LIKE REALLY OLD AND STUPID.
WHAT'S WRONG?
GIVE IT, MATT.
ROLLING STONE.
WHAT KIND OF MAGAZINE IS THAT?
DUNNO.
IT'S... Um... IT'S LIKE MUSIC AND STUFF.
COOL. IT'S NOT OLD, THOUGH.
WHAT?
IT'S ONLY LIKE A *WEEK* OLD. WHERE'D YOU FIND IT?

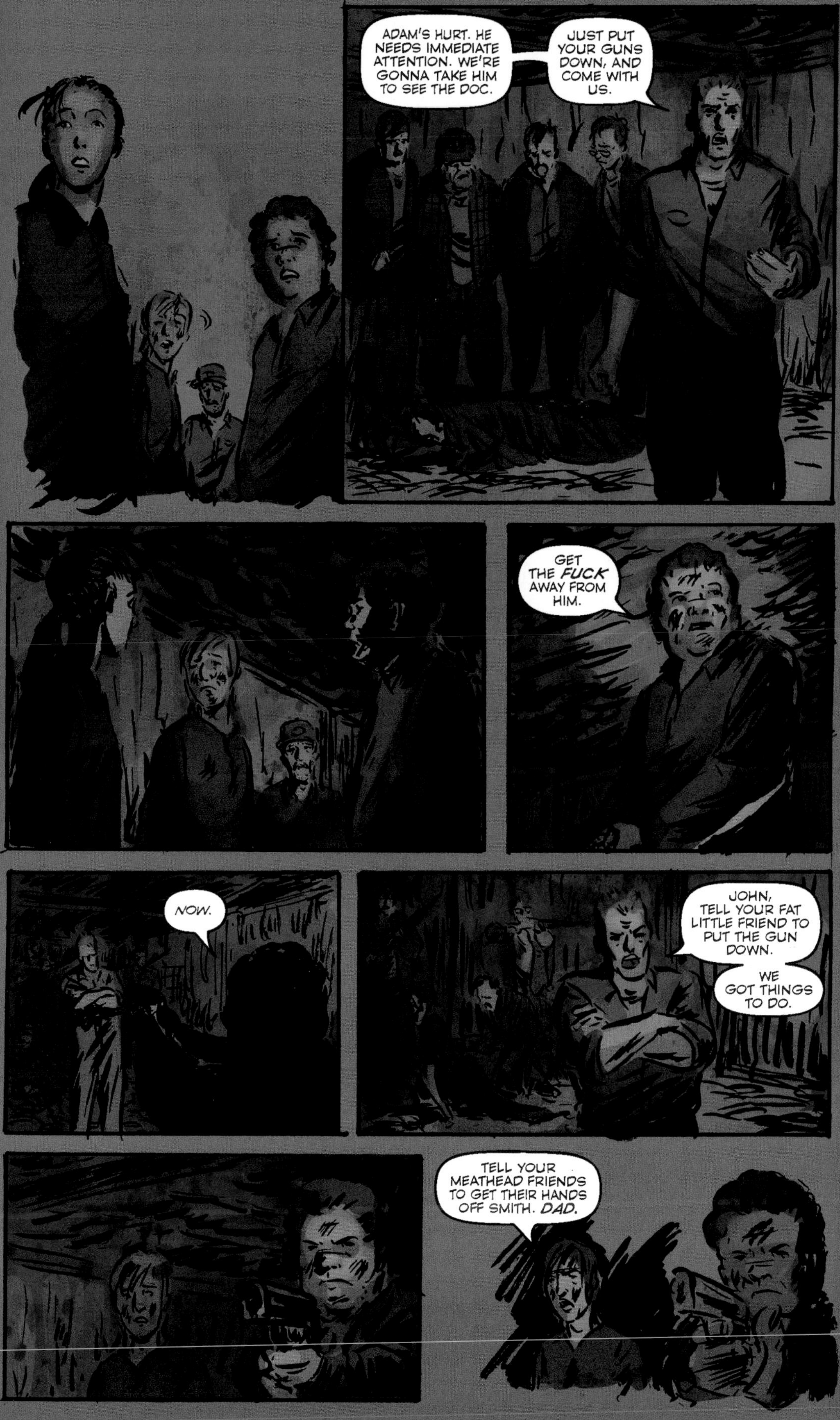
ADAM'S HURT. HE NEEDS IMMEDIATE ATTENTION. WE'RE GONNA TAKE HIM TO SEE THE DOC.
JUST PUT YOUR GUNS DOWN, AND COME WITH US.
GET THE *FUCK* AWAY FROM HIM.
NOW.
JOHN, TELL YOUR FAT LITTLE FRIEND TO PUT THE GUN DOWN.
WE GOT THINGS TO DO.
TELL YOUR MEATHEAD FRIENDS TO GET THEIR HANDS OFF SMITH. *DAD.*

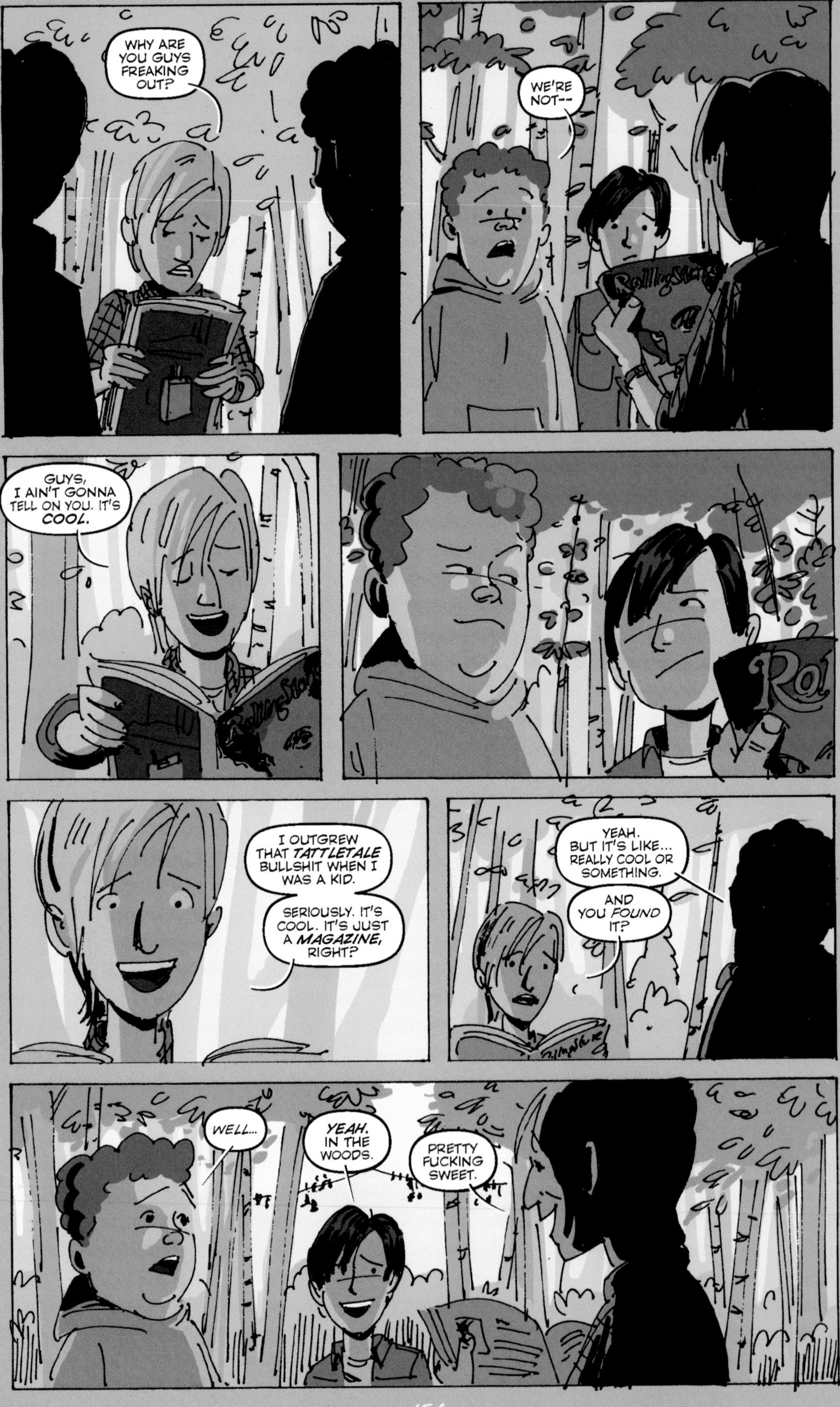

WHY ARE YOU GUYS FREAKING OUT?
WE'RE NOT--
GUYS, I AIN'T GONNA TELL ON YOU. IT'S *COOL.*
I OUTGREW THAT *TATTLETALE* BULLSHIT WHEN I WAS A KID.
SERIOUSLY. IT'S COOL. IT'S JUST A *MAGAZINE,* RIGHT?
YEAH. BUT IT'S LIKE... REALLY COOL OR SOMETHING.
AND YOU *FOUND* IT?
WELL...
YEAH. IN THE WOODS.
PRETTY FUCKING SWEET.

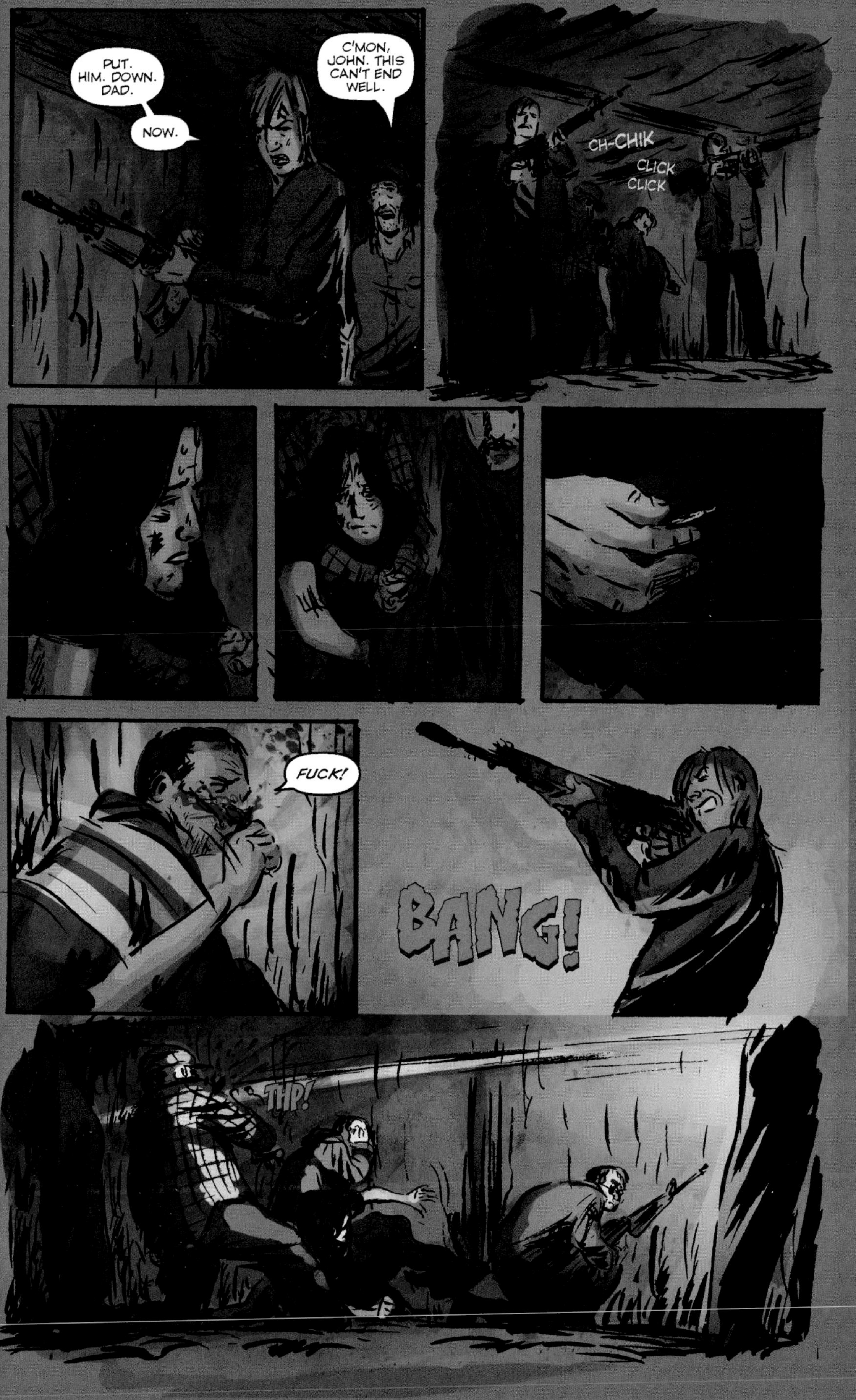
PUT. HIM. DOWN. DAD.
NOW.
C'MON, JOHN. THIS CAN'T END WELL.
CH-CHIK
CLICK CLICK
FUCK!
BANG!
THP!

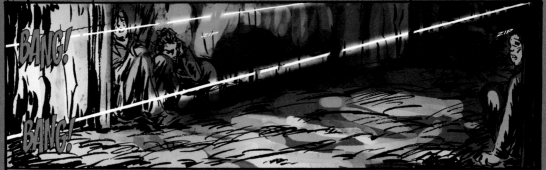

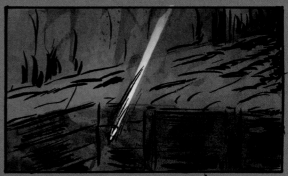

BANG!
BANG!
BANG!
BANG!
ZIP
ZIP
BANG!
SPNNG!
WHAT'S THAT SMELL?
SOMETHING'S BURNING...
SMELLS LIKE A TIRE FIRE.
JOHN... THE NAPALM.

RUMMBLE

RUMMBLIE

CRACK!

ADAM!!

WHY WOULD YOU GUYS THINK I'D TELL?

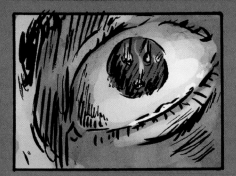

'CAUSE YOU'RE AS SCARED OF YOUR DAD AS WE ARE.

I'M NOT SCARED OF HIM.

I JUST FUCKING HATE HIM.

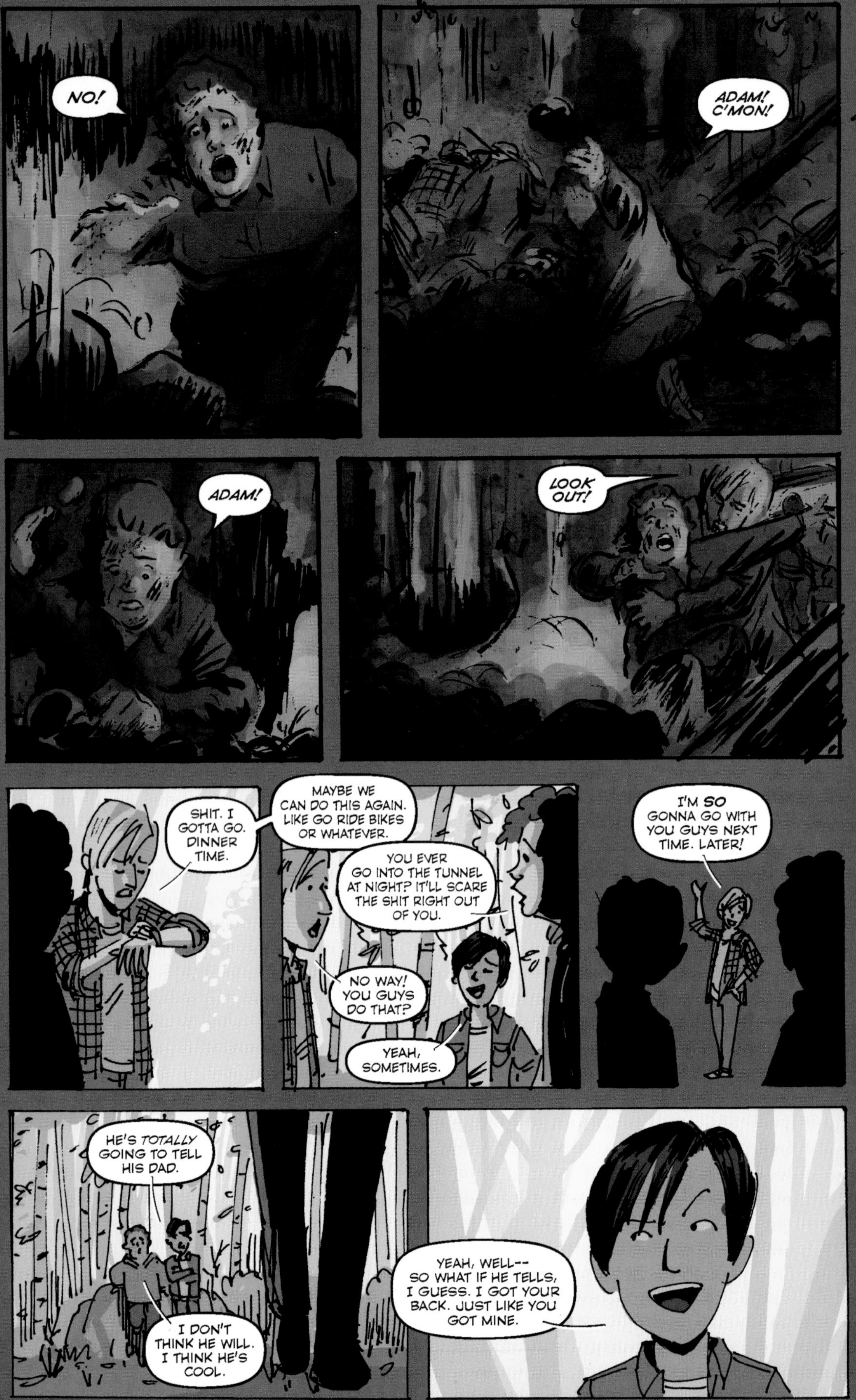
NO!
ADAM! C'MON!
ADAM!
LOOK OUT!
SHIT. I GOTTA GO. DINNER TIME.
MAYBE WE CAN DO THIS AGAIN. LIKE GO RIDE BIKES OR WHATEVER.
YOU EVER GO INTO THE TUNNEL AT NIGHT? IT'LL SCARE THE SHIT RIGHT OUT OF YOU.
NO WAY! YOU GUYS DO THAT?
YEAH, SOMETIMES.
I'M SO GONNA GO WITH YOU GUYS NEXT TIME. LATER!
HE'S TOTALLY GOING TO TELL HIS DAD.
I DON'T THINK HE WILL. I THINK HE'S COOL.
YEAH, WELL-- SO WHAT IF HE TELLS, I GUESS. I GOT YOUR BACK. JUST LIKE YOU GOT MINE.

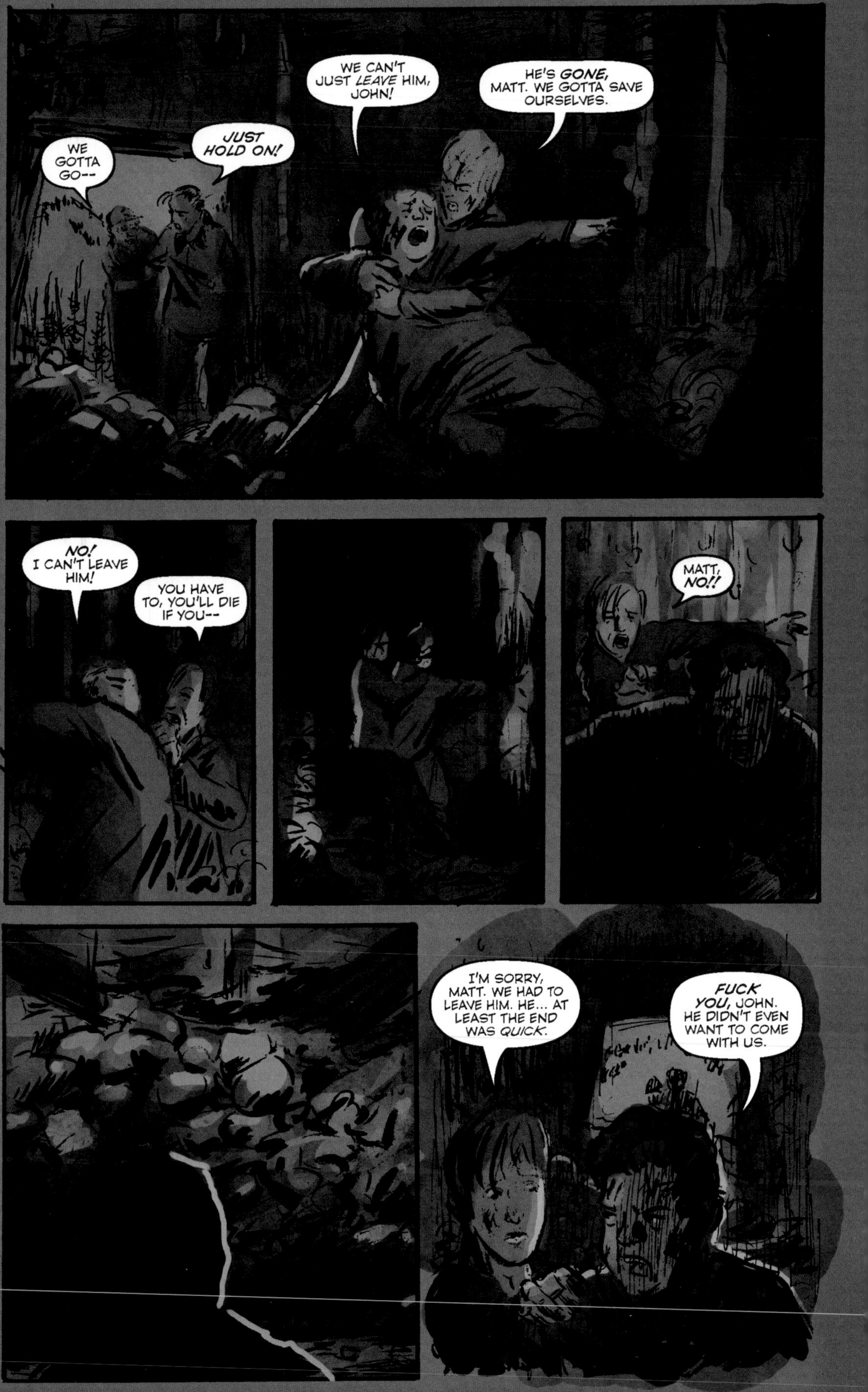
WE GOTTA GO--
JUST HOLD ON!
WE CAN'T JUST LEAVE HIM, JOHN!
HE'S GONE, MATT. WE GOTTA SAVE OURSELVES.
NO! I CAN'T LEAVE HIM!
YOU HAVE TO, YOU'LL DIE IF YOU--
MATT, NO!!
I'M SORRY, MATT. WE HAD TO LEAVE HIM. HE... AT LEAST THE END WAS QUICK.
FUCK YOU, JOHN. HE DIDN'T EVEN WANT TO COME WITH US.

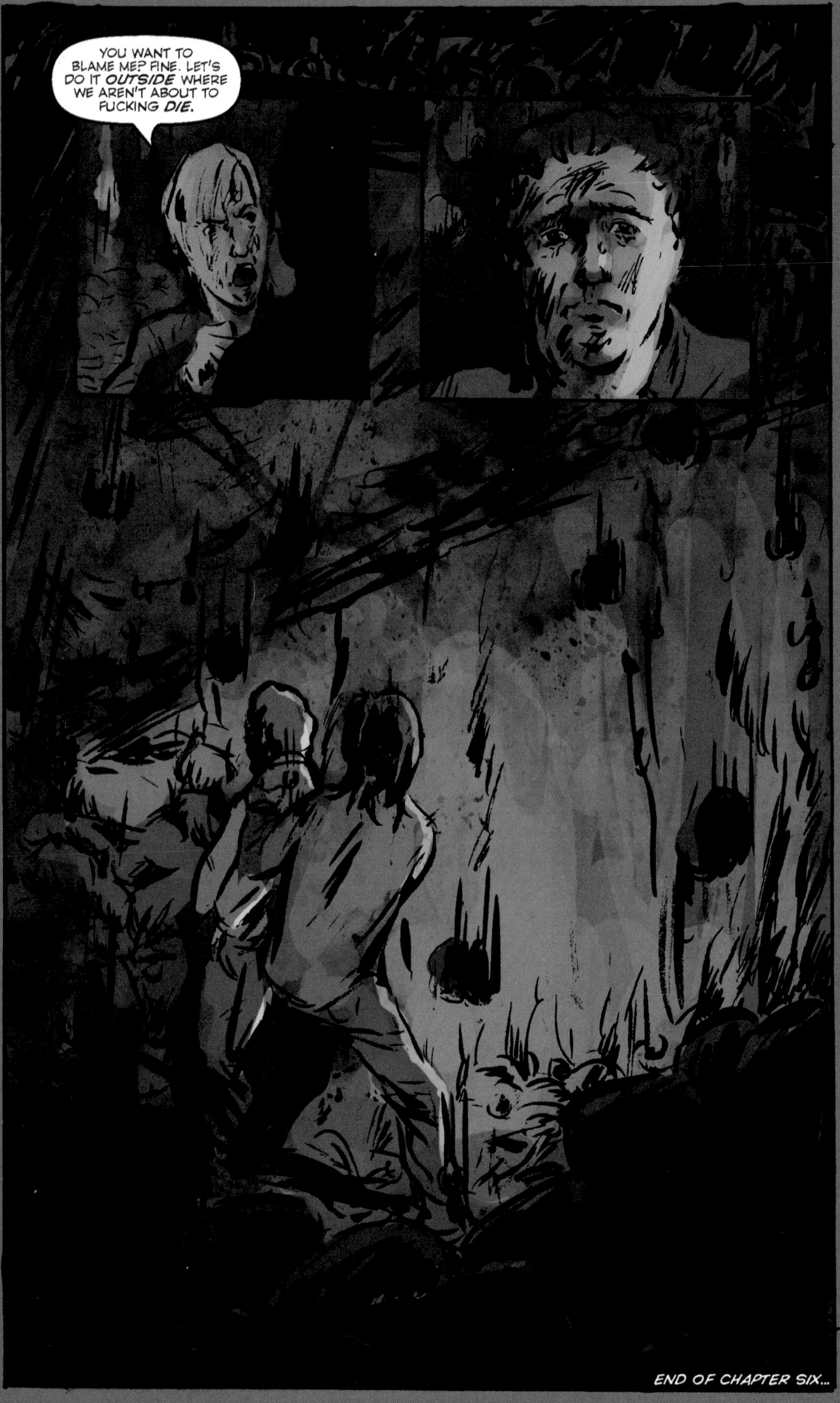
YOU WANT TO BLAME ME? FINE. LET'S DO IT OUTSIDE WHERE WE AREN'T ABOUT TO FUCKING DIE.
END OF CHAPTER SIX...

Chapter Seven: Chaos

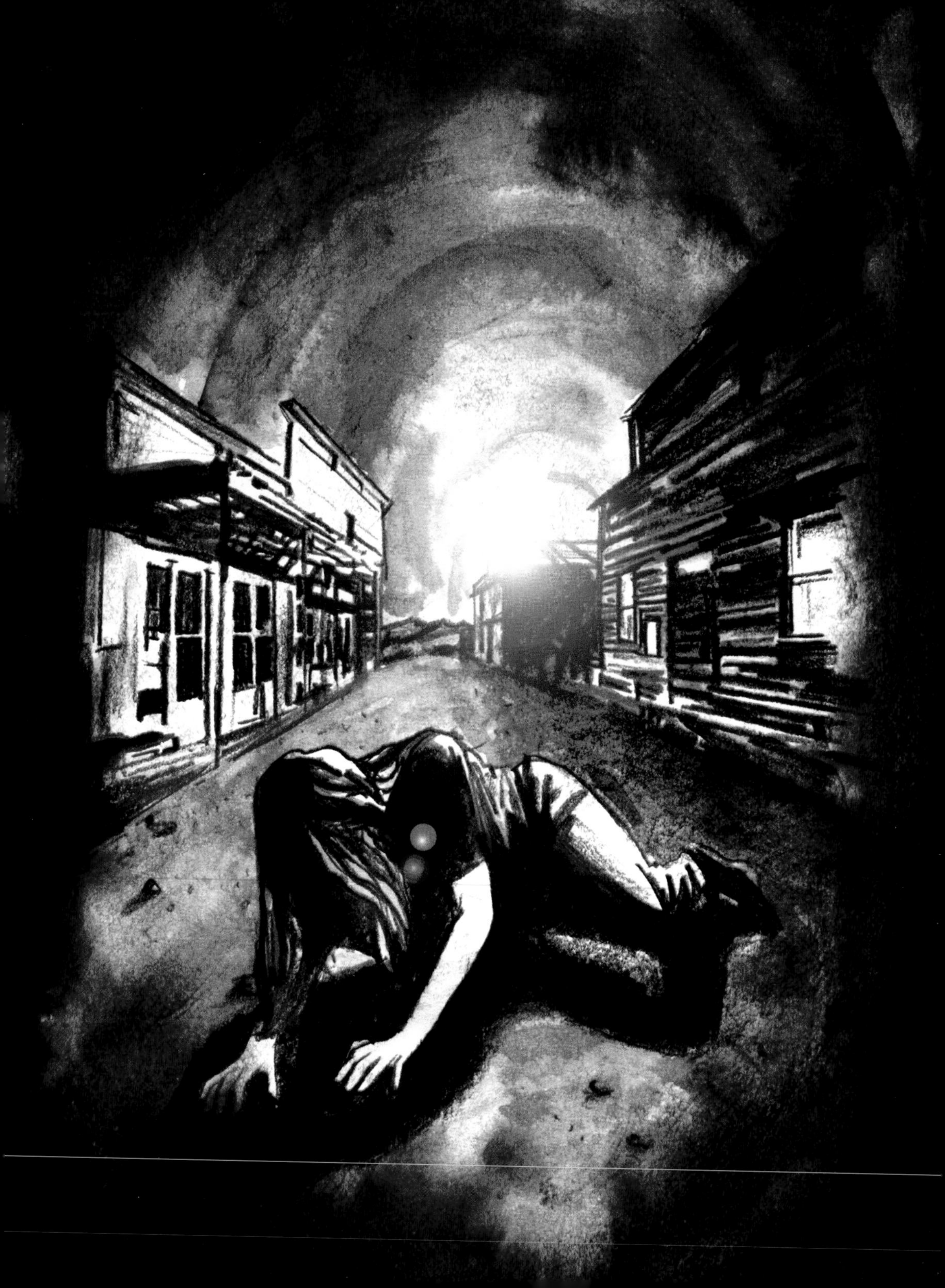

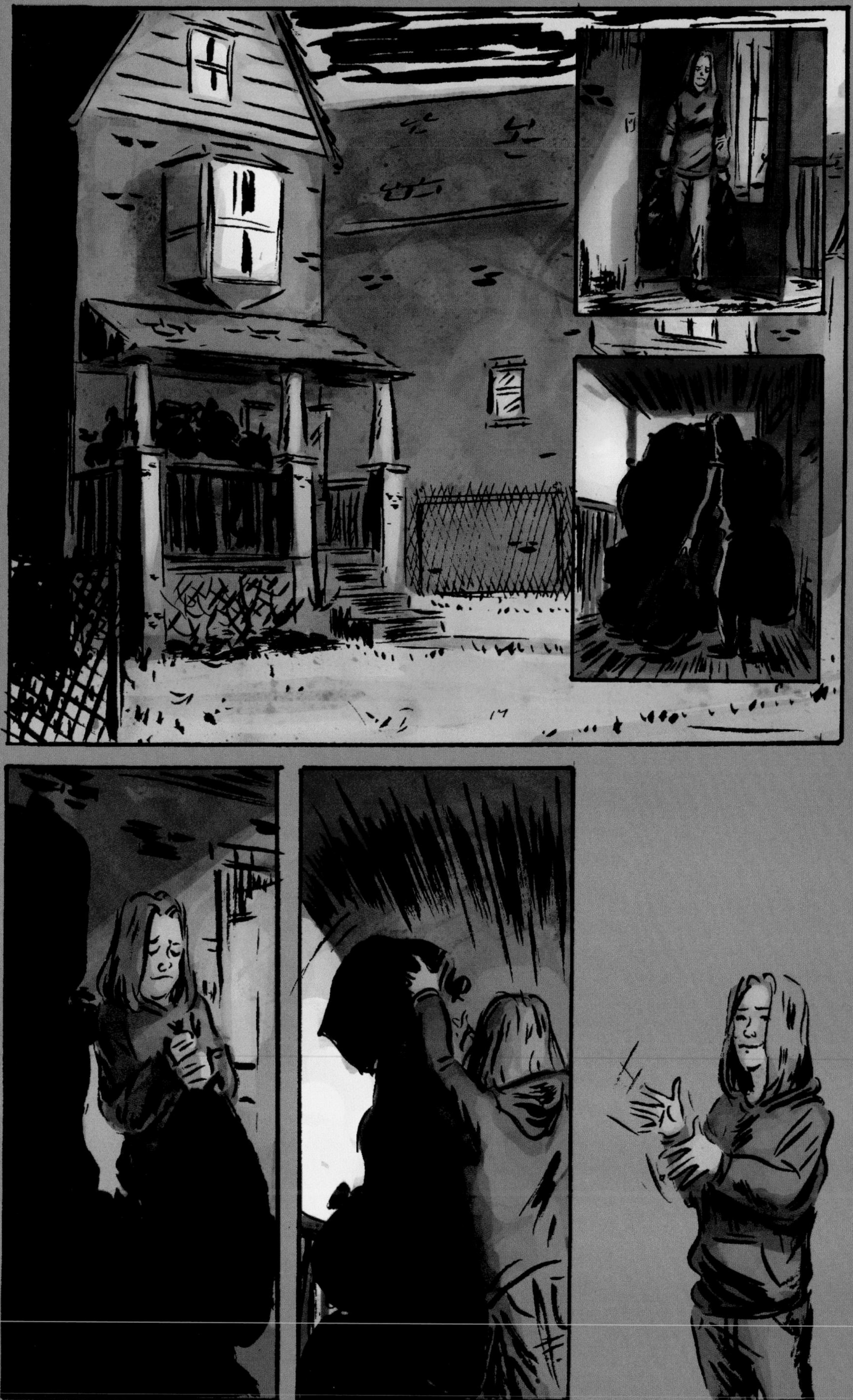

SARA...
WE NEED TO
TALK.

SURE, LINDA,
WHAT'S--

THIS
NEEDS TO
STOP.

I UNDERSTAND
THE GUNS, AND THE
FENCE, AND THE RULES.
IT'S *FINE*, IT'S THE LIFE
OUR HUSBANDS CHOSE
FOR US.

BUT THOSE
POLICEMEN... THEY
WERE JUST DOING
THEIR *JOB*.

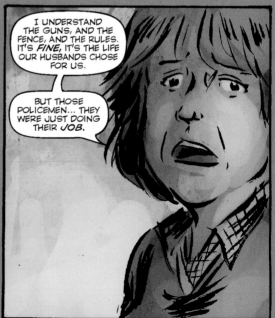

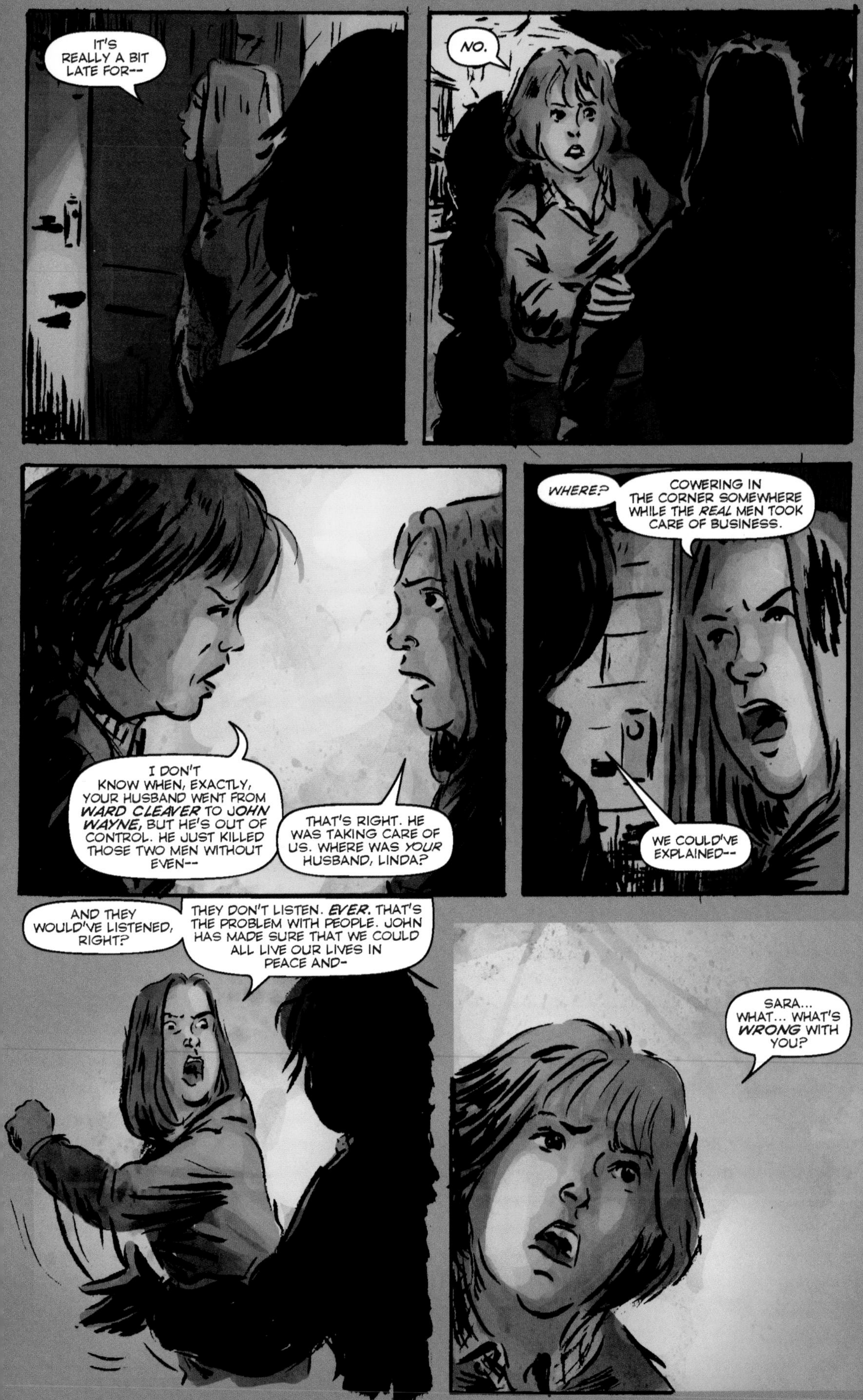
IT'S REALLY A BIT LATE FOR--
NO.
I DON'T KNOW WHEN, EXACTLY, YOUR HUSBAND WENT FROM WARD CLEAVER TO JOHN WAYNE, BUT HE'S OUT OF CONTROL. HE JUST KILLED THOSE TWO MEN WITHOUT EVEN--
THAT'S RIGHT. HE WAS TAKING CARE OF US. WHERE WAS YOUR HUSBAND, LINDA?
WHERE?
COWERING IN THE CORNER SOMEWHERE WHILE THE REAL MEN TOOK CARE OF BUSINESS.
WE COULD'VE EXPLAINED--
AND THEY WOULD'VE LISTENED, RIGHT?
THEY DON'T LISTEN. EVER. THAT'S THE PROBLEM WITH PEOPLE. JOHN HAS MADE SURE THAT WE COULD ALL LIVE OUR LIVES IN PEACE AND-
SARA... WHAT... WHAT'S WRONG WITH YOU?

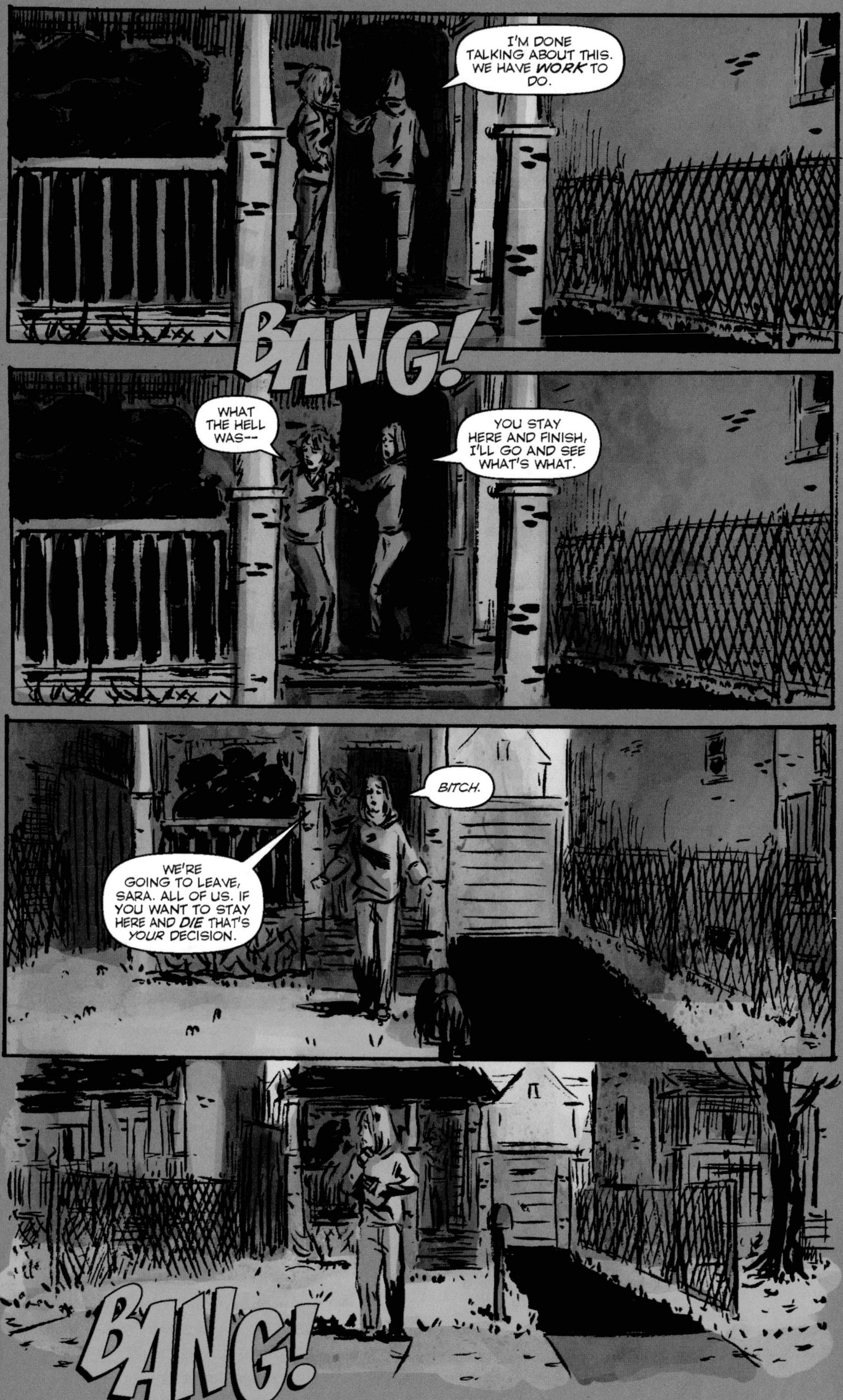
I'M DONE TALKING ABOUT THIS. WE HAVE WORK TO DO.
BANG!
WHAT THE HELL WAS--
YOU STAY HERE AND FINISH, I'LL GO AND SEE WHAT'S WHAT.
BITCH.
WE'RE GOING TO LEAVE, SARA. ALL OF US. IF YOU WANT TO STAY HERE AND DIE THAT'S YOUR DECISION.
BANG!

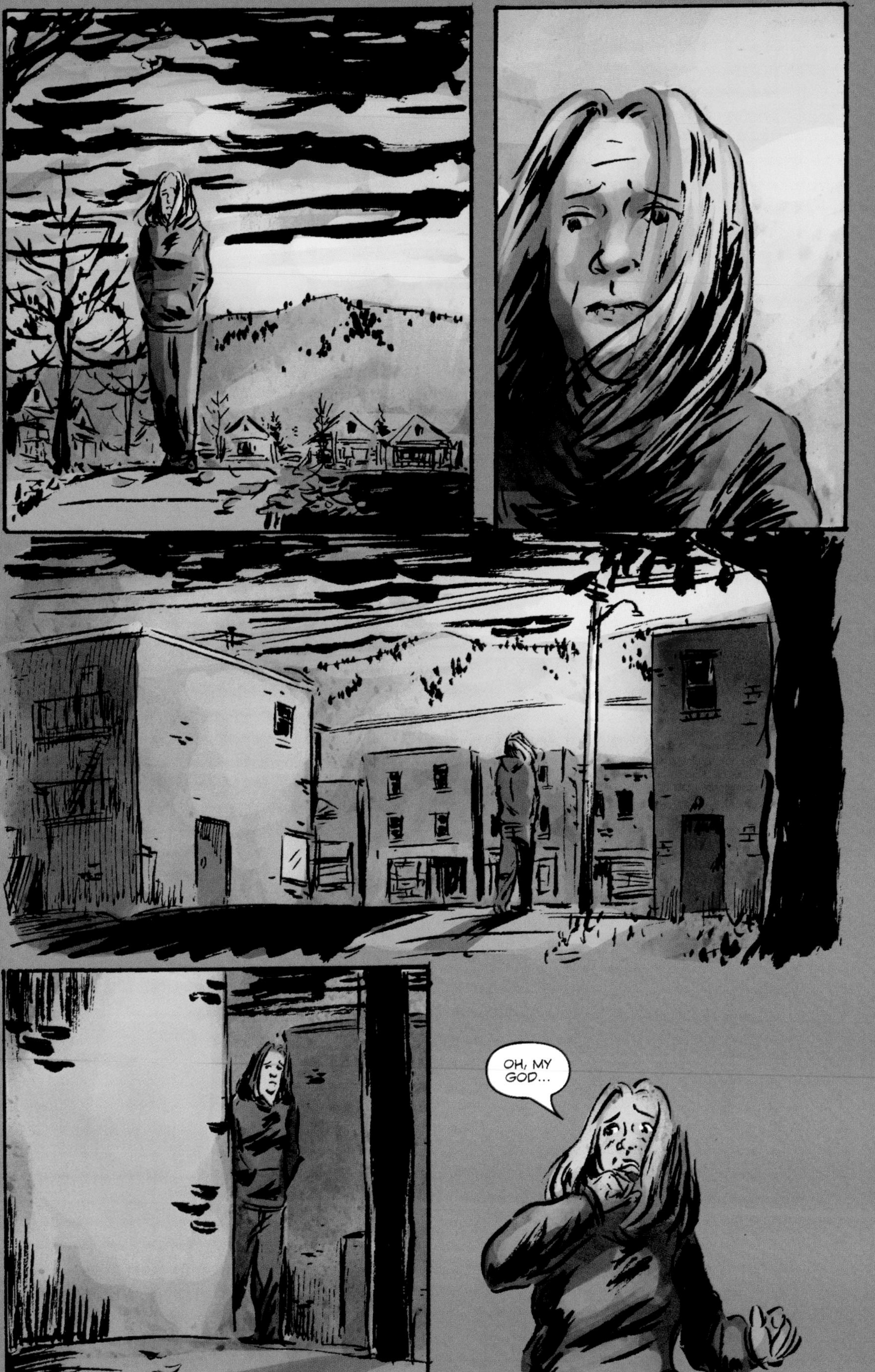
OH, MY GOD...

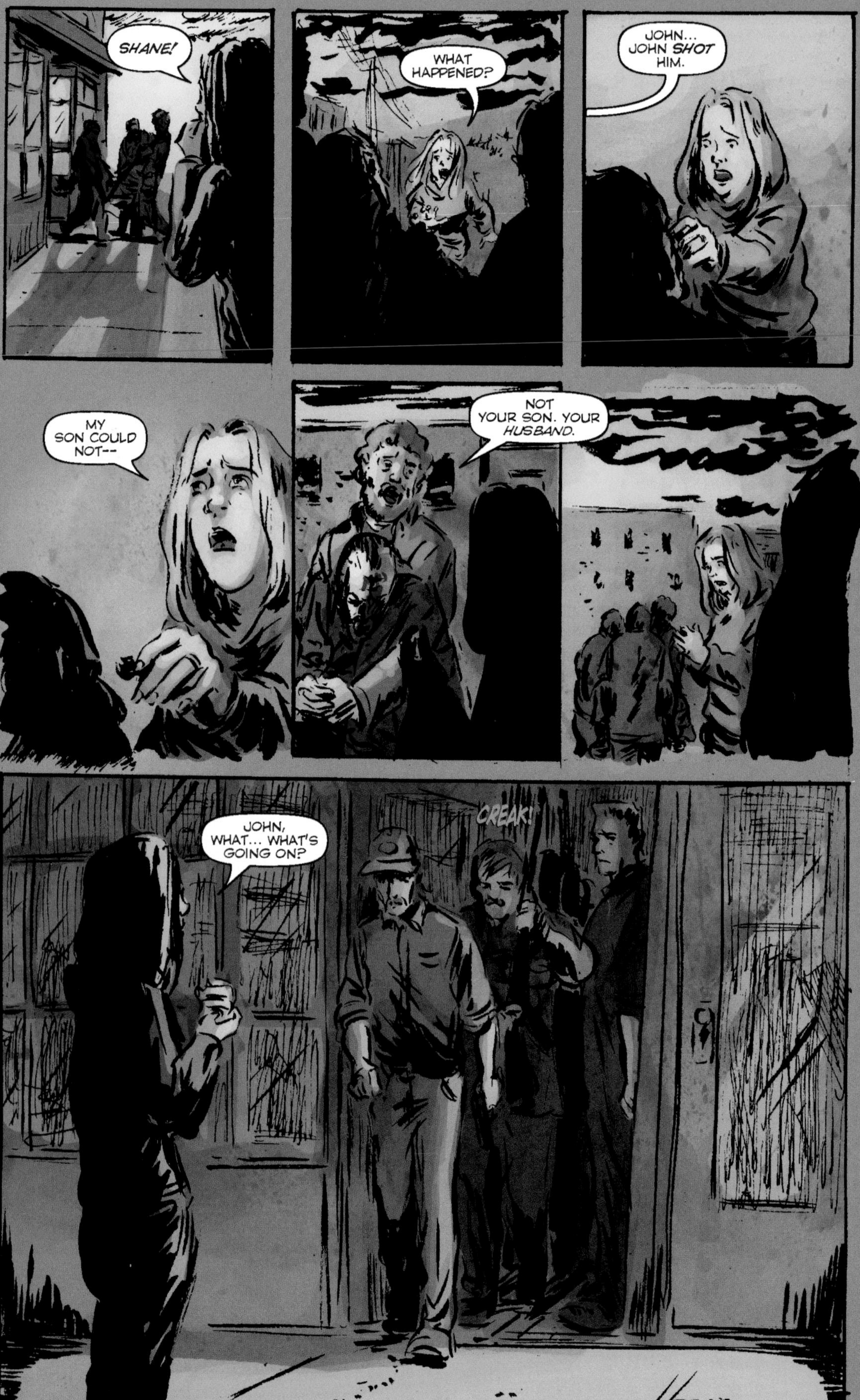
SHANE!
WHAT HAPPENED?
JOHN... JOHN SHOT HIM.
MY SON COULD NOT--
NOT YOUR SON. YOUR HUSBAND.
JOHN, WHAT... WHAT'S GOING ON?
CREAK!

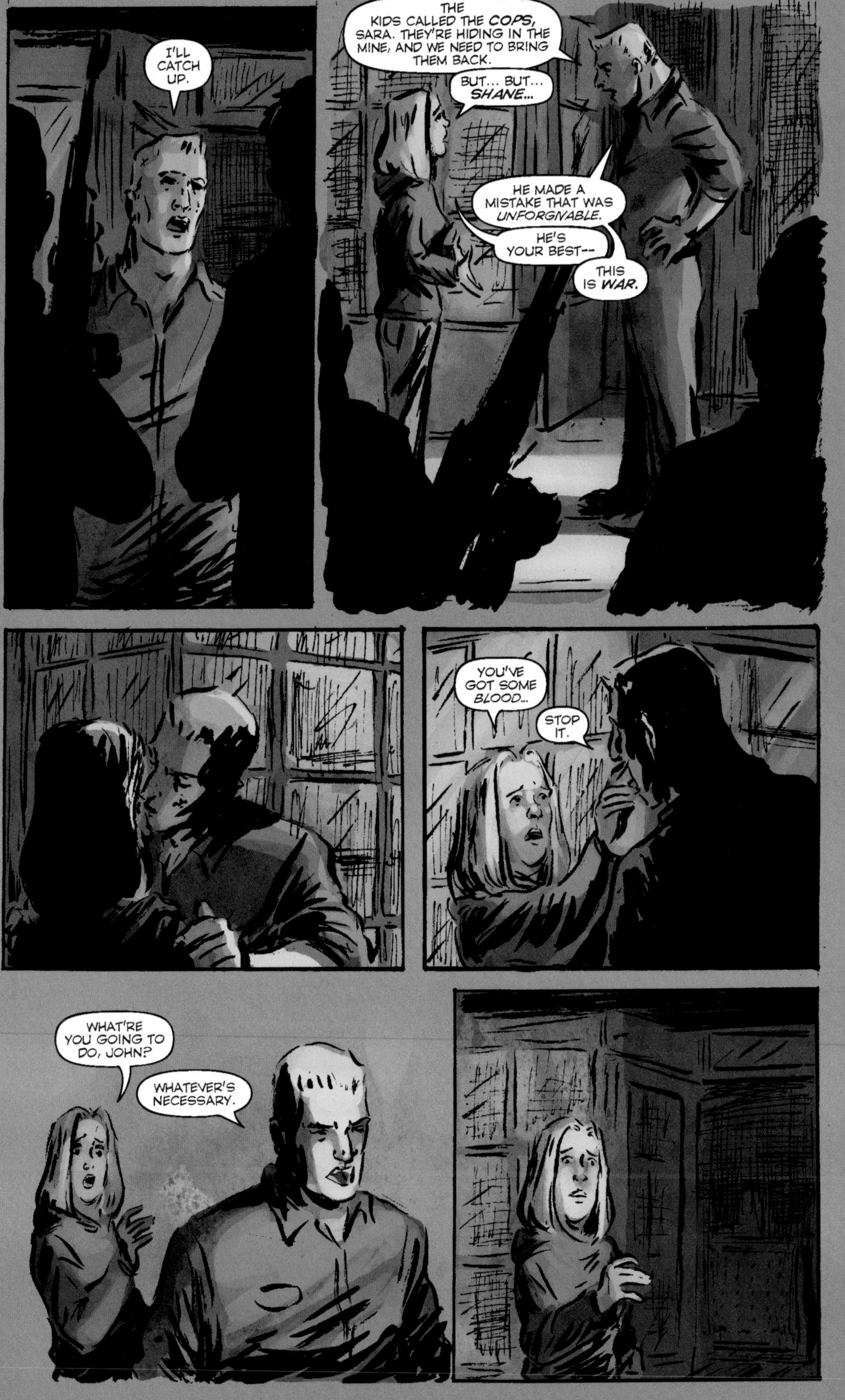
I'LL CATCH UP.
THE KIDS CALLED THE COPS, SARA. THEY'RE HIDING IN THE MINE, AND WE NEED TO BRING THEM BACK.
BUT... BUT... SHANE...
HE MADE A MISTAKE THAT WAS UNFORGIVABLE.
HE'S YOUR BEST--
THIS IS WAR.
YOU'VE GOT SOME BLOOD...
STOP IT.
WHAT'RE YOU GOING TO DO, JOHN?
WHATEVER'S NECESSARY.

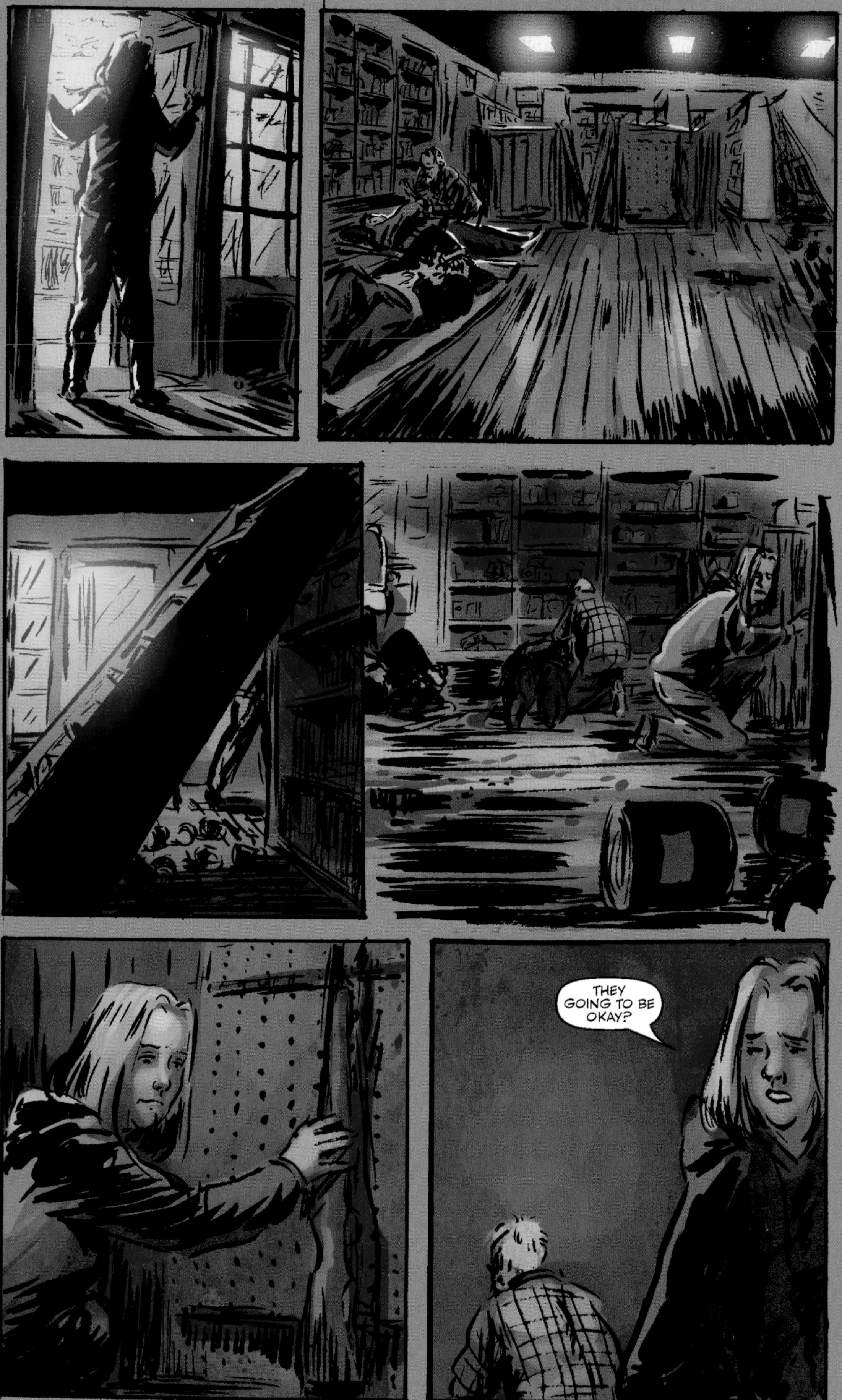
THEY GOING TO BE OKAY?

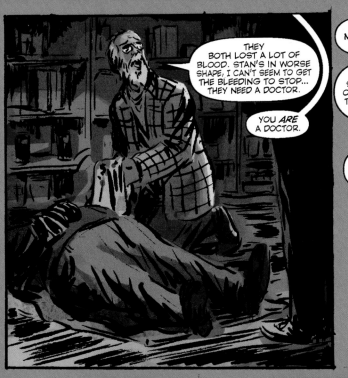

THEY BOTH LOST A LOT OF BLOOD. STAN'S IN WORSE SHAPE, I CAN'T SEEM TO GET THE BLEEDING TO STOP... THEY NEED A DOCTOR.

YOU *ARE* A DOCTOR.

NO. I WAS A MEDIC IN THE WAR 25 YEARS AGO, SARA.

I CAN BANDAGE A SCRAPED KNEE, OR PUT A *SLING* ON SOMEONE. HELL, I'VE EVEN TAKEN BULLETS OUTTA SOME OF THESE KNUCKLEHEADS. BUT THIS IS WORSE. THESE MEN NEED SOMEONE WHO KNOWS WHAT IN THE *HELL* THEY'RE DOING.

STEVE'S CONCUSSED ALL TO HELL AND HE--

YOU'LL HAVE TO MAKE DO.

THESE MEN WILL--

DIE LIKE SOLDIERS.

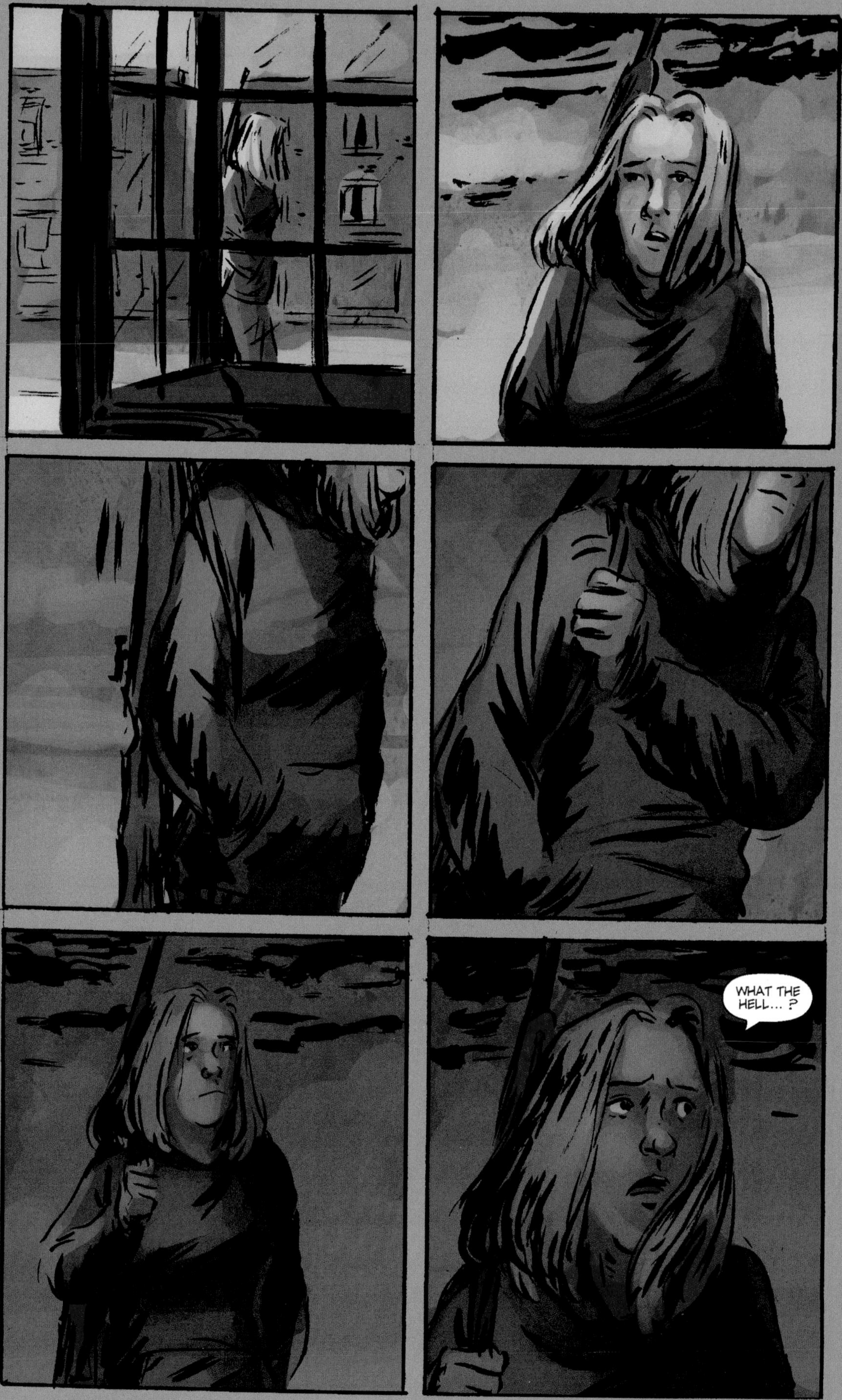
WHAT THE HELL... ?

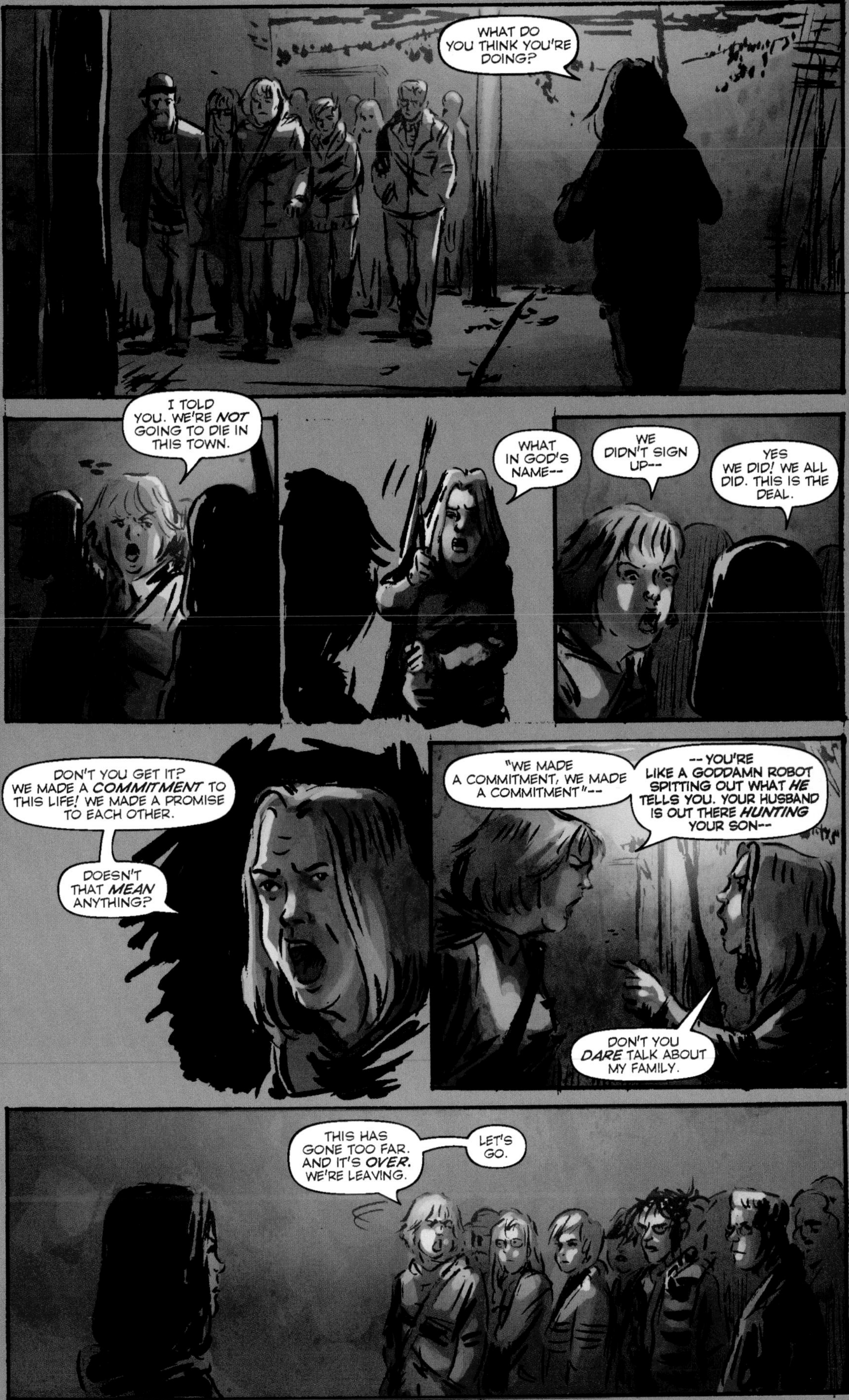
WHAT DO YOU THINK YOU'RE DOING?
I TOLD YOU. WE'RE NOT GOING TO DIE IN THIS TOWN.
WHAT IN GOD'S NAME--
WE DIDN'T SIGN UP--
YES WE DID! WE ALL DID. THIS IS THE DEAL.
DON'T YOU GET IT? WE MADE A COMMITMENT TO THIS LIFE! WE MADE A PROMISE TO EACH OTHER.
DOESN'T THAT MEAN ANYTHING?
"WE MADE A COMMITMENT, WE MADE A COMMITMENT"--
--YOU'RE LIKE A GODDAMN ROBOT SPITTING OUT WHAT HE TELLS YOU. YOUR HUSBAND IS OUT THERE HUNTING YOUR SON--
DON'T YOU DARE TALK ABOUT MY FAMILY.
THIS HAS GONE TOO FAR. AND IT'S OVER. WE'RE LEAVING.
LET'S GO.

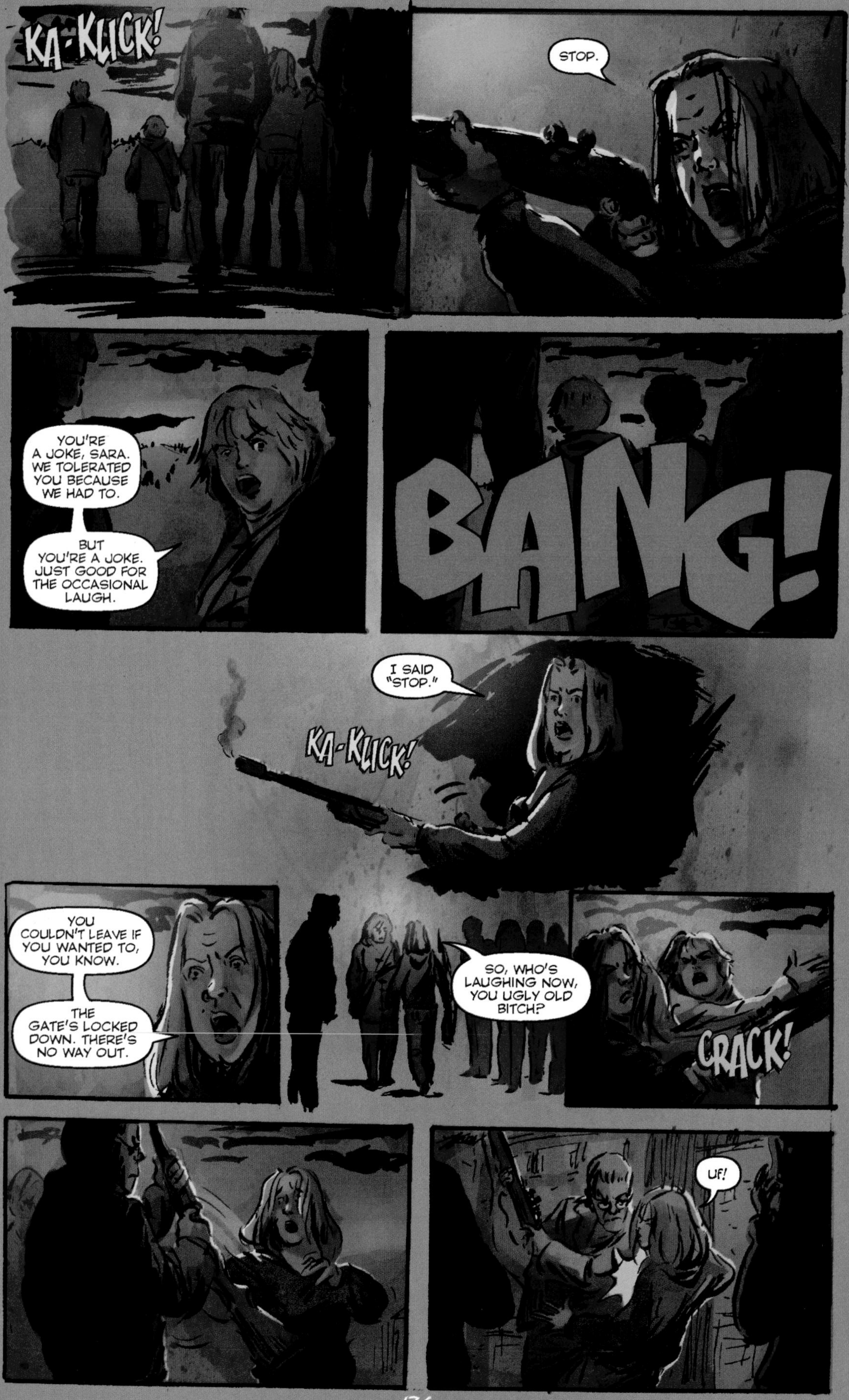
KA-KLICK!
STOP.
YOU'RE A JOKE, SARA. WE TOLERATED YOU BECAUSE WE HAD TO.
BUT YOU'RE A JOKE. JUST GOOD FOR THE OCCASIONAL LAUGH.
BANG!
I SAID "STOP."
KA-KLICK!
YOU COULDN'T LEAVE IF YOU WANTED TO, YOU KNOW.
THE GATE'S LOCKED DOWN. THERE'S NO WAY OUT.
SO, WHO'S LAUGHING NOW, YOU UGLY OLD BITCH?
CRACK!
UF!

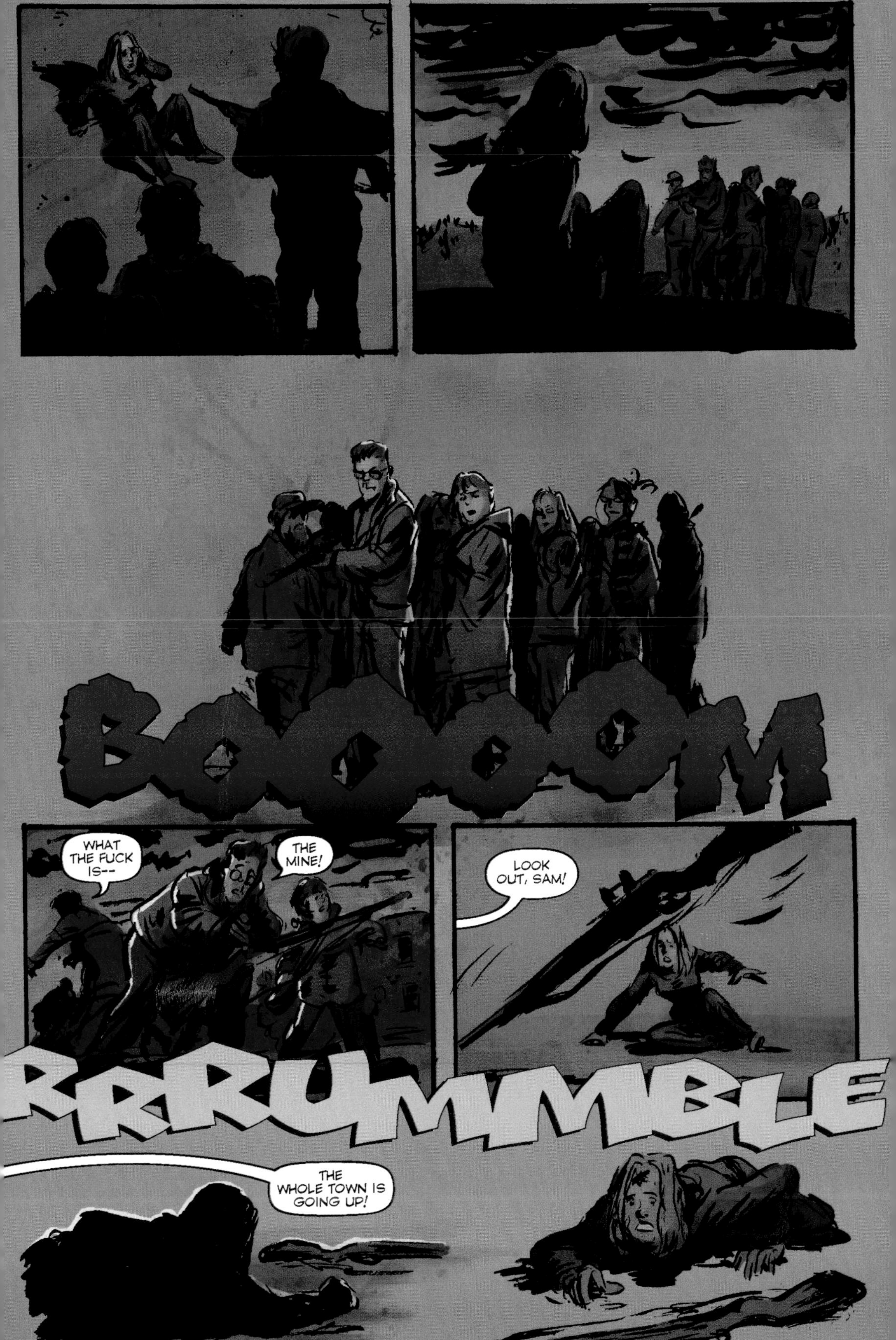
BOOOOM
WHAT THE FUCK IS--
THE MINE!
LOOK OUT, SAM!
RRRUMMBLE
THE WHOLE TOWN IS GOING UP!

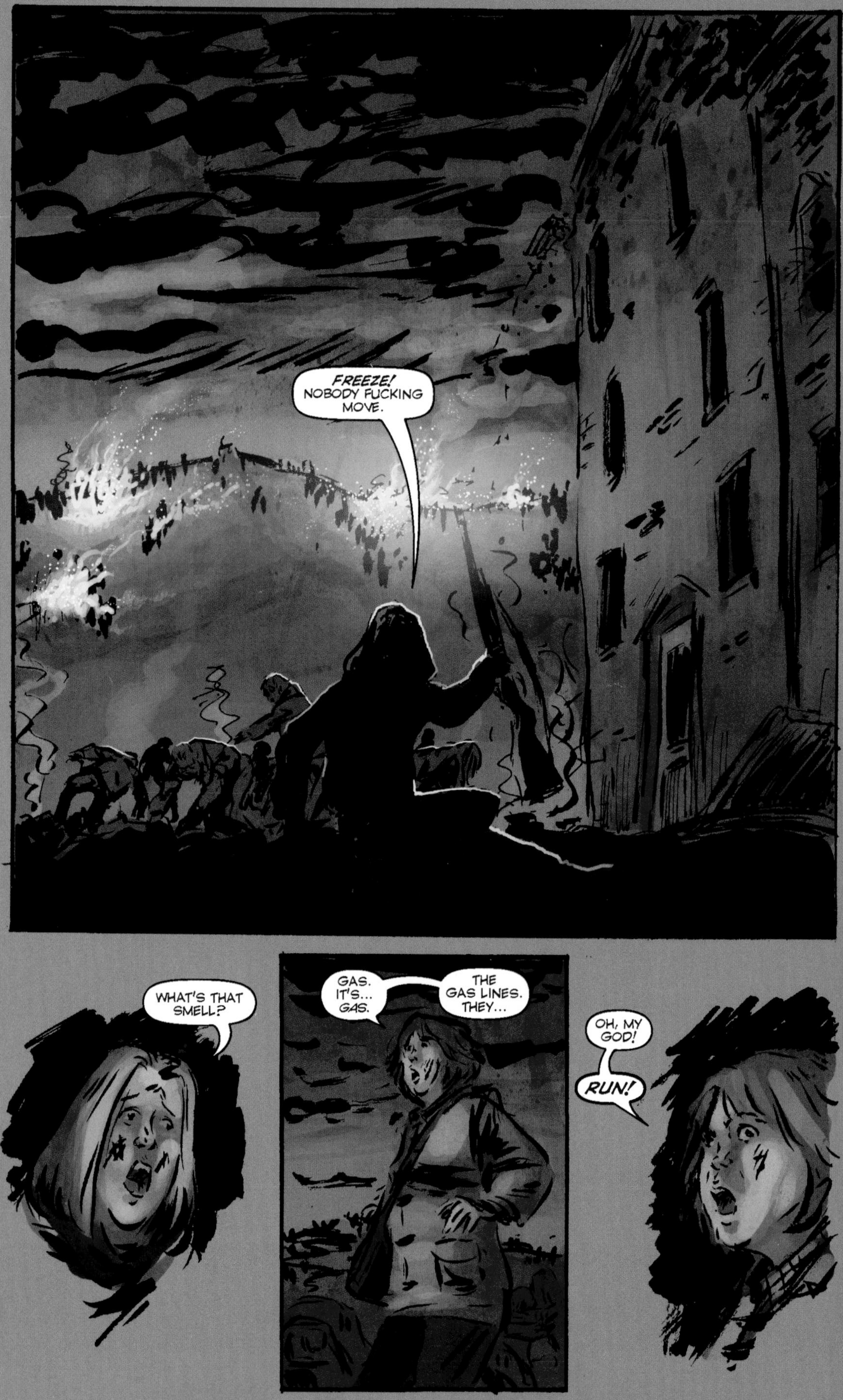
FREEZE! NOBODY FUCKING MOVE.
WHAT'S THAT SMELL?
GAS. IT'S... GAS.
THE GAS LINES. THEY...
OH, MY GOD!
RUN!

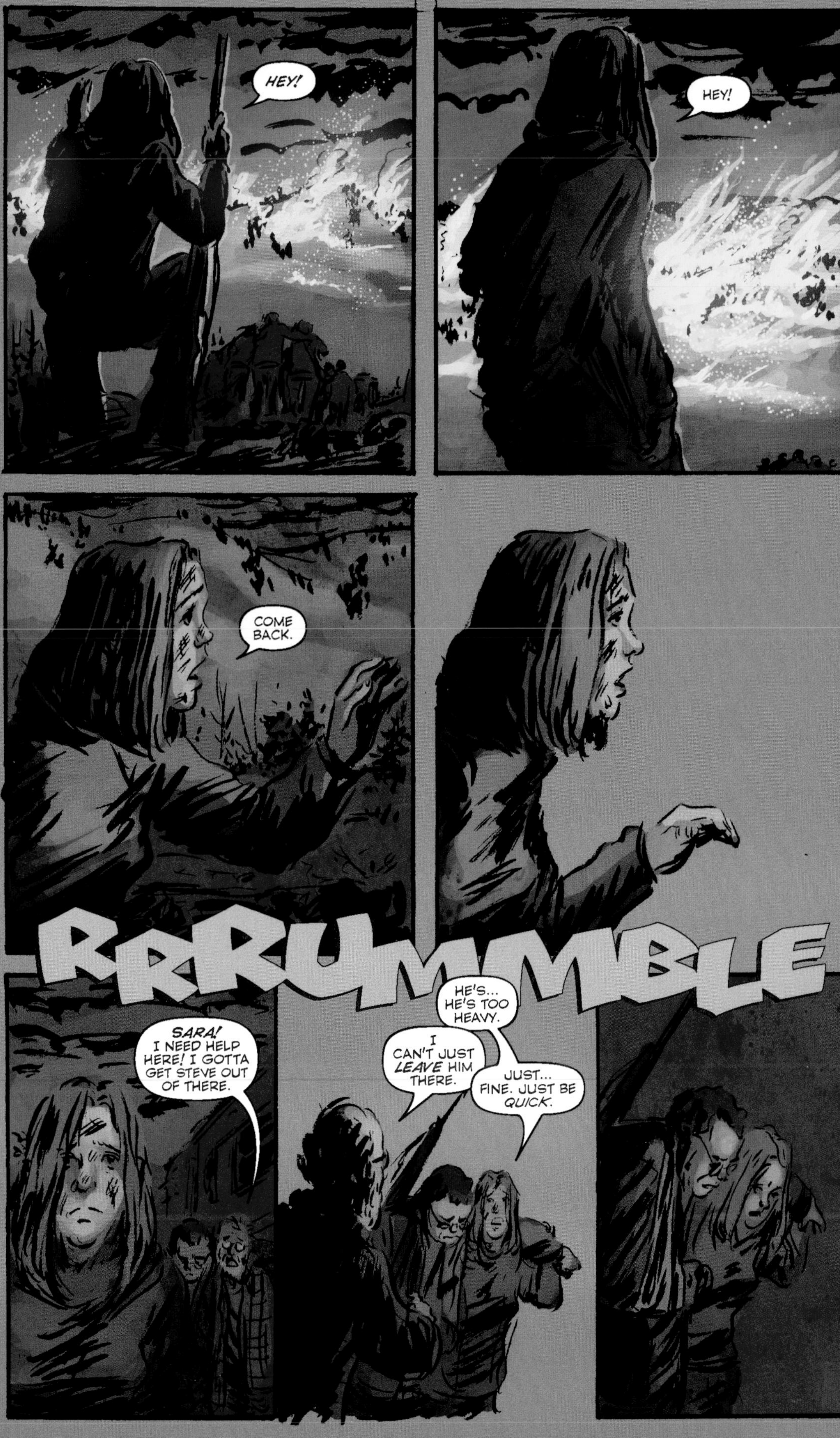
HEY!
HEY!
COME BACK.
RRRUMMBLE
SARA! I NEED HELP HERE! I GOTTA GET STEVE OUT OF THERE.
HE'S... HE'S TOO HEAVY.
I CAN'T JUST LEAVE HIM THERE.
JUST... FINE. JUST BE QUICK.

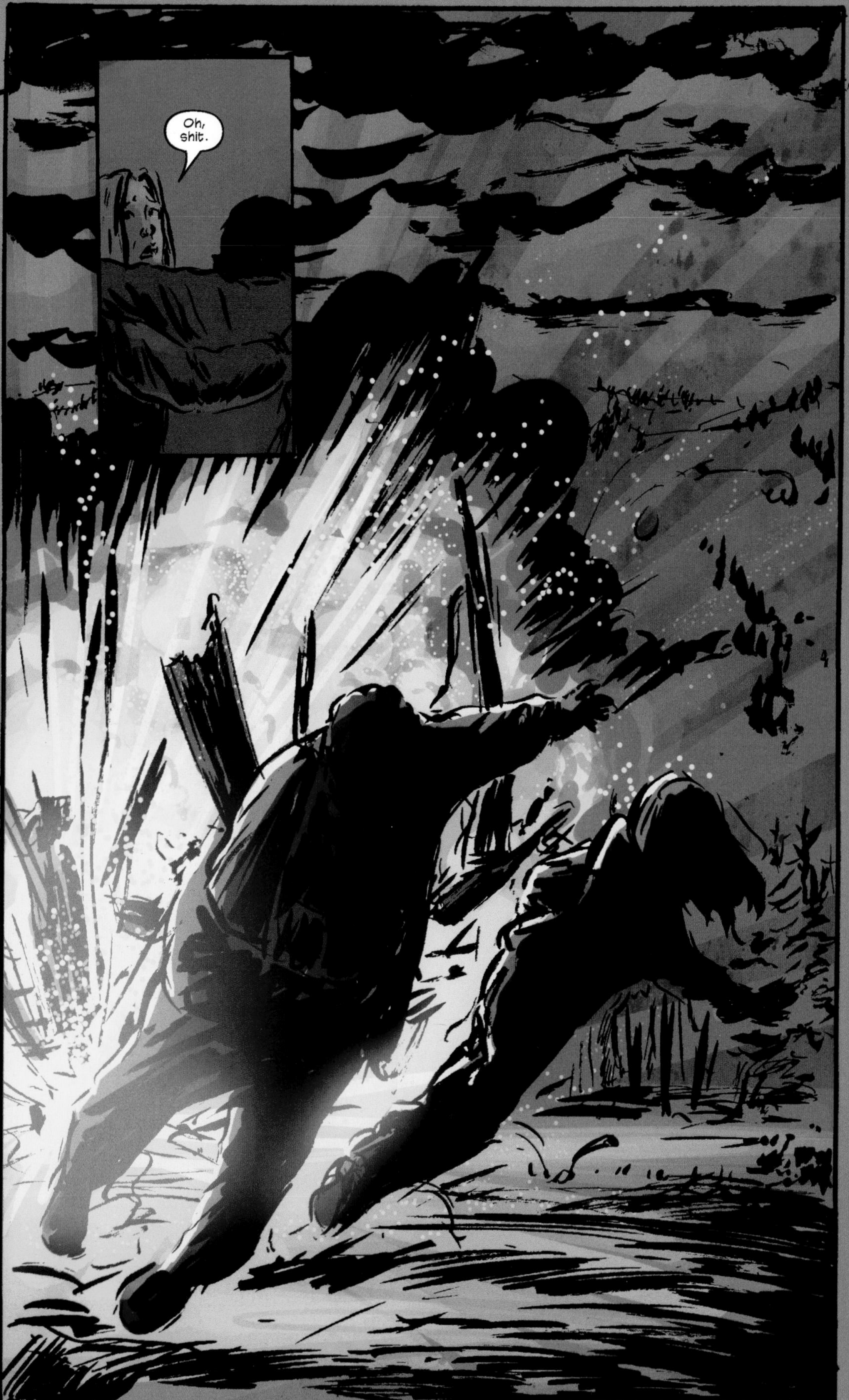
Oh, shit.

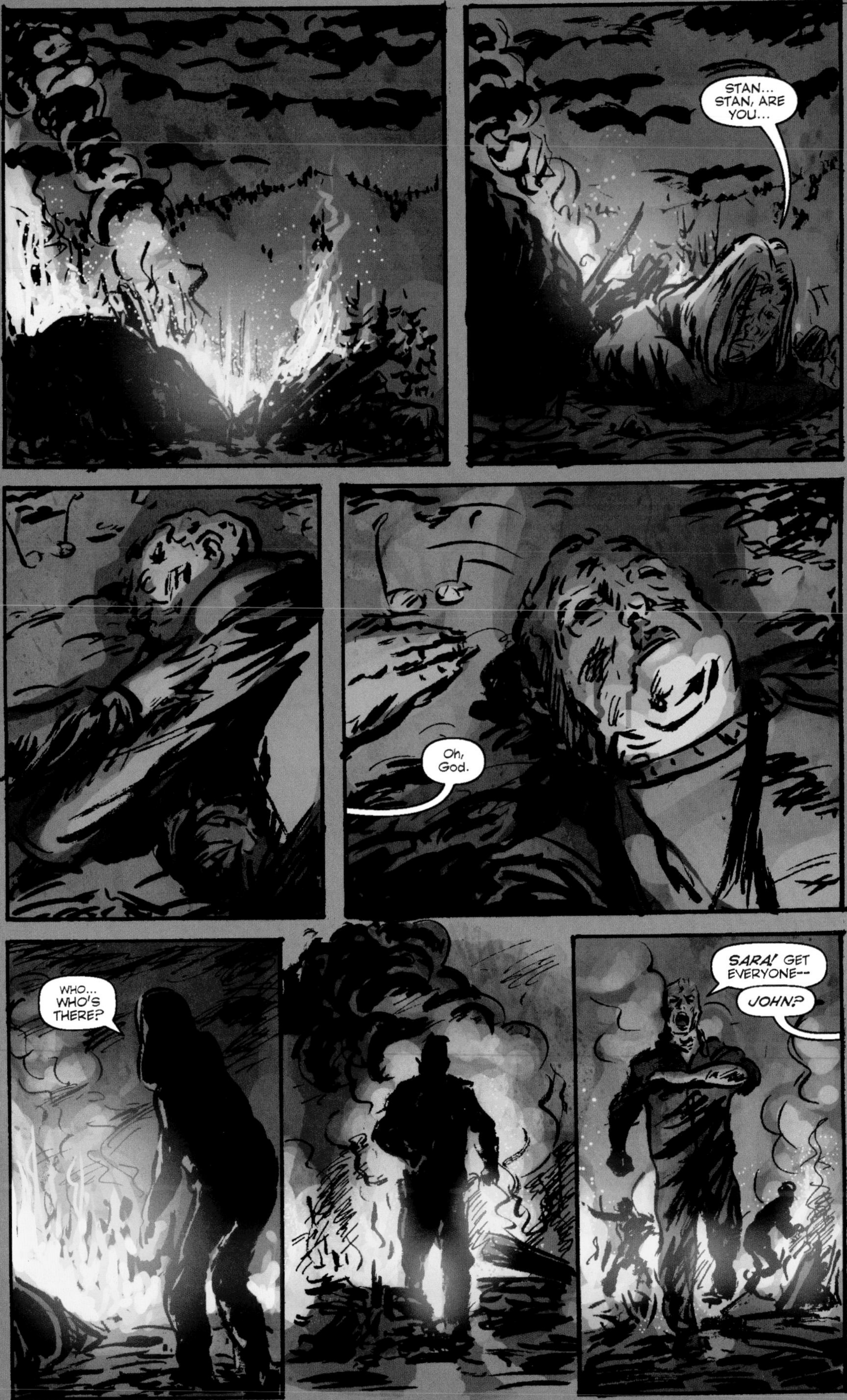
STAN...
STAN, ARE
YOU...
Oh,
God.
WHO...
WHO'S
THERE?
SARA! GET
EVERYONE--
JOHN?

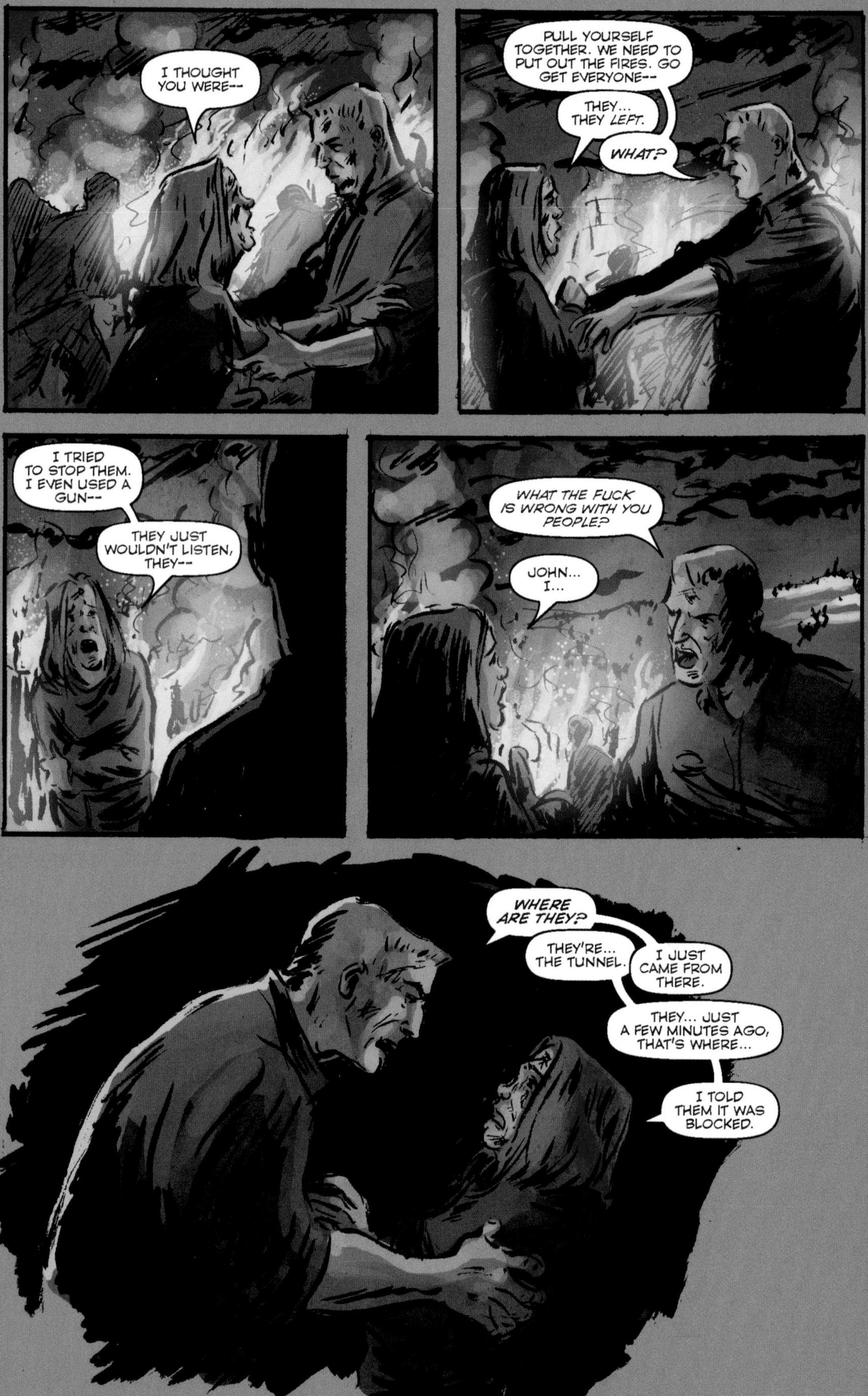
I THOUGHT YOU WERE--
PULL YOURSELF TOGETHER. WE NEED TO PUT OUT THE FIRES. GO GET EVERYONE--
THEY... THEY *LEFT*.
WHAT?
I TRIED TO STOP THEM. I EVEN USED A GUN--
THEY JUST WOULDN'T LISTEN, THEY--
WHAT THE FUCK IS WRONG WITH YOU PEOPLE?
JOHN... I...
WHERE ARE THEY?
THEY'RE... THE TUNNEL.
I JUST CAME FROM THERE.
THEY... JUST A FEW MINUTES AGO, THAT'S WHERE...
I TOLD THEM IT WAS BLOCKED.

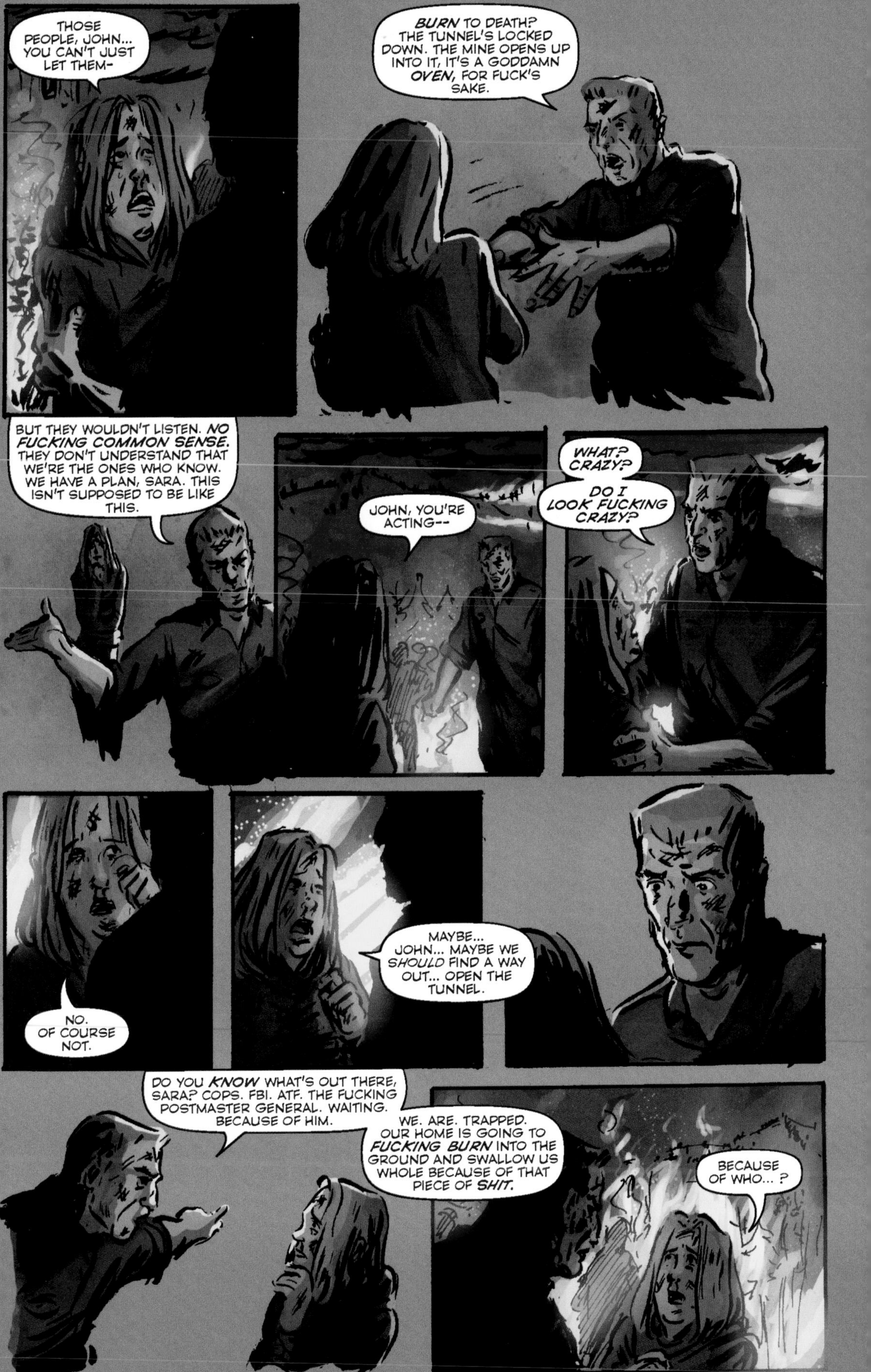
THOSE PEOPLE, JOHN... YOU CAN'T JUST LET THEM-
BURN TO DEATH? THE TUNNEL'S LOCKED DOWN. THE MINE OPENS UP INTO IT, IT'S A GODDAMN OVEN, FOR FUCK'S SAKE.
BUT THEY WOULDN'T LISTEN. NO FUCKING COMMON SENSE. THEY DON'T UNDERSTAND THAT WE'RE THE ONES WHO KNOW. WE HAVE A PLAN, SARA. THIS ISN'T SUPPOSED TO BE LIKE THIS.
JOHN, YOU'RE ACTING--
WHAT? CRAZY?
DO I LOOK FUCKING CRAZY?
NO. OF COURSE NOT.
MAYBE... JOHN... MAYBE WE SHOULD FIND A WAY OUT... OPEN THE TUNNEL.
DO YOU KNOW WHAT'S OUT THERE, SARA? COPS. FBI. ATF. THE FUCKING POSTMASTER GENERAL. WAITING. BECAUSE OF HIM.
WE. ARE. TRAPPED. OUR HOME IS GOING TO FUCKING BURN INTO THE GROUND AND SWALLOW US WHOLE BECAUSE OF THAT PIECE OF SHIT.
BECAUSE OF WHO... ?

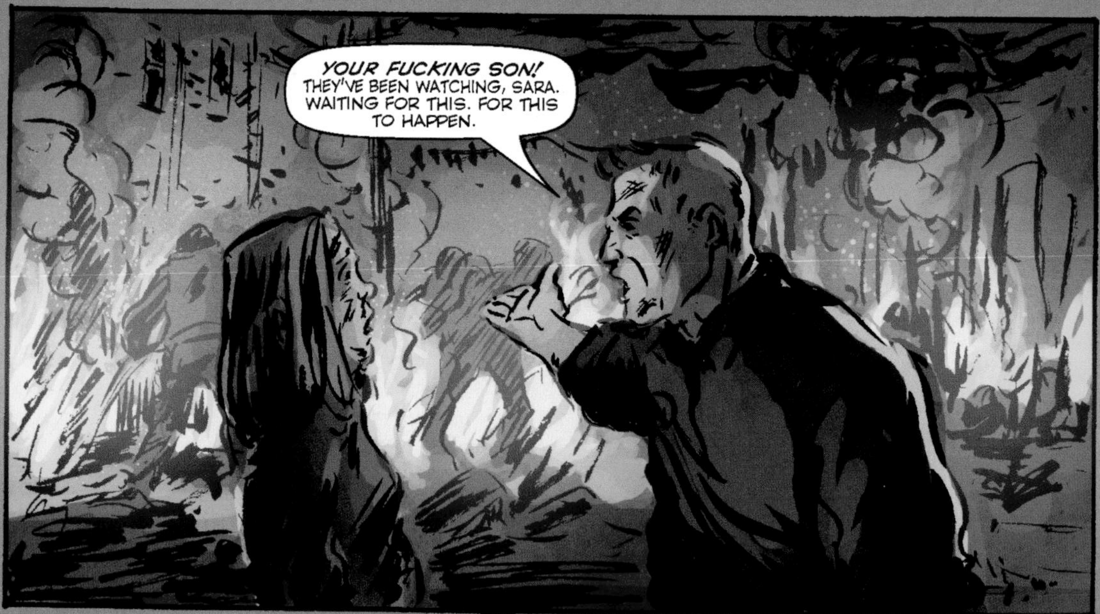
YOUR FUCKING SON! THEY'VE BEEN WATCHING, SARA. WAITING FOR THIS. FOR THIS TO HAPPEN.

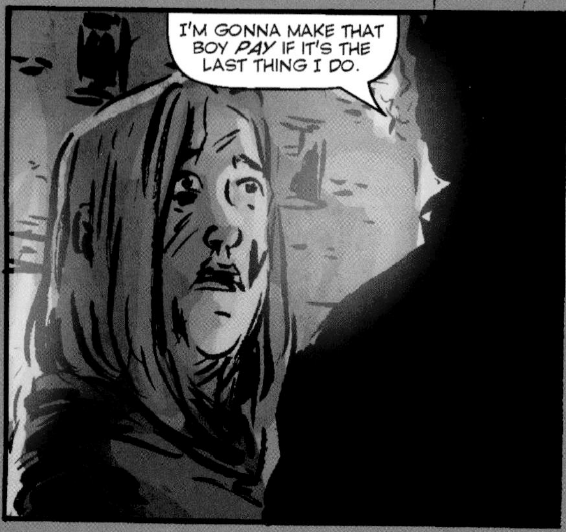
I'M GONNA MAKE THAT BOY PAY IF IT'S THE LAST THING I DO.

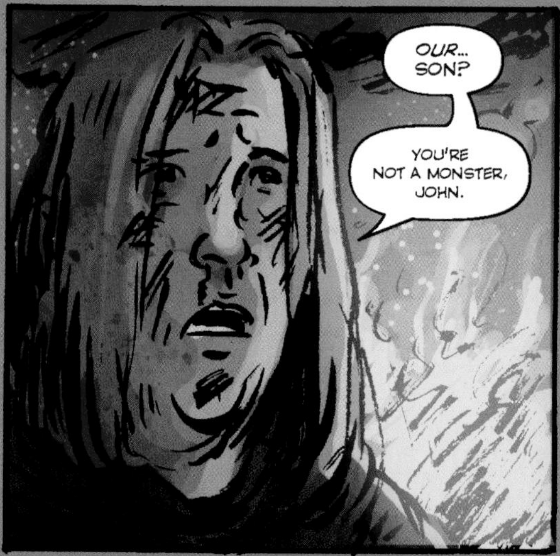
OUR... SON?
YOU'RE NOT A MONSTER, JOHN.

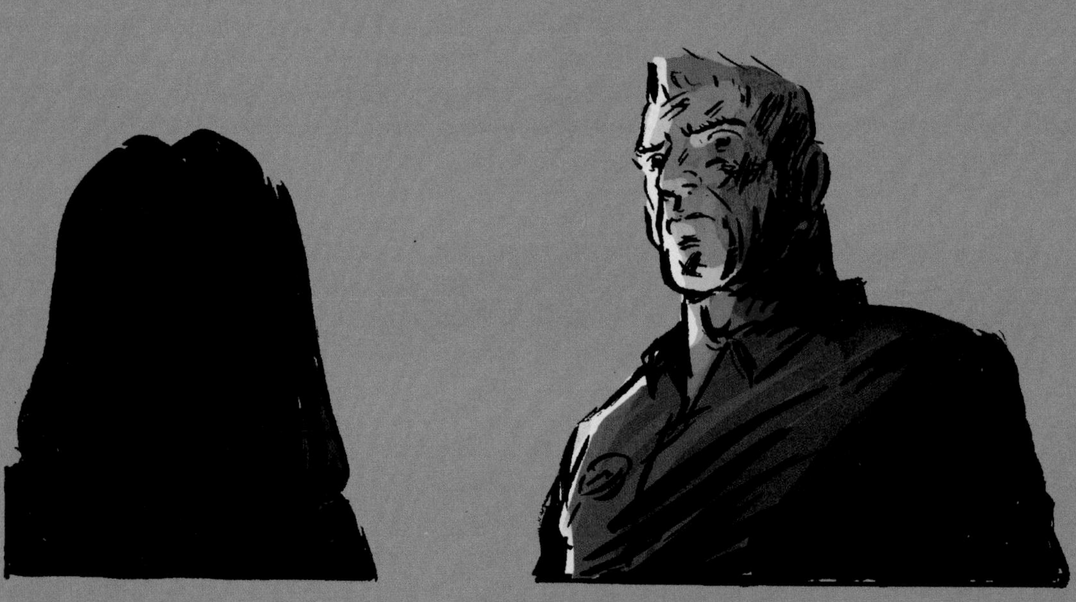

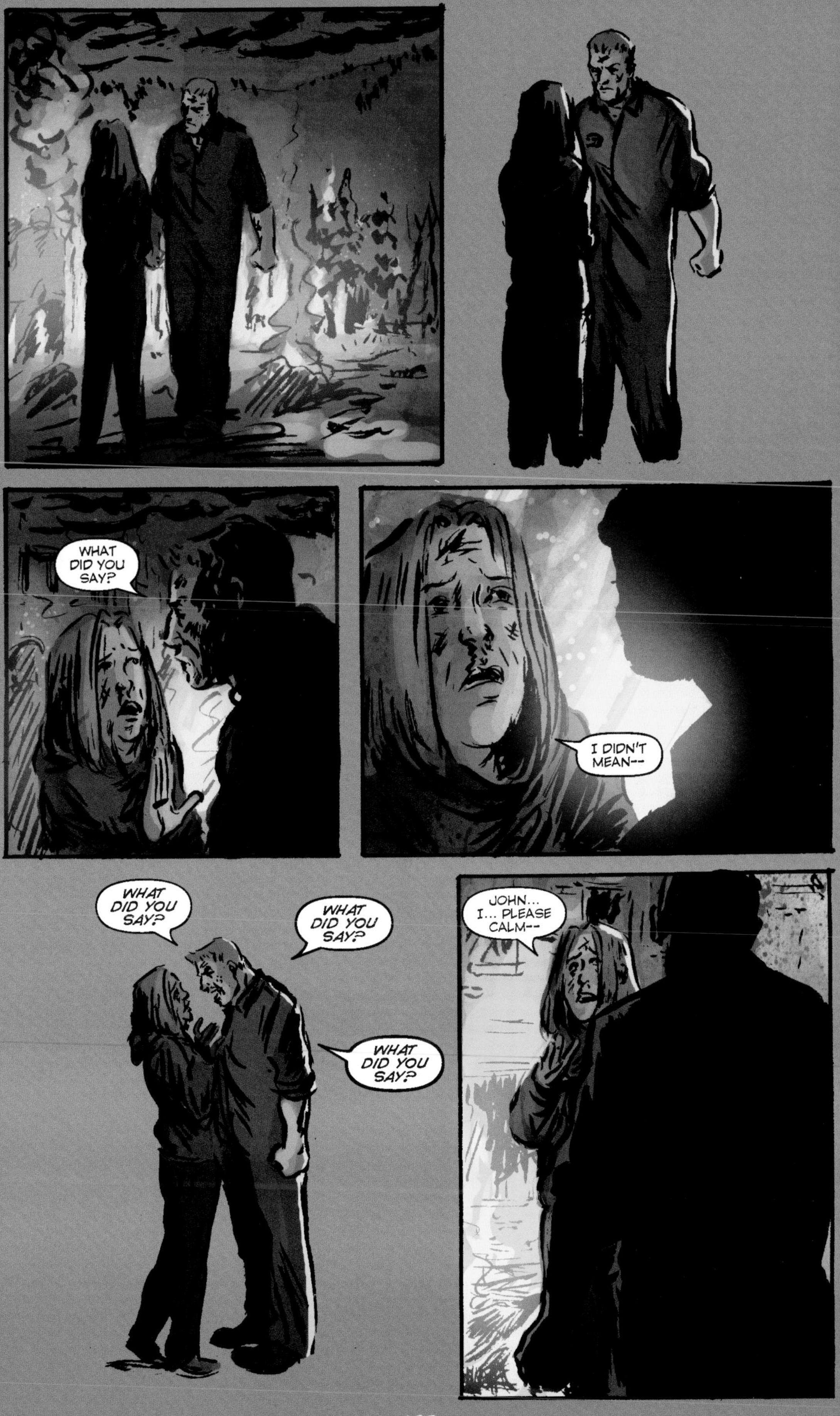
WHAT DID YOU SAY?
I DIDN'T MEAN--
WHAT DID YOU SAY?
WHAT DID YOU SAY?
WHAT DID YOU SAY?
JOHN... I... PLEASE CALM--

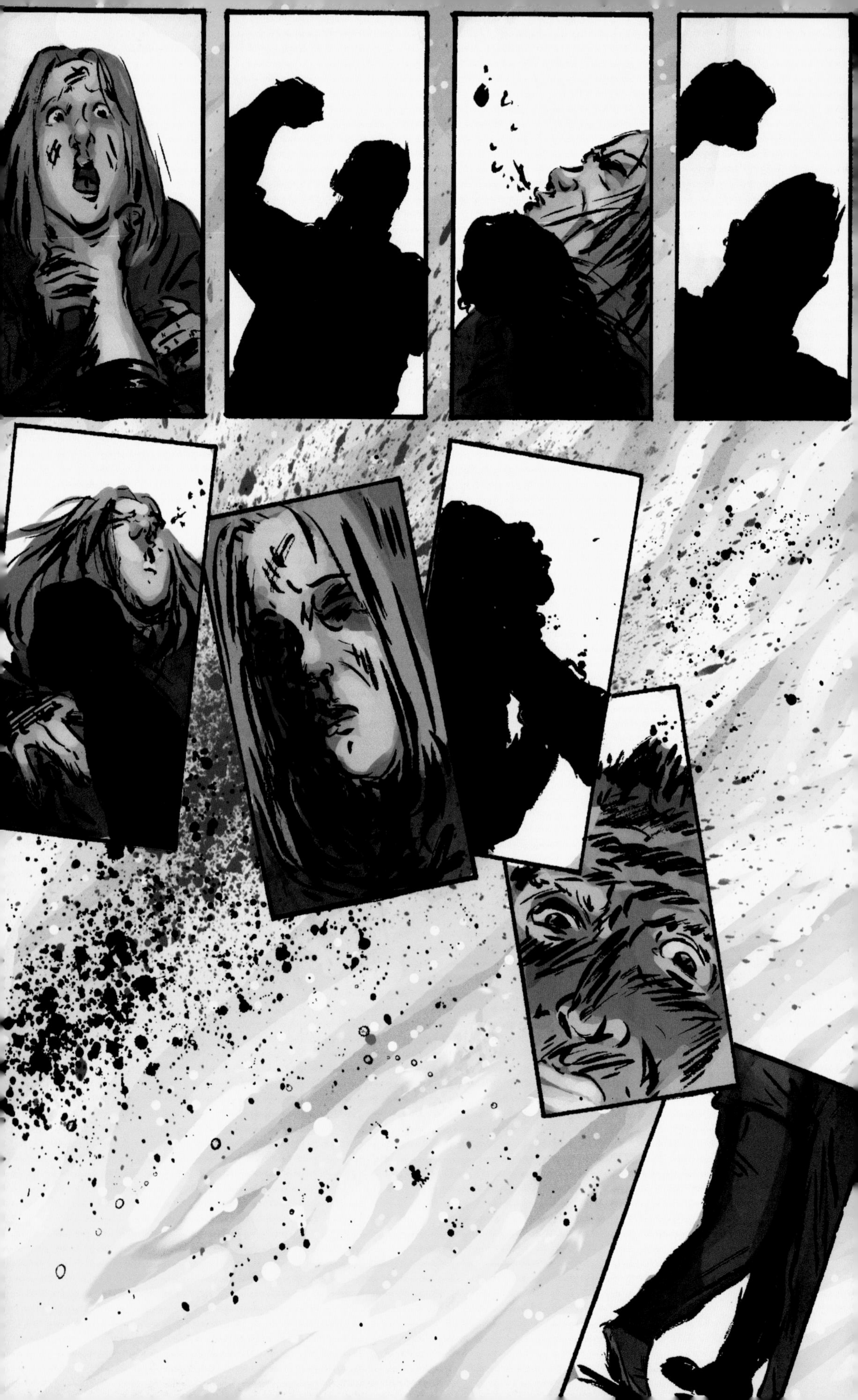

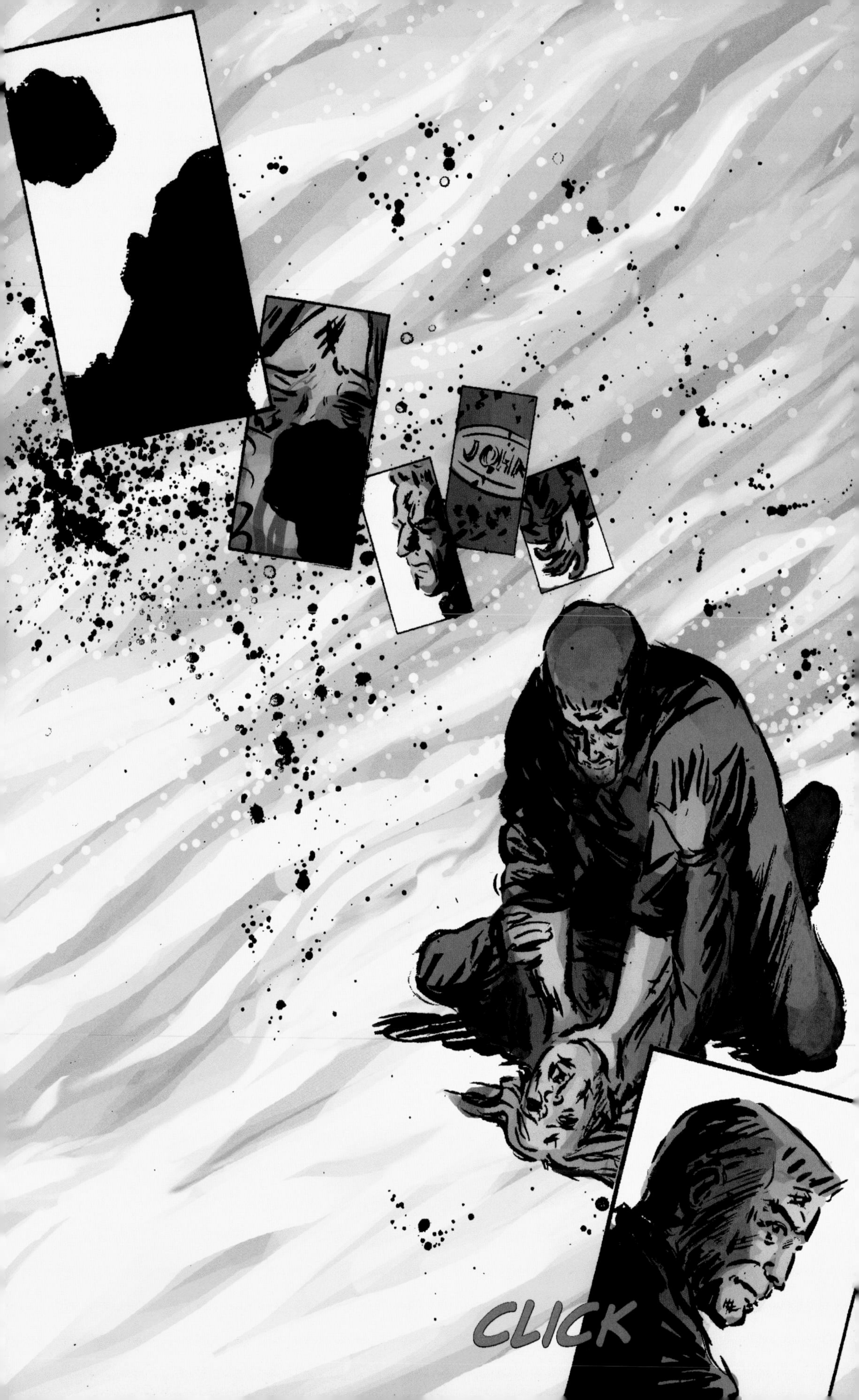
CLICK

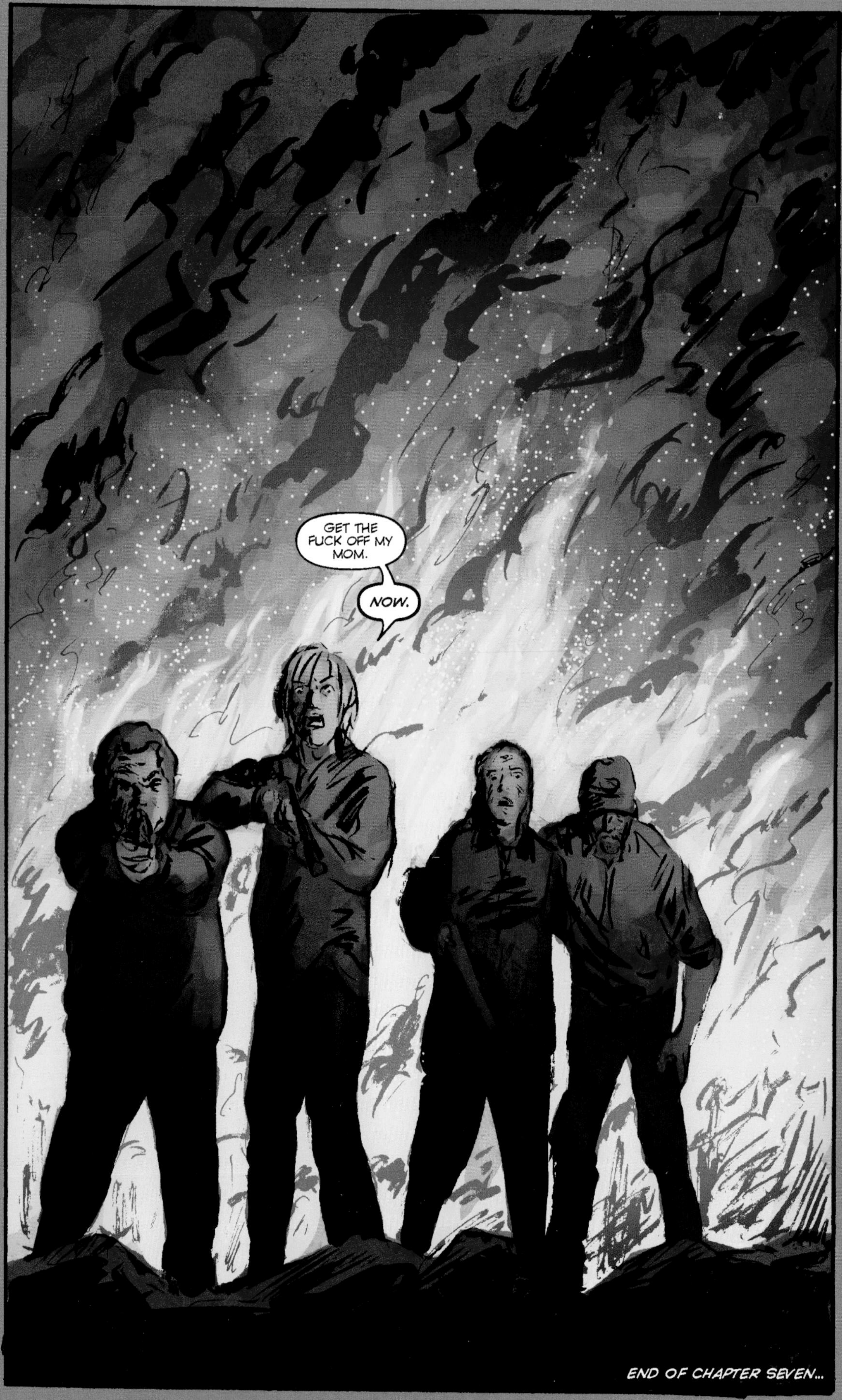
GET THE FUCK OFF MY MOM.
NOW.
END OF CHAPTER SEVEN...

Chapter Eight: Rockslide

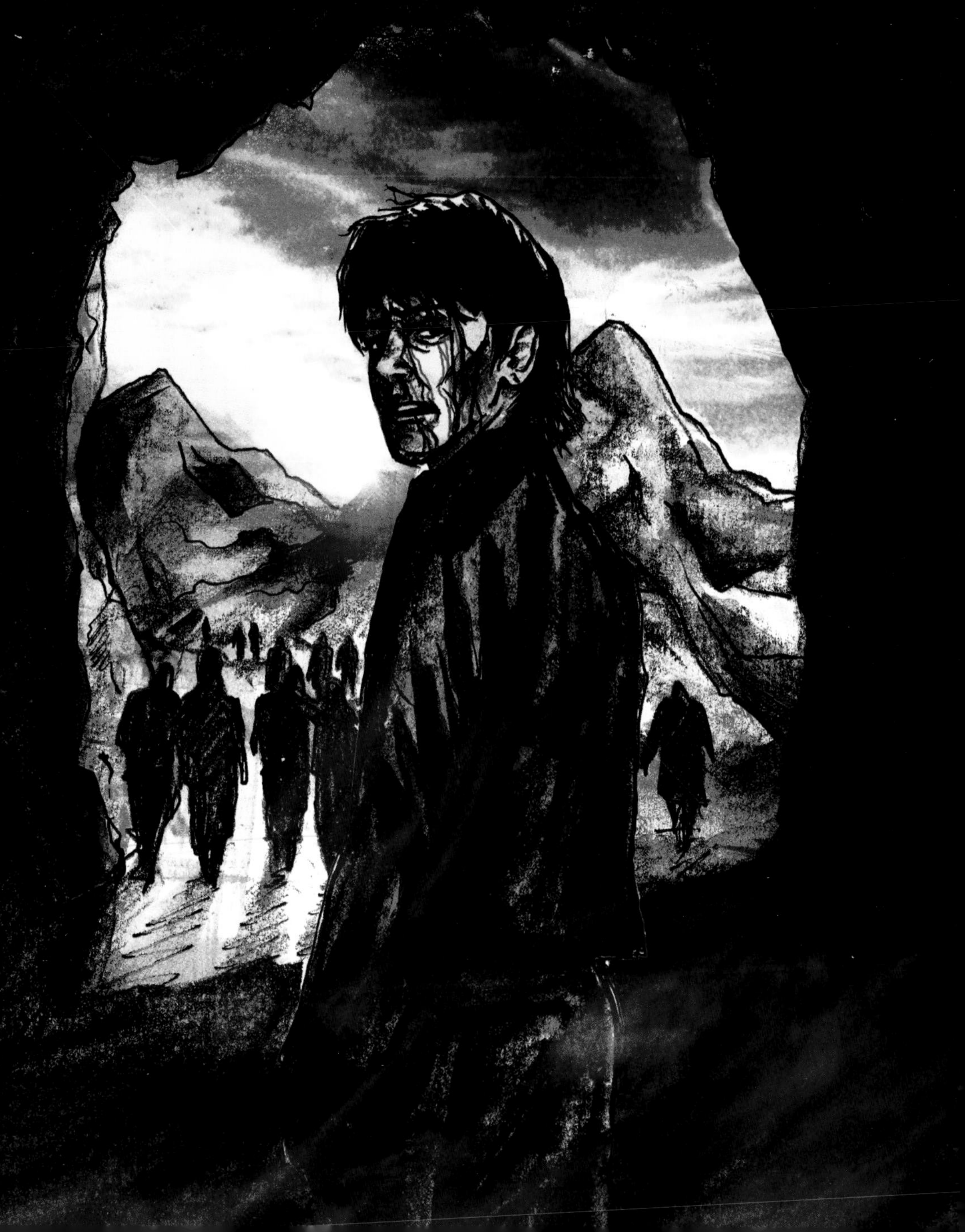

IT ALWAYS STARTS *SMALL*...

A ROCKSLIDE STARTS WITH A FEW LOOSE PEBBLES.

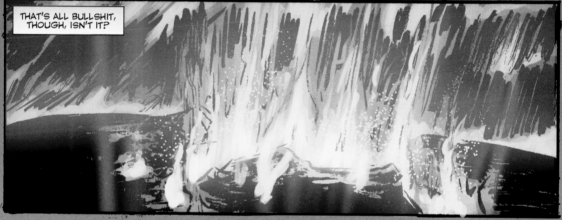

THAT'S ALL BULLSHIT, THOUGH, ISN'T IT?

THIS HAS ALWAYS BEEN *BIG*.

OUR VISION WAS JUST *TOO NARROW* TO SEE THE WHOLE PICTURE.

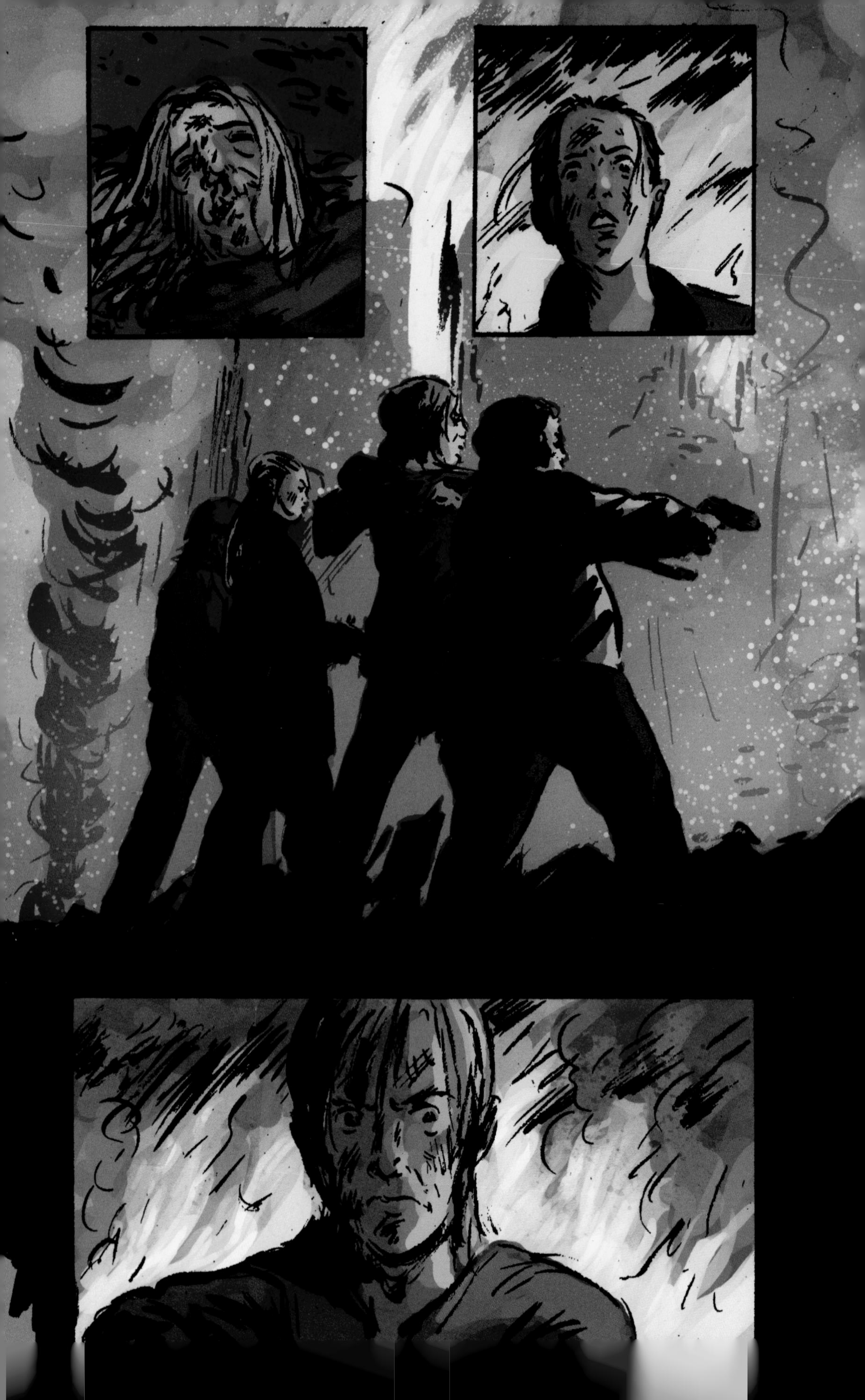

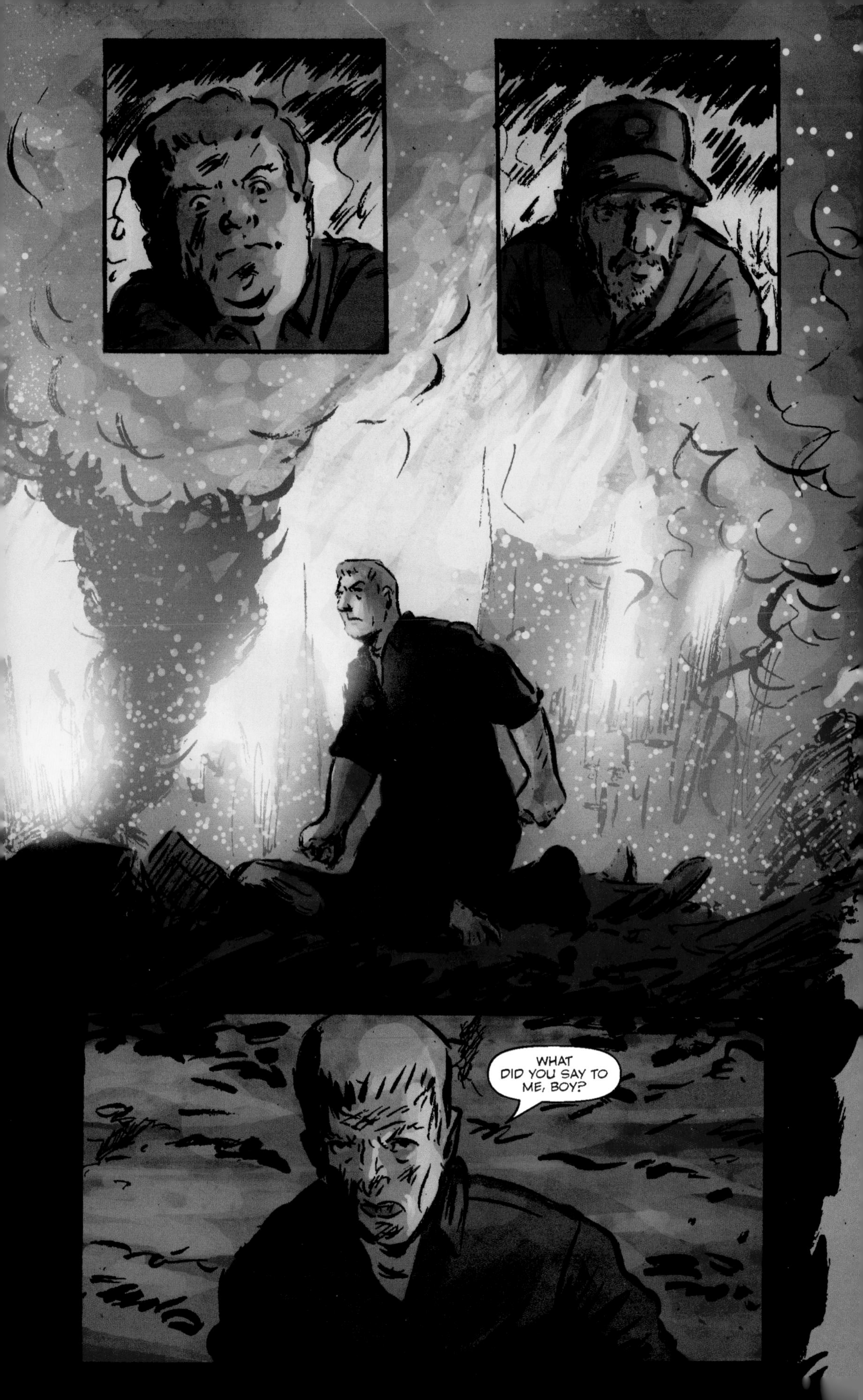
WHAT DID YOU SAY TO ME, BOY?

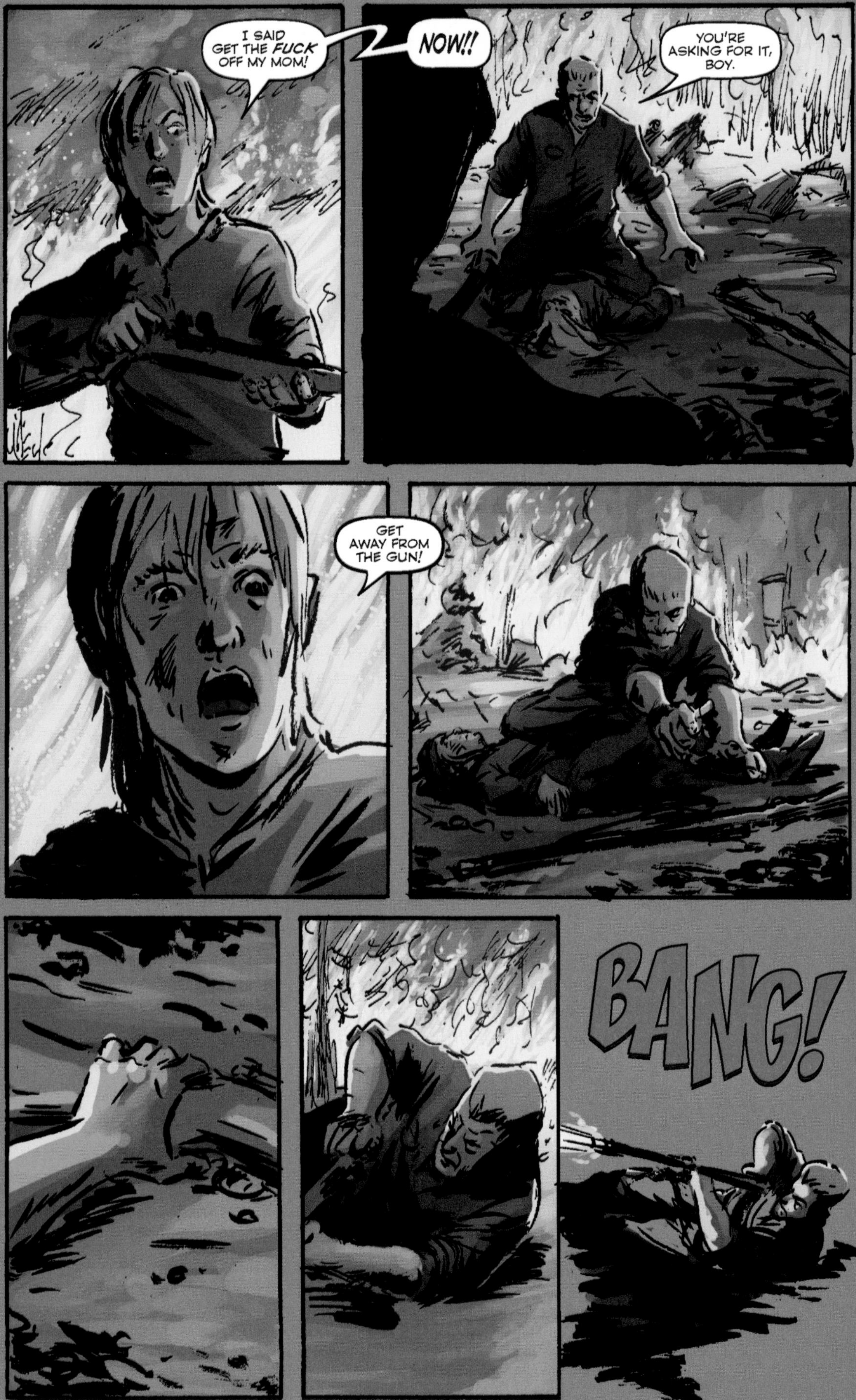
I SAID GET THE *FUCK* OFF MY MOM!
NOW!!
YOU'RE ASKING FOR IT, BOY.
GET AWAY FROM THE GUN!
BANG!

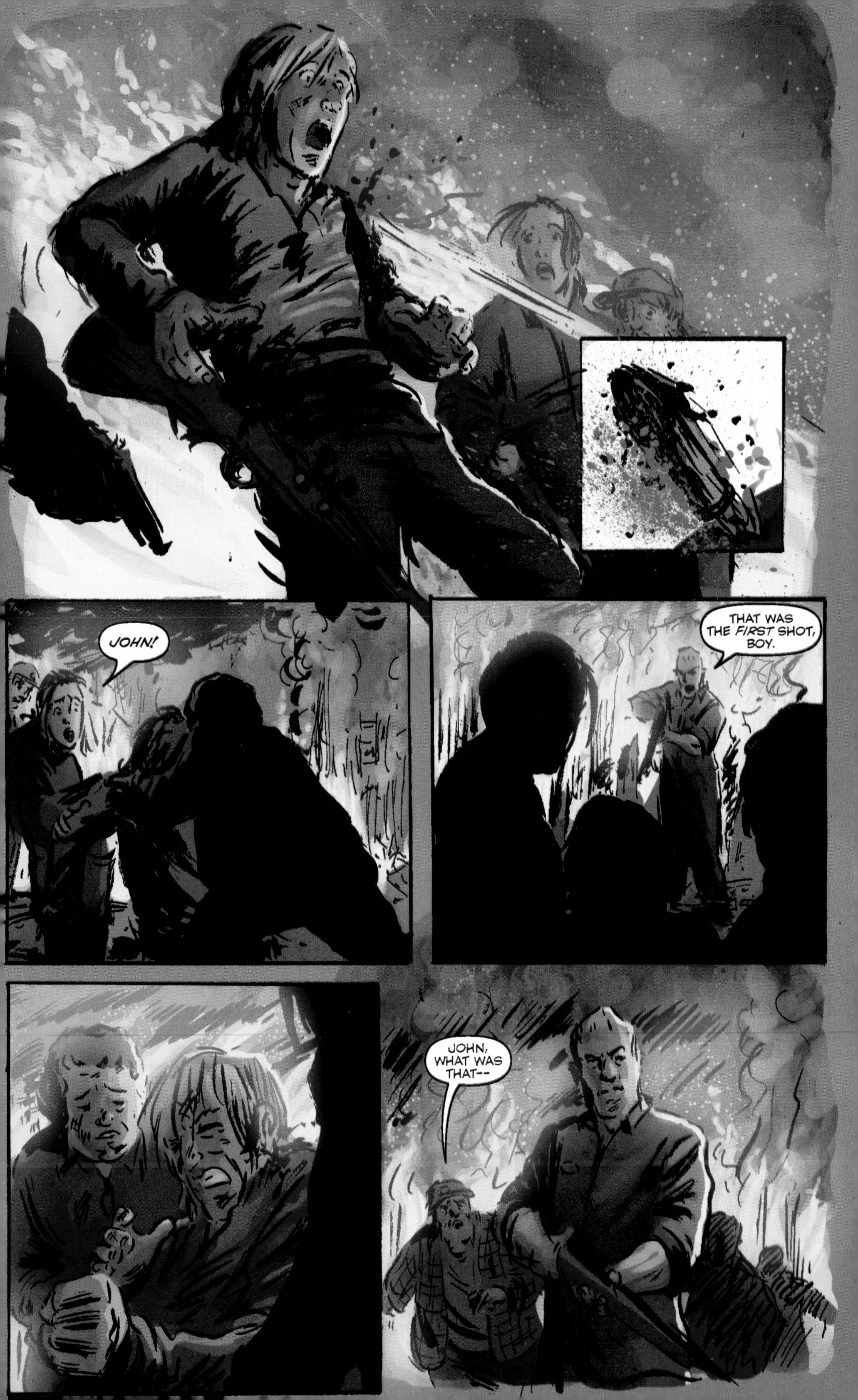
JOHN!
THAT WAS THE FIRST SHOT, BOY.
JOHN, WHAT WAS THAT--

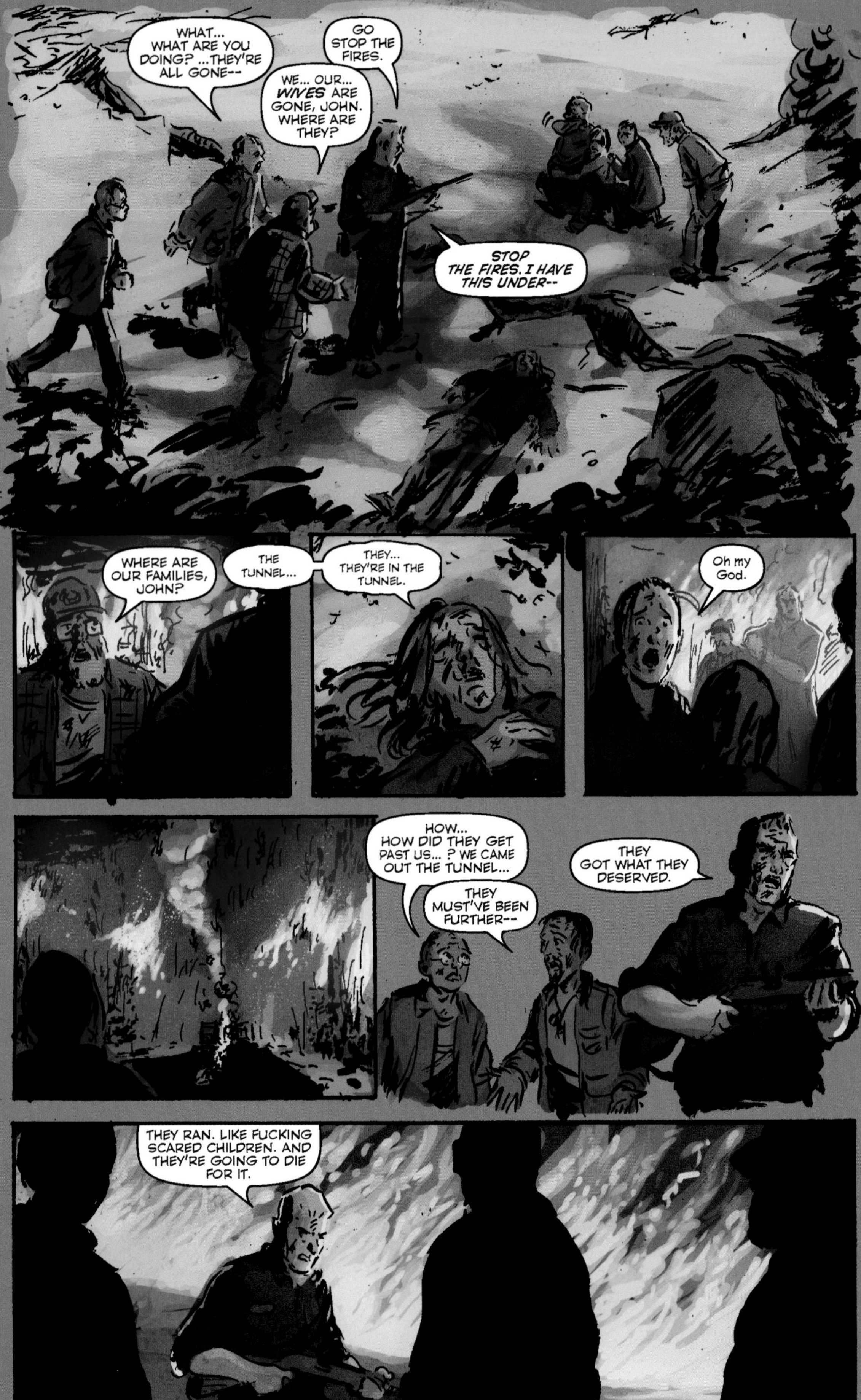
WHAT... WHAT ARE YOU DOING? ...THEY'RE ALL GONE--
GO STOP THE FIRES.
WE... OUR... WIVES ARE GONE, JOHN. WHERE ARE THEY?
STOP THE FIRES. I HAVE THIS UNDER--
WHERE ARE OUR FAMILIES, JOHN?
THE TUNNEL...
THEY... THEY'RE IN THE TUNNEL.
Oh my God.
HOW... HOW DID THEY GET PAST US... ? WE CAME OUT THE TUNNEL...
THEY MUST'VE BEEN FURTHER--
THEY GOT WHAT THEY DESERVED.
THEY RAN. LIKE FUCKING SCARED CHILDREN. AND THEY'RE GOING TO DIE FOR IT.

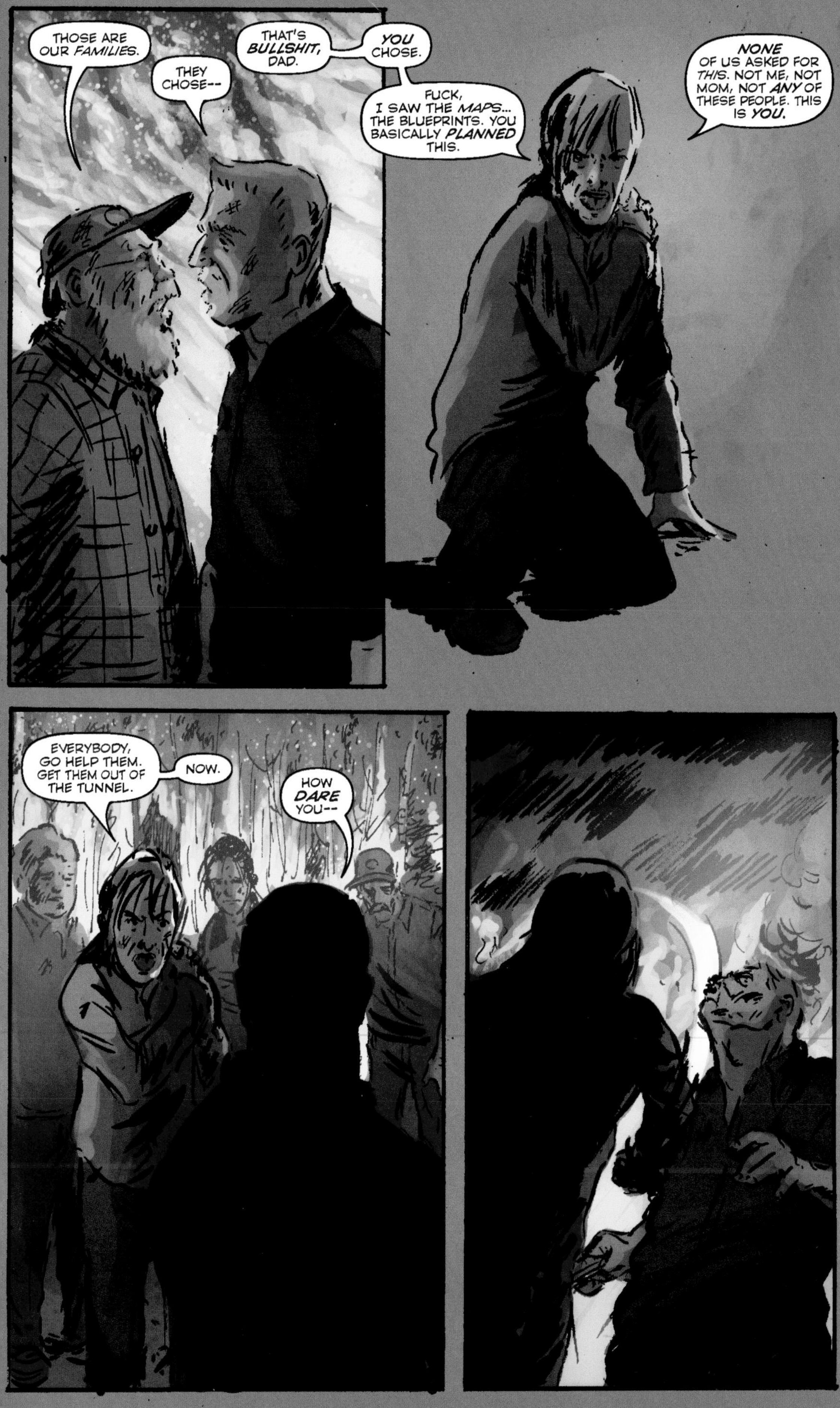
THOSE ARE OUR FAMILIES.
THEY CHOSE--
THAT'S BULLSHIT, DAD.
YOU CHOSE.
FUCK, I SAW THE MAPS... THE BLUEPRINTS. YOU BASICALLY PLANNED THIS.
NONE OF US ASKED FOR THIS. NOT ME, NOT MOM, NOT ANY OF THESE PEOPLE. THIS IS YOU.
EVERYBODY, GO HELP THEM. GET THEM OUT OF THE TUNNEL.
NOW.
HOW DARE YOU--

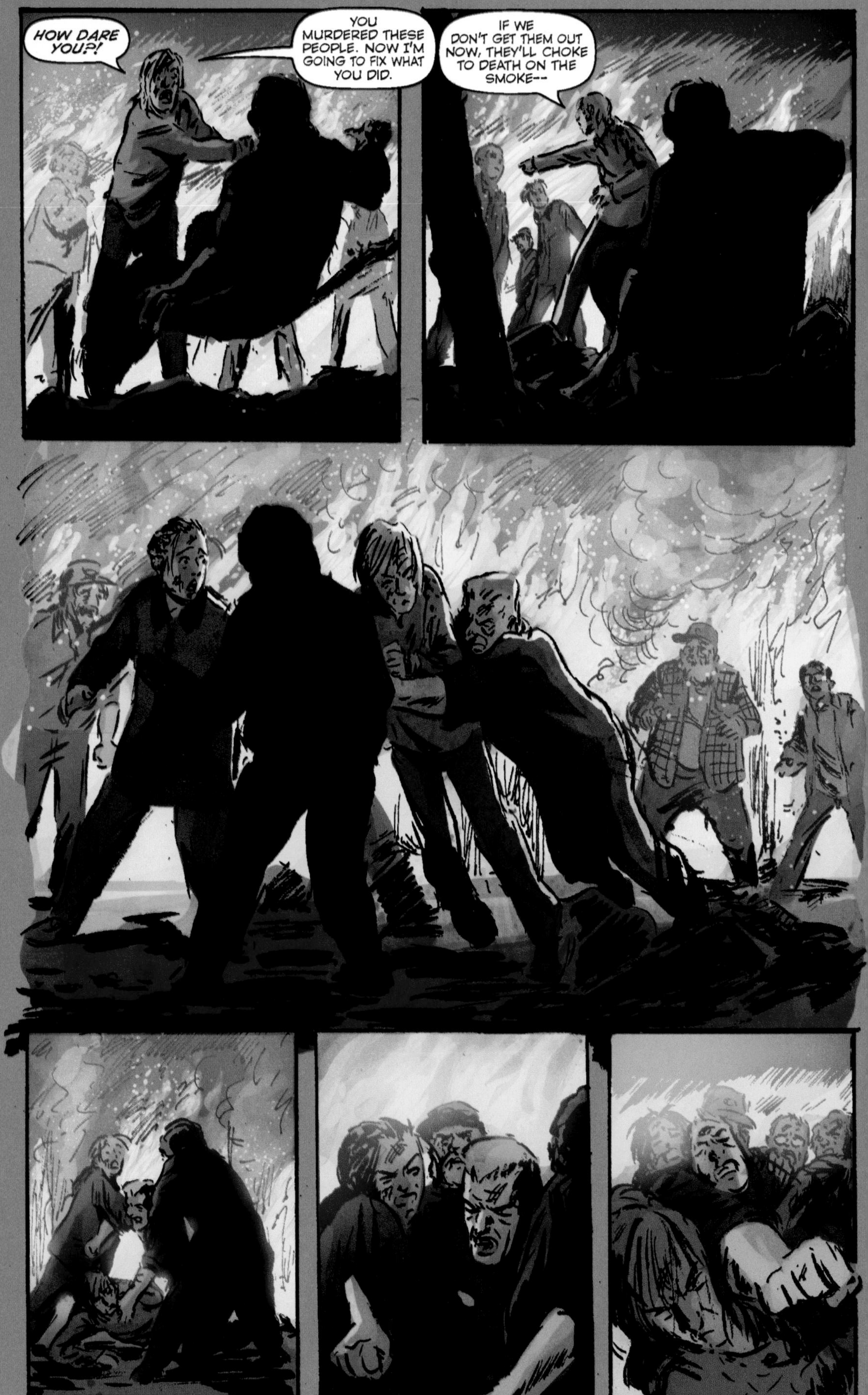
HOW DARE YOU?!
YOU MURDERED THESE PEOPLE. NOW I'M GOING TO FIX WHAT YOU DID.
IF WE DON'T GET THEM OUT NOW, THEY'LL CHOKE TO DEATH ON THE SMOKE--

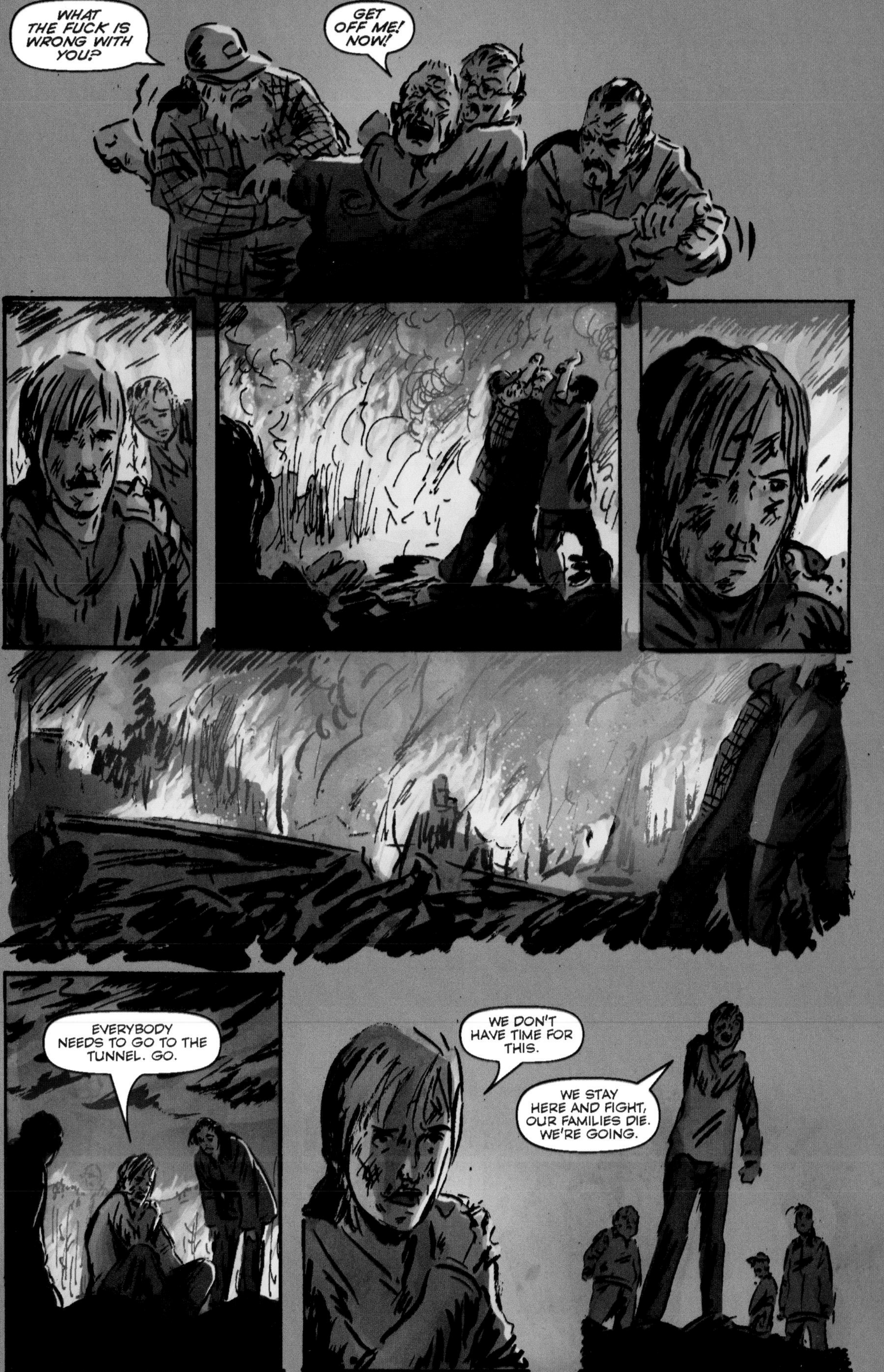
WHAT THE FUCK IS WRONG WITH YOU?
GET OFF ME! NOW!
EVERYBODY NEEDS TO GO TO THE TUNNEL. GO.
WE DON'T HAVE TIME FOR THIS.
WE STAY HERE AND FIGHT, OUR FAMILIES DIE. WE'RE GOING.

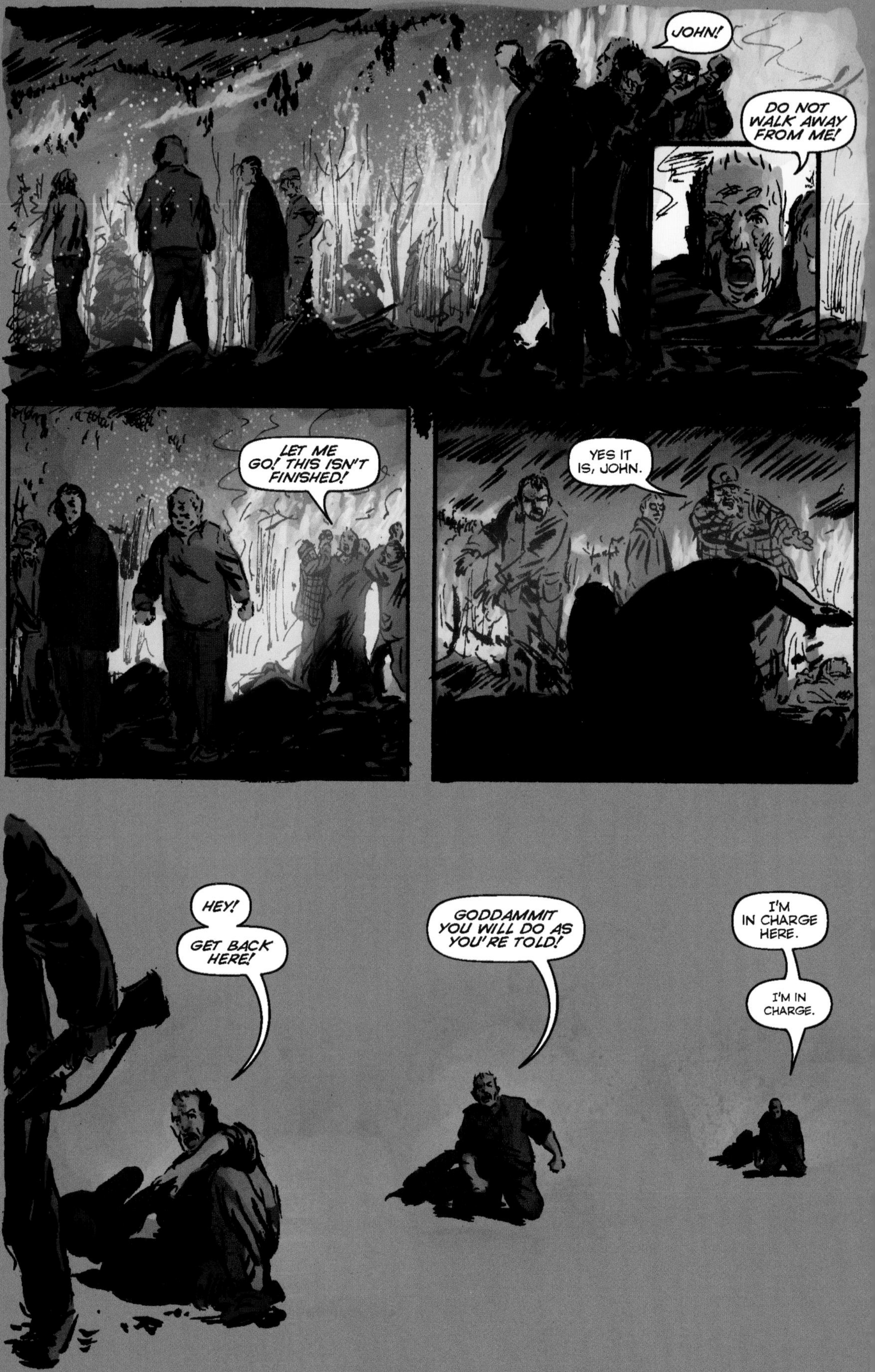
JOHN!
DO NOT WALK AWAY FROM ME!
LET ME GO! THIS ISN'T FINISHED!
YES IT IS, JOHN.
HEY!
GET BACK HERE!
GODDAMMIT YOU WILL DO AS YOU'RE TOLD!
I'M IN CHARGE HERE.
I'M IN CHARGE.

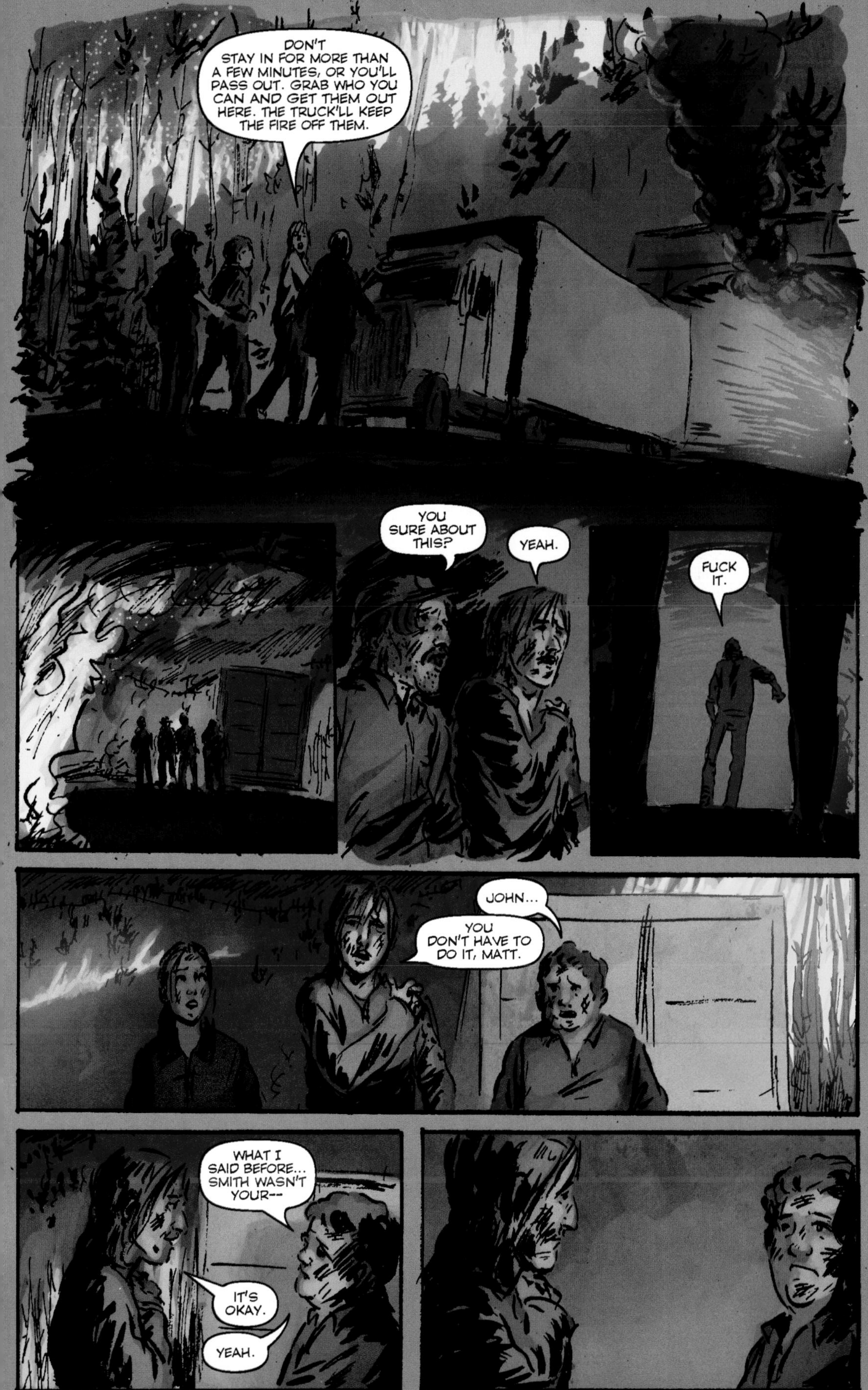
DON'T STAY IN FOR MORE THAN A FEW MINUTES, OR YOU'LL PASS OUT. GRAB WHO YOU CAN AND GET THEM OUT HERE. THE TRUCK'LL KEEP THE FIRE OFF THEM.
YOU SURE ABOUT THIS?
YEAH.
FUCK IT.
JOHN...
YOU DON'T HAVE TO DO IT, MATT.
WHAT I SAID BEFORE... SMITH WASN'T YOUR--
IT'S OKAY.
YEAH.

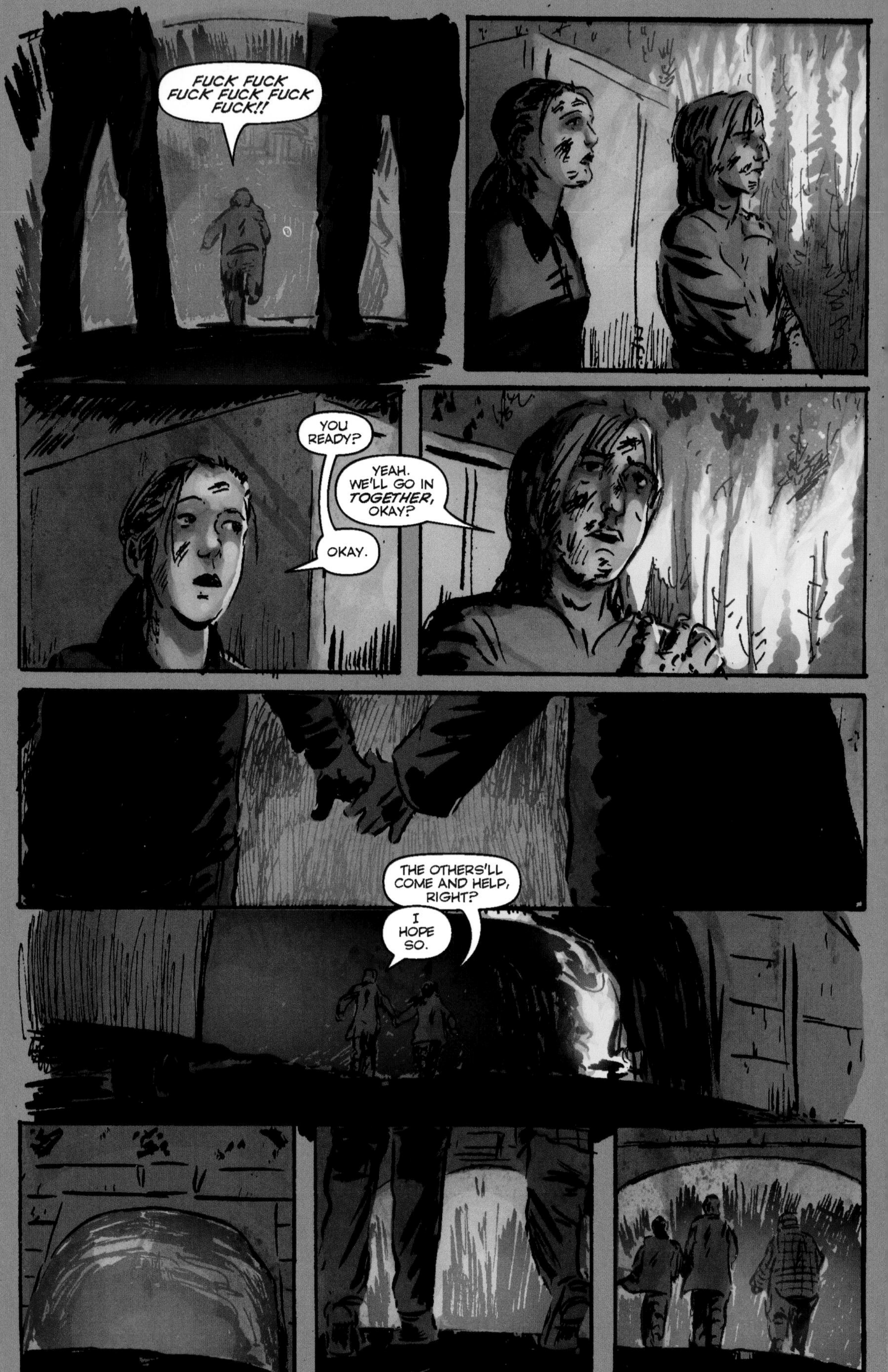
FUCK FUCK FUCK FUCK FUCK FUCK!!
YOU READY?
YEAH. WE'LL GO IN *TOGETHER*, OKAY?
OKAY.
THE OTHERS'LL COME AND HELP, RIGHT?
I HOPE SO.

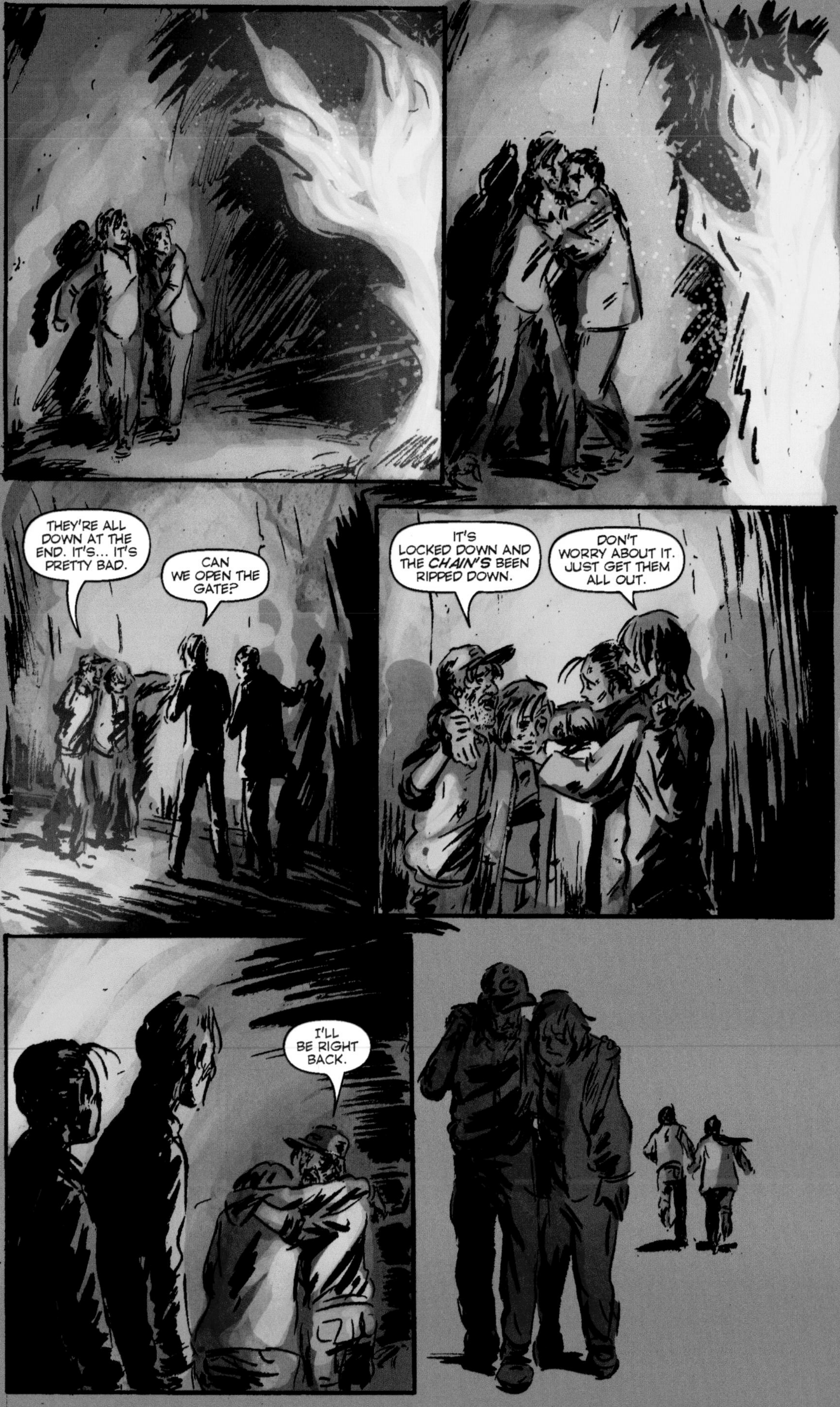
THEY'RE ALL DOWN AT THE END. IT'S... IT'S PRETTY BAD.
CAN WE OPEN THE GATE?
IT'S LOCKED DOWN AND THE CHAIN'S BEEN RIPPED DOWN.
DON'T WORRY ABOUT IT. JUST GET THEM ALL OUT.
I'LL BE RIGHT BACK.

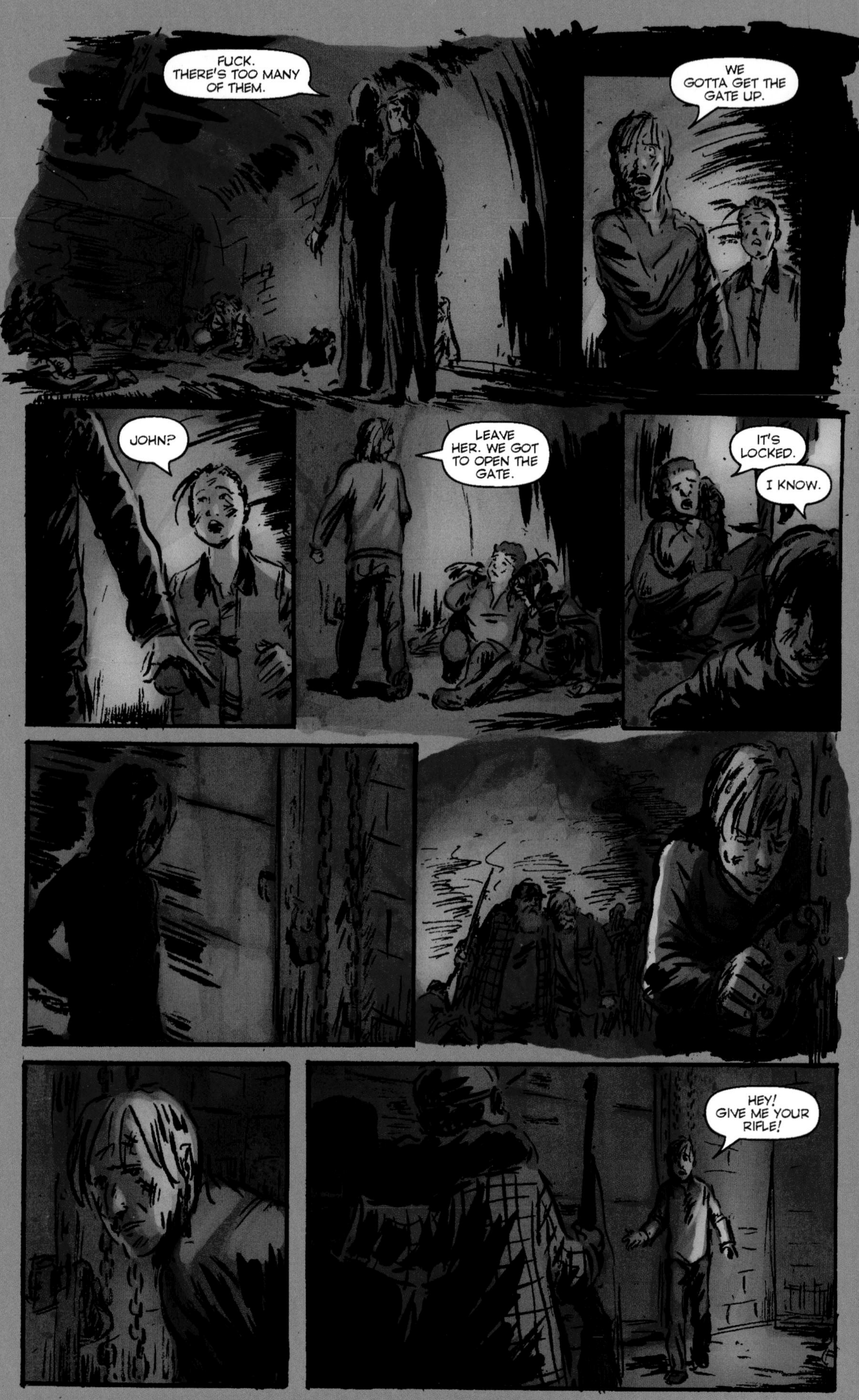
FUCK. THERE'S TOO MANY OF THEM.
WE GOTTA GET THE GATE UP.
JOHN?
LEAVE HER. WE GOT TO OPEN THE GATE.
IT'S LOCKED.
I KNOW.
HEY! GIVE ME YOUR RIFLE!

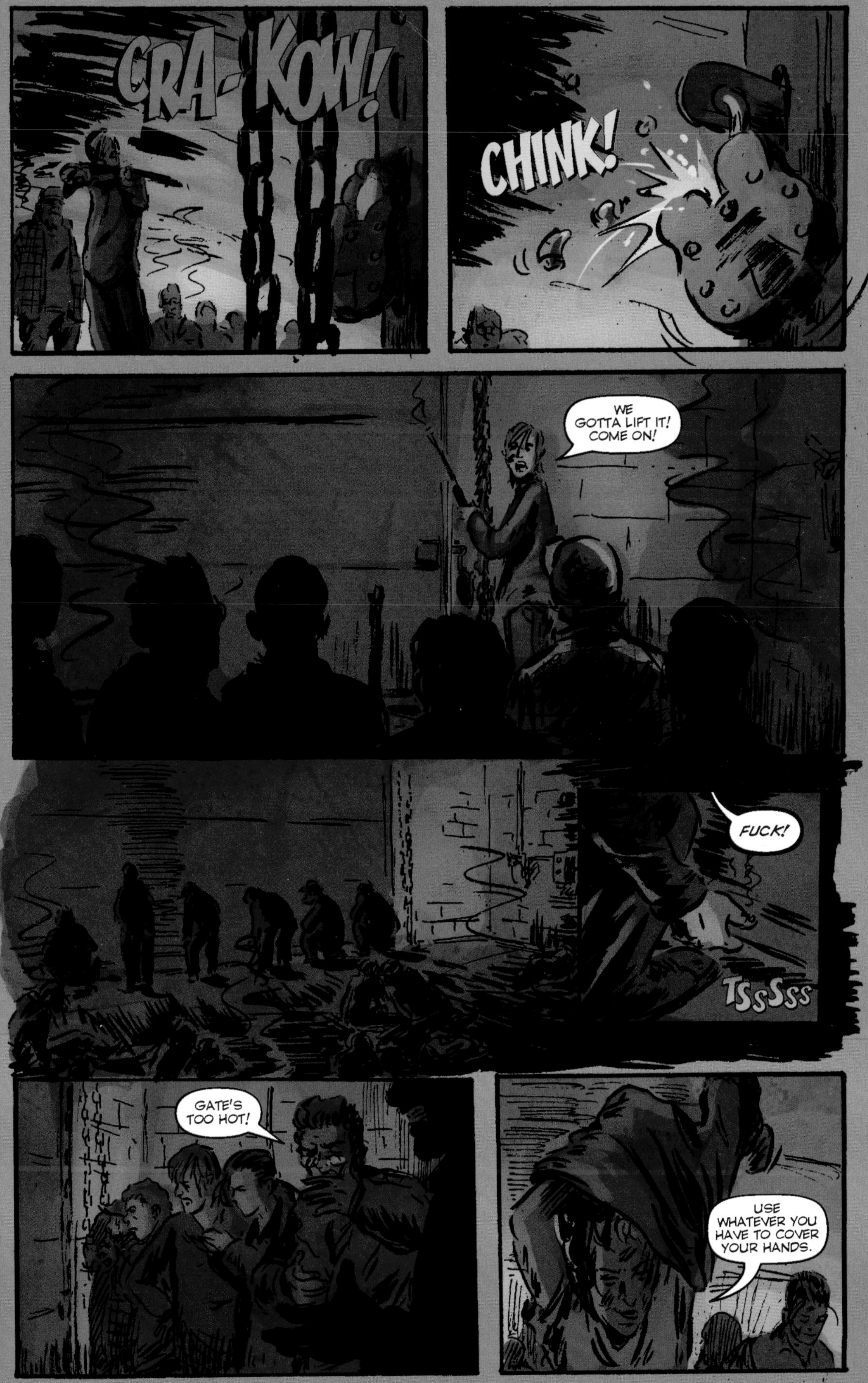
CRA-KOW!
CHINK!
WE GOTTA LIFT IT! COME ON!
FUCK!
TSSSSS
GATE'S TOO HOT!
USE WHATEVER YOU HAVE TO COVER YOUR HANDS.

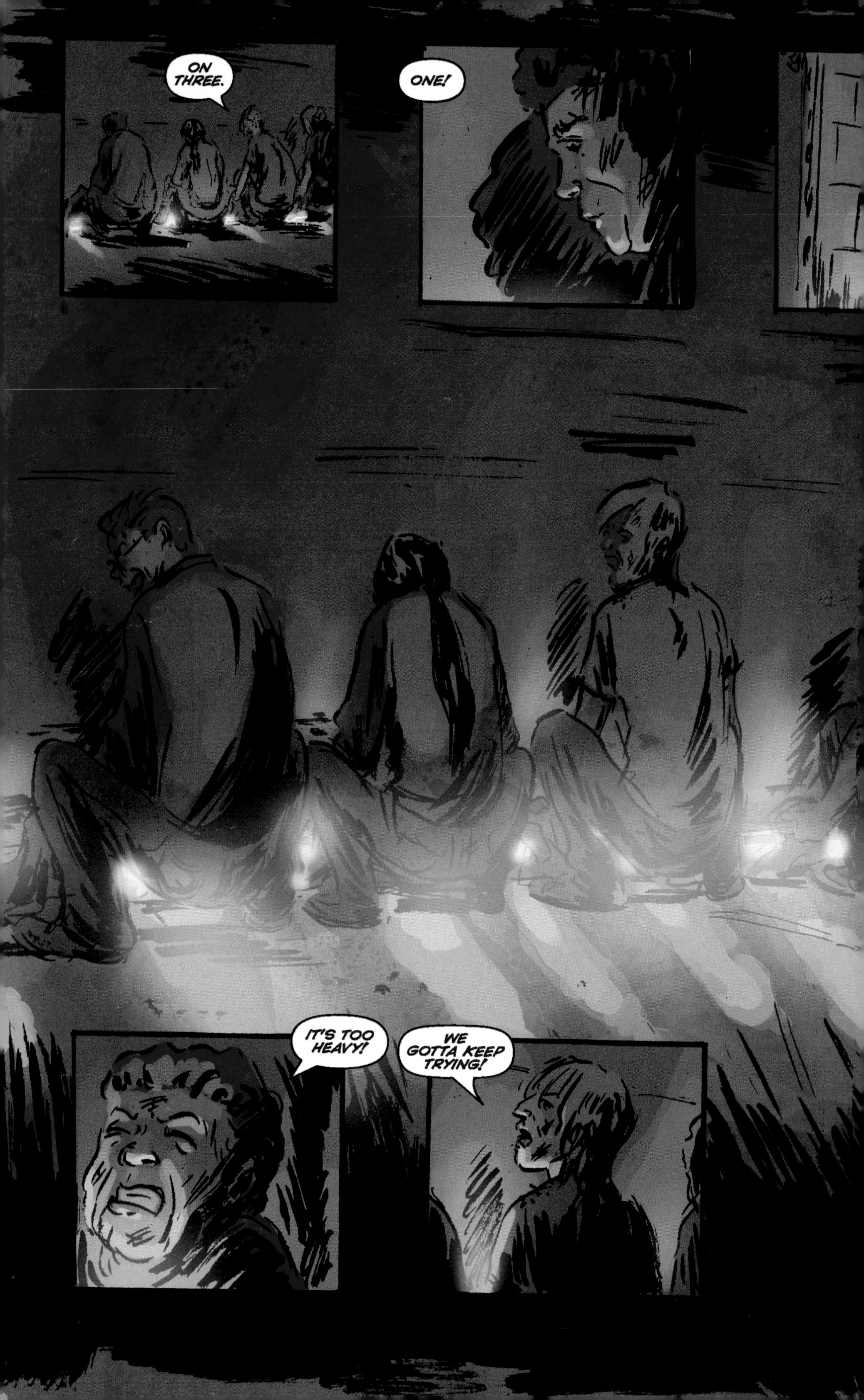
ON THREE.
ONE!
IT'S TOO HEAVY!
WE GOTTA KEEP TRYING!

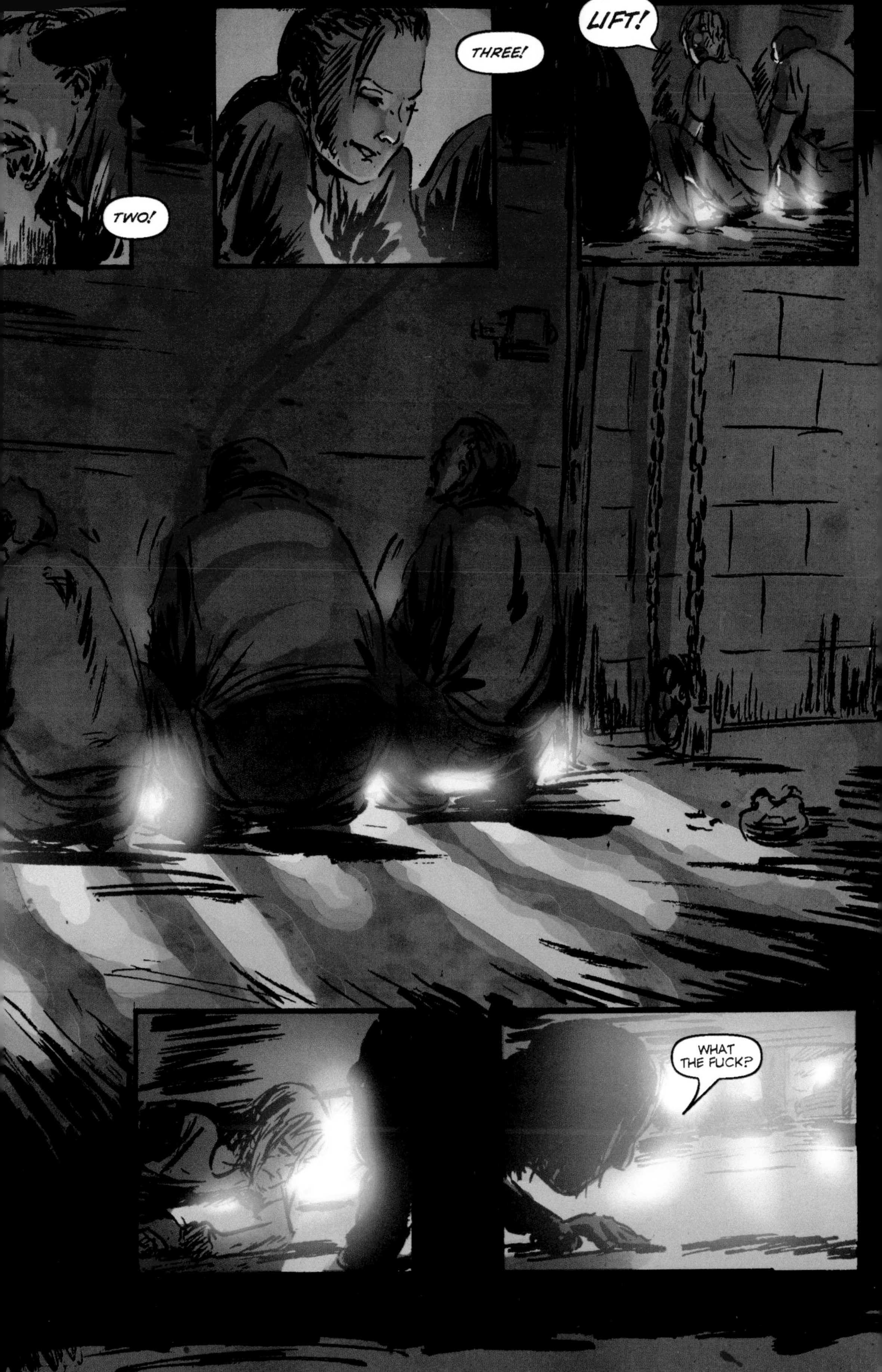
TWO!
THREE!
LIFT!
WHAT THE FUCK?

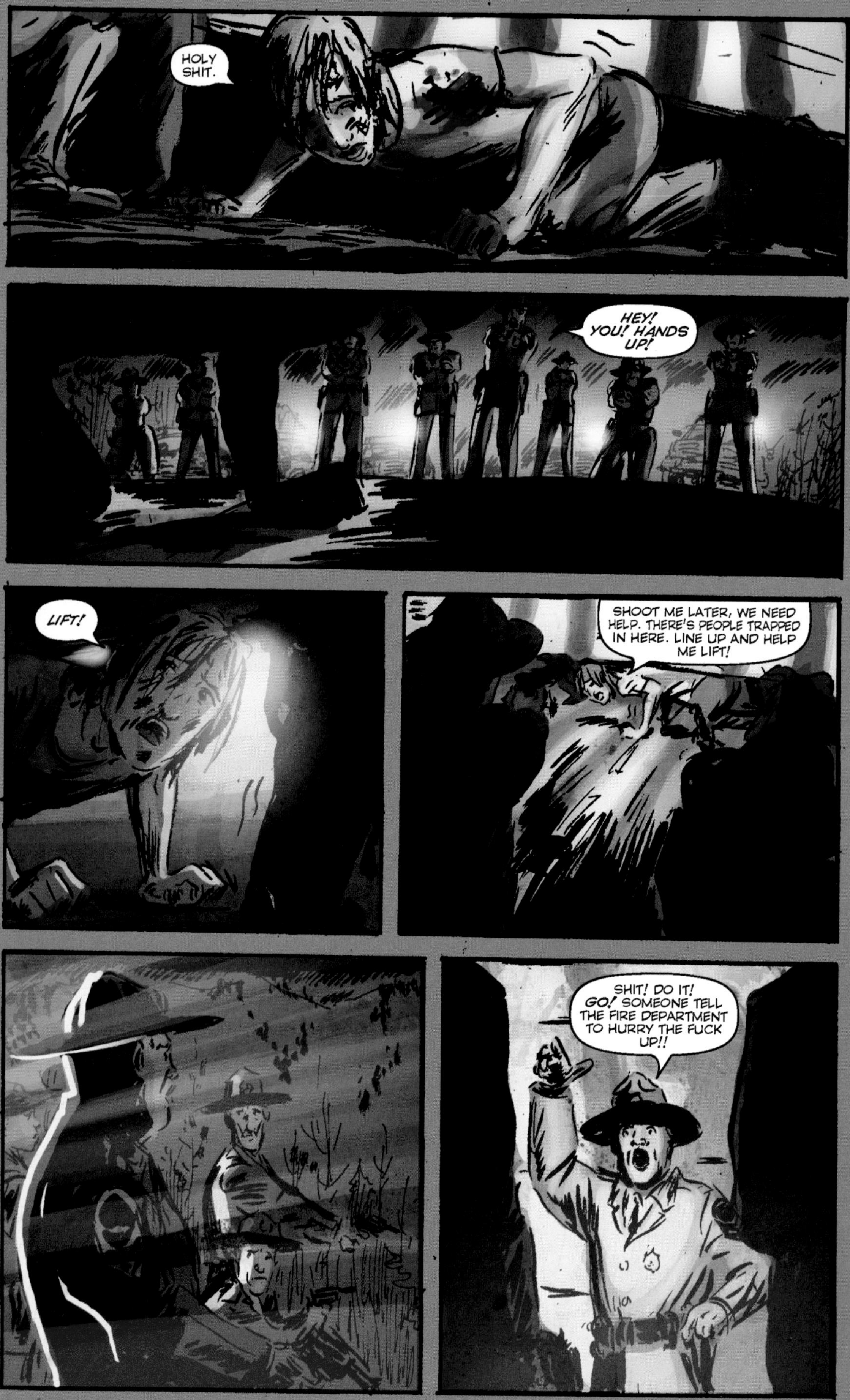
HOLY SHIT.
HEY! YOU! HANDS UP!
LIFT!
SHOOT ME LATER, WE NEED HELP. THERE'S PEOPLE TRAPPED IN HERE. LINE UP AND HELP ME LIFT!
SHIT! DO IT! GO! SOMEONE TELL THE FIRE DEPARTMENT TO HURRY THE FUCK UP!!

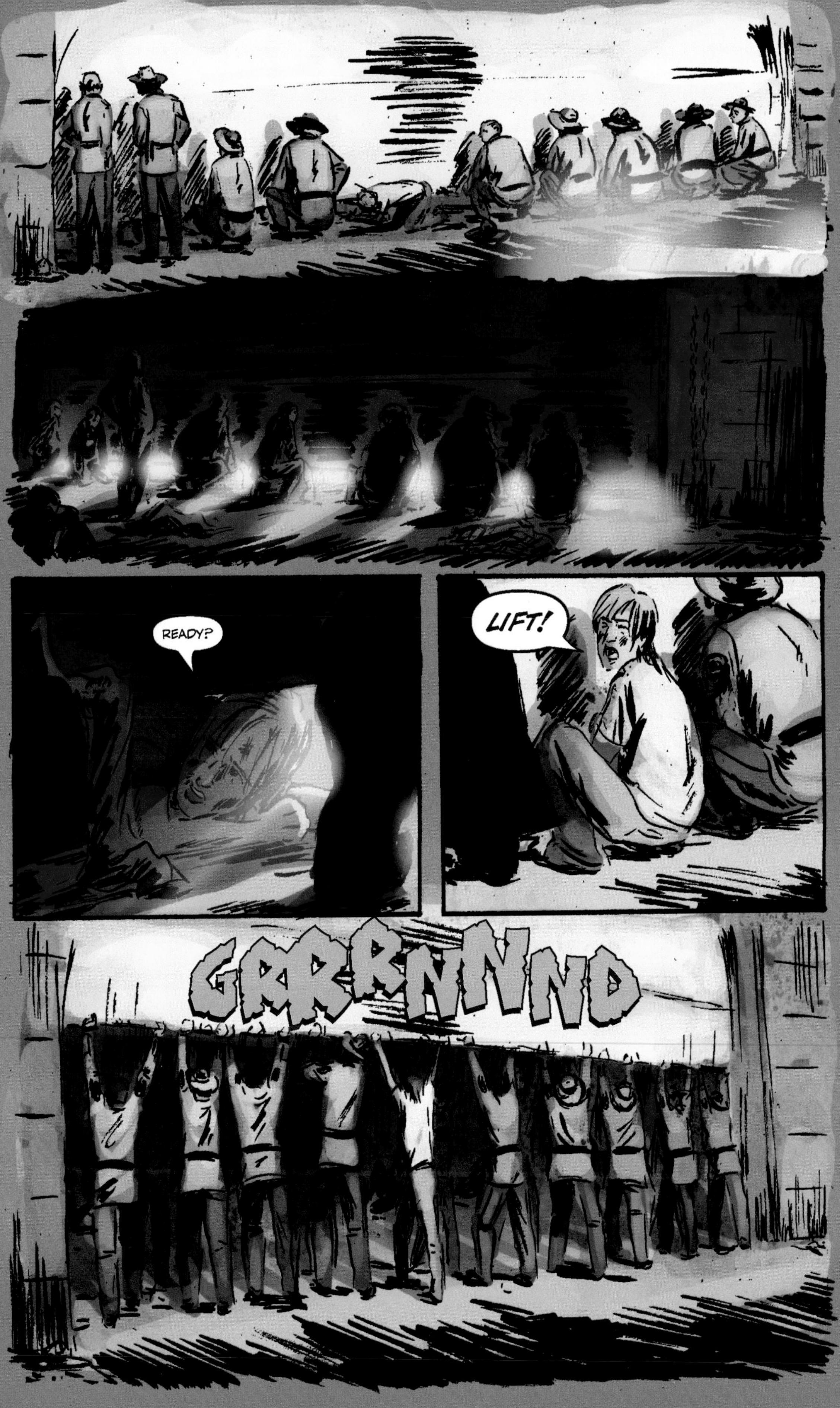
READY?
LIFT!
GRRRNNND

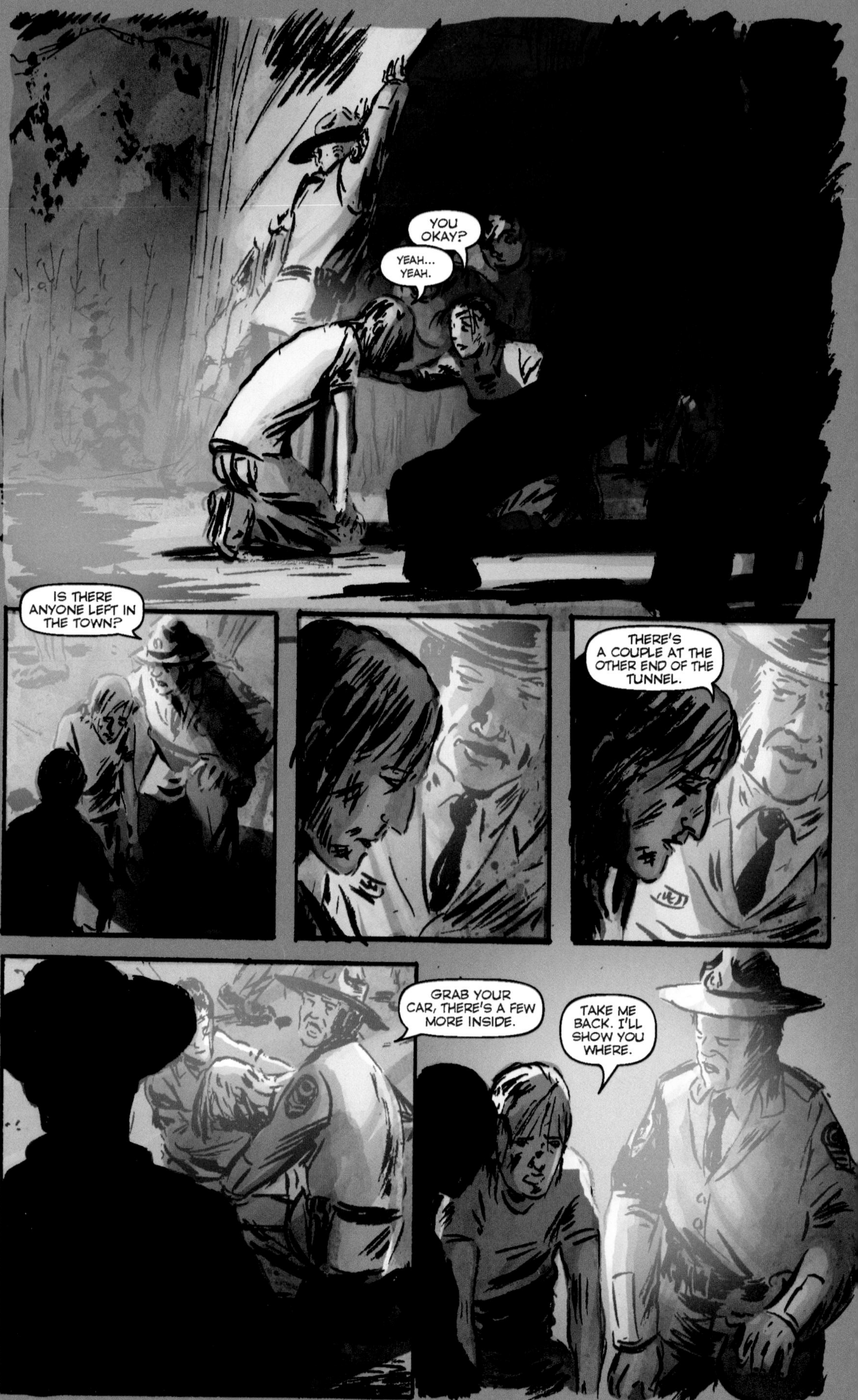
YOU OKAY?
YEAH... YEAH.
IS THERE ANYONE LEFT IN THE TOWN?
THERE'S A COUPLE AT THE OTHER END OF THE TUNNEL.
GRAB YOUR CAR, THERE'S A FEW MORE INSIDE.
TAKE ME BACK. I'LL SHOW YOU WHERE.

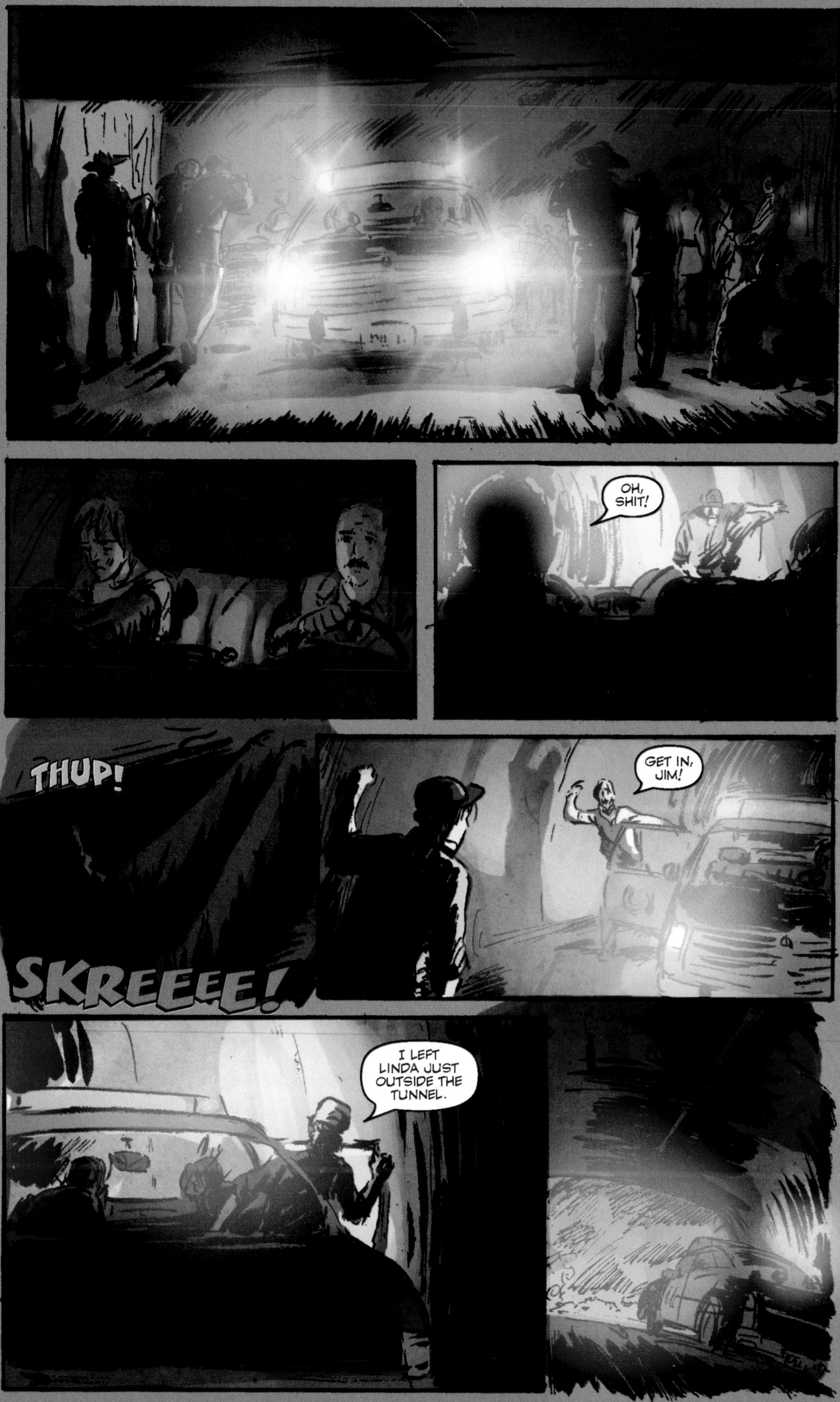
OH, SHIT!
THUP!
SKREEEE!
GET IN, JIM!
I LEFT LINDA JUST OUTSIDE THE TUNNEL.

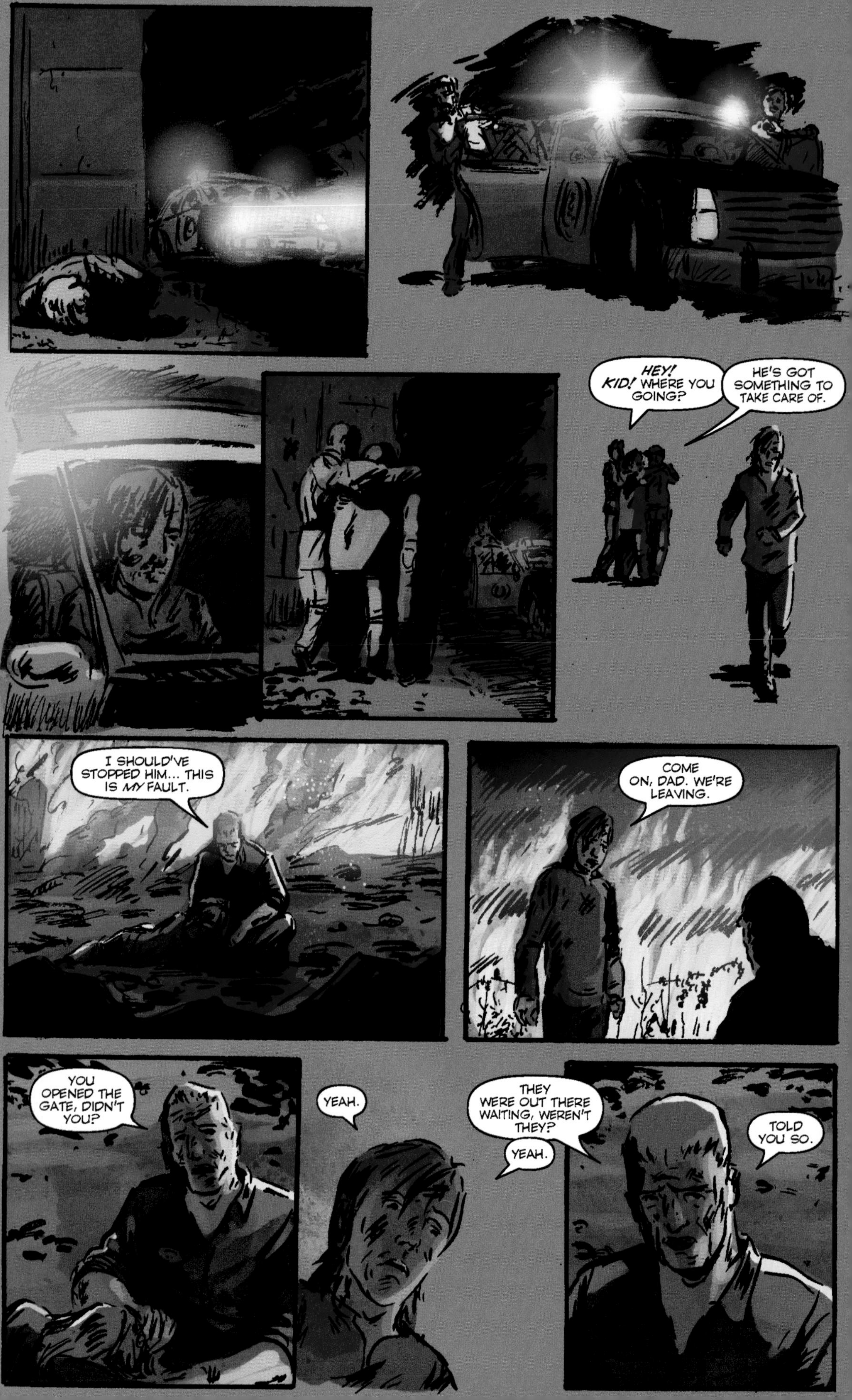
HEY! KID! WHERE YOU GOING?
HE'S GOT SOMETHING TO TAKE CARE OF.
I SHOULD'VE STOPPED HIM... THIS IS MY FAULT.
COME ON, DAD. WE'RE LEAVING.
YOU OPENED THE GATE, DIDN'T YOU?
YEAH.
THEY WERE OUT THERE WAITING, WEREN'T THEY?
YEAH.
TOLD YOU SO.

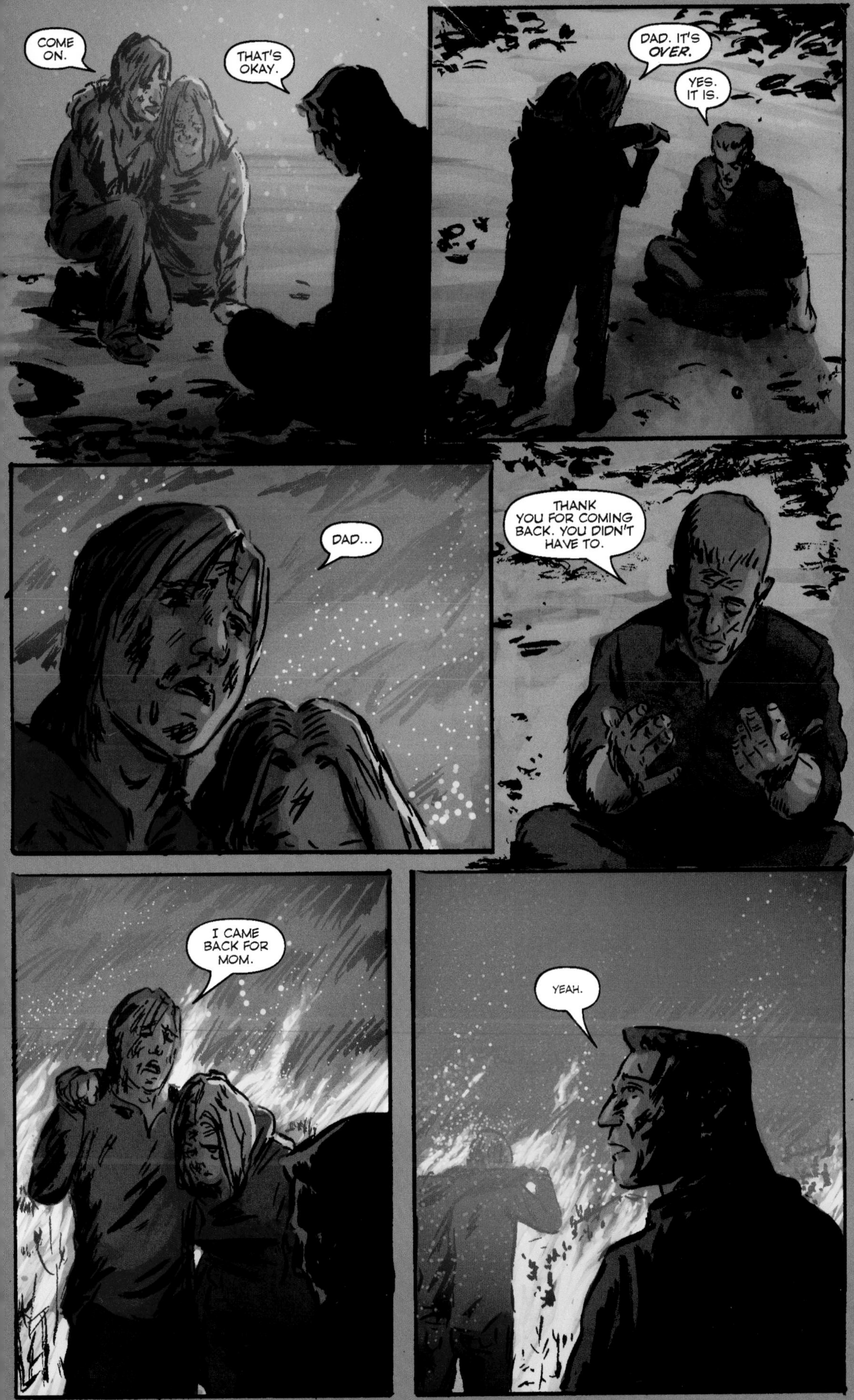
COME ON.
THAT'S OKAY.
DAD. IT'S OVER.
YES. IT IS.
DAD...
THANK YOU FOR COMING BACK. YOU DIDN'T HAVE TO.
I CAME BACK FOR MOM.
YEAH.

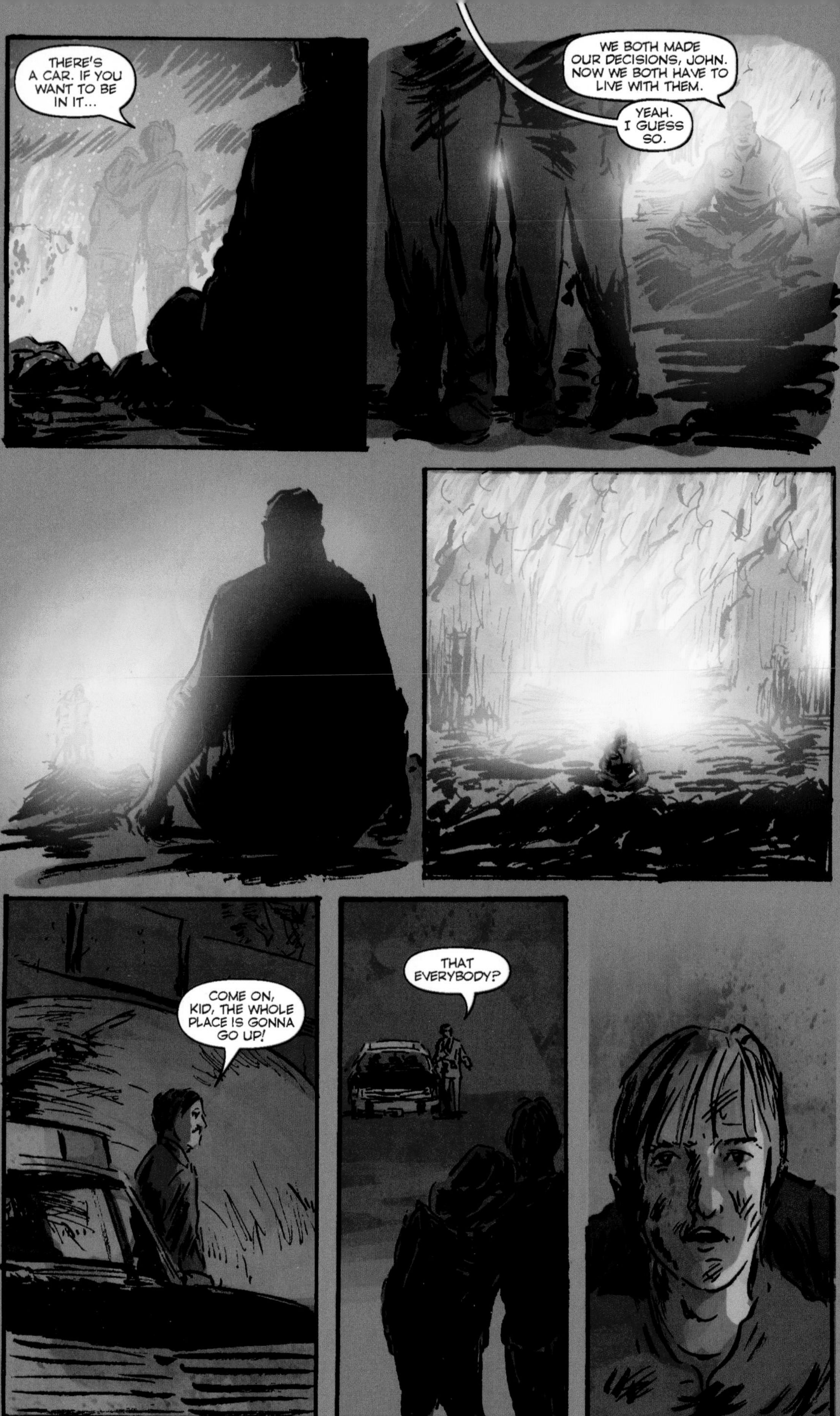
THERE'S A CAR. IF YOU WANT TO BE IN IT...
WE BOTH MADE OUR DECISIONS, JOHN. NOW WE BOTH HAVE TO LIVE WITH THEM.
YEAH. I GUESS SO.
COME ON, KID, THE WHOLE PLACE IS GONNA GO UP!
THAT EVERYBODY?

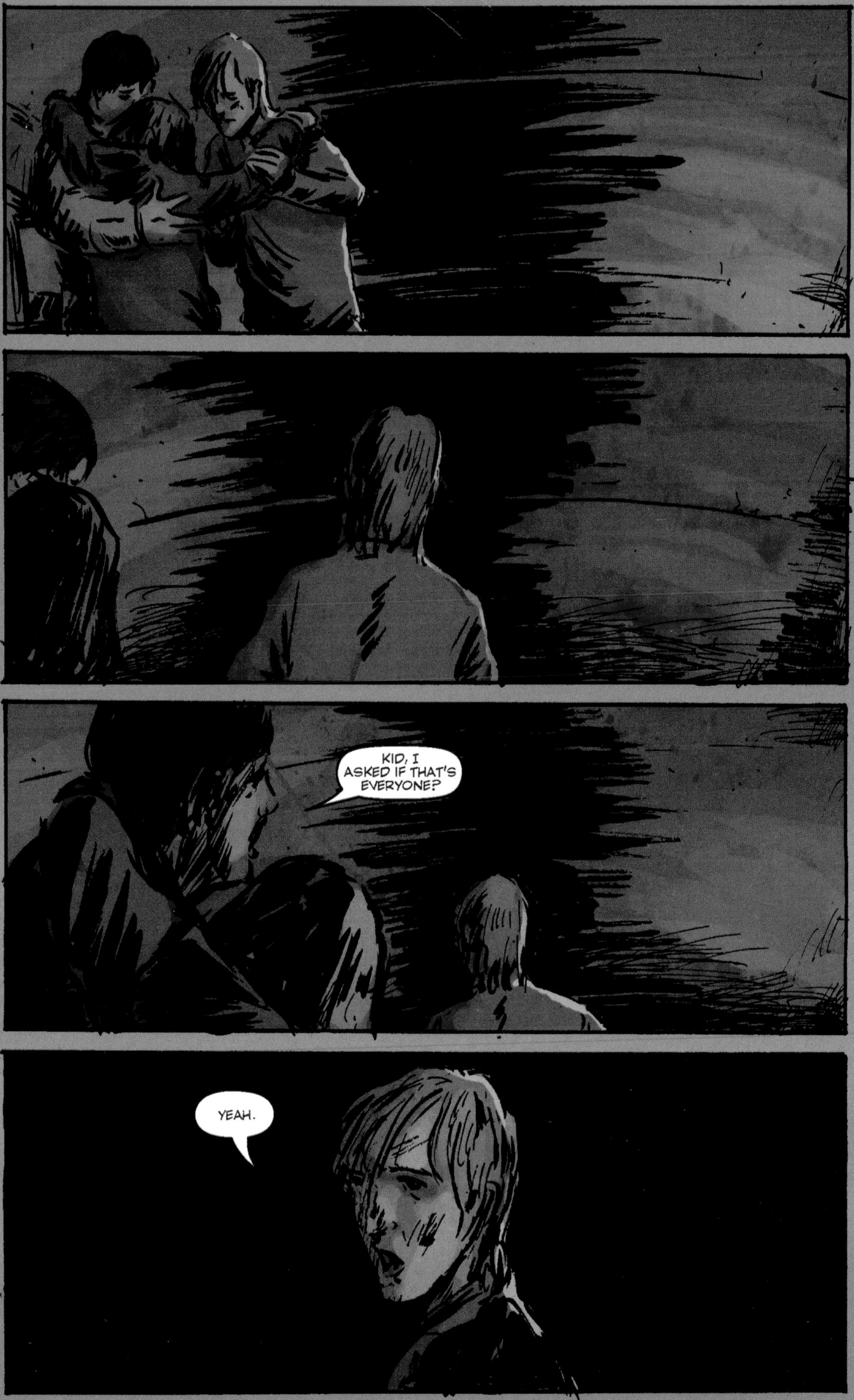
KID, I ASKED IF THAT'S EVERYONE?
YEAH.

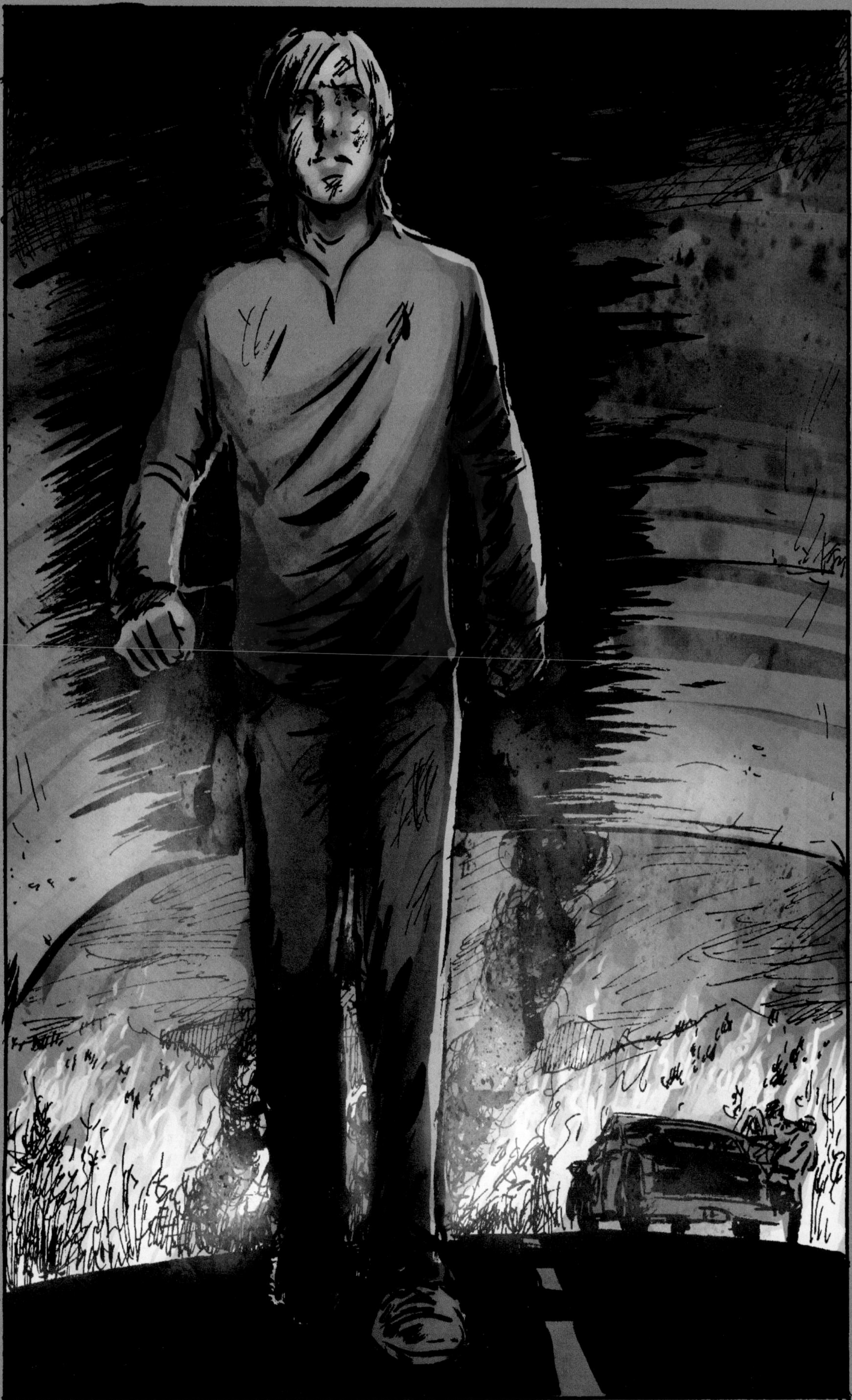

Afterword

After three long years working on this book, it's time to sit down and write the afterword. It's not the last thing I'll ever write about the book, but it's the last time I'll ever write anything that will go into it. Into this permanent record. And, frankly, I've covered it all before. So I called on my brain trust—my friends, family, and colleagues—to tell me what I haven't said . . . or at least what I should say now.

My girlfriend, Christina, told me to write about where the story came from: growing up in the suburbs of Pittsburgh, living for a year in a town that was at least somewhat reminiscent of Elk's Ridge. . . . But I've covered that. My screenwriting partner, Mark, told me to talk about the politics, about the post-9/11 culture of fear that the book delves into. But, well, Charlie's introduction pretty much covers that. Jason Rodriguez, this book's editor from nearly day one, told me to do the one thing we can never do enough of—thank everyone involved, from my creative team (to whom there is no equal) and the fans (who stood on rooftops shouting in a tidal wave of support) to the book's original publisher, Chris Arundel (whose hard work and commitment got the book in front of people for the first time), and the kind folks at Random House (who, quite frankly, made it possible for me to tell the story I wanted to tell in the format I always wanted.)

But come on, all of that shit's old hat. That's what some asshole says when going to claim his retirement clock radio and faux-gold plaque after drunkenly punching out at the factory for the last time.

So instead, to keep things moving along here, I'll simply dedicate the book to the people who deserve it most.

To our parents.

To the ones who made us who we are, sometimes against their own intents, but never to our detriment. Our lives, our purposes, and even, for some of us, our unsightly gigantic nasal protuberances—we owe all to you.

Joshua Hale Fialkov
Los Angeles, California
October 15, 2006

About the Creators

JOSHUA HALE FIALKOV (writer), Harvey Award nominee for best new talent and best writer, is the creator of the hit indie anthology *Western Tales of Terror* as well as the Internet cult hit *Poorly Drawn Animals*. His comic work has appeared in books from Marvel Comics, Harris Comics, Boom! Studios, and IDW Publishing, and all across the Internet. He was raised in Pittsburgh and currently enjoys a writer's life in Los Angeles.

NOEL TUAZON (artist), Harvey Award nominee for best artist, was born in the Philippines but has lived most of his life in Toronto, Ontario. His work has appeared in several anthologies (including *Taboo Especial, Cerebus Bi-Weekly, Dennis Eichhorn's Real Stuff, Drawing the Line* and *Drawing the Line Again, Frecklebean Comics and Stories, Fleshrot 2* and its *Halloween Special*) and a handful of miniseries (*Arianne* by Rafael Nieves, *Redchapel* by Caleb Monroe). He also illustrated the children's book *Sunny Bear's Rainy Day* by Caryn A. Tate.

SCOTT KEATING (colorist) received a bachelor of fine arts degree (in visual art) in 2003 and has worked in graphic design and illustration since. After showing his artwork in local galleries and providing illustrations for Fantasy Flight Games' collectible card game *A Game of Thrones,* he moved into the realm of comic books in order to pursue his love of visual storytelling. His coloring work has been featured in books such as *The Wicked West* and *CSI: Secret Identity*. Scott lives in Saint John's, Newfoundland.

JASON RODRIGUEZ (editor) is best known as an Internet personality and as the editor of the hit indie anthology *Western Tales of Terror.* He has spent entire afternoons in antique shops across America, purchasing one-paragraph glimpses into people's lives for inclusion in *Postcards,* his most ambitious project to date. He currently resides in Arlington, Virginia, where he spends his evenings editing graphic novels and correcting his girlfriend, Robin, when she calls them "the funnies."

DATSUN TRAN (chapter title art) spends most of his time painting in his garage or sitting in front of the computer, working out new animation styles. He likes chimpanzees and drinking gin martinis.

JASON HANLEY (letterer) lives in Lincoln, New Brunswick, Canada. Deciding that he no longer wanted to work for "the man," Jason quit his day job to create and letter comics full-time. He has done lettering and logo work for Image Comics, Automatic Pictures, Raw Entertainment, Shadowline, and Lionsgate films. He spends hours every day arranging letters and words into little balloon shapes. His mom is very proud.

Nominated for seven Harvey awards, *Elk's Run* was originally self-published by Joshua Hale Fialkov. He switched publication of the book to Speakeasy in 2005, only to have the indie publishing house fall into bankruptcy and leave the eight-issue series unfinished.